TROUBLED YOUTH, TROUBLED FAMILIES

Understanding Families
At-Risk for
Adolescent Maltreatment

ABOUT THE AUTHORS

James Garbarino, is President, Erikson Institute for Advanced Study in Child Development, Chicago, and was formerly an Associate Professor of Human Development at Pennsylvania State University. He has authored more than sixty articles on social development, child welfare, and education. Dr. Garbarino is the author of seven books including: *Protecting Children from Abuse and Neglect, Understanding Abusive Families, Successful Schools and Competent Students, Children and Families in the Social Environment,* and *Social Support Networks: Informal Helping in the Social Environment.* In 1985 he received the first C. Henry Kempe award for the "outstanding professional contribution to the field of child abuse and neglect."

Cynthia J. Schellenbach, is currently Assistant Professor, University of Notre Dame. Her current interest is in the field of human development and family studies.

Janet Sebes, is a postdoctoral clinical fellow at Devereux Foundation, Philadelphia, Pennsylvania. She was formerly the Research Director for the Family Interaction Project.

ISBN 0-202-36039-3

CONTRIBUTORS TO THIS VOLUME

AARON T. EBATA

TERESA M. COONEY

ANNE C. GARBARINO

JAMES GARBARINO

LOUISE GUERNEY

EDNA GUTTMANN

ANDREW F. KELLY

MARK KREJCI

JAMES W. MIKESELL

MARGARET C. PLANTZ

CYNTHIA J. SCHELLENBACH

JANET M. SEBES

JANIS WILSON

JOAN I. VONDRA

TROUBLED YOUTH, TROUBLED FAMILIES

Understanding Families
At-Risk for
Adolescent Maltreatment

JAMES GARBARINO
CYNTHIA J. SCHELLENBACH
JANET M. SEBES
and Associates

ALDINE
Publishing Company
New York

ABOUT THE AUTHORS

James Garbarino, is President, Erikson Institute for Advanced Study in Child Development, Chicago, and was formerly an Associate Professor of Human Development at Pennsylvania State University. He has authored more than sixty articles on social development, child welfare, and education. Dr. Garbarino is the author of seven books including: *Protecting Children from Abuse and Neglect, Understanding Abusive Families, Successful Schools and Competent Students, Children and Families in the Social Environment,* and *Social Support Networks: Informal Helping in the Social Environment.* In 1985 he received the first C. Henry Kempe award for the "outstanding professional contribution to the field of child abuse and neglect."

Cynthia J. Schellenbach, is currently Assistant Professor, University of Notre Dame. Her current interest is in the field of human development and family studies.

Janet Sebes, is a postdoctoral clinical fellow at Devereux Foundation, Philadelphia, Pennsylvania. She was formerly the Research Director for the Family Interaction Project.

Copyright © 1986, James Garbarino, Cynthia J. Schellenbach, Janet M. Sebes
All rights reserved. No part of this publication may be reproduced or transmitted in any form or by any means, electronic or mechanical, including photocopy, recording, or any information storage and retrieval system, without permission in writing from the publisher.

Aldine Publishing Company
200 Saw Mill River Road
Hawthorne, New York 10532

Library of Congress Cataloging in Publication Data
Garbarino, James.
    Troubled youth, troubled families.

    Bibliography: p.
    Includes index.
    1. Problem families—United States—Addresses, essays, lectures. 2. Youth—United States—Family relationships—Addresses, essays, lectures. 3. Adolescent psychology—United States—Addresses, essays, lectures. 4. Child abuse—United States—Addresses, essays, lectures. 5. Problem children—United States—Addresses, essays, lectures. I. Schellenbach, Cynthia J. II. Sebes, Janet M. III. Title.
HV699.G34   1986   362.7'044   85-20154
ISBN 0-202-36039-3 (lib. bdg.)
ISBN 0-202-36040-7 (pbk.)

Printed in the United States of America
10 9 8 7 6 5 4 3 2 1

To Tom Gregory,
A Friend

CONTENTS

FOREWORD

Writing of the evolution of science and the science of evolution, Steven Jay Gould argues for a mid course between *inductivism* and *deductivism* ("eurekaism"):

> ... theory, the inductivists claimed, can only arise from a firm foundation of facts . . . each fact is a brick in a structure built without blueprints. Any talk or thought about theory (the building) is fatuous and premature before the bricks are set . . . [*deduction*] substitute(s) an alternative equally extreme and unproductive in its emphasis on the essential subjectivity of creative thought. In this "eureka" view, creativity is an ineffable something, accessible only to persons of genius. . . .
>
> Might we not marry the good features of each view, and abandon both the elitism of eurekaism and the pedestrian qualities of inductivism. (*The Panda's Thumb.* Norton: 1980, 60–61.)

Gould argues, in short, that good science—and the prediction and understanding that flow from it—requires both the "building blocks" of observed fact and the "blueprints" of integrative theory. In examining the complex precursors and sequelae of adolescent abuse, James Garbarino, Cynthia Schellenbach, Janet Sebes, and their associates have provided an ample measure of both. Their work is theoretically provocative and empirically sound. Moreover, it is rich in its implications for both identifying the conditions that lead to adolescent abuse, as well as for intervening to prevent or ameliorate its effects. Child abuse researchers and practitioners will each find much of value here: in fact, this book goes a long way to reduce the gap between these latter two groups by offering a model, in the empirical study reported here, of research in the service of more effective practice. Beyond its specific subject matter, the authors provide interesting speculation on family violence across the life span. Their analyses contain numerous implications for child abuse, spouse abuse, and abuse of the elderly.

One feature of this present effort is particularly worthy of note. Garbarino and his colleagues approach their subject from an *ecological perspective*. Consequently, they view multiple factors within the adolescent and the environments he/she inhabits as potential factors in both prediction and prevention. The unmistakable emphasis of the book is on efforts at coping, mastery, and adaptation—some highly successful, some markedly unsuccessful—and not per se on psychopathology. Consistent with the ecological paradigm, there is a dual focus on personal competencies and social supports—reflected both in assessment and intervention. Precisely how the components will be joined in a design for intervention will await future practice experiments, based, one hopes, on the hypotheses generated from this present study and review. But if the authors have not given us a prescriptive model for preventing/remediating adolescent abuse, they have provided, nonetheless, a valuable contribution to practice and research by pointing us away from both unicausal explanations and singular treatments. Whether "chaotically enmeshed" or coping adequately with the difficult life transition of adolescence, the families portrayed here are viewed neither as "empty vessels" waiting to be filled with professional advice/insight, nor as hapless victims of errant biology or pathogenic environments. Rather they stand, in the aggregate, as evidence of society's need to buttress, complement, and enhance the capabilities of families to prepare well the next generation of its citizens. To ignore the public policy message embedded in this very pracatical book about troubled youth and troubled families is to put society itself "at risk."

James K. Whittaker
The University of Washington
Seattle, Washington

PREFACE

I began my efforts to understand the maltreatment of adolescents about a decade ago. As a Fellow at the newly created Boys Town Center for the Study of Youth Development, I worked with a group of researchers, practitioners, and science writers to create what we called the *Maltreatment of Youth Project.* Through that project we joined the growing number of professionals around the country who were attempting to understand the origins, dynamics, and outcomes of abuse and neglect in the lives of adolescents. We undertook research, arranged consultations, developed pilot programs for professional and public awareness as well as intervention, and produced a film on adolescent maltreatment (*Don't Get Stuck There*) that went on to win a Silver Award at the International Film and Television Festival of New York in 1981.

When we began our work it had been only little more than a decade since Henry Kempe had coined the term "the battered baby syndrome" and stimulated a national effort to identify and treat child abuse. As we passed through the mid-1970s, professional and public awareness of child abuse and neglect grew. The federal government created the National Center on Child Abuse and Neglect under the auspices of 1974's legislation. Henry Kempe and his colleagues established a national center for treatment, research, and advocacy in Denver, and Donna Stone founded the volunteer-oriented National Committee for the Prevention of Child Abuse. But the maltreatment of adolescents remained a topic largely neglected by professionals and public alike.

However, as the decade of the 1970s came to a close, efforts were underway to focus attention on the special issues of adolescent maltreatment. The National Institute of Mental Health sponsored several demonstration intervention programs, prompted by the efforts of Ira Lourie. The Youth Development Bureau funded a national review of services through a grant to Urban Rural System Associates—with Bruce Fisher and Jane Berdie taking the lead. My colleague Gwen Gilliam and I synthesized the fruits of these and other labors (including our own pilot studies) in our book *Understanding Abusive Families* (Lexington Books, 1980).

The 1980s have brought forth a series of studies and intervention projects aimed at adolescent maltreatment. They provide the foundation for this book. In it, my colleagues and I have set the phenomenon of adolescent maltreatment within the broader issues of "destructive parent—adolescent relations" and "troubled youth." This approach reflects our reading of the research and clinical evidence concerning adolescent maltreatment and our conviction that to understand abuse and neglect we must examine the entire human ecology in which these problems occur. My colleagues and I have presented the background and rationale for this "ecological perspective" in two other books—*Children and Families in the Social Environment* (Aldine Publishing Company, 1982) and *Adolescent Development: An Ecological Perspective* (Charles E. Merrill Publishing Company, 1985).

Since this book and the work it represented are a collaboration, I must acknowledge many contributors. Cindy Schellenbach and Jan Sebes were my principal collaborators in this volume. As doctoral students in Individual and Family Studies at Pennsylvania State University, where I made my faculty home, Jan and Cindy were the principal research associates for the federally funded research project (National Center on Child Abuse and Neglect grant #90CA835/01) that forms the core of this volume. They took on responsibility for the study above and beyond the call of duty. For her doctoral dissertation project, Jan Sebes developed the instrument to assess risk for adolescent maltreatment that is the focal point for the study. Cindy played a pivotal role in the study and a leadership role in developing this book. Jan is now a practicing clinician/researcher, and Cindy has gone on to join the faculty of Notre Dame University in the Psychology Department.

My faculty colleague Donald Ford served as a co-investigator for the original grant, playing an important role in the design and data collection stages of the project. Louise Guerney, who is a contributor to this volume, was the co-investigator working on the development of appropriate interventions for high-risk families facing troubled adolescents.

Of course, we acknowledge the contributors to this volume. Each has taken on special responsibility for exploring an important topic and bringing intelligence to bear on the research and clinical evidence available. All but one are or were graduate students at Penn State. Andrew Kelly, Margaret Plantz, Janis Lee Wilson, Anne Garbarino, Edna Guttmann, Aaron Ebata, Terri Cooney, Joan Vondra, and Jim Mikesell are from Penn State. Mark Krejci is from Notre Dame. We were aided in the research by a cadre of graduate and undergraduate students: John Schulenberg, Earl Merritt, Anne Dolan, Margie Niehenke, Alycia Chambers, Rhonda Richardson, Joan Speicher, Wendy Groninger, Rosemary Rixie, Joyce White, Melinda Spyler, Pat Grandjean, Betsy Stumpf, Christy Demchak, Paul Kobilk, and Susan Ward. A special vote of thanks goes to Cheryl Freeman who took on the task of tracking down and interviewing family members 2½ years after the initial study. In preparing the manuscript we called upon and received the assistance of the staff of the Department of Individual and Family Studies, most notably Alice Saxion and Joy Barger. Throughout the project we received assistance from the administration of the College of Human Development at Penn State.

Two additional acknowledgments are in order. The first goes to Jim Whittaker who agreed to write the foreword to this volume, and whose counsel and friendship sustain me. The second goes to Tom Gregory, who was director of the Research Use and Public Service Division at Boys Town (now Director of External Affairs). He inspired the Maltreatment of Youth Project in the first place and nurtured it with his concern, his many skills, and his good humor. I dedicate this book to him.

James Garbarino

DESTRUCTIVE FAMILY RELATIONS IN ADOLESCENCE

I

In Part I, we offer our view of how family dysfunction relates to the broad spectrum of adolescent problems. Chapter 1 examines the concept of psychosocial normality in adolescence. We review evidence concerning the costs and benefits of alternative childrearing models with an eye to their implications for adolescence. Finally, we review the evidence on adolescent maltreatment and propose a series of hypotheses. Chapter 2 explores the links between abuse and delinquency. We document several possible relationships: Abuse causes socially incompetent behavior which leads to delinquency; efforts to escape abusive families lead to delinquency; institutional responses to delinquency precipitate abuse; both abuse and delinquency result from socially impoverished dysfunctional families. Evidence exists in support of all four. Chapter 3 documents the significant role of family conflict (and particularly abuse and neglect) in adolescent running away.

AN INTRODUCTION TO TROUBLED YOUTH IN TROUBLED FAMILIES

1

JAMES GARBARINO
ANDREW F. KELLY

ADOLESCENCE IN CONTEXT

Human development is the science of human biology and psychology in social context. When asked, "Does X cause Y?" the appropriate answer for a student of human development is always, "It depends." It depends upon who is involved, and when and where in historical time and cultural place a particular X is acting to produce a specific Y. This emphasis on context and contingency is an ever-present aspect of the scientific landscape, nowhere more so than in studying adolescence.

Adolescence is embedded in contingencies of social context. It is clear the onset and duration of the *social* dimensions of adolescence exist as an institutionalized figment of our cultural imagination. The observed variability in the very existence and experience of adolescence testifies to this. As for the intricacies of what it means to be an adolescent—expectations regarding dress, speech, schooling, sexuality, the transition to adulthood, and the rites of passage—these manifestly depend upon context.

Even the biological events of adolescence, even these physiological X's and Y's, depend upon the contingencies of context. What Tanner (1973) has called the "secular trend" (in which the onset of puberty has come ever earlier over the last 100 years) demonstrates that even the biology of adolescence is enmeshed in a complex web of cultural and socioeconomic contingencies that are manifest through variations in diet and health care. The contingencies of context are evident in the cognitive developments of adolescence as well. The prevalence and rapidity of the shift from childlike reasoning to the more sophisticated thinking that Jean Piaget (1952) called "formal operational thought" depend upon a host of social influences.

Having said all this, it should come as no surprise that our efforts to understand adolescent maltreatment are beset by contextual contingencies. Just as we have learned that child abuse and neglect are not the simple product of any one factor operating uniformly in all situations, so we are beginning to see that to understand adolescent maltreatment we must identify the special blend of circumstances surrounding and enveloping troubled youth in troubled families. If we include intervention in our mission, then we are all the more faced with the task of establishing the context in which troubled families play out the painful dramas of adolescent maltreatment. Our efforts to act are bound up by the way our society views and feels about its adolescents and its families, particularly its troubled adolescents and families.

IMAGES OF ADOLESCENCE

Many adults recall adolescence as a bittersweet time. The nineteenth century British poet, Wordsworth, captured this feeling of exquisite poignancy in his "Ode. Intimations of Immortality" (1807): Though nothing can bring back the hour/Of splendor in the grass, of glory in the flowers,/We will grieve not, rather find/Strength in what remains behind . . . / Consider the following anonymous poetic tribute to youth that captures one way people attribute social meaning to adolescence.

On Youth
   Youth is not entirely a time of life, it is a state of
mind. It is not wholly a matter of ripe cheeks, red lips, or
supple knees. It is a temper of will, a quality of the
imagination, a vigor of the emotions.
   Nobody grows old by merely living a number of years.
People grow old only by deserting their ideals. You are as
young as your faith, as old as your doubt; as young as your
self-confidence, as old as your fears; as young as your hope,
as old as your despair.
   In the central place of every heart, there is a recording
chamber; so long as it receives messages of beauty, hope,
cheer and courage, you are young.
   When the wires are all down and your heart is covered
with the snows of pessimism and the ice of cynicism, then and
then only have you grown old.

In understanding the origins and significance of adolescent maltreatment, we need to go beyond nostalgic images of adolescents (which usually apply to teenagers in ones or twos) to recognize the sinister images of adolescents as a class. These images have a lot to do with how sympathetic or hostile people are to the "victims" of adolescent maltreatment. For all the positive nostalgia, adolescents nonetheless suffer from bad press. Negative stereotypes of adolescents abound in the mass media and in the hearts and minds of most adults—even many professionals.

Some of the most prominent observers of adolescence in the 1950s and 1960s saw these negative stereotypes of youth as both the cause and effect of adolescent alienation from the adult world. Classics such as Paul Goodman's *Growing Up Absurd* (1956) and Edgar Friedenberg's *The Vanishing Adolescent* (1959) and *The Dignity of Youth and Other Atavisms* (1965) explored this pessimistic theme. Goodman's title is self-explanatory. Friedenberg emphasized the way adults often regard adolescents in general with fear and often contempt. High schools are the principal arena in which adults society plays out this theme.

> They are problem-oriented and the feelings and needs for growth of their captives and unenfranchised clientele are the least of their problems; for the status of the "teenager" in the community is so low that even if he rebels, the school is not blamed for the conditions against which he is rebelling. What high school personnel become specialists in, ultimately, is the *control* of large groups of students . . . (Friedenberg, 1965, pp. 92–93).

Twenty years later, as controlling school crime and meeting basic scholastic requirements have become dominant issues, Friedenberg's analysis remains timely.

In her book, *Children Without Childhood*, social critic Marie Winn (1983) speaks of "The Myth of the Teenage Werewolf":

> A pervasive myth has taken hold of parents' imagination these days, contributing to their feeling of being powerless to control the fates of their children: the myth of the teenage werewolf. Its message is that no matter how pleasant and sweet and innocent their child might be at the moment, how amiable and docile and friendly, come the first hormonal surge of puberty and the child will turn into an uncontrollable monster (p. 14).

This monsterous imagery is not without precedent. Consider this view of adolescents discovered in a 1972 book by Leonard Wolf entitled *A Dream of Dracula: In Search of the Living Dead*:

> Adolescents recognize him at once. (His bad breath, his red, red lips.) If he kissed you once, will he kiss you again? They lie in the torpor of their pupa stage, waiting for something better to happen to them, dreaming about transformations. Pimpled, gawky, swollen with blood and other juices they do not quite understand, they know about being loathed, and loathing. . . .

Blood surges in and soils the young. Hearing the word "suck," they look about warily, in the grip of strange confusions: they know what all those films are about—ego, power, parasitism, loneliness, immortality, youth, youth, youth and thirty-eight kinds of sex. The living-dead. Finally it comes down to this: When Dracula's lips approach the delicate throat of the beautiful girl on the screen, *they* know . . . (p. 17).

This cultural context is important in understanding how families deal with adolescence. These images of adolescence contribute to the context in which the dynamics of adolescent maltreatment take place. Of equal or greater importance is how we define what is normal and abnormal conflict in adolescence, particularly in relation to parents.

WHAT IS NORMAL FOR ADOLESCENTS?
PROFESSIONAL STEREOTYPES AND
EMPIRICAL REALITIES

Public images of adolescents as monsters find their professional parallel in the widely held image of adolescence as necessarily "stormy and stressful" (translated from the German "Sturm und Drang") (Garbarino *et al.*, 1985; Kelly and Garbarino, 1985). In this view, adolescents experience conflict and turmoil as a *normal* part of their development. Many who hold this view most strongly have studied or worked professionally with disturbed adolescents engaged in deviant behavior.

The roots of the storm and stress stereotype lie in the work of psychologist G. Stanley Hall (1844–1924), who was the first to publish a textbook on adolescence, in 1904. Hall was very much influenced by Darwin and the nineteenth-century biologist Ernst Haeckel. Darwin hypothesized that human beings have evolved from "lower" forms of life—with apes, monkeys, and other mammals being our closest relatives. Haeckel studied the development of human embryos and compared this process to the development of the embryos of other species. With the primitive equipment available in his day, Haeckel mistakenly observed that the human embryo changed in such a fashion as to first resemble a fully developed fish embryo, then a frog embryo, later a rat embryo, a monkey embryo, and at last an ape embryo. In Haeckel's view, this was a manifestation of the evolutionary development of man as hypothesized by Darwin. Thus, it was said that *ontogeny* (the biological development of an individual organism) *recapitulates phylogeny* (the historical evolution of a species).

Hall grasped this notion and applied it to the postnatal development of the human. Thus, as he saw it, the stages of childhood reflected the stages in human evolution. As Gallatin (1975, p. 30) has described Hall's theory:

During early infancy the child was recapitulating a "monkey-like" stage in the history of the human species. The years between eight and twelve allegedly represented a reenactment of a more advanced but still rather primitive form of mankind, perhaps a tribe that had managed to support itself through hunting and fishing. Similarly, adolescence was supposed to be a recapitulation of a stage midway between savagery and civilization—when still-primitive man had begun to develop the rudiments of a culture.

In Hall's view, the adolescent is struggling to balance the more primitive impulses of the savage with the more humane ones of the civilized person. This attempt to reconcile these two divergent sources of influence results in the turmoil or "storm and stress" that Hall defined as an inevitable part of adolescence.

This early formulation of human development did not gain wide acceptance, due in part to its reliance on the tenuous extension of Darwin's evolutionary theory. One of the problems with the theory was addressed immediately by the psychologist Thorndike (1904). He pointed out that one could not account for the behavior of a 2-year-old child by stating that he was "recapitulating" a monkey-like stage of human evolution, because the 2-year-old is already more advanced than monkeys, apes, or any of the creatures the developing human is supposed to be "recapitulating." For an in-depth review of the specific critiques leveled at the theory, the interested reader should seek out Gallatin (1975) or Thorndike (1904).

Although Hall's specific theory of human development as reflecting the Darwinian evolutionary process did not gain wide acceptance, Hall was responsible for starting off the field in the view that human behavior was more under the influence of genetic rather than environmental determinants, nature rather than nurture. The general idea that adolescence is characterized by storm and stress also exerted an enduring influence on psychological theories of adolescent development.

Sigmund Freud's psychoanalytic view of adolescence is one of these theories, one that has had a profound impact on the way social service and mental health professionals deal with adolescents. While the theory is very different from Hall's formulation in content, it shares Hall's view of adolescence as being necessarily stormy and chaotic and is rooted in biological influences. Along these lines, Anna Freud (1958) wrote of the difficulty of distinguishing normality from psychopathology in adolescence:

Adolescence constitutes by definition an interruption of peaceful growth which resembles in appearance a variety of other emotional upsets and structural upheavals. The adolescent manifestations come close to symptom formation of the neurotic, psychotic or dissocial order and merge almost imperceptibly into borderline states, initial, frustrated or fully fledged forms of almost all the mental illnesses. Consequently, the differential diagnosis between the adolescent upsets and true pathology becomes a difficult task (p. 267).

Anna Freud viewed adolescence as a developmental disturbance derived from the reawakening of libidinal impulses that marks the movement from the latency period into the pubertal period.

Teenagers experience psychic conflict as they try to balance their Oedipal impulses with what society dictates as correct behavior. Childhood defenses (repression, rationalization, and projection) keep these Oedipal desires from awareness and thereby permit escape from uncomfortable and threatening turmoil. As the individual moves out of childhood, this defensive balance becomes ("preliminary and precarious" as it is) more and more inappropriate. It cannot handle the powerful sexual drives that are resurgent in adolescence as the primary force propelling personality (Id) makes itself felt. Adolescents must overthrow their old systems and build new ones. This process results in the rebellion, the ups and downs, and the dramatic changes that Anna Freud saw as being typical of adolescence.

This "period of upheaval" is a healthy, normal expression of development, but during it adolescents will reject their parents (in response to the unacceptable desire to possess the opposite sex parent) and enter into a series of intense but brief romantic involvements with their peers (as they learn to accept and adapt to their new-found sexuality). Parents and other adults will perceive this behavior as "rebellion." This provides a theoretical explanation for the stereotyped view of adolescents as being necessarily "rebellious." It is interesting to recall what Anna Freud (1958) wrote concerning what is occurring when such "structural upheavals" and "rebellious" activities do *not* occur.

> We all know individual children who as late as the ages of 14, 15, or 16 show no such outer evidence of inner unrest. They remain, as they have been in dealing with the latency period, "good" children, wrapped up in their family relationships, considerate sons of their mothers, submissive to their fathers, in accord with the atmosphere, ideas, and ideals of the childhood background. Convenient as this may be, it signifies a delay of normal development and is, as such, a sign to be taken seriously. . . . These are children who have built up excessive defenses against their drive activities and are now crippled by the results, which act as barriers against the normal maturational processes of phase development. They are, perhaps more than any others, in need of therapeutic help to remove the inner restrictions and clear the path for normal development, however "upsetting" the latter may prove to be (p. 265).

From Anna Freud's psychoanalytic perspective, the exhibition of "storm and stress" in the form of conflict with parents not only is a *natural* experience but it is also a *necessary* occurrence for normal adolescent development to take place. The "upholding of a steady equilibrium during the adolescent process is in itself abnormal" (A. Freud, 1958, p. 275). This undermines the validity of adolescent acting out behaviors as indicators of disrupted development, family conflict, or psychopathology. As such it may undermine our ability to intervene in adolescent maltreatment by casting its results as "just as phase," when in fact they represent a genuine crisis.

But is this view correct? Anthropologists such as Margaret Mead and Ruth Benedict challenged it on the basis of their observations in other cultures. What is more, survey research in the United States indicates that while adolescence is usually a time of family challenge, *adolescents are not normally either crazy or highly rebellious.*

The first systematic research evidence that teenagers in modern Western-ized societies do not necessarily experience major problems of adjustment was presented by two sociologists, Westley and Elkin (1956). Their small sample of middle-class adolescents in Montreal, Canada, reported little turmoil. Instead, they presented a picture of relative calm and stability. Douvan and Adelson (1966) conducted a study in which they extensively interviewed over 3000 adolescents. The sample was constructed in such a way as to be representative of the entire United States population of boys and girls facing adolescence, although it was restricted to teenagers in school and somewhat underrepresented low-income and racial-minority youth. In this broad, more representative sample, there also was little evidence of *major* turmoil and conflict. In fact, their data presented a picture of the "typical" adolescent as a somewhat conservative and conforming individual (to which Anna Freud might respond that this only shows how widespread is the problem of pathological placidity).

> The adolescent at the extremes responds to the instinctual and psychosocial upheaval of puberty by disorder, by failures of egosynthesis, and by a tendency to abandon earlier values and object attachments. In the normative response to adolescence, however, we more commonly find an avoidance of inner and outer conflict, premature identity consolidation, ego and ideological constric-tion, and a general unwillingness to take psychic risks. The great advantage of the survey technique is that it allows us to study these adolescents who make up the middle majority, who evoke neither grief nor wonder, and who all too often escape our notice (p. 351).

As an aside, it is important to make note of this last point. Many observers have noted that psychologists and psychiatrists see a rather selected sample of adolescents—those who are brought to professional attention usually because they are experiencing some form of psychological distress. Due to this restricted outlook, psychologists and psychiatrists may have a rather limited, skewed perception of what most adolescents are like.

Some critics challenged Douvan and Adelson's study on the grounds that their interviewers were not mental health professionals (and thus presum-ably were more likely to miss signs of distress), but subsequent studies that

have employed mental health professionals interviewing nonpatient populations have confirmed the finding that the majority of adolescents do *not*
show overt signs of disorder. (Of course, the psychoanalytically oriented
could respond that this shows that most adolescents suffer from the "problem" of no problems.)

One of the most extensive studies of adolescent normality was the
Normal Adolescent Project carried out by Daniel Offer and his colleagues
(Offer, 1969; Offer and Offer, 1973, 1974, 1975; Offer *et al.*, 1981). Offer
directed an 8-year project using a sample of 73 typical middle-class, male
teenagers in the Midwest United States. The boys were assessed at various
times from their freshman to senior years of high school. The assessment
procedure consisted of parent interviews, psychological tests, and psychiatric interviews. In addition, 61 of the original 73 subjects were assessed in the
same manner during their 4 years of college (and this reference to college
attendance indicates the relative affluence of the sample).

Offer identified three major patterns of growth for these adolescents.
Continuous growth refers to a gradual, smooth transition from adolescence
to young adulthood, free from the turbulence and turmoil predicted by the
"storm and stress" theorists. *Surgent growth* refers to a less gradual developmental pattern, where growth occurs in "spurts," between which
development appears arrested. Most of the teenagers in this study developed
in one of these two modes—experiencing little or no signficant stress and
discomfort on their way to normal, adaptive adjustment to adulthood. A
third pattern of growth was termed *tumultuous growth* and corresponds to
the kind of turmoil and crisis pattern the storm and stress hypothesis predicts
for all adolescents. Of the sample, 21% evidenced this kind of developmental process, a large enough minority to show that there are
sufficient troubled adolescents to sustain the professional stereotype of storm
and stress, but too few to validate the claim that it is the typical adolescent
pattern.

In another study, Rutter *et al.* (1976) studied a large representative sample
of all of the 14 to 15-year-olds on the Isle of Wight (in Great Britain). They
found only a very slight increase in psychopathology from middle childhood
to adolescence and a very low incidence of rejection or relationship
difficulties between adolescents and parents. Interestingly, however, they
found that about 22% of their sample reported that they *often* felt miserable
or depressed and were having trouble sleeping. This is almost the exact
percentage that reported this pattern in the studies by Offer (1973, 1974,
1975). About 44% reported feeling miserable and depressed *at times*. We
should note that in Rutter *et al.*'s study (1976), the incidence of psychopathology (as assessed by a formal psychiatric interview) was 16.3%, so
that there is a difference between reporting depression and being considered
clinically depressed.

Therefore, we have evidence from two fairly large-scale studies that about 20% of nonpatient adolescents report experiencing serious turmoil as they grow up. This is far short of the majority predicted by storm and stress theorists, and it tells us that we should be alert to adolescents and families that are experiencing a high level of conflict, for it is not typical or "normal" to do so. In a survey of college students, Balswick and Macrides (1975) found that only 22% reported that they had been rebellious as teenagers.

In their study of middle-class families of adolescent boys, Bandura and Walters (1959) also found little evidence of storm and stress. When teenagers did exhibit aggressive behavior, such as fighting physically with their parents, it was found that these kids presented the same problems as children—but only when they became bigger and stronger could they overpower their parents, a finding to which we will return. Bandura and Walters concluded: "Our findings suggest . . . that the behavioral characteristics exhibited by children during the so-called adolescent stage are lawfully related to, and consistent with, pre-adolescent behavior" (Bandura and Walters, 1952, p. 196).

The general conclusion that profound conflict and turmoil across all life's domains is not the typical pattern of development for adolescents receives support from other studies of nonclinical populations (Grinker et al., 1962; Hamburg et al., 1974; Oldham, 1978; Weiner, 1982). It seems fairly well established then that when one looks at the data, the typical adolescent is not one who is experiencing far-reaching psychic disturbance as a matter of predetermined developmental course. Keep in mind, also, that no period in the human life course is totally free from stress and conflict. Adolescents certainly have no monopoly on storm and stress, no more so than toddlers or middle agers.

Freudian psychoanalytic theory is not the only theoretical perspective from which to view adolescence, of course. "Ego psychology" presents a useful alternative, one that is perhaps more in tune with the empirical evidence. In the early work of Hartmann (1958), we find an effort to base personality development on Ego (rather than Id) as the primary force. Rather than relying upon Id for its energy (as Ego must do in Freudian psychoanalytic theory), in Hartmann's view Ego has its own primary energy (the "mastery drive" as it is often called) and thus is an independent rather than a dependent agent. This somewhat simplified presentation of what is in reality a highly complicated analysis should make clear why it comes as no surprise to ego psychologists that adolescents are not normally crazy and rebellious, as the Freudian analysis asserts they are (must be, should be).

The adolescent who is well equipped with a healthy maturing ego is ready to face the physiological, social, and psychological changes of adolescence (Erikson, 1956). Because Ego is independent it serves as a vehicle for dealing with the unsettling demands of Id (and Superego for that matter). Were it a dependent entity, Ego would be highly vulnerable to a "traitorous" Id, and thus storm and stress would be the normal condition of adolescents. However, this same line of analysis tells us that impaired ego development is related to psychopathology (Noam et al., 1984). The ego psychologist's assumptions are that at the normal level of ego development [the "conformist" level in Loevinger's (1976) terminology], adolescents respond well to the challenges of change but

> that lower levels of ego development are characterized by less impulse control and are geared toward gratification of needs with little ability for delay. The concrete and physical orientation toward self and others would make internally experienced guilt, anxiety, and depression, unlikely. At the conformist level subjects are more oriented toward how others view them and they possess more impulse control. Conflicts lead to experienced sadness and depression rather than to anger and acting out. Needs can be delayed in the service of maintaining relationships and conformity to social norms (Noam et al., 1984, p. 189).

Just as ego psychologists find normal teenagers are not crazy and rebellious (Masterson, 1968, 1972), they report that adolescents evidencing serious psychopathology manifest impaired ego development (Noam et al., 1984).

All this tells us is that seriously troubled youth should be taken seriously, and that the behaviors often identified as symptoms of adolescent maltreatment are usually indicators of genuinely serious problems, often problems of family breakdown associated with the special challenges of adolescence.

THE CHALLENGE OF BEING PARENT TO AN ADOLESCENT

What does adolescence mean for the family as a whole? For one thing, it means adjusting patterns of authority and interaction to incorporate a new person. Developmental psychologist John Hill (1980) has looked at the research on this matter, and his conclusions are these:

> Studies where family interaction is directly observed suggest that there may be a period of temporary disequilibrium in early adolescence while the family adjusts to having a "new person" in the household—"new" in stature, "new" in approaching reproductive capability, "new" in cognitive competence—but this disequilibrium in no way approaches the shoot-out that many parents are led to expect from media reports. Instead, in most families, there appears to be a period of adaptation to the primary changes, a period when both parents and their newly adolescent children work out—often not consciously—what these changes mean for their relationships (1980, p. 33).

At its heart, the task of being parent to an adolescent (and adolescent to a parent) is substantially different from the parent–child relationship in several ways, each of which has implications for the origins and impact of adolescent maltreatment (Garbarino and Gilliam, 1980).

The adolescent's power is much greater than the child's. This includes physical power, of course, including the capability for physical retaliation if assaulted by a parent. It goes beyond this, however, to include the power to stimulate and influence family conflict, to leave the family situation, to harm self and others, to embarrass the parents, to compare parents with other adults, and to help oneself and others. This enhanced power that comes with adolescence is often a destabilizing force, particularly when parents and/or adolescents have little motive or facility for flexible negotiation and compromise.

The adolescent has a broader field of other significant individuals with whom the parents must come to terms. Autonomous relationships with other adults and with peers increase, including sexual relationships that many parents may perceive as threatening. This broader field is a special challenge for parents who seek and expect social isolation.

The adolescent's cognitive abilities are likely to be more advanced than are the child's. Adolescents tend to reason much more like adults, and this injects a new element of complexity into the parent's task. It may also increase the relevance of cognitive sophistication for harmonious family relationships.

In some ways, parents can "get away with more" in their interactions with young children than in their treatment of adolescents. The latter have a broader base of experience with which to compare parental actions. If treated badly, teenagers are more likely than young children to perceive the deviance of their treatment and to report it to someone outside the family (Garbarino and Gilliam, 1980). Adolescents have developed the mental capacity to enable them to understand better flaws in parental reasoning and character and the physical capacity to do something about it. On the economic side, U. S. Department of Agriculture figures indicate that the yearly cost of maintaining a teenager is about 140% that of a young child. This increased cost is stressful for many families and may be a source of family conflict, particularly in larger families where the increased financial demands of adolescence are not matched by increasing income.

Put it all together and it is little wonder that surveys such as that done by Pasley and Gecas (1984) report that a majority of parents say that the adolescent years are the most difficult ones for child rearing. They found that the ages 14–18 were ranked most difficult, followed by the 10- to 13-year-old period. One reason for this is the pressure to rearrange family power relationships and adjust to new actors in the child's social field.

Many parents may feel rejected by the natural shift of attention and affection away from them to others (Dreyfus, 1976). Some may be specially vulnerable to this feeling because of their own life histories and contemporary needs (Pelcovitz et al., 1984). During this period, the power and affectional fabric in the family may be torn. This situation is particularly unfortunate because it occurs at a time when adolescents may most need parental support. On their side, parents need adolescent support if the parents are facing mid-life crisis or "midolescence" (McMorrow, 1977). Olson et al. (1979a, b) have developed a model of family functioning that seems useful in understanding why families differ in their ability to respond effectively to the challenge of adolescence. They view families along two dimensions—adaptability and cohesion. Extremes of either reduce the family's effectiveness. Too much cohesion is termed enmeshed; too little, detached. Too much adaptability is chaotic; too little is rigidity. As we shall see, this approach to characterizing the family system is useful in understanding what places a family at risk for destructive parent–child relations in adolescence, particularly when coupled with an analysis of affection and modes of discipline.

Offer (1969) has described families with adolescents as being in a state of "transitional crisis characterized by confusion." The family reaches a time when there is a need for adjustment and accommodation. It is a difficult time; there are few clear-cut answers as to how much control parents should seek to maintain and how much freedom to grant the adolescent. Diana Baumrind (1979) contends that in the current climate, in which "the rights of youth" are emphasized, parents have all the obligations but few rights. She believes that the current emphasis on the rights of children and adolescents leads to narcissistic, selfish behavior in adolescents, behavior that can precipitate crisis in some families. Baumrind holds that while adolescents depend upon their parents economically and socially, it is unwise to grant them the full freedom and independence accorded to truly independent individuals. As Baumrind sees it, adolescents lack the natural limits imposed by society that arise from the experience of supporting oneself and therefore develop unrealistic expectations concerning the future. This exemplifies how broad social influences can shape the family, and how the meaning of specific parental behavior depends upon the context in which it occurs.

The manner in which parents respond to the adolescent quest for autonomy depends partly upon the type of family structure present, as defined by cohesion, flexibility, authority, and affection (Gamble and Garbarino, 1985). In authoritarian homes, there is little or no allowance for freedom on the adolescent's part. If authoritarian parents are unwilling to divest themselves of any power and continue trying to maintain their dominance over the adolescent, they run the risk of facing a combination of rebellion and dependency on the adolescent's part (Balswick and Macrides,

1975; Douvan and Adelson, 1966; Nye, 1958; Scheck et al., 1973). If adolescents are successful in challenging parental authority, they may become rebellious; if parental discipline has been severe and unjust without much love and affection, teenagers may become overtly aggressive and hostile (Weiner, 1970). The adolescent may leave home and become involved in delinquent activities (Nye, 1958). On the other hand, if children are completely dominated and have no success in challenging parental authority, they may become meek and conform to the parent's dictates. Both usually show some emotional difficulty (Weiner, 1970) and have trouble proceeding to mature identity.

Conflict of all kinds during adolescence is found more frequently in authoritarian or permissive homes than in authoritative homes. In the authoritarian home, the parents are the boss and issue unilateral directives, with no process of negotiation. In the permissive home, the children are in charge, and their demands run the show. It is in the authoritative home that parents negotiate with children to a degree appropriate to the child's development and in ways that enhance further development.

There is more conflict over spending money, friends, social life, home chores, and activities outside of the home in authoritarian households (Edwards and Brauberger, 1973). The autocratically controlled adolescent is likely to harbor resentfulness toward the parents and is less likely to identify with them (Flacks, 1971). Receiving little or no acceptance at home, the adolescent children of authoritarian parents may be driven outside the home for assurance. They may seek it from other adults or become peer dependent. In an effort to garner attention, they may become disruptive and antisocial. They may seek peer acceptance, sociability, and attention from membership in a delinquent gang (Martin, 1975). Thus, for authoritarian parents unwilling to adjust to the adolescent need for independence, attention, and affection, the period of adolescence is likely to be conflict-ridden and stressful. It is, in fact, a vicious cycle: The teenager's wild behavior seems to justify the parent's harsh treatment, and vice versa.

Conversely, permissive parents who cater to their offspring's every need may engender resentment in the adolescent if they are viewed as being overly protective, overly indulgent, or overly detached (all of which are likely perceptions of a "permissive" approach). Adolescents may resent this babying ("infantilizing") approach as their contact with the world beyond the family increases. Adolescents sometimes complain that their parents are sticking too close, trying to be their "best friend" (Daly, 1963). Such "smothering" behavior can produce conflict when the adolescent finally does establish competing relationships, especially sexual ones. The adolescent may also feel confused and resentful at the lack of direction in the home. Or, the adolescent who has experienced permissiveness as benign neglect may cause problems during adolescence both from a lack of supervision and a feeling of having been rejected.

Authoritative parents have the best relationships with their adolescents— at least in families in the mainstream of North American, middle-class society (Balswick and Macrides, 1975; Devereux et al., 1969; Scheck, et al., 1973; Baumrind, 1975). They are willing to grant their children sufficient autonomy to engender the development of self-governorship and ego control but not so much responsibility that it would lead to feelings of omnipotence and social irresponsibility. Their life-long experience with negotiation and shared control prepares them for adolescence in settings away from home as well as in the family.

With the emergence of the period of formal operational thought, many adolescents have the capacity to evaluate parental directions and become increasingly aware of alternatives. Parents are then in the position of having to defend their points of view, a position authoritative parents have already adopted and become used to. Baumrind (1975) has concluded that parents of adolescents will find the use of power assertion ineffectual; "She (the authoritative mother) makes limited use of power to settle parent–child differences, and then primarily to guard her personal interests or to break a stalemate when the adolescent's objection is based, not on principle, but on pique" (p. 143). Authoritative parents have the advantage during adolescence because they can "state and defend their own thesis vigorously, and yet will not limit the freedom of the adolescent to express and argue for his antithesis" (Baumrind, 1975, p. 143).

The job of being a parent, particularly to an adolescent, requires flexibility, the ability to adapt general principles (e.g., "be supportive") and techniques (e.g., "reward positive behavior") to the specifics of a particular adolescent. It is very difficult to understand what life is like for a family member if we can only look from the outside in on a family. This should make us cautious about jumping to conclusions (good or bad) about a family until we have really tried to get an insider's view. Jane Austen said it well when she wrote: "Nobody who has not been in the interior of a family can say what the difficulties of any individual of that family may be " (Emma, 1816–1819). It is hard to know a family from the outside, "objectively," because so much of family life is bound up in what special meaning members attach to each other and their behavior.

No discussion of families will succeed unless it recognizes the special bond between parent and child. To develop well, children need to bask in that crazy feeling parents have. They need to know that someone loves them intensely and unconditionally. We cannot understand families without understanding that to be a parent is to have a special feeling of responsibility for a special being. Perhaps the Russian novelist Leo Tolstoy best captured the miracle of seeing *your* child become an adolescent and then an adult. In his epic, *War and Peace*, he writes:

> The universal experience of the ages, showing that children grow from the cradle to manhood, did not exist for the Countess. The growth of her son had been for her at every stage as extraordinary as though millions and millions of men had not already developed in the same way. Just as twenty years before it had seemed unbelievable that the little creature lying under her heart would ever cry, nurse at the breast, or talk, so now she could not believe that this same little creature could be that strange brave officer, that paragon of sons and men, which judging from his letter he now was. (Tolstoy, pp. 291–292)

As Rogers (1981) points out, the diverse and contradictory nature of research on family relationships cautions us against making specific "how to" prescriptions for parents. Many successful individuals—particularly writers of dramatic fiction—come from families that seem to violate basic principles for effective families (Goertzel and Goertzel, 1972), although, of course, most socially incompetent individuals do as well. The point is that while we can say something about general principles, we cannot offer specific prescriptions on how to *guarantee* effective socialization. Good parent advice books, consultants, and programs should reflect this (Newson and Newson, 1974) rather than offer a "how to" manual, as many have done in the past (Bronfenbrenner, 1958). We *can* say, however, that both adolescents and parents need support. To increase the likelihood of families succeeding in adapting to adolescence, we need a community that is rich in social support—formal support services such as parent education programs and counseling services, as well as informal support services such as social networks, mutual help groups, and positive neighborhoods (Whittaker *et al.*, 1983). To increase the probability that adolescents will make a successful transition to adulthood, adolescents need stable, supportive, and protective relationships with their parents.

For better or for worse, parents do not *determine* what their adolescents will become. The most caring and wise parents do not always succeed in producing competent, caring, and wise offspring. Likewise, even when children have been abused and neglected by their parents, they do not *necessarily* become socially incompetent, vicious, and uncaring. For all its importance, the family is not all-determining, and parents cannot always predict the effects of their actions. Peers, the community, the "times in which we live," and the temperament of the individual play big roles.

Having said all that, we *still* maintain that no other social system has greater influence on development than the family. The family meets most of the young child's biological, emotional, and intellectual needs, and interaction with family members constitutes the greatest portion of the child's early experience. However, it is the very essence of development for the child's world to expand beyond the family to include schools, community organizations, and, most significantly, peers. As adolescents become more actively involved in the wider society, attempt to establish their own independence, and gain a sense of their own unique identities, other influences join, rival, and in some cases may even surpass the family's impact on development. The family retains a critical role in enhancing or impeding development, however. Parents may encourage adolescents to discover their potentials, while providing security and affection when appropriate, or they may inhibit psychological growth through insensitive, excessively demanding, overly restrictive parenting, or overtly abusive treatment. Maltreatment is the bottom line in our analysis, and to it we next turn.

ADOLESCENT MALTREATMENT: AN OVERVIEW

For all its importance and the attention given it in the public and professional press, the transmission of abuse from generation to generation is not the only pertinent developmental consideration in the issue of domestic violence. A more sophisticated developmental approach proceeds to investigate changes in the meaning, causes, correlates, and effects of mistreatment as a function of development and maturation (Cicchetti and Rizley, 1981). The issues for school-age children differ from those for infants, or even for 3-year-olds, for that matter. The infant can do virtually nothing to protect itself from abuse and is totally defenseless against neglect. The battered baby is victimized in direct proportion to the parent's impulses and the presence of internal and external constraints (which are often few). The infant experiences neglect in exact proportion to the parent's failure to provide care, thus being liable to nonorganic failure to thrive. What is more, the infant's capacity to signal its plight to others is limited and largely unconscious. School-age children, on the other hand, have better resources. They can adapt to the parents to minimize abuse by assuming whatever role will appease the parent (e.g., by being extremely compliant, innocuous, or responsible). They can counteract neglect by fending for themselves to some degree. Their ability to communicate their plight is greater because of language skills, and attending school offers many opportunities to do so. Finally, they are likely to have larger independent social networks from which to draw nurturance, support, and protection. This sort of developmental contrast is essential when we consider adolescent maltreatment.

These factors and others come together to shift the standards that guide appropriate behavior in family relationships when a child reaches adolescence. Some forms of behavior by parents toward their offspring that were appropriate (if not particularly wise) in childhood may become abusive in adolescence. For example, the psychological connotations and behavioral responses to spanking a 3- or 4-year-old ("control through force") are usually different from those of spanking a 15-year-old. Likewise, a permissive policy of "control through indulgence" that is possible in response to the child's relatively benign impulses may become untenable in adolescence, for even the most permissive parent cannot fully indulge the more powerful impulses of the adolescent. Also, managing every detail of a 4-year-old's daily existence ("control through intrusion") may be acceptable, while the same intrusiveness with a teenager would be entirely inappropriate and is likely to produce a strong adverse reaction leading to family conflict.

This is crucial because observational research (Reid, in press) shows that abusive families are behaviorally differentiated from nonabusive families in their handling of the 5–10% of parent–child interactions that are negative. Nonabusive families are able to conclude (or at least terminate) these negative interactions quickly. Abusive families are ineffective and become enmeshed in escalating conflict. It is possible that some of the families using the strategies enumerated earlier (control through force, indulgence, or intrusion) become abusive in adolescence because these approaches are no longer sufficient to prevent or put the lid on negative exchanges and prevent the escalation of conflict.

Adolescents typically demand a more nearly equal role in family decision making (Steinberg and Hill, 1980). Observational research presents a picture of the youth challenging the parents (particularly the father) for a more active role in leading family discussions and decision making.

These factors, combined with differences in our culture's view of adolescents (with suspicion) and in our institutional treatment of them (with little compassion), predict the phenomenon of destructive parent–child relations in adolescence will differ from child maltreatment. In fact, as we shall see, in their interpersonal dynamics and cultural interpretation, such destructive relations may more closely resemble spouse abuse than the mistreatment of children, and efforts to understand adolescent maltreatment may serve as a bridge to constructing a much needed, general life-course theory of domestic violence.

Figure 1.1 places abused adolescents on a circular continuum relating abused wives, mistreated children, and abused elders. The central issue is power: the ability to determine one's own behavior and influence the actions of others. Children and the frail elderly are nearly powerless (though their behavior can have a significant effect on what happens to them). Teenagers gain power because of increases in the ability to think, argue, and

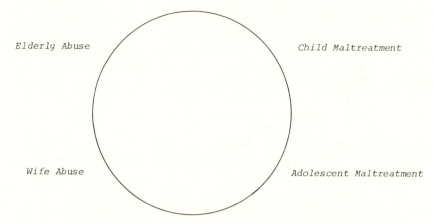

Figure 1.1. A life-course continuum of maltreatment.

act that adolescence brings. Just as wives in a patriarchal and sexist society are powerful enough to threaten the authority of husbands, teenagers challenge parental authority. Paradoxically, because children and the elderly are powerless, they are perfect victims for two reasons. First, they are easily victimized. Second, they elicit sympathy once they are abused. Teenagers are closer to wives in being imperfect victims, in both respects. One evidence of the greater power of abused teens and wives is the fact they sometimes are involved in reciprocal assault. Obviously, children and elderly cannot match the strength of the parent generation, but abuse has been identified as a contributing factor in many assaults by adolescents, from relatively minor incidents to parricide (Garbarino and Gilliam, 1980). Likewise, wives who murder their husbands do so often in retaliation for abuse, usually as the culmination of a long period of mutual assault in which wives are the chronic losers (Straus *et al.*, 1980). Straus *et al.* (1980) reported assault by youth against their parents in some 10% of American families. The likeness between adolescent and wife abuse extends beyond these power dynamics, of course. The two groups are likely to face similar psychodynamic issues, including ambivalence about dependency and separation in their relationships with family authority figures.

Research on adolescent maltreatment is limited to a handful of small-scale studies and several major surveys. The surveys are the National Incidence Study (NIS) (National Center on Child Abuse and Neglect, 1981), the American Humane Association's annual tabulation (1982), and the national probability sample assessed for domestic violence by Straus *et al.* (1980). The small-scale studies include clinical and questionnaire studies of identified or suspected cases of adolescent maltreatment (e.g., Berdie et al., 1983; Farber and Joseph, 1985; Garbarino and Gilliam, 1980; Garbarino et al., 1984; Libbey and Bybee, 1979; Lourie, 1979; Pelcovitz, et al., 1984).

The NIS (National Center on Child Abuse and Neglect, 1981) collected data on suspected abuse and neglect occurring in a sample of 26 United States counties located in 10 states. In addition to child protective service agencies, other local agencies were surveyed (including schools, hospitals, police, and courts). This resulted in the identification of what would be projected nationally to be approximately 650,000 distinct cases. Olsen and Holmes (1983) undertook an analysis of these data contrasting child (11 and younger) with adolescent victims (12–17 years of age). The American Humane Association's National Study of Child Abuse and Neglect Report tabulates and analyzes cases reported to (and "accepted" by) official child protective service agencies, as computed on a state by state basis (with approximately 80% of the states participating in the program). Straus et al. (1980) undertook to assess the level of violence in a national sample of more than 1000 United States families (containing two parents and at least one child 3 years of age or older).

Berdie and her colleagues (1983) studied 163 families (from two separate samples) being serviced by specialized adolescent maltreatment programs after having been identified as cases of adolescent abuse. Farber and his colleagues (Farber and Joseph, 1985; Farber and Kinast, 1984) studied 77 families in which an adolescent was being served by a demonstration treatment project aimed at victims of adolescent maltreatment. These adolescents had been identified by a local protective service agency (40% of the sample), a runaway youth center (31%), a hospital abuse team (20%), or some other agency (9%). Garbarino and Gilliam (1980) studied a sample of 209 cases of maltreatment (100 of which involved adolescents) reported to a local child protective service agency. Libbey and Bybee (1979) studied 25 cases of adolescent abuse, all such cases reported to a local child protection agency over a 10-month period (but excluding all sexual abuse cases from the analysis). Lourie (1977) surveyed 258 cases and conducted an in-depth clinical assessment of 70% of these cases of confirmed adolescent abuse reported to a local child protective agency. Pelcovitz and his colleagues (1984) studied 33 adolescents (from 22 families) reported to a local child protective service agency and referred to a hospital-based treatment program.

RESEARCH-BASED HYPOTHESES

Drawing upon the available research we are in a position to put forth a series of hypotheses concerning adolescent maltreatment. Each reflects an attempt to synthesize critically existing findings.

Hypothesis 1: The incidence of adolescent maltreatment equals or exceeds the incidence of child maltreatment. The National Incidence Study indicates that despite public and professional emphasis on *child* abuse and neglect, adolescent maltreatment accounts for some 47% of the known cases of maltreatment [42% of the cases according to Olsen and Holmes' analysis (1983) which eliminated all "unsubstantiated" cases], although teenagers account for only 38% of the population under the age of 18. The American Humane Association cites a figure of 23% of all reported cases of abuse. As noted earlier, adolescent cases are less likely to be reported, and this is the presumable source of this discrepancy. Studies confined to specific localities (and thus differing on the basis of both local reporting/ definitional practices *and* ecological factors) vary between the NIS and American Humane Association figures (e.g., Morgan, 1977).

Much of the existing body of research on abuse and neglect is based on hospital and protective service samples. This has biased designs and findings against adolescent victims who are less likely to be identified and served by these agencies. One finding of the NIS was that adolescent abuse cases were less likely to be reported to the protective services system than were cases involving abuse of other age groups (24% for children versus 61% for adolescents). An analysis conducted by the American Humane Association (Trainor, 1984) indicates, however, that the likelihood of adolescents receiving services once reported to protective agencies has risen as professional awareness of the problem has grown (from 33% receiving services in 1976 to 55% in 1982). Adolescent maltreatment tends to be associated with problematic acting-out behavior of the teenager or dysfunction within the familiy and is dealt with as such by agencies other than protective services. These cases may often be buried under the labels of "dysfunctional families," "school adjustment problems," "running away," "acting-out," or "marital problems," even when there is no apparent difference in the level of abuse experienced by these groups (Farber and Kinast, 1984). This has implications for sampling in studying adolescent maltreatment, as we shall see.

Hypothesis 2: Adolescent maltreatment includes all forms of abuse and neglect, but psychological and sexual abuse appear to be particularly prevalent. Psychological maltreatment includes "terrorizing," "rejecting," and "isolating" (Garbarino and Vondra, in press). The sexual abuse data reflect the fact that minors are neither fully capable of giving nor free to give informed consent in sexual relationships with adults—particularly authority figures like parents and guardians (Finkelhor, 1979). The NIS reports that adolescents receive less severe physical injuries, more psychological maltreatment, and experience more sexual abuse than do children (Olsen and Holmes, 1983). The small-scale studies present a mixed picture with respect to this hypothesis. The significance of these discrepancies is difficult to establish, however. Some studies are explicitly limited to physical abuse (e.g., Libbey and Bybee, 1979). Others seem to depend upon selective referral that may distort the relative proportion of each type of maltreatment (e.g., Berdie et al., 1983; Pelcovitz et al., 1984). At this point, it seems wise to accept the NIS's findings as the best report on this matter, namely that physical assault constitutes smaller proportions of adolescent cases (42%) than for children (52%), while psychological abuse accounts for a larger proportion (32% for adolescents versus 25% for children).

Hypothesis 3: Females appear to be more likely to be abused as they pass through adolescence than they are in childhood, while risk for males peaks early and generally declines through adolescence. This is evident in the NIS in which female adolescent victims outnumber males 2 to 1 (Olsen and Holmes, 1983). Small-scale studies tend to confirm this: 65% female (Farber and Joseph, 1985); 72% female (Lourie, 1977); 64% female (Libbey and Bybee, 1979); with few exceptions (e.g., 45% female in Pelcovitz et al., 1984).

Hypothesis 4: Some cases of adolescent maltreatment are simply the continuation of abuse and neglect begun in childhood; others represent the deterioration of unwise childhood patterns or the inability of a family that functioned well in childhood to meet new challenges in adolescence. The relative proportion of adolescent maltreatment cases in each category varies from study to study (based in part, it seems, on differences in definition and/or sampling). Lourie (1977) concluded that 90% of the adolescent abuse cases begin in adolescence. In Libbey and Bybee's study (1979) 80% were so described. Garbarino and Gilliam (1980) report a 50–50 split. Pelcovitz et al. (1984) report a 57% adolescent onset. Farber and Joseph (1985) report 29% displayed adolescent onset, while 51% began in childhood but became qualitatively more severe in adolescence. Berdie and her colleagues concluded that 24% of their adolescent cases began in adolescence (Berdie et al., 1983).

Hypothesis 5: Unlike families at high risk for child maltreatment, families at high risk for destructive parent–adolescent relations are socioeconomically equivalent to low-risk families—although a feeling of deprivation and the strain on resources associated with larger family size may play a role (Vondra, this volume, Chapter 9). The big social class differences found to characterize child maltreatment cases are largely absent (or at least are attentuated). This is evident in the NIS. Adolescent abuse cases were one-half as likely as child maltreatment cases to be earning less than $7000 per year, and three times as likely to be earning $15,000 per year or more. Nonetheless, 66% of the adolescent maltreatment cases had family incomes below $15,000—with 25% below $7000 and 33% above $15,000 (Olsen and Holmes, 1983). Berdie and her colleagues (1983) reported that about 51% of the families in her study earned incomes less than $15,000.

Garbarino and Gilliam (1980) reported findings consistent with the NIS. What is more, when they compared adolescent onset with childhood onset adolescent maltreatment cases they found even more striking differences— with the adolescent onset cases being about one-half as likely to be in the poverty group than the child onset (and child maltreatment) cases. In that protective service-based sample, adolescent onset families were four times as likely to earn incomes in excess of $11,000 (in 1978 dollars): 42% versus 11%.

Several studies have used measures of social class apart from income. The NIS reports higher educational levels for parents of maltreated adolescents than for maltreated children (Olsen and Holmes, 1983). Farber and Joseph (1985) report that their families were predominantly lower class (average Hollingshead Index of 53). Pelcovitz and his colleagues report that 59% of their families were classified in the two top socioeconomic groups (5 point Hollingshead Index). Libbey and Bybee (1979) indicate that only 12% of their families were located in the lowest (of 8) socioeconomic status categories.

Hypothesis 6: Families at high risk in adolescence are more likely to contain stepparents. A variety of analyses point to the stepparent–adolescent relationship as a very risky one, particularly among families in which adolescents exhibit developmental pathology (cf. Burgess and Garbarino, 1983; Daly and Wilson, 1981; Kalter, 1977). Research on adolescent maltreatment tends to confirm this. Libbey and Bybee (1979) report 28% of their families were stepfamilies (and an additional 8% were adoptive). Berdie and her colleagues (1983) reported that 25% of their families were step- (and 31% had no father figure in the home). Olsen and Holmes' (1983) analysis of the NIS data revealed that 40% of the adolescent maltreatment cases contained a stepparent. Farber and Joseph (1985) reported that only 30% of their adolescents were living with both biological parents. Overall, 12–15% of children live with stepparents.

Hypothesis 7: Adolescents at high risk for maltreatment are less socially competent and exhibit more developmental problems than their peers. Most studies comment upon the aversive and/or dysfunctional character of the adolescent victim of maltreatment. Libbey and Bybee (1979) report that in more than 90% of the cases they studied, specific abusive incidents were preceded by negative adolescent behavior (such as disobeying or arguing). Farber and Joseph (1985) present the most complex analysis. They have grouped the problems of physically abused adolescents into six clinical patterns, observed in their sample of abused runaways (served by a shelter).

1. *Acting out* (running away, theft, drug abuse, provocative behavior, and truancy)—17% of the adolescents.
2. *Generalized anxiety* (lack of trust, rationalization and manipulative

behavior, poor concentration, poor identity development, and academic failure)—13%.

3. *Depression* (lethargy, social isolation, fluctuations in weight, fatigue, and low self-esteem)—22%.

4. *Adjustment reactions* (extreme and age-inappropriate alcohol misuse, school misconduct, inaccessibility of feelings, eating disorders, auditory hallucinations)—16%.

5. *Emotional thought disorder* (homicidal actions, speech disorders, hypomanic symptoms, disordered thinking)—12%.

6. *Helplessness and dependency* (homicidal and suicidal ideation, extreme sibling conflict, family role problems, denial as a frequent defense mechanism)—21%.

Of the 77 adolescents in the study, five were classified in two categories: one mixed "generalized anxiety" and "acting out"; two mixed "depression" and "helplessness/dependency"; and two mixed "helplessness/delinquency" and "generalized anxiety." Berdie and her colleagues (1983) report that 49% of their adolescent maltreatment victims exhibited significant clinical indicators of depression and problems such as "nervous habits," "isolation," "poor social skills with peers," "lethargy," "low self-esteem; low frustration tolerance," "temper outbursts," and "stubbornness" characterized from 45 to 70% of the adolescents (depending upon which problem is being considered in the analysis).

Hypothesis 8: Families characterized as high risk for adolescent maltreatment are also at high risk on the dimensions of adaptability, cohesion, support, discipline, and interparental conflict. Lourie's (1979) model of family functioning offered three categories of adolescent abuse: (1) families that continued a childhood pattern; (2) families that escalated from harsh (though nonabusive by community standards) punishment in childhood to abuse in adolescence; and (3) families that functioned normally in childhood but in which the transition to adolescence precipitated abuse. This early formulation figures prominently in many subsequent analyses of family functioning in adolescent maltreatment.

Libbey and Bybee (1979) reported that 13 of their 25 cases could be characterized as "reasonably well-functioning families who had recently been under stress." The other 12 cases were characterized by "psychopathology or disturbed behavior by either the adolescent or parents." Few cases seemed to be attributable to the high stress/social isolation syndrome characteristic of many child maltreatment families. In contrast, Berdie et al. (1983) concluded that "adolescent maltreatment families, like many child maltreated families, are multi-problem families with high rates of divorce and separation, financial stresses and family conflict." Farber and Joseph (1985) do not comment directly on family functioning but do report that an analysis of adolescent problems did not find differences based upon Lourie's (1979) classification of maltreatment types (with its implicit classification of families).

Pelcovitz *et al.* (1984) conducted a clinical analysis of their 22 adolescent maltreatment families. They classified cases into childhood and adolescent onset. The eight childhood onset families (14 adolescents) were characterized in the multiproblem child abuse mode—intergenerational abuse, spouse abuse, developmentally inappropriate demands, all the elements of what Helfer and Kempe (1968) termed "the world of abnormal rearing." The 14 adolescent onset families (19 adolescents) fell into two categories (on the basis of multiple, independent clinical assessments): 7 "authoritarian" and 7 "overindulgent."

The authoritarian families were characterized by paternalistic, harsh, rigid, domineering styles of child rearing. This was coupled with denial— denial of parental feelings toward each other and about the family system. Abuse typically arose from adolescent challenge (acting out and testing behavior) that was met with overwhelming force. The high priority placed upon control provided the foundation for high levels of force.

In contrast, the overindulgent families were characterized by parental efforts to compensate for the emotional deprivation they had experienced in their own childhood (12 of the 14 parents had lost one or both of their parents during childhood). These families made few demands upon their children, set few limits, and desired a high level of emotional gratification from them. When the children reached adolescence and sought not only to form primary attachments outside the home but also began to act impulsively in important social settings, the overindulgent parents reacted with excessive force.

Hypothesis 9: Adolescent abuse is less likely to be transmitted intergenerationally than is child abuse. Pelcovitz and his colleagues (1984) report that 75% of the parents in families with childhood onset of abuse had themselves been abused in childhood, as opposed to 25% of the parents in the adolescent onset group. Garbarino and Gilliam (1980) reported that 21% of the childhood onset cases (being served by child protective services) had parental history of abuse versus 10% for the adolescent onset group. Berdie *et al.* (1983) report a trend in this direction.

In conclusion, it seems clear that our understanding of the meaning, origins, and impact of adolescent maltreatment is progressing. We can see that it does seem to represent a set of phenomena that differentiate it from child maltreatment. With the preceding hypotheses as a guide we can proceed. Chapters 2 and 3 explore the links between abuse and two major juvenile problems, delinquency and running away from home. These analyses of consequences set the stage for our efforts to understand the origins of maltreatment.

2

CHILD ABUSE AND JUVENILE DELINQUENCY: WHAT ARE THE LINKS?

JAMES GARBARINO
MARGARET C. PLANTZ

INTRODUCTION

Child maltreatment and juvenile delinquency are two of the most compelling and perplexing social problems facing the United States in the 1980s. Both meet the criteria proposed by Manis (1974) for classification as "serious" problems: They are *prevalent* (involving millions of people); they are *severe* (being implicated in many thousands of injuries and deaths as well as widespread emotional anguish); and they are *primary* (being intertwined with a host of other problems such as poverty, alienation, stress, and economic dysfunction). The evident seriousness of both problems justifies the current high level of public and professional concern. As we have seen in Chapter 1, adolescent maltreatment is intertwined with issues of social competence and social relationships for the adolescent. In this and the chapter to follow, we explore the dynamic processes that link together destructive family relations and the adolescent's relations with the world outside the family. Here we discuss the full range of juvenile delinquency. Chapter 3 focuses on the phenomenon of running away from home. In both chapters, we are setting the stage for further, more detailed explorations of troubled youth and troubled families.

Despite the lack of consensus concerning the precise causes of maltreatment and delinquency, grounds exist for wondering whether these two social problems are themselves linked. This hypothesis arises from the common observation that lives containing delinquent behavior often seem to contain maltreatment as well. As we shall see in the review that follows, it is not the existence of this coincidence that is so difficult to establish (although some researchers do doubt even this) but the magnitude, meaning, direction, and significance of the apparent association. Is the relationship simply and unidirectionally causal? Does abuse cause delinquency? If so, how? Or, is it reciprocally causal? Does delinquency also cause abuse? Or, is there some third cause of both, some set of family problems, individual dysfunctions, and/or social conditions that produces *both* maltreatment *and* delinquency? What prevents these causal links from operating? What exacerbates them? All these questions stand in need of answers. Our review examines the empirical evidence available to answer them.

The first section of the chapter contains research findings that may indicate whether or not there is some link between maltreatment and delinquency. Following that, we discuss methodological problems and noncomparability issues that are associated with much of the research in this area. In the third section, we present current hypotheses and related evidence about the links between these two social problems.

EVIDENCE OF AN ASSOCIATION BETWEEN MALTREATMENT AND DELINQUENCY

In this section, we present the results of empirical efforts to test the existence of a link between being maltreated as a child and being involved in delinquent activities as a juvenile. Reported first are retrospective studies of delinquent juveniles that sought evidence of maltreatment in their backgrounds. Next are follow-up studies of maltreated children that looked for delinquent behavior when the child reached adolescence. The final set of studies addressed the link between one type of maltreatment—physical abuse—and delinquency characterized by violence. We cite in this section only studies in which the researchers used the terms *abuse* or *abuse and neglect* to describe the mistreatment they were studying. We present research that examined "harsh" or "severe punishment" as a variable related to delinquent behavior later in the chapter.

Maltreatment in the Histories of Juvenile Delinquents

One way of establishing an association between maltreatment and delinquency is to show that juvenile delinquents have experienced maltreatment at a rate higher than that of the general population. That National Incidence Study (NIS) on child abuse and neglect (National Center on Child Abuse and Neglect, 1981) estimated that 3.4 children per thousand (or roughly 0.34% of all children) are known to suffer demonstrable physical harm at the hands of a parent or other in-home caretaker in this country each year (pp. 1, 4). The report also estimated that 5.7 children per thousand (0.57%) are victims of some type of abuse—physical, sexual, and/or emotional—and 5.3 children per thousand (0.53%) endure physical, educational, and/or emotional neglect (p. 4). Among the low-income populations, the rate of maltreatment (abuse and neglect combined) was estimated (p. 10) at 27 children per thousand (2.7%). Of course, these rates are incidence figures per year. At issue is the total *prevalence* rate—that is, how many children experience maltreatment over the course of their childhood (until age 18 under law). The overall prevalence rates are, of course, higher than the yearly incidence rates. How much higher? We do not know. If each case identified by the NIS was a "once in a childhood" situation, and if maltreatment typically begins to occur with equal frequency across the age space from birth to age 18, then we might simply add up the incidence rates for each of the 18 years involved to get a total prevalence rate. Using the NIS data, this would result in a 61.0 per 1000 children (6.1%) overall. This figure is very unlikely, however. For example, most estimates of the proportion of adolescent victims who are the recipients of maltreatment for the first time in adolescence average around 50%. This alone would lower the figure to 48.2 per 1000 (4.8%). Also, most cases of child maltreatment are long-term. Thus, the *same* children who were identified as 2-year-old victims might (if undetected) be picked up as 4- or 6-year-old victims in succeeding years. We can thus expect that the 6.1% prevalence rate is an upper limit, and a significantly lower figure is more likely.

If we simply extrapolate the low-income incidence rate of 2.7% to an *upper-limit* prevalence rate of 55%, the same problems arise. In addition, the link between low income and maltreatment seems to operate mostly during childhood (particularly infancy and early childhood) and to diminish dramatically in adolescence. This would mean that most low-income-related cases would occur early in childhood and tend to be chronic. A plausible estimate is an overall prevalence of 30% for low-income children and youth (based on an initial 2.7% incidence rate that declines gradually to a 1% incidence rate by age 17). All these figures reflect guesses about the relation between incidence and prevalence, of course. As we shall see, however, even the high estimates used still permit the conclusion that juvenile delinquents report maltreatment at disproportionately high rates.

> Case files of 863 delinquent male adolescents incarcerated in Ohio showed that 26% had been physically abused, and 86% of this group had been abused more than once (Kratcoski, 1982).
>
> When girls in an Arkansas diagnostic center and school who had been adjudicated as delinquent or in need of supervision were asked to complete questionnaires, 53% of 60 who responded indicated that they had been sexually abused, while 25% recalled scars, 38% recalled beatings, and 51% recalled bruises resulting from physical punishment (Mouzakitis, 1981).

Of 1963 children reported as delinquent or ungovernable in eight New York counties in 1971 and 1972, 21% of the boys and 29% of the girls had been reported to authorities earlier as abused or neglected. Figures for each county ranged from 8 to 41% for boys and from 11 to 53% for girls (Alfaro, 1978, 1981).

Child abuse had been noted in the medical records of 15% of 81 delinquents of both sexes incarcerated in a Connecticut correctional school (Shanok and Lewis, 1981).

At a private residential treatment program in New Hampshire for court-referred delinquents, 66% of 150 youths referred over an 8-year period were found to have been abused or severely neglected (Sandberg, 1983).

Two hundred juvenile offenders being held in a Denver detention center after being picked up by police for the first time were interviewed about their backgrounds. Eighty-four percent of 100 whose statements later were confirmed and 72% of 100 whose statements could not be confirmed reported being abused or neglected before the age of six. Of the confirmed-report group, 92% had been bruised, lacerated, or fractured by their parents within 18 months prior to being picked up (Steele, 1975; credited to Hopkins in Steele, 1976).

Interviews with 100 juvenile offenders in Philadelphia yielded reports that 82% had been abused or neglected, with 43% recalling having been knocked unconscious by a parent (Weston, reported in Steele, 1976).

In a study of 653 delinquents, 43% were found to have been abused, neglected, or abandoned at some time in their lives (Weinbach, et al., 1981).

From questionnaires completed by 191 residents of juvenile delinquent centers in Oregon, researchers found that 58% had experienced abusive discipline by their fathers, and 40% were disciplined abusively by their mothers (Rhoades and Parker, 1981).

When medical records for 109 delinquents referred to a Connecticut juvenile court were matched with those of 109 nondelinquents, it was found that 9% of the delinquents, compared to 1% of the nondelinquents, had received services from one near-by hospital for child abuse injuries (Lewis and Shanok, 1977). In a follow-up study an indepth analyses revealed that 69% of the delinquents had been abused in contrast to 15% of the nondelinquents (Lewis, 1985).

Delinquent Behavior by Maltreated Children

A second way of demonstrating a link between maltreatment and delinquency is to show that victims of child maltreatment are involved in delinquency at a higher rate than juveniles who have not been maltreated. Estimates of the prevalence of delinquency vary dramatically as a function of whether self-reports or official reports are used as the basis for calculations and whether the definition is broad—including the most commonplace minor offenses—or narrow—including only the most serious offenses. Poulin et al., (1980) used state-by-state data in their estimate that 13 juveniles per 1000 youth population (or up to 1.3%) were being admitted annually to juvenile detention centers and adult jails in the mid-1970s. Corbett and Vereb (1974) used census figures and juvenile court reports to estimate that 37.5 delinquency cases per 1000 children in the population were disposed of by juvenile courts in 1974. Because one child could be involved in more than one case, this figure means that something less than 3.75% of all children were involved in a juvenile court case that year. Griffin and Griffin (1978) reported estimates that, before attaining adult status, 3% of all youths are adjudicated delinquents, 17% are referred to juvenile court, 34% are taken into police custody, and as many as 90% commit some act for which they could be adjudicated if caught and legally processed.

Identifying rates of delinquency among children who were maltreated requires following up on such children either in person or through agency records. Most of the longitudinal and follow-up studies of maltreated children considered issues other than delinquency rates in their search for information (e.g., Baher *et al.*, 1976; Elmer, 1977; Friedman and Morse, 1974; Herrenkohl and Herrenkohl, 1981; Kent, 1976; Lynch and Roberts, 1982; Martin and Beezley, 1977; Martin *et al.*, 1974; Morse *et al.*, 1970; Terr, 1970). Few follow-up studies have examined delinquency rates of abused children. Whether or not the first three findings reported below indicate an association between maltreatment and delinquency depends upon the delinquency rates in the general population with which they are compared. The last result reported does include a comparison figure.

Following up 4 years later on 34 victims of child abuse from a Washington, D.C. hospital, researchers found that 20% had come to the court's attention because of delinquency (Silver *et al.*, 1969).

When 5392 Arizona children referred to a state agency because of child abuse were followed up in juvenile court records, after 5 years, 14% were found to have been brought before the court for juvenile crimes or status offenses (Bolton *et al.*, 1977) and after 10 years, 32% had been adjudicated (Bolton, personal communication).

From 1952 and 1953, through court and other records, researchers followed 4465 children from 1423 families in eight New York counties who had been reported for suspected child abuse and neglect. Of the 3637 victims of substantiated abuse or neglect, 19% had been reported as delinquent or ungovernable. For each county, the figures ranged from 8 to 32% of the boys and from 2 to 24% of the girls (Alfaro, 1978, 1981).

In one of the counties in the New York study (Alfaro, 1978, 1981), almost 10% of the children who had been abused or neglected were reported as delinquent or ungovernable, compared to 2% of all children in the county during the same time period.

Physical Abuse and Violent Delinquency

Guided by psychodynamic and modeling theories, some investigators have hypothesized that experiencing physical abuse as a child relates not just to general delinquent behavior but to delinquent behavior that involves violence. Some studies have found that violent delinquents are more likely to have experienced abuse than nonviolent delinquents.

Among 97 male juvenile offenders in a Connecticut correctional school, 75% of the 78 boys who had committed violent acts had experienced abuse in statistically significant contrast to one-third of the 19 boys whose offenses were nonviolent, and the youths' degree of violence was correlated with having been abused (Lewis, Shanok, Pincus, and Glaser, 1979).

A group of 80 incarcerated delinquents in the same correctional school were found to be significantly more violent than a matched group of 77 nonincarcerated delinquents, with 50% of the former and 27% of the latter having been involved in violent acts. Researchers found that 10% of the incarcerated (more violent) group compared to 4% of the nonincarcerated (less violent) group had notations of child abuse in their medical records (Lewis, Shanok, and Balla, 1979).

A relationship between abuse and delinquent violence is indicated also by findings that delinquents who were abused or neglected are involved in violent offenses more often than nonmaltreated delinquents.

In the New York study of 1963 delinquents, while only small percentages had been referred to authorities for one or more of seven types of violent acts (from 0.2 to 12% implicated in each type of offense), those delinquents who were found to have been victims of abuse or neglect had been involved in violence at much higher rates (between 12 and 29% for each type of violent act) (Alfaro, 1978, 1981).

In contrast to the "violence begets violence" hypothesis that abuse relates positively to violent delinquency is the hypothesis that being a victim of family violence *decreases* violent behavior and increases withdrawal. In this view, being abused as a child is related negatively to violent delinquency, contributing instead to escape acts such as truancy and running away.

An Arizona research team found that 774 juvenile delinquents who had been referred earlier for child abuse were less likely than their siblings or 900 nonabused offenders to have engaged in aggressive crimes and much more likely to have committed escape acts such as truancy and running away (Bolton et al., 1977; Gutierres and Reich, 1981). At a later follow-up, however, the differences between aggressive crimes and escape acts had disappeared (Bolton, personal communication).

Summary

The first section of this chapter has covered empirical tests of an association between child maltreatment and juvenile delinquency. Retrospective studies of juvenile delinquents consistently have found that these youth experienced maltreatment at rates much higher than the general population. The strength of the evidence presented by follow-up studies of maltreated children is less clear. While rates of delinquency among these children appear high, it is not always clearer whether they are higher than those of other subgroups of the population. Data on the relationship between physical abuse and violent delinquency are sparse, but findings indicate that an association may be present.

Shortcomings of the Research

Taken as a group, the studies presented in the first section suggest an association between child maltreatment and juvenile delinquency. Methodological flaws and differences among these research efforts, however, make it difficult to draw firm conclusions from their findings.

There is notable inconsistency among the specific behaviors that were measured and labeled as "delinquency" for each study. Some studies examined only violent delinquency, some included property crimes and/or status offenses, and some included various forms of youthful mischief-making. Inhibiting comparisons further, some researchers recorded only adjudicated instances of delinquency, others measured reported incidents, and still others, using self-report methods, included incidents unknown to authorities.

The variation among behaviors measured as "abuse" or "maltreatment" seems to be nearly as great, although several reports do not include the researchers' operational definition of the term. Different degrees of force are labeled as abusive. Physical, sexual, and emotional abuse are variously grouped or separated, and different types of abuse are at times grouped with some form of neglect. The noncomparability of the key variables in these studies makes it unlikely that they can provide a definitive answer to the question of an association between maltreatment and delinquency, although a carefully executed meta-analysis might yield some needed clarification.

A methodological shortcoming of many of the studies cited in the previous section is their lack of appropriate comparison groups. This problem may be particularly troubling for studies assessing the rates of delinquency among maltreated children because rates can be unexpectedly high for various delinquent offenses in different population groups, and thus high rates among maltreated children are not necessarily indicative of an association. Lack of comparison groups is related to another methodological deficiency: absence of inferential statistics assessing the significance of findings.

A problem associated with many of the retrospective studies of delinquents is their use of reports from the juveniles themselves to identify child abuse or neglect in the histories of juvenile offenders. Such reliance on self-report data may result in inflated estimates of abuse. The New York study of delinquent and ungovernable children (Alfaro, 1978, 1981) and the

Connecticut study of correctional school and juvenile court wards (Lewis and Shanok, 1977; Lewis, Shanok, and Balla, 1979; Shanok and Lewis, 1981) are notable exceptions. The former relied on records from public and private child protective agencies and children's court for documentation of past abuse and neglect; the latter used hospital medical records to identify abuse. While research relying on self-reports may produce inflated estimates of past maltreatment, the New York study's finding that 21% of the boys and 29% of the girls had been identified earlier as abused or neglected and the Connecticut findings that 9% of court-referred delinquents (Lewis and Shanok, 1981), 10% of an incarcerated and 4% of a nonincarcerated group (Lewis, Shanok, and Balla, 1979), and 15% of another incarcerated group (Shanok and Lewis, 1981) had been treated at the same hospital for abuse injuries, probably are conservative estimates of the actual incidence of maltreatment in these groups.

ATTEMPTS TO IDENTIFY THE LINKS

Despite methodological issues, the body of available evidence suggests that involvement in delinquent acts as an adolescent is linked to an increased likelihood of having experienced maltreatment as a child. The assertion that there are links between these two problems is not new. The larger question is, What are those links? How is it that a child who is maltreated may be more likely to encounter the juvenile justice system than one who is not, or that a delinquent adolescent is more likely to have been abused or neglected than a nondelinquent adolescent?

There undoubtedly is no simple cause–effect mechanism operating here. Many intervening and confounding factors appear to be present. Unraveling the connections is complicated by the possibility that the links are different for different types of maltreatment and different types of proscribed adolescent behavior. One might suspect that family and other social network variables, as well as economic and perhaps cultural ones, shape the relationship. Finally, of course, are the basic individual differences such as temperament and sex, even height and weight, that personalize any general equations describing the situation. In this section, we present findings pertaining to several explanations of how these two variables may be linked.

Severe Punishment and Delinquency

One formulation of the relationship holds that it is not just abuse but severe physical punishment, whether termed abuse or not, that is linked to later delinquent behavior. Some studies have examined the association between harsh discipline (which might or might not have been considered abuse in some of the studies reported earlier) and delinquency.

Twenty-six delinquent boys were found to have experienced significantly higher rates of physical punishment by their fathers than was the case for 26 nondelinquents (Bandura and Walters, 1959).

Of 48 juveniles referred for psychological services by juvenile court, 100% of the 29 boys and 63% of the 19 girls indicated they had experienced severe parental punishment (Welsh, 1976).

When 58 consecutive court-referred boys were asked what their parents normally did when they misbehaved, 97% said they had been disciplined by belt, board, extension cord, fist, or similar object (Welsh, 1976).

The proposition that severe punishment is related not just to general delinquency but to juvenile violence also has been investigated.

The strongest support for this link comes from a British longitudinal study of 411 boys begun when they were age eight. Twenty-seven of the group (7%) had been convicted of a violent offense by age 18, and 98 (24%) had been convicted of a nonviolent offense. Parents of 62% of the violent boys had been judged to use harsh discipline and have a harsh attitude toward their child, while parents of 33% of the nonviolent delinquents and 27% of the 286 nondelinquents were identified in this category (Farrington, 1978; West, 1969, 1982; West and Farrington, 1973, 1977).

In a retrospective study, severity of corporal punishment and aggressiveness of delinquent crime were significantly related in the earlier mentioned groups of 58 court-referred delinquent males (Welsh, 1976).

Central Nervous System Disorders

Another line of evidence concerns the possibility that early trauma and/or congenital abnormality places the child at risk for subsequent (or further) maltreatment *and* for delinquency—particularly violent delinquency.

Over 30% of the children in a follow-up study of abused children evidenced central nervous system damage, and 57% had IQ scores of 80 or less (Elmer, 1977).

Of the abused children in another sample, 43% evidenced neurological damage, and 33% had IQs of less than 80 (Martin, 1972).

Among 19 nonviolent incarcerated delinquents, 7% were found to evidence major neurological damage, and 67% showed minor damage. For 78 violent incarcerated delinquents, the figures were 46% for major and 99% for minor damage. Thirty percent of the violent (but none of the nonviolent) delinquents had abnormal EEGs and/or a history of grand mal epilepsy (Lewis, Shanok, Pincus, and Glaser, 1979). A group of 80 incarcerated delinquents had been significantly more involved in violent acts than a group of 77 nonincarcerated delinquents. Sixty-two percent of the former and 44% of the latter had been treated at a local hospital during childhood for head or face injury. Injuries were not only significantly more prevalent in the incarcerated (more violent) group, but also more severe (Lewis, Shanok, and Balla, 1979). In a follow-up study, Lewis found that 28% of the incarcerated delinquents had been hospitalized for psychiatric reasons in contrast to none of an otherwise comparable sample of nondelinquents (Lewis, 1985).

Here, as with the broader question before us of the causal nature of the link between abuse and delinquency, the *sequence* of events is crucial. Some researchers dispute the contention that the child's disabilities stimulate abuse and argue that, rather than being congenital, the central nervous system and intellectual deficits noted are consequences of early maltreatment (cf. Starr, 1982b). A complete review of this issue is beyond the scope of the present discussion, however. Our purpose in raising the issue is simply to establish that sorting out the sequences and causal relations involved in maltreatment and delinquency is as complex and difficult as it is vital, as empirically intractable as it is scientifically important. At any rate, maltreatment and delinquency do seem to bear a family resemblance, including but not necessarily limited to both being products of high-stress, low-resource, multiple-problem families.

Family Factors

The possibility that certain stressful family situations or characteristics press toward both maltreatment and delinquent behavior by family members would seem to be fertile ground for research. Many studies have examined the relationship between various family characteristics and child maltreatment, and many others have considered family variables related to delinquency. Little has been done, however, to integrate the two groups (but see Weinbach, *et al.*, 1981). A review and comparison of the literature from both areas would be instructive, but we do not attempt it here.

> An opportunity to identify family characteristics common to both problems was presented by the New York study (Alfaro, 1978, 1981) that not only followed up children from families reported for abuse and neglect but also searched for evidence of abuse in the histories of ungovernable or delinquent adolescents. Data from this study indicated that children from larger families and children from homes where a paramour was present were more likely to be both maltreated and later identified as delinquent or ungovernable (Carr, 1977).

Delinquent Responses to Maltreatment

Another hypothesis about the link between maltreatment and delinquency suggests that delinquency is one *eventual* consequence of maltreatment because some of the behavioral responses to maltreatment either lead to delinquency or are defined as delinquent. For example, if one consequence of maltreatment is to become estranged from prosocial adults and peers, then a maltreated child is more likely to have antisocial friends, and association with delinquent peers is a powerful predictor of juvenile delinquency (Gold and Petronio, 1980).

As we shall see in Chapter 3, frequently a link between maltreatment and delinquency is forged when victims of maltreatment attempt to remedy their situation by retaliating or running away—either choice being considered a delinquent act. While no studies have been found of the proportion of abused children who leave home while still under age, several studies indicate that a large proportion of this country's adolescent runaways have been abused, and many left home because of the abuse. We should note that, while many adolescents leave home voluntarily to escape abuse, there is evidence that some "runaway" delinquents are actually "castaways": children put out of their homes by their parents. These victims of extreme child neglect constitute a special class of cases in which maltreatment "causes" delinquency.

> In the Connecticut runaway housing program, 24% of the 308 adolescents studied were found to be castaways (Gullotta, 1977). Of 33,000 youths served by the Department of Health, Education and Welfare (DHEW) runaway projects in 1976–77, 10% had been pushed out of their homes by their parents or legal guardian (Youth Development Bureau, 1978).

The frequency with which physical abuse leads to physical retaliation rather than running away is less well studied.

> This abuse-delinquency link may be reflected in findings that 26% of 223 abused delinquents incarcerated in Ohio had directed violence toward immediate family members or caretakers, while 12% of 640 nonabused incarcerated delinquents had attacked a family member. Of those youths who had committed a violent offense against any person, 45% of the abused and 18% of the nonabused had acted against a family member (Kratcoski, 1982).

> Case studies of four juveniles who fatally shot their adult caregivers show that all four were victims of on-going physical abuse, and two of the killings occurred during an abusive episode (Post, 1982).

> In another study of five youths who had killed or threatened to kill a parent, researchers concluded that parental brutality had led to at least two killings (Duncan and Duncan, 1971).

Delinquency Leading to Abuse

A further link to be explored is the extent to which delinquent behavior puts an adolescent at risk for abuse, be it in the home, on the street, or in an institution. A special issue here is whether such abuse represents a new experience or the continuation or resumption of earlier maltreatment that itself might have contributed to the particular delinquent acts that resulted in the *current* experience of abuse. The possibilities for seemingly endless chains of causality appear to exist unless intervention occurs to alter the abuse–delinquency–abuse or delinquency–abuse–delinquency cycle.

> One study of 25 physically abused adolescents revealed that the majority had shown serious behavior problems (chronic truancy, stealing, and running away) prior to the abusive incident (Libbey and Bybee, 1979).

Many runaway delinquents become victims of pornographers and pimps who subject the runaways to sexual exploitation. In turn, teenage prostitutes, who are classed as "delinquent" if apprehended by authorities, are frequent victims of physical and sexual abuse by both pimps and customers (Fisher et al., 1982).

Many children who are picked up for juvenile offenses are held in adult jails. While it is debated whether this in itself is an inappropriate response to the child's situation and constitutes maltreatment, there is little doubt that the conditions and treatment inflicted on many jailed children are severely abusive (Children's Defense Fund, 1976; Wooden, 1976).

Not only jails, but also juvenile detention centers, training schools, and some types of foster homes have been indicted for their conditions and practices (see Haeuser et al., 1981).

System-Created Links

An additional possibility is that links between maltreatment and delinquency are created by juvenile justice practices that label and adjudicate maltreatment victims as juvenile offenders (Smith et al., 1980). Related to this are assertions that child welfare and judicial system practices are more likely to intervene with low-income parents and children than with families of greater financial means (Griffin and Griffin, 1978; Pagelow, 1982; Weinbach et al., 1981), so that these systems not only create links between maltreatment and delinquency but also create them disproportionately among youth from low-income backgrounds. While this bias is alleged often and empirically documented in some cases, we cannot determine whether or not it accounts for the disproportionate rates of both reported maltreatment and reported delinquency among low-income populations.

CONCLUSIONS

What, then, are the links between child maltreatment and juvenile delinquency? Our review tells us that there is some empirical evidence to support the existence of several links. It does appear that child maltreatment (particularly when defined broadly) is associated with juvenile delinquency (particularly when defined narrowly). The links may be causal in both directions, as well as being the result of common etiology in disrupted, ineffectual families and culturally based practices that legitimate family violence, decrease social control in adolescence, and support institutional practices that respond punitively to adolescent reactions to family disruption.

The relative importance and strength of these links remain undetermined, however. What is more, the available evidence does not address many historical and cultural issues of great relevance. For example, we do not know whether recent efforts to deinstitutionalize status offenders (and separate them from criminally delinquent youths) have strengthened or weakened the link between maltreatment and delinquency. Neither do we know the effects of recent increases in reported abuse (and particularly sexual abuse). Nor do we know if the presumed causal links between maltreatment and delinquency operate differently for different groups within society—more or less powerfully, for instance, for impoverished versus affluent families and communities.

Also unclear is the relevance of these links for intervention. How relevant is a history of maltreatment to therapeutic and correctional intervention in juvenile delinquency? Is it more relevant for some subgroups than others? What are the scientific, administrative, and constitutional implications of accepting a history of victimization as grounds for specifying treatment and/or correctional goals?

Our meager knowledge in this area is a promise of future understanding. Our ignorance is a challenge to researchers and policymakers alike, one that we will confront throughout this volume. We face it first in Chapter 3 as we review what is known about adolescent runaways.

THE ADOLESCENT RUNAWAY

3

JAMES GARBARINO
JANIS WILSON
ANNE C. GARBARINO

Running away to and, more significantly, running away in America has traditionally grown out of a mixture of youthful expectations and the hope for a better life away from home as well as out of frustrations and despair over current life circumstances.

Liebertoff, 1980, pp. 151–152

Yeah, I ran. I ran to get away from that house and the people in it. I wanted to be on my own without all the hassles. . . . Yeah, right, so I ended up on the street. No job because I was too young; no place to stay because I didn't have any money. So when this dude approached me I went with him. . . . You know the rest of the story.

A 15-year-old runaway

INTRODUCTION

Running away from home has a long tradition in America. It played an important role in the settlement of the Western frontier and has been immortalized in Mark Twain's classic *Huck Finn*. During the nineteenth and early twentieth centuries, most adolescents who ran away from home had a relatively easy time integrating into new communities given the economics of the times. As full-time, unskilled, and uncredentialized work was the norm for adolescents, runaways, for the most part, were able to secure legitimate work roles. Unfortunately, even under these circumstances, some runaways were unable to integrate so easily and thus became prey to neglect and exploitation. Liebertoff (1980), in his excellent historical review, cites

41

the observations of George Matsell, a nineteenth-century police official in New York City (as reported in Bremner, 1970, p. 755): "A large proportion of these juvenile vagrants are in the daily practice of pilfering whatever offers and begging where they cannot steal. . . . The female portion of the youngest class, those who have only seen some eight or twelve summers, are addicted to immoralities of the most loathsome descriptions."

Today, running away from home has become increasingly prevalent *and* problematic. It is one of the primary issues linked to troubled youth in troubled families. While traditional reasons for leaving home may continue to motivate young people to "hit the road," the social stakes are higher and the challenges greater for today's runaway. The prolonged period of adolescence as a moratorium from adultlike responsibilities such as work has destroyed many of the legitimate economic roles into which runaway youth once could fit. Now, there are few legitimate work roles for the runaway adolescent, and this creates a dangerous push into socially illegitimate economic activities such as prostitution, robbery, the drug trade, and other forms of hustling. Like high school dropouts, runaways have become social deviants as their place in the social order has been displayed by changes in the economic and educational systems. These social changes have accompanied a general aging of the population that has pushed the entrance into adulthood further and further away from the typical 16-year-old runaway and nonrunaway alike. In this chapter we will be examining the adolescent runaway as a human service problem in this changed social, economic, and educational context.

DEFINITION AND SCOPE OF THE PROBLEM

What is a runaway? And, how many are there? These two questions are the obvious starting points for our discussion. Just how many runaways are there? The number depends, of course, on the precise definition used in counting them. In 1976, the *National Statistical Survey on Runaway Youth* conducted by Opinion Research Corporation (1976), reported that there were about 733,000 youth aged 10–17 who were absent from home at least overnight without parental permission. Only when the definition of running away as "absent without parental permission for two hours or more" was used did the figure reach 1 million. To complicate the picture even further, the *National Statistical Survey* reported that in nearly one-half the cases of 10- to 17-year-olds absent from home without permission, the parents knew where the AWOL youth had gone, expected them to return, and thus did not define the incident as "running away." In our discussion, we will reserve the term *runaway* for youth who leave home without permission, are gone at least one night, and intend to remove themselves from the parents' awareness and control (cf. Nye and Edelbrock, 1980). As we shall see, the issues of where one goes, how long one stays away, and why one goes are very important from the professional's perspective in properly diagnosing the meaning and significance of running away.

According to the *National Statistical Survey*, runaways come from across our society, but the likelihood that a family will produce a runner bears some relation to its socioeconomic and demographic character. Low-income families and, to some extent, upper-income families have more than their share of runners. Middle-income families have the lowest rate. Likewise, very small families (one parent, one child) and very large families (six or more children) have higher rates than medium-sized families. Overall, about 3% of American families produce an adolescent runaway in a given year, and about 12% of America's youth run away by the time they are 18 years old. Age 16 seems to be the peak year for running away (with about 31% being that age). The rate is about the same for males and females; for Anglos and Blacks; for white-collar and blue-collar. In their review of this evidence, Nye and Edelbrock (1980) comment on the fact that these national figures depart somewhat from the caseloads of agencies that serve runaways. As of the 1978 Annual Report on the Runaway Youth Act, 166 projects had been established to aid runaways [Department of Health, Education and Welfare (hereafter DHEW), 1980, p. 33]. In that year, these projects aided 12,936 runaway youth, a comparatively small proportion of those who are estimated to be in need (DHEW, 1980, p. 41). Of this number, 66.9% were females and 33.1% were males (DHEW, 1980, p. 114). The majority were between the ages of 14 and 16 years old (DHEW, 1980, p. 114) and were mainly Caucasian (76.9%) (DHEW, 1980, p. 114).

Nye and Edelbrock also note that the *National Statistical Survey* reports some significant regional differences, with lower rates in the Northeast (1.5%) and Southeast (2.1%) and higher rates in the Northwest (5.0%) and West–Midwest (4.1%). This can be a significant factor for those responsible for community-based programs. The picture is especially complex for those who work in areas such as New York and San Francisco that experience significant runaway "immigration," as youth from other regions join the pool of "indigenous" runaways. Of course, these runaway meccas face special problems and have special service needs. In New York City, for example, officials estimate that "some 20,000 to 30,000 runaway youth are wandering the streets" and unofficial estimates put the numbers much higher (Children's Defense Fund, 1981). As a result, intensive programs exist in major metropolitan areas that can serve as laboratories or research and demonstration projects for developing and evaluating services for runaways. In New York, for example, the Group Live In Experience (GLIE) has been in the business of identifying and meeting needs for service since 1968. Of course, smaller communities may find it difficult to translate such metropolitan-oriented programs to the smaller scale and often substantially different needs they face when dealing with mainly or even exclusively local runaways.

We will have more to say later about how far runaways typically travel, but let us note here that according to the *National Statistical Survey*, only 18% of the runners travel more than 50 miles from home, and 70% had returned home within a week of their departure. Most run no farther than a friend's or relative's home (Brennan et al., 1978; Nye and Edelbrock, 1980). This is an important piece of information because it helps to "normalize" the problem. For most adolescents, most of the time, running away from home is best thought of as an "episode." It may grow out of a chronic personal or family problem, but the running incident itself is typically a short-term phenomenon. Of course, it may set in motion a long-term process of conflict and/or reorganization in parent–child relations once it is over. Nonetheless, when we consider the magnitude of the runaway problem, we must always remember that most running away is, in a sense, self-correcting.

THE LINKS BETWEEN RUNNING AWAY AND OTHER ADOLESCENT TROUBLES

It is clear from survey research and case studies that running away means different things to different people. Like most behaviors, it can result *from* diverse circumstances and result *in* a variety of consequences. Given our problem-orientation, we think it is appropriate to look at running away as both the effect and cause of adolescent troubles.

Running away is an effect of adolescent troubles when it results from problems in the youth's day-to-day existence. Research demonstrates that these problems take three principal forms: personal maladjustment, family conflict, and parental mistreatment. All three are significant "causes" of running away and can interact with each other in negative ways.

Personal Maladjustment

Runaway behavior has been associated with various types and degrees of personal maladjustment. In one empirically grounded study, Edelbrock (1980) used the Child Behavior Checklist in matched samples of children and youth—1300 referred to mental health services ("disturbed"), and 1300 not referred ("normal") and found that, as a group, runaways were more likely to exhibit a pattern of disturbed social functioning. The difference between the "disturbed" and "normal" groups was most evident in the runaway behavior of the girls as 30% of the "disturbed group" had run away in the past year, while only 2% of the "normal" group had run. For males, the ratio was not so significant as only 10% of the "disturbed" males had run in the previous year, and only 1% of the "normal" males had run. In this study, running away was also associated with five problem behaviors: truancy, use of alcohol or drugs, delinquency, incorrigible misbehavior at home, and attempted suicide.

As Edelbrock (1980, p. 218) points out, however, "these behaviors are not necessarily *predictive* of running away," since the study did not assess the children and youth systematically before this occurred. Other studies have examined personal maladjustment in relation to runaway behavior. M. Goldberg (1972) found that runaways had multiple problems, including school problems, alcohol abuse, and delinquency. These individuals were further characterized as dependent, hostile, and impulsive loners. A study by Jenkins and Boyer (1968) indicated that runaway delinquents seemed to have the least well-organized personality of three delinquent groups studied. Further, there is evidence of substantial personal maladjustment among those who run far and stay away a long time. The evidence comes from a variety of studies of diverse methodological rigor, and includes findings of less favorable self-concepts, poorer interpersonal relationships, greater defensiveness, depression, and feelings of powerlessness and failure (Brennan et al., 1978; D'Angelo, 1974; Jenkins, 1971; Reilly, 1978; Reismer, 1940; Shellow et al., 1967; Wolk and Brandon, 1977).

It is important that personal maladjustment as a "cause" of runaway behavior be viewed in the proper perspective. Personal maladjustment is estimated to be a characteristic of a substantial minority of runaways. As Edelbrock indicates, although "disturbed" youth are more likely to run away, most runners are not disturbed. The low rate among the "normal" population produces a greater number of runners than the high rate among the "disturbed" youth population, as most youth fall into the "normal" category and relatively few into the "disturbed" group. Thus, we must recognize that family conflict involving otherwise psychologically normal youth can produce running away.

Family Conflict

Familial relationships and interactions have long been recognized as factors leading to runaway behavior. The 1978 Annual Report on the Runaway Youth Act reported that 80% of runaways indicated that they left home because of family problems (DHEW, 1980, p. 90). Family problems cover a broad spectrum and range from divorce to parent–child conflicts over dating and peers. Poor conflict resolution, inadequate communication patterns, and ineffective parental supervision characterize the families of runaway youth.

Behaviorally oriented researchers and clinicians have made an important contribution to our understanding of family dynamics by documenting and explicating how what seem to be innocuous behavioral interactions can build up into full blown "pathological" patterns of family conflict. Parents and children can become entrapped in coercive, conflictual behavior patterns through a gradual process of escalating reinforcements (Patterson, 1976). Some families permit minor conflicts to evolve into major confrontations (Troll, 1972). In some situations, disputes over issues like dinner time, hairstyle, and curfews can divert attention from more basic commitments of love and regard and result in a running incident (Kimball, 1970). Further complicating poor conflict resolution is the lack of effective communication patterns in the families of runaways. In the 1978 Annual Report on the Runaway Youth Act, 58.1% of the population stated that poor or no communication with parents was the main reason for running (DHEW, 1980, p. 90). Thus, resolution of problem areas within their families was limited by lack of understanding resulting from poor communication patterns.

In regard to parental supervision, an interesting sex difference has been reported. In Wolk and Brandon's study of runaways' perceptions of self and parents (1977), they report that runaway girls indicate excessive control as a critical issue while runaway boys indicate inadequate control as an issue. This coincides with the general impression gained from youth that overcontrol is usually more of a problem for females. It may tie in with the finding that teenage boys with single parents and teenage girls with stepparents are at greatest risk for mental health referrals (Kalter, 1977). The former is more likely to be an undercontrol situation, whereas the latter is more likely to bring to the fore the issue of overcontrol.

While these "normal" runaways may become enmeshed in the web of victimization and exploitation that will be discussed later as an effect of running away, most engage in a short run and a relatively quick return. Much more serious seem to be incidents of running that are a response to parental mistreatment.

Parental Mistreatment

Evidence continues to accumulate documenting the role of parental mistreatment, including physical abuse, neglect, and incest, in producing runaway behavior. Several studies have linked parental mistreatment to running away from home, particularly in cases where the adolescent goes far and stays away a long time (Garbarino and Gilliam, 1980). For youth exposed to chronic mistreatment at the hands of parents or guardians, running away from home may constitute a "healthy and adaptive response to an impossible situation" (Silbert and Pines, 1981). What is more, some "runaways" are actually "throwaways" in the sense that parental mistreatment has led to a runaway response.

Houghten and Golembiewski (1976) concluded that more than 80% of all "serious" runaways flee serious family problems, particularly abuse and alcoholism. Gutierres and Reich (1981) indicated that a violent home life created stresses that led to runaway behavior. Farber and Kinast (1984), in their study, found that three-fourths of those who ran reported having been subjected to severe maltreatment in the year prior to their runaway behavior (p. 2981). An HEW report estimated that mistreatment figured in one-third to one-half the cases of running away served by agencies. Many "throwaways" report incestual or abusive problems as the major cause of leaving home (Young et al., 1983, p. 277). Other researchers, including Fisher et al. (1979) who have produced the only existing national study of abused adolescents, concur that parental mistreatment is a significant "cause" of running away (e.g., Ambrosino, 1971; Crowley, 1977; D'Angelo, 1974; Liebertoff, 1980).

Clearly, all three "causes" of running can interact. Personal maladjustment, family conflict, and parental mistreatment can become a self-reinforcing, vicious cycle. Victim can become victimizer (Garbarino, 1980), and the effects of damaging family interaction can produce deficits in social competence that precipitate still more conflict. Running away is often bound up in this cycle. All of these causes have a bearing on running itself as a "cause" of adolescent troubles.

As we move from considering running away as an *effect* of adolescent troubles to running away as a *cause* of adolescent troubles, we encounter a pattern of developmentally disastrous victimization. Naturally, the personal maladjustment, family conflict, and parental mistreatment that often precipitate running also make the adolescent specially vulnerable to the risks that running away itself produces. The deficits in social competence and self-esteem highlighted earlier as correlates of running will tend to make an adolescent particularly vulnerable to the psychosocial threats of life on the streets. Runaway adolescents who do not return home quickly have inadequate financial resources to meet their basic needs because of their poor prospects for legitimate employment. Thus, they are candidates for recruitment into the illicit economy—dealing drugs, larceny, hustling, and prostitution–pornography. It is a damning indictment of the larger society, of course, that the "opportunities" for such illicit activities are institutionalized by predatory and exploitative elements of adult society and tolerated by "legitimate" society.

The link between running away and prostitution has been most clearly demonstrated, but we assume that the results for illicit sex parallel those for drugs and related activities. Silbert and Pines (1981) have reviewed the available evidence and conducted their own study. The conclusion they offer is that the runaway–prostitution link is a clear causal connection. Adolescent runaways cannot meet basic economic needs on the street. They eventually choose or fall into one of three courses: get off the street, steal what they need, or sell what they have. Silbert and Pines report that nearly all the juvenile female prostitutes they interviewed were runaways, and nearly 90% cited "needed money, was hungry" as "the main reason for their initial involvement in prostitution." Of course, there are adults who are ready, willing, and able to facilitate this entry into "the life."

Pimps are known to cruise bus stations and runaway hangouts looking for recruits. Once having identified the runaway youth, these predatory adults (perhaps through their adolescent representatives) will offer housing, food, cash, and perhaps even emotional support as a way of engaging the youth for future service. Any runaway youth can be taken in or captured in this way, but many "disturbed" youth are particularly vulnerable. Of special concern are adolescents who have a history of having been sexually abused. These adolescents seem most readily channeled into the runaway–prostitution system (cf. Crowley, 1977; Meyerding, 1977). Silbert and Pines (1981) indicate that 60% of the runaway–prostitutes in their sample reported sexual abuse at home prior to running away. Involvement in the sex industry generally brings with it a vicious cycle of victimization—rape, assault, incarceration, and other degrading experiences. And, although most research has focused on female runaways in the sex business, experts generally agree that many male runaways face the same pattern of exploitation and victimization (Meyerding, 1977). Several recent infamous cases have involved male runaways in homosexual victimization and murder. Running away can be truly a case of escaping the frying pan of a disturbed family only to find oneself in the scorching fire of victimization on the streets. How can the professional helper offer assistance to the runaway? To that question we next turn our attention.

DIAGNOSTIC ISSUES AND TYPOLOGIES

We have shown that the motives for running away from home differ significantly among adolescents. Some youth are psychologically "normal" and leave home seeking adventure. Others are suffering serious personal maladjustment and leave home driven by their inner turmoil. Still others are fleeing conflict or mistreatment. Once on the road, differences in motivation continue to be a significant factor. Although any adolescent on the run can be victimized by predatory elements, run afoul of the law (perhaps through the very act of being AWOL from the family), and otherwise become embroiled in trouble, we believe those who leave home because of trouble are most likely to become involved in trouble. Furthermore, these youth may be most difficult to serve, to return home, and to restore to the family. It is for this reason that we believe issues of diagnosis and typology are so very important in dealing with adolescent runaways.

Several investigators have suggested dichotomous classification of run-aways. It is always appealing to say, "There are two kinds of people in the world: those who X and those who Y." Such dichotomies may even be sufficient for the purpose of a particular agency or professional. For ex-ample, a number of professionals and researchers are most concerned with distinguishing between those who go far and stay away a long time and those who stay near home and return home quickly (e.g., Haupt and Offord, 1972; Houghten and Golembiewski, 1976). A related interest is in contrast-ing those who run once and return permanently and those who run repeatedly. Indeed, a follow-up study by Olson *et al.* (1980) found that repeaters showed much higher levels of personal and social dysfunction as young adults than did one time runners. The repeaters were characterized by academic and vocational failure coupled with court involvement. They also appeared to have had disrupted family relationships even before they ran that became worse when they returned (or were returned). This suggests that professionals be especially concerned about adolescents who run more than once. Orten and Soll (1980) have incorporated this concern into their treatment typology. They focus on the degree of alienation and ambivalence between youth and parents and suggest alternative counseling orientations. It appears that many runners are able to reintegrate themselves into their families after the dramatic act of running away. As we shall see later, however, one important area for professional activity may be in preparing families to accomplish this process of reintegration.

Other dichotomies used to characterize runaways are *running from* versus *running to* (Homer, 1973)—terms that are analogous to Berger and Schmidt's (1958) "reactive runaway" versus "spontaneous runaway" and Tsunts' (1966) "escapist runaway" versus "romantic adventurer." Pro-fessionals may find these dichotomies useful. Another classification with much appeal is Scientific Analysis Corporation's (1974, 1976) designation of runaways who are "sick," "bad," or "free" (i.e., disturbed, delinquent, or adventure-seeking). This trichotomy is useful in highlighting the diversity of needs and resources among the runaway group as well as cautioning against a simplistic view of runaways as uniformly "reasonable," "noble," or "victimized."

Brennan (1980) and Brennan and his colleagues (1978) have produced the most sophisticated typology of runaways. Based on a variety of statistical clustering techniques, Brennan both alone and with his group used in-terview data gathered from 183 runaways to generate seven types of runaways in two broad categories. Once they had statistically grouped the cases, they examined the characteristics of each type to give it a label.

Class 1: Not Highly Delinquent, Non-alienated Runaways
Type 1: Young, overcontrolled escapists
Type 2: Middle-class loners
Type 3: Unbonded, peer-oriented runaways

Class 2: Delinquent, Alienated Runaways
Type 4: Rejected, peer-oriented runaways
Type 5: Rebellious and constrained middle-class drop-out girls
Type 6: Normless, rejected, unrestrained youth
Type 7: Rejected push-outs

In their efforts to assess the validity of these categories, Brennan and his colleagues (1978) have found differences among them in specific aspects of the running syndrome. For example, they report that Type 1 runners were most likely to return home within a day and stay close to home, Type 5 youth were most serious about actually planning a long-term break, and Type 7 adolescents were most likely to be repeaters and to elicit minimal parental interest upon their return (Brennan et al., 1978).

Ideally, agencies and individual professionals will be able to match their service to the specific needs of each individual runaway using the most sophisticated and elaborated diagnostic categories available. The Brennan typology may be particularly useful for agencies planning a large-scale institutional response to runaways and who therefore need a sophisticated system of classification. For the individual professional or small agency, the simpler dichotomies or trichotomies may suffice to highlight important issues in assessment and case management. In fact, however, only the grossest discriminations are often possible because of limited information (e.g., the absence of a family contact), legal restrictions (e.g., confidentiality, "innocent until proven guilty" and "least restrictive alternative" mandates) and scarcity of resources (e.g., having only a small fraction of the residential facilities needed). Therefore, practitioners will need to adapt and simplify the typologies to meet their needs and resources.

We should note here that all the typologies discussed earlier deal with running away from home. This, of course, is our principal concern. Just as most discussions of child maltreatment focus on abuse and neglect in the family context, most discussions of running away are limited to running away from parents. However, a second form of both maltreatment and running away concerns institutions. Running away is one of the more difficult problems faced by many residential facilities. In fact, the runaway rate is one of the commonly used indicators of program operation used by those charged with the responsibility of managing such institutions. For example, the "Teaching Family Program" at Boys Town in Nebraska reports a decline in the facility's runaway rate (from a monthly average of 7.3% to just 1.5%) as testimony to the program's success (Phillips et al., 1979). Running from foster home placements is a related and vexing problem where troubled adolescents are concerned (Friedman, and Zeigler, 1979).

SERVICE ISSUES

The general service issues facing those who would assist runaways are protection, assessment, and placement—either family restoration or alternative living arrangements. Protection is first on the list because we know that all juvenile runaways are potential marks for exploitation and victimization, particularly from the illicit sex industry. This protection takes two forms. The first is a secure and supportive place for runaways to go to get off the street, when they want off. The second is an economic buffer to provide runaway and professional helper alike some time to move to the assessment phase of intervention without economic crisis pushing the youth into illicit activities—whether it be the sex industry, the drug trade, or some other form of illicit hustling. Runaway houses appear to offer a vehicle for providing both forms of basic protection. They provide a safe point in time and space. These facilities provide short-term services, however. The protection they provide is usually but the first chapter in meeting the needs of runaways. The second chapter is assessment.

Once the runaway is protected from exploitation and victimization, the professional helper can get on with the business of assessing the causes of running and the steps necessary either to restore the youth to the family or to implement an alternative living arrangement. The assessment should focus on discovering whether the principal cause of running is adventure, on the one hand, or personal maladjustment, family conflict, and parental mistreatment, on the other. However, no matter what the decision, the runaway may need assistance in reentering the family.

Friedman (1978) suggests that working with the parents while the adolescent is still out of the home is a key to achieving successful restoration of the runaway to the family. Whittaker (1979) sees this coordination as a crucial generic issue in youth work, namely, ensuring that the home and youth care institution form an integrated system. The effectiveness of this link plays a very significant role in the long-term prospects for the runaway's return to family and community (i.e., school, peer group).

We should remember that most runaways return home and stay home after their (usually brief and short) trip. The survey research cited earlier (e.g., Brennan et al., 1978; Opinion Research Corporation, 1976) makes this clear. The typologies illuminate this finding by showing that many adolescents run away from home seeking relief from exaggerated problems at home, at school, with peers, or within themselves. On their own for a while, they may develop a better perspective on these problems, feel they have "made their point," or simply find that life on the run is no better and maybe much worse than the imperfect life afforded by home and family. Often no professional intervention is necessary at all in these cases. Sometimes all that is needed is the practical help required to make contact and arrange for the trip home. The toll-free runaway hotline (1-800-621-4000) maintained by the National Runaway Network and its local cousins can and do meet this need in a way that augments the informal networks of friends, neighbors, relatives, and good samaritans that can help an adolescent find that sometimes you really can go home again.

Smooth restoration to the family is not the only concern when personal maladjustment, family conflict, or parental maltreatment are involved, of course. Where the assessment reveals personal maladjustment, a mental health referral should accompany the restoration process. Where family conflict is present, a family counseling referral is in order. Where parental mistreatment is the issue, a protective services referral is imperative. All of these steps are based on family restoration as the goal of case management. We must recognize that family restoration is not the only appropriate goal, however. Maybe you really can't go home again.

The assessment may reveal a very poor prognosis for family restoration. Where the level of personal maladjustment is high, the family chronically conflictual and inflexibly resistant, or a pattern of parental mistreatment with high probability of reoccurrence evident, the appropriate goal for case management may well be some alternative placement such as a group home, foster care, a residential treatment program, or even an independent living arrangement (where this is a legal option). The experiences of programs serving runaways around the country suggests that each of these options has merit when matched appropriately to the needs and resources of the individual runaway. Appendix I (p. 54) lists some programs that appear to present good models for service to runaways.

One of the important potential resources available to those who would help runaways is the peer social network. Early adolescence is a time of heightened sensitivity to influence. While the influence of parents and other adults remains strong and typically preeminent in most important matters, the influence of peers *is* consequential. Peer groups can serve a useful function in several aspects of the services-to-runaways system. First, they may be an instrument for preventing the running incident itself. Professionals and other concerned adults may establish connections with adolescent peer groups and then use these connections to "pass the word" about alternatives to running such as counseling and group home placement. This may be particularly important in forestalling running to escape family conflict or parental maltreatment where grounds for professional intervention are present. Our experience with this sort of liaison role for peer groups is encouraging (cf. Garbarino and Jacobson, 1978).

A second role for adolescent peer networks is as a referral agent for runaway houses and related programs. The runaway youth may be skeptical of adult agencies—particularly if they have had bad experiences with professional services, if their personal maladjustment makes trust difficult, or if involvement in illicit activities makes them wary. Thus, the runaway program may need the help of adolescent peer networks to establish and communicate their credibility. Multipurpose youth service centers like The Door in New York City rely upon "satisfied customers" to make referrals. A runaway youth agency that *is* doing a good job of serving clients should not neglect its "alumni" in this regard.

A third role for adolescent peers in the process of helping runaways is as formalized youth self-help groups. The self-help model has enormous appeal in many domains of human service. Services to runaway youth are no exception. Although most runaway youth programs operate on a short term, revolving door basis (in and out in a few days or weeks), they still can make use of structured group experiences to stabilize and enhance the social–psychological development of their young clients. Where more long-term services are provided, the self-help group setting may be an excellent context for teaching needed social skills and assessing mental health status. We are aware of one model of such a social skills orientation to the youth helping youth group that seems promising (Longberg et al., 1980). All in all, peer-oriented approaches to identifying and serving runaways promise added effectiveness for professionals and their agencies.

CONCLUSION

Running away from home is not a new phenomenon, but contemporary society makes it especially risky. The costs to the adolescents, to their families, and to society are substantial. The link between running away and illicit activity is now well established—particularly for repeaters, of whom roughly one-half admit illicit activities such as theft, according to survey data (Brennan et al., 1978). The link between running away and the sex industry is particularly disturbing.

The causes of running are multiple and often benign, particularly for the majority of runners who do not go far and who return home relatively quickly. However, those who run to escape serious personal and family trouble are a serious social problem. Their troubles tend to be exacerbated and multiplied by life on the run and on the streets. They require intensive and sustained intervention by savvy professionals who are willing and able to handle these troubled and often troublesome youth.

APPENDIX I: PROGRAM INFORMATION

1. Clearinghouse
   National Youth Work Alliance
   1346 Connecticut Ave., N.W.
   Washington, D.C. 20036

   For general information and information about aftercare
   (request *It's Me Again*)

2. National Network of Runaway and
   Youth Services
   1705 DeSales St., N.W., 8th Floor
   Washington, D.C. 20036

   For general information about runaway houses

3. New York City Runaway
   Coordinator
   618 Avenue of the Americas
   New York, New York 10011

   For information about community coordination of services

4. Youth Care Division
   Father Flanagan's Boys' Home
   Boys Town, Nebraska 68010

   For information on social skills training for runaways via The Family Teaching Model

5. The Shelter Program Office
   Suite 509, Jones Building
   Seattle, Washington 98101

   For information about dealing with runaways as part of the larger status offender population

6. D.C. Coalition for Youth
   P.O. Box 9035
   Washington, D.C. 20003

   For information about continuing care for runaways

7. GLIE Community Youth Program
   2021 Grand Concourse
   7th and 8th Floors
   Bronx, New York 10453

   For information on their metropolitan programs for runaways

8. Youth Helping Youth Project
   Division of External Affairs
   Boys Town, Nebraska 68010

   For information about setting up and running a youth self-help group

STUDYING
TROUBLED YOUTH
AND TROUBLED
FAMILIES

II

The first three chapters in Part I introduced many of the themes with which we will be concerned throughout this volume, and presented a microcosm of troubled youth in troubled families. We have seen the way the context presented by the family serves as both cause and effect of troubled youth development. We have seen how the quality of care in the family is implicated in delinquency and running away—two youth problems of disturbing prevalence and seriousness. Now we move on to the task of untangling these issues, in general, and in the lives of 62 families we studied.

Part II examines methodological and conceptual issues in studying families at risk for adolescent maltreatment and presents an overall picture of our families from the perspective of mother, father, and adolescent. In Chapter 4 we present an overview. It includes a look at the implications of systems theory for studying families, particularly high-risk families. We then examine a series of research assessment issues as they apply to our own study of troubled youth in troubled families. This includes a look at the instruments we used in our investigation. Chapter 5 focuses on the measurement of high risk. We examine the history of efforts to devise an instrument to predict who will abuse and who will not, and note the many fundamental technical and ethical problems involved. We then present our own efforts to develop an instrument for identifying families at risk for adolescent maltreatment. In Chapter 6, we present an overview of our findings. We contrast the pattern typical of troubled youth in high-risk families with their counterparts in low-risk families and illustrate each comparison with family case studies. The overall picture is one marked by more adolescent problems, a pattern of "chaotically enmeshed" relations, less parental support and more punishment, more parent–adolescent discrepancies, more stressful life changes, and more parental conflict in the high-risk families.

METHODOLOGICAL CONSIDERATIONS IN STUDYING TROUBLED YOUTH AND TROUBLED FAMILIES

4

CYNTHIA J. SCHELLENBACH
MARK KREJCI

The family and youth problems with which we are concerned in this volume are created not on the basis of one person but as a product of the interaction of all family members acting as a unit. There are characteristics of individual parents that may be likely to be associated with dysfunction, however. Parents whose values fall on extreme poles of a continuum from extreme rigidity to extreme adaptability (laissez-faire) may be more likely to be abusive. We know from research (Baumrind, 1975) on parenting styles that these extreme attitudes toward parenting are not optimal. Rather, the ability to allow independence within limits is necessary. This is the authoritative style of discipline. Individual family members may demonstrate a lower level of functioning reasoning in general. Dysfunction is not limited to parents, however. Children may distinguish themselves by a tendency to display a high degree of pathology that intensifies in adolescence. Specifically, abused adolescents tend to have experienced a greater number of stressful life events and to display problems in interpersonal relationships.

We think that adolescent abuse may be viewed as both a symptom and a result of dysfunction in the family system. Adolescent maltreatment exemplifies the heterogeneity of abuse as a phenomenon. Therefore, one of the objectives of this chapter is to illustrate recent advances in conceptual work and in methodology that may be utilized to bring about a clearer understanding of adolescent abuse.

DEFINITION OF ADOLESCENT MALTREATMENT

Specifically, abuse must be defined on a continuum of parent–child interaction embedded within a developmental perspective on family functioning. The developmental course of each individual family member must be in synchrony with those of the others to achieve effective family functioning. Abuse may be the result of ineffective equilibration of the dynamic interactions within the family. According to the open living systems conceptual framework, there are three sets of dynamically interacting variables that compose the family system (Ford, 1984). First, each family member is a dynamic unit. The intrapersonal factors inherent in producing a coherent pattern of behavior must be in place. For each member, behavior occurs on a continuum of developmental change over the life course, that is traced on the trajectory of intraindividual development. One way of examining the changing constellations of behaviors is to look at development as a series of behavioral reorganizations focused on specific developmental tasks. As many developmental theories suggest, the unsuccessful resolution of a normal developmental task may be indicative of dysfunction on the individual level of functioning (Erikson, 1963).

As a member of a family, the interpersonal needs of individual family members must also be equilibrated. In other words, the internal dynamics of family members must be organized to effect a coherent pattern of behavior in response to changing demands between and among family members. This is referred to as *effective interpersonal equilibration*. Changes within family structure may be plotted against a developmental course of family development (Aldous, 1978). Deviations or inability to coordinate behavior of the family system may result in ineffective resolution of family developmental tasks.

Finally, the family does not exist in a vacuum. It is embedded within a community. Effective family functioning is also influenced by the degree to which the family is able to meet the challenges imposed by the larger social structure. For example, social support or social isolation, employment or unemployment, problems or strengths in the community, must be confronted to deal effectively with family–environment interactions. This is analogous to the larger ecological system described by Bronfenbrenner (1979). Further, these three levels of equilibration are also interacting reciprocally. That is, a change in one may effect a "ripple" effect in other systems, as suggested in the social interactional model.

In the next section, we outline our concept of abuse. Second, we set forth a systems framework for understanding family functioning, and third, we explore the family from a developmental perspective.

Conceptualization of Maltreatment

There has been much debate regarding current definitions of child maltreatment. Most accepted components in definitions of abuse focus on the type of abuse, the intentionality of the abuser, the scope of abuse, and the community standards of discipline. In part, the attitudes of society and the community in which the family is embedded define the problem under investigation. Alvy (1975) suggests that abuse must be analyzed from a comprehensive approach that defines abuse as collective, institutional, and individual in nature. Collective abuse refers to those specific societal attitudes that impede the psychological and physical development of children. The denial of children's rights and belief in excessive physical punishment are good examples of collective abuse. A recent example is the controversy surrounding the administration of regular physical beatings to young children as part of an accepted system of religious values. Institutional abuse refers to abusive and developmentally damaging policies and behaviors toward children and families, such as judicial intervention which commonly separates children from other families. These values and policies in the larger environment provide the conditions that make abuse more likely to occur.

Abusive incidents are best studied within the family system as a whole. Working from within this perspective, abuse is based upon the criteria of outcome to the child and the intentionality of the parent (Parke and Collmer, 1975). In terms of outcome, abuse is defined as any behavior that results in the injury of a child under the age of 18. This definition is valuable because it seeks to be objective and fulfills the need for scientific precision by defining abuse in terms of a quantifiable observable outcome to the child. There are several problems that limit the usefulness of the definition, however. Identical behavioral outcomes for children as judged by observable severity of abuse may have different meanings. For example, two children may sustain the same injuries yet the context may be very different. For one child, the injury might have been accidentally incurred by a peer, or it might have occurred as a punishment at the hands of his parents. The age of the child may affect the outcome of abuse. Younger children may be more physically vulnerable and, thus, sustain more serious injury. For these reasons, it is important to include a consideration of intentionality. This is a difficult criterion, however, since it is often impossible to determine whether or not the behavior was accidental.

A further distinction must be clarified. The outcome of abuse may not always be observable. The blow to self-esteem may be more harmful developmentally than the physical injury. Rejection or excessive restriction by the parent is a powerful source of developmental damage. Although psychological abuse is exceedingly difficult to define, emotional rejection must be considered abusive behavior toward children. An early work defined emotional abuse (Garbarino and Gilliam, 1980) involving two facets of emotional maltreatment: (1) punishment of self-esteem; (2) restriction of social competence and developmental progress. From this definition, any parental behavior that functions to delay the normal developmental course would be considered emotional abuse.

The definition of abuse that incorporates these components is "Any non-accidental physical or psychological injury sustained by a child under the age of 18 resulting from acts of omission or commission" (Burgess and Richardson, 1981).

In attempts to operationalize the effects of psychological maltreatment, Garbarino and Gilliam (1980) suggest that is is crucial to ground one's definition in the broader social context. An addition to the definition of abuse is included: "Acts of omission or commission by a parent or guardian that are judged by a mixture of community values and professional expertise to be inappropriate and damaging"(Garbarino and Gilliam, 1980, p. 7).

The assumptions that underlie this definition of abuse have limited our understanding of the phenomenon of maltreatment. From the statement of the definition, one may deduce that the categories are discrete. In fact, emotional maltreatment is most likely to coexist with physical abuse and certainly will accompany sexual abuse. The lack of precision in defining different types of abuse has been underscored by several researchers (Lourie, 1979; Burgess, 1980; Garbarino et al., 1984; Cicchetti and Rizley, 1981). As Lourie (1979) suggested, the use of the term *maltreatment* is about as useful and ambiguous as the term *insanity*. The broad conception of abuse has limited our understanding of abusive behavior. Such heterogeneity of abusive behavior is one that is beginning to be acknowledged (Cicchetti and Rizley, 1981). In a parallel movement in the field of research methodology, attempts are being made to identify different correlates and patterns associated with different types of abuse.

Burgess (1979) has suggested that abusive behavior must be viewed on a continuum from positive interchanges to severe physical abuse. The assumption underlying the continuum definition of abuse is that the act of physical abuse is actually a rare occurrence, a low-frequency event even in highly abusive families. It may be more profitable to view physical abuse as both a result and a symptom of more pervasive dysfunction in the family system. Moreover, the physically abusive incident that occurs in an otherwise warm emotional climate is expected to have very different developmental consequences and correlates compared to the abusive incident that occurs within a highly restrictive, emotionally abusive family context.

Indeed, the behaviorally oriented research of Burgess (Burgess and Conger, 1978; Burgess et al., 1981) showed that abusive families were significantly different from nonabusive families in their daily interactional styles. Abusive families tended to interact less frequently. When the members did interact, they tended to be more negative in their interactions. Physically abusive incidents tended to occur within verbally impoverished, highly negative patterns of negative interactions. If one were to impose the framework cited earlier, the accompanying hypothesis would suggest an impoverished community network for abusive families as well. Research also supports the notion of the abusive family as a socially impoverished unit (Garbarino and Sherman, 1980), and that impoverished families operate on a system marked by lack of balance in resources and needs, favoring the latter. These families are likely to be deficient in support and feedback.

In the same way that abusive interactions occur on a continuum from positive, affectionate interchanges to negative, abusive exchanges, so neglect toward adolescents may also be viewed on a continuum. There are a number of parallels between abuse and neglect. Although our thinking tends to be guided by a dichotomous viewpoint of neglect/nonneglect, neglect is more appropriately pictured on a continuum of severely neglectful to quality care, psychologically and physically nurturing. The family's placement on such a continuum is the product of the measurement of several different levels of care-taking. With these considerations in mind, Polansky et al. (1975) suggest the following definition of child neglect:

> Child neglect may be defined as a condition in which a caretaker responsible for the child either deliberately or by extraordinary inattentiveness permits the child to experience avoidable present suffering and/or fails to provide one or more of the ingredients deemed essential for developing a person's physical, intellectual, and emotional capacities.

When this definition is translated into legal standards, Meier (1969, p. 157) suggests that

> the conditions that constitute neglect are variously defined, but rather characteristically the laws cite these circumstances: (1) inadequate physical care; (2) absence of or inadequate medical care; (3) cruel or abusive treatment; (4) improper supervision; (5) exploitation of the child's earning capacity; (6) unlawfully keeping the child out of school; (7) exposing the child to criminal or immoral influence that endangers his morals.

We can imagine neglectful situations that occur precisely because of the developmental characteristics of the adolescent. An adolescent being forced by a parent to care for younger brothers and sisters rather than permitted to attend school on a regular basis is an example of neglect. The parent who forces her adolescent sons to be locked in the basement with cots as beds, so that she can control the "excessive eating" that strained the family food budget, and the parent who engages in drug experimentation or sexually promiscuous behavior in the presence of an impressionable teenager is also considered neglectful.

There are several areas in which neglect may differ from abuse. In contrast to abuse, which tends to occur in a burst phenomenon, neglect is more likely to be a chronic, ongoing condition that persists for several years. Neglect is likely to be an act of omission, a lack of attention to the adolescent, a lack of supervision appropriate to the age of the adolescent. Again, what is appropriate for the young child may not be appropriate for the adolescent.

We have tried to understand neglect in light of the family's functioning in the larger social context. There have been productive attempts to view neglectful behavior as it relates to economic deprivation (poverty in the social system, as exemplified in extremely deprived environments in Appalachia), in ecological environment (in social support at the community and neighborhood environments), and in the family system (the interaction of individuals in the smaller family unit). We suggest that the adolescent provides an impetus for reorganization of family rules and changes in parent–child relationships. The new problems present a challenge to equilibrium in well-adjusted families. We suspect that the additional challenges related to adolescent adjustment may exacerbate problems in a family already strained in resources.

This larger body of research describes the correlates found in child abuse. There may be different types of abuse, as there are different constellations of variables for adolescent abuse as a special case. Indeed, Lourie (1979) was the first to suggest specific patterns of family system variables in differentiating three types of adolescent abuse that are derived from a family systems model viewed within a developmental framework. This begins with the phase-specific developmental issues of both adolescent and parent.

Adolescent Maltreatment

For the adolescent, the problems presented to the parent are those of age-appropriate rebellion, testing limits of the family, rapid shifts in mood, one minute depending on the parent and striking out against them in another, spending more time away from home—all of these are important in the establishment of individual identity.

For the parent, the developmental tasks of mid-life are quite different. According to the research on adult personality development, adults are also involved in a process of self-evaluation, a realization that their years are finite and all must be accomplished within a brief period of time (Gould,

1978). Physical energy and stamina may be on the decline, there may be marital problems, and symptoms of depression that may lower parental tolerance. This intrafamilial conflict is described by Lourie (1979, p. 968):

> Compounding any trouble the parent has in these mid-life tasks is the fact that characteristics of adolescence naturally conflict. Adolescents are planning their lives, not reassessing; they are denying mortality rather than facing death; they are perceived as having boundless energy in comparison to decreasing energy; they are falling in love, not divorcing. . . . Whatever problems parents might have, the lives of their adolescents rub salt in the wounds.

As we noted in Chapter 1, Lourie (1979) proposed three different patterns of behavior in the family system to characterize the special case of adolescent abuse: (1) abuse continuing from childhood to adolescence; (2) abuse that occurs as a quality change in severity of punishment beginning in adolescence; (3) abuse in which physically violent behavior toward the child begins only when the child reaches adolescence. Each of these patterns is marked by a unique constellation of factors in the family system.

Ongoing abuse is marked by deficits in parenting skills and problem behavior of the child. The family is very chaotic, seemingly overwhelmed with the problems of daily living. This child often remains undetected until he/she appears in juvenile court.

Quality change is abuse that has intensified due to the child. Parents are highly controlling and restrictive, and when they discover that methods of discipline are no longer effective with the adolescent, the response is to intensify the punishment.

The adolescent-only pattern of abuse is abusive behavior that begins in adolescence. The abusive incidents occur very infrequently and are linked to outbursts of problems in the family. The developmental problems of the child are handled through explosive incidents in the family.

From a developmental viewpoint, it may be expected that these constellations or family types may be a concrete example of the heterogeneity of abuse. This is one area of inquiry in which research may be very productive. Although there is much evidence to believe that different family types are discernible (Kent et al., 1983), there is little systematic evidence for development of a taxonomy for differentiating among manifestations of abuse. Further, there is a lack of integrative theory for specifying the mechanisms by which known risk factors lead to abuse. An enduring question concerns why some families with the same factors may become abusive, whereas others do not. Perhaps the problem is one of a lack of precision in defining the family interaction variables—the risks and the buffers for each family (Cicchetti and Rizley, 1981).

A Systems Perspective to Family Functioning

The family is a semiclosed system of interrelated positions. George Herbert Mead suggested that the family is the integral link between the individual and the larger society. The individual both creates and reacts to the world within the context of the family, and each family member occupies a specific role or fulfills a set of normative expectations regarding appropriate behavior. These roles commonly are organized in such a way to accomplish equilibrium within the family system. The family performs functions that are vital to the maintenance of society. As represented by Duvall (1971), there are a number of developmental tasks that are necessary for the maintenance of the family. These functional requisites include (1) physical maintenance; (2) effective allocation of resources; (3) division of labor; (4) socialization of family members; (5) reproduction, recruitment, and release of family members; (6) maintenance of order; (7) maintenance of motivation and morale. These developmental tasks represent the forces that push for gradual change in the family

According to Aldous (1978), these tasks wax and wane in importance for the family. Chronological time is important as the family progresses through the achievement of these tasks, and the unit of time that has meaning for the family is the process by which the family achieves these tasks. Thus, there are normative expectations regarding the timing of these events and the roles attendant to the developmental turning points. The social expectations are age-graded. That is, appropriate behavior of parents and children is partially a result of acceptable norms in society. To the extent that a family is unable to provide conditions for resolution of developmental tasks, the family may be considered dysfunctional. Following is a description of the open systems framework.

The family may be characterized as an open, living self-constructing system of interrelated roles. The family is considered open since members exchange information, energy, and material with the environment. There are three dimensions of change over time for the family unit. First, each individual member of the family has a developmental course of change over the life span. This incorporates the changes in physical, cognitive, and social development that have long formed the substance of inquiry for developmental psychology. Second, related to these individual changes, the family structure or roles within the family unit may change, particularly in relation to the developmental course of the family career. In fact, the life course changes in the family career are energized by changes in individuals. The third dimension of change is the family in society or changes in the family unit affected by historical influences. A family with an adolescent who has a problem with drugs may be affected by a cutback in funds for drug abuse services on a national level. The difficulty Blacks have in breaking out of the welfare system may be related to early pregnancy of adolescent girls in urban settings.

In the systems perspective, each dimension of change must follow a path of reorganization or equilibration. The family will display both consistency and variability over the life course. As a system, the family is purposeful in its actions and functions to achieve specified goals necessary for successful growth of its members. The functions of the family are organized to provide for a set of interrelated actions in the family. Each subunit of the family (the individual, the family unit, the family in society) is a complete dimension itself, and these are organized in hierarchal form so that each system is a component of the broader, more encompassing system. In this way, the world may be considered a set of nested systems (Bronfenbrenner, 1979).

The family unit is constituted by a physical entity that distinguishes the unit from the larger contexts of society and history. The physical structure is marked by a closer set of relationships than the surrounding contexts. This physical structure makes possible four types of functions that maintain the structure and provide conditions for future growth.

First, the biological functions provide for the transformation of energy and material to maintain the physical entity of the family. This system refers to the activities necessary to physical maintenance of the family. Tasks such as provision of housing, adequate income, neighborhood, and variables related to physical health and individual characteristics would fall into this category.

The second function is the governing function. These processes refer to the direction, control, and regulation of systems that maintain the family system. The goals of this category are appropriate allocation of available resources, both in physical energy and material resources. Rules for division of labor within the household are necessary for clear definition and functioning of role structure for the family. This may be particularly difficult given the changes in traditional structure. That is, role structure is no longer dictated by society so that family members may be forced to negotiate adequate solutions for family members. Finally, flexibility must be inherent in the family's ability to respond to the unpredictable changes in environment demands. One need only to conjure up an image of the family juggling the schedules of two or more adolescents with those of two working parents in order to predict the importance of these skills. Finally, the family must have adequate problem-solving skills in order to maintain order and discipline in the family.

The transactional function is the third function, and it actually carries out the exchanges of material, energy, and information with the environment. In the family, this category refers to communication functions between parents in the marital relationship and among family members. These types of functions are most clearly related to the appropriate socialization of family members. The child-rearing techniques of the parents are also important components of transactional process.

The fourth function, the arousal function, regulates variations in rate or intensity related to other areas of functioning. In the family setting, the arousal system is responsible for the maintenance of motivation and morale within the family system. Similarly, variations in emotional functioning may exist within the family. A positive emotional climate is characterized by respect, affection, and love among family members. In contrast, a negative emotional climate is characterized by fear, anger, and guilt among family members.

The presence or absence of these factors is not indicative of healthy family functioning. Rather, a balance of positive factors against negative factors would indicate an equilibrium between stresses and supports. Each family may have a unique location on the continuum for a constellation of factors. In the following section, the literature describing healthy family functioning has been summarized in the organization of the open systems framework.

HEALTHY FAMILY FUNCTIONING AND
THE SYSTEMS FRAMEWORK

Biological Functions

The provision of adequate housing for the family is a prerequisite for the family. The physical condition of the home reflects a commitment by family members to the welfare of the family unit. General physical health of the family may be dependent, in part, on the stability of the physical environment. The socioeconomic stability of the family is linked to the strength of the family unit (Carter and Glick, 1976; Cutright, 1971; Hampton, 1975; Udry, 1966). The impact of socioeconomic status may be variable depending upon mediating factors in the family. One of the primary conditions of stability is employment. The impact of unemployment may not be severe— some families will unite to support the family in times of financial crisis (Stinnett, 1979). Physical problems in the family linked to the stress of unemployment and the unavailability of resources to pay for health care services may produce additional stress.

The Governing Subsystems

The governing processes are those cognitively based abilities of the family to solve problems, maintain order, and provide socialization to the young. The method of child rearing may shift power in the family. For example, an authoritarian model of discipline may be functional for young children but will easily incite rebellion among adolescents. Moreover, children raised with authoritarian methods are likely to be rigid and conforming in later life (Baumrind, 1975). Particularly relevant for the changes during adolescence is the necessity for flexibility in parenting styles.

The distribution of power is a frequent focal point for conflict during adolescence. The normal desire for the adolescent to rebel against authority may be exacerbated by a restrictive environment. In fact, the locus of power within the family is the primary influence on healthy family interaction (Lewis et al., 1976). Not only does the power structure assure the implementation of the family policy, but the parents provide an important model for education of children in values. Each family member should know the rules for the organization of the family, including the emphasis on the unique contributions of each family member. Healthy families have reciprocity in which the unique contributions of family members complement the behaviors of others (Lederer and Jackson, 1968). Dysfunctional family systems do not have a clear structure.

Transactional Functions

The transactional functions refer not only to the actual interaction of the individuals within the family but also to the individual family members with the community. The primary channels of communication have been outlined by Aldous (1978) as marital dyad and parent toward children. The basis for healthy interaction is the marital dyad (Mace and Mace, 1980). Within the dyad, transactions must be open and effective so that natural conflicts of married life are resolved as issues arise. In this way, unresolved tensions are less likely to influence interaction with children. An unhealthy system does not confront stressful situations openly and thus represses the issues.

A consistent approach to child rearing is an important variable for communication. Haley (1962; 1967) suggests that the amount of authority used to curb original or nonconforming behavior may be destructive in the family. In fact, the parents' ability to allow individual expression is a reaffirmation of the value of the individual. The authoritarian style of parenting may inhibit the differentiation of the child through a rigid set of rules. The totally permissive parent will produce an adolescent who is aggressive and uninhibited and will have difficulty setting guidelines for appropriate behavior in the teens. The optimal style of parenting is authoritative, that of a parent who imposes guidelines for behavior but allows flexibility within these boundaries. The amount of time spent together is an important indicator of healthy family functioning (Stinnet, 1979). As that author notes, time is spent by choice to be a commitment to the family. Healthy family time may be active or passive but generally geared to participation by all family members. In contrast, unhealthy families spend little time together nurturing relationships; time in dysfunctional families is largely noninteractive. When interactions do occur, members may accentuate the negative (Stinnet, 1979). Within a context of minimal interaction, this interaction is more rejecting. Abusive family interaction styles have been distinguished from nonabusive families on the basis of these negative interactional styles in observational research (Burgess and Conger, 1978; Burgess et al., 1981). Open and positive communication within the family system is the foundation for implementation of rules, child rearing, and support. The healthy family system maintains open communication patterns, and all members listen with respect to varying viewpoints (Otto, 1971). The inevitable disagreements that occur are confronted openly and resolved quickly (Haley, 1967; Jackson, 1965).

The degree of interpersonal competence is evident not only within the family but in effective communication and positive relationships outside the family. The healthy family is characterized by active connections to a network of social support of extended family and friends. An inwardly focused family will be likely to preserve a boundary between family and external world; dysfunctional families may be highly enmeshed (Fisher, 1981; Olson et al., 1979), thus limiting interaction with the outside world. Indeed, abusive families are distinguished by the lack of social support, whereas healthy family systems are open to others external to the family. External support systems are vital to the development of family (Caplan, 1976; Otto, 1971).

Evaluative/Regulatory Functioning

The evaluative functions refer to the intensity or variation in atmosphere in the family. The emotional exchange or the affect that regulates the atmosphere, the boundaries of roles that permit differentiation, the positive evaluations of self and others, and flexibility in roles are important.

Healthy family functioning is characterized by a high degree of empathy among family members and frequent, positive interactions. Stinnet (1979) describes positive interaction as a commitment to concern, intimacy, and emotional closeness.

Individuals must have clear perceptions of themselves and others, specifically, self-evaluation of one's positive and negative contributions to the family. An understanding of role structure must be clear; Barnhill suggests the existence of generational differences.

Two descriptions of families based on this pattern of variables will illustrate the interactive components. Family A consists of two parents of middle age ($-$) with two adolescent children, one aged 15 (apex $-$) and one aged 12 (+). The father is now self-employed in real estate after a series of severe heart ailments that forced him to leave his earlier employment with a corporation (−). The mother works part-time in order to supplement the family income (−). Mother has good health (+). One adolescent male has a number of learning disabilities for which he has been placed in a special classroom (−). The modest home is well-kept (+), and all appear to share a commitment to maintenance of the home (+).

The family appears average in cognitive problem-solving (+) although parents remark humorously that adolescents argue and break parental rules (−). The parents share responsibility for setting rules, making a family discussion mandatory once weekly (+). The adolescents express their viewpoints freely but respectfully (+). Child-rearing techniques appear authoritative with parents explaining rules to adolescents. All members participate in a common commitment to religious activities (+). There are frequent contacts with extended family and neighbors and friends (+).

Although there are frequent disagreements, there is an atmosphere of humor and affectionate interchanges (+). The older adolescent has many insecurities related to his school problems (−), but the family shows a high degree of sensitivity and empathy for his problems (+). Similarly, the mother reports that the family suffered a series of crises during the health problems of the father (−). The father felt his health significantly decreased his perception of himself as a wage-earner (−). The family then worked together to decrease expenses so that the father could set up a business at home (+). In return, the father attempts to be flexible in performing extra chores around the house during the day while his wife is at work (+).

In summary, this family has a number of factors that could place them at risk for abuse if viewed as isolated risk factors. The developmental status of the parents and adolescents places them in direct opposition in developmental crises. The age of one adolescent at apex puberal level has been correlated with a higher degree of rebellion. The serious health problems of the father are offset by the mother's physical strength. The strengths of the family are the positive emotional interchanges, the clear organization of the family, and an internal problem-solving skill with high external support from the church and community.

In contrast, a high-risk family that does exhibit significant problems leading to abuse is described as follows. The family has a low to moderate level of income, but the number of children is greater (5) (−). The health of both parents is quite good (+), but the mother has a severe problem with obesity which appears to constrain her activity level (−). She appears to be suffering from depression (−) and spends days in bed or watching television. The children range in age from 9 to 15, thus presenting a variety of age-related developmental problems. The family lives in a small, crowded apartment (−). The adolescent girl is psychologically impaired and over-weight (−).

The rules of the family are unclear, as mother is the organizer. When mother is depressed, the daughter fulfills the role of organizer for the younger children. Father is very withdrawn from involvement since he works nights. The mother is responsible for child rearing but seems to vary her enforcement of rules, depending upon her mood.

The marital relationship has almost completely deteriorated, with little communication. There is a generally low rate of interaction among family members, and when they do interact, it is task-oriented with a high degree of negative emotional overtones. Positive, humorous interaction is initiated only by the children, and this interaction can be nurturant at times. Family members spend a great deal of time away from home. Each individual family member has a few friends but none seems dependable. The mother and daughter appear lonely. There is virtually no social support from the larger community.

In terms of interpersonal equilibration, the family appears to have differing perceptions of roles and needs. There is a large disagreement on rules and goals. This family is abusive. The father is the perpetrator of outbursts of physical abuse toward the older daughter.

One of the objectives of the Family Interaction Project was to identify constellations of variables that would occur in common patterns that may differentiate healthy from dysfunctional families.

SAMPLING

Consistent with the concept of abuse on a continuum, one of the goals of the project was to identify a range of families on a continuum of dysfunction—some with adolescent problems, some at risk for abuse yet not abusive, some at risk and presently abusive, and others low-risk and not abusive. In this way, the sampling strategy was more consistent with our general interest in examining why parent–child relationships may become negative or destructive during adolescence. The criteria for destructive parent–child relationships were on a continuum in physical, psychological, and sexual domains. Based on the systems framework, the measurement of correlates of abuse must include the family as a system, their immediate ecological context (i.e., the neighborhood or community), and the individuals who contribute to the family system. Questionnaires and interviews tapped multiple levels of interaction including the individual and the family. A sample of 62 families consisting of a mother, father, and adolescent was constructed through referrals from diverse community institutions including schools, youth groups, churches, as well as social service agencies and self-referrals. Through this sampling strategy, a range of families was constructed from those experiencing normal adjustment problems related to adolescence but handling them well (low-risk for abuse) to those having serious problems (high-risk for abuse) in addition to identified cases of abuse. In this way, group comparisons were conducted within this range of families rather than through the use of a nonabusive "control" group. With problems of definition of abuse and somewhat arbitrary labels related to reporting problems, it seemed more appropriate to analyze families based on specific variables (education, income, rating of problem in family) and to conduct comparisons within the group. In this way, variables could be controlled naturally rather than by assuming that the only variability in a control/abuse comparison was the degree of abuse.

The total sample consisted of 62 families, defined by themselves or a community professional as confronting a significant problem in family life: problem behavior of adolescent, marital adjustment problems, or family system problems. All families contained at least one child between the ages of 10 and 16. The sample of target children consisted of 27 females and 35 males. The families included a man and a woman living together conjugally in the same dwelling (although not necessarily married). Both were assumed to share responsibility for raising the adolescent. The families were representative of the central Pennsylvania region (lower and middle socioeconomic status, low to high education).

Procedures

The assessment battery of instruments was derived from the living systems conceptual framework (Ford, 1984). Three sets of measures were derived from the framework: family system characteristics, parental (individual) characteristics, adolescent characteristics. A three-member research team administered the battery of instruments described in Table 4.1. Each family member was interviewed privately to protect the confidentiality of subjects and to encourage honesty in the replies to potentially sensitive topics such as adolescent attitudes toward parental discipline. Identical measures on some dimensions were administered in order to analyze discrepancies in judgments among family members. Research on behavior problems and competencies (Jessop, 1981) has indicated that discrepancies in judgments of family functioning may characterize dysfunctional families with adolescents. A brief description of the procedures, instruments, and variables is included in Table 4.2.

1. The Telephone Interview. Following the return of the consent form allowing the research staff to contact families, one of the project leaders phoned the family to describe the research and ask the family if they wished

Table 4.1. Format for Home Observations

	Time (minutes)
Parents (To be filled out by each parent individually)	
1. FACES	20
2. Cornell (CPBD)	15
3. Demographics (Part 1)	20
4. Achenbach	25
5. Vignettes (*write response on inside of folder*)	5
Break 10 minutes	
6. AAI	20
7. Demographics (Part 2)	15
8. Peel	
Separately	10
Whole family	10
9. Observations of family free play	
(when indicated)	10
10. Observer Perception Forms	
(*after interviews and filled out by all interviewers*)	
Adolescent	
1. Interparental Influence (IPI)	30
Interparental Conflict Scale (IPC)	
2. FACES	20
3. Support networks	15
4. Achenbach	25
Break 10 minutes	
5. Tanner Scale (*filled out by observer immediately following break*)	
6. Vignettes	5
7. Cornell (CPBD)	15
8. Peel	
Separately	20
Whole family	
9. Observation of family free play	10

to participate. If the family consented, basic information was recorded on the number of children, relationship to parents (step- or biological parent), employment, and schools attended by children. At this time, the parent was asked which adolescent (in the case of multiple adolescents in a family) presented the greater challenge in rearing. This adolescent was then chosen as the target for the procedures.

2. *Family Demographic Interview.* This measure was adapted from Garbarino and Sherman's (1980) Family Interview Questionnaire. The interview

combined open-ended and scaled items to describe the family itself (names and ages of children), health status, resources in financial and emotional support in the family, and the perceptions of the family relationship to the community. Income and an assessment of present financial strain were included. Employment histories (including number of hours and changes in occupation or job), physical problems, and parental perceptions of changes associated with adolescence were also part of the interview. The division of labor reflected in role structure and amount of time as well as perceived satisfaction with time spent together was assessed. Examples of the type of questions included were "How much time do you have to do the things you would like to do?" Choices were: Too much; about right; too little; none. "How do you divide your time outside work?" "What percentage of time would you allot to the following"—alone; children; spouse; children and spouse. Each major area of questions such as health, employment, recreation, finances, and service was followed by a general rating on a scale from excellent to poor. This rating was completed by both the respondent and the interviewer. Finally, there was a measure of social support and quality of relationships.

3. *Interparental Influence/Interparental Conflict Scale.* A series of studies that looked for "configural effects" has afforded consistent evidence that possible "sets" of familial characteristics are present in troubled families and that these are predictive of later psychopathology in the child (see Schwarz, 1979; Schwarz and Zurloff, 1979, for review). Gassner and Murray (1969) observed that interactions between children diagnosed as "neurotic" and their parents were marked by more conflict than "normals." They also found the "neurotic" children were predominantly opposite in sex to the dominant parent. In simple terms, this meant that the parental dyads of neurotic boys were characterized by maternal dominance, whereas the parental dyads of neurotic girls were paternally dominated. This study not only offered information on what "effects" abuse could have on the child and how this may escalate problems but also offered information on family interactions involving adolescent females.

Parental dominance and enforcement of rules was measured by way of Schwarz and Getter's (Schwarz, 1979) adaptation of the work of Klein et al. (1973). The first, a decision-making dominance scale contained items such as the following: "Chooses family car," "Decides when to visit relatives," etc. The adolescent rated each item on a scale ranging from 1, "always mother," to 5, "always father" with the intermediate value of 3 labeled, "mother and father about equal." Sums greater than 27 indicated relatively greater paternal decision-making dominance.

The dominance or assertiveness scale included items such as: "Interrupts others during discussion," and "Is timid about asserting his/her opinion."

Table 4.2 Relation of Family Systems Perspective to Research Procedures

Family systems characteristic	Variables	Measure	Hypotheses: more likely for risk
A. Biological maintenance and functioning			
1. Age of parents Age of adolescents	Age	Telephone interview	1. Middle adulthood and apex adolescent
2. Gender	Adolescent age; male, female		2. Cross-gender relationship
3. Biological or step relationship			3. Step-parenthood
4. Family structure			4. Large families
5. Health of family members			5. Chronic health problems of any family member
6. Family size			6. Large family size
B. Transactional functioning			
1. Marital status	Conflict	IPI/IPC	1. Single parenthood or conflict
2. Amount and type of recreation		Demographic interview	2. Less time spent in recreation

74

3. Parental dominance		
4. Child-rearing attitudes	IPI	3. One dominant parent
Cornell	CPBD	4. High in punishment, low in support
At-risk rating		
5. Emotional support network	Demographic interview	5. Quality support in community which is used

C. Governing functions
1. Role distribution — Interview
2. Level of cognitive functioning — Interview / Peel (1971)
3. Constructive decision making — Discussion task
4. Adaptability — Family Adaptability and Cohesiveness Scale
5. Cohesion
6. Mutuality of goals
7. Social competence — Achenbach
8. Financial pressure — 8. Overcommitment

D. Evaluative functions
1. Family classification — Adolescent Abuse Inventory
2. Emotional climate — Warm, positive

The adolescent was asked to complete the assertiveness scale for his/her parents. Information about reliability is included in the Appendix.

Parental conflict was measured by the Schwarz–Getter Interparental Conflict Scale (Schwarz and Zurloff, 1979). Construction and validation of this scale followed a three-step process of development of an item-pool from substantive considerations, items selected by validation against an external criterion, and cross-validation against the criterion using a new sample. An example of an item was "How often would you say there are disagreements over how to spend money at your house? Over drinking? Flirting with opposite sex? Having manners at the table?" The answer was rated on a 5-point scale.

4. Family Adaptability and Cohesiveness Evaluation Scales (FACES). This self-report instrument was designed to assess family cohesion and adaptability (Olson et al., 1978). The scale was based on the development of the Circumplex Model which uses two dimensions: adaptability and cohesion. The model is described in greater detail in a paper entitled "Circumplex Model of Marital and Family Systems" (Olson et al., 1979). The scale is used to provide an assessment of cohesion and adaptability as perceived by each family member on items designed to tap nine concepts (54 items) to the former dimension and seven concepts (42 items) related to the latter dimension. Items used to tap cohesion included the following:

- Family members are totally involved in each other's lives.
- Family members share almost all interests and hobbies with each other.

Items related to adaptability were:

- Family members feel free to say what is on their mind.
- It seems as if males and females never have the same chores in our family.

Each item was rated by the family member on a 4-point scale from 1 ("true none of the time") to 4 ("true all the time").

In addition, 15 items from the Edmond's Social Desirability Scale were included; FACES is composed of 111 items.

5. Cornell Parent Behavior Description (CPBD). A report of each parent's and adolescent's perception of the parents' child-rearing practices was obtained by way of the Cornell Parent Behavior Description (CPBD). This instrument consists of 11 items that are responded to by each parent and by the adolescent for each parent. The CPBD yields three subscale scores: support (whether the parent is available for counseling, support, and assistance); punishment (use of physical and nonphysical punishment); and control (parental demandingness, protectiveness, and intrusiveness). Examples of items were rated on a 5-point scale from "never" (1) to "very often" (5).

• She keeps pushing me to do my best in whatever I do.
• I know what she expects of me and how she wants me to act.

The validity of the scale has been established in the research literature (Devereux, Bronfenbrenner and Rodgers, 1969), including correlations with direct observation of parent–child interactions.

6. *Adolescent Abuse Inventory (AAI).* Families are classified on the basis of their status on the criterion measure (i.e., the Adolescent Abuse Inventory (AAI). The AAI was developed by Janet Sebes to assess retrospectively the prior occurrence of specific events and behavior that fell within the definitions of abuse and neglect used in the NCCAN sponsored National Incidence Study. It is described in Chapter 5, which discusses the issues involved in assessing risk for maltreatment.

7. *Peel's Assessment of Cognitive Functioning.* Participants' responses to two personal judgment vignettes were utilized to determine their level of cognitive functioning. The vignettes, which were adapted from Peel (1971), were read to each participant and their open-ended responses tape recorded. Each vignette consisted of two parts. The first part provided background information and a request for personal judgment.

> The Baseball Hall of Fame is full of trophies, balls, gloves, and other things which belonged to famous baseball players. Many people travel to Cooperstown, New York, especially to enjoy these things. Recently, there have been several robberies and break-ins into the Hall of Fame and many things have been damaged or stolen. These things are valuable and should be safely guarded. Are the police in Cooperstown to blame for the loss of these valuable baseball treasures?

The second part of the vignettes provided more specific information about the situation and again, a request for personal judgment.

> The authorities knew the Hall of Fame had been broken into at least once a week over the past month and that the security system did not stop the robberies before. Are the police in Cooperstown to blame for the loss of these valuable baseball treasures?

If necessary, the interviewers probed for background reasoning in the participants' responses; however, they did not provide further information.

The responses were rated according to a 4-point scale. This scale was adapted from Petersen's (1982) adaptation of Peel's (1971) rating procedure. The four categories and explanations and examples of each are as follows:

1. *Illogical or totally concrete*—The response is nothing more than either irrelevant statements or a repeat of the text (e.g., "Yes, because these things were valuable," and after additional information, "I don't know; they were stolen and valuable").

2. *Logical and concrete*—The response is a concrete explanation of the

text. The explanation includes information that is in or follows directly from the text. The response is more than a repeat of the text, but alternative explanations are not considered (e.g., "Yes, there were robberies, and the police are supposed to stop robberies," and after additional information, "Yes, they should have stopped the robbers").

3. *Alternative explanations*—The response includes consideration of alternative explanations that may or may not follow directly from the text. The response does not include hypothetical thinking (e.g., "Yes, they should have realized it had been broken into several times, and they should have guarded it better," and after the additional information, "Well, in that case, you can't blame the police all the way—the Hall of Fame authorities are partly to blame as well as the thieves").

4. *Hypothetical thinking*—The response contains consideration of alternative and hypothesis information. The response may or may not fully analyze all of the available data and logical alternatives (e.g., "Well, I don't know for sure. There's so many different levels that need to be considered. First of all, the police should have been on the alert—but then maybe they had more important emergencies. Or perhaps they were on strike. Second, the Hall of Fame should have had a security system—if they didn't, then it's partly their fault. Third, while people shouldn't steal, crime is a community problem, so perhaps the community at large is at fault. I really don't have enough information to give you a yes or a no," and after additional information, "Well, if they knew about the security system, then they should've met with the Hall of Fame personnel. But again, with the information provided, it's hard to give a clear cut yes or no").

This last category encompasses a wide range of functioning levels. Petersen (1982) divided this category into two categories (i.e., hypothetical thinking and fully formal). However, for the purpose of the present study, it was decided that the ability to think hypothetically was the major issue, and further categorization of each was unnecessary.

Three trained raters participated in rating the responses. The raters were naive to the other measured characteristics of the participants and their families. From the responses to the two vignettes, one rating was determined for each participant. In the event that a participant's responses covered a range of categories, either within or between vignettes, the highest dominant category that was evident became that participant's rating. Admittedly, the ratings were somewhat subjective and several "gray areas" were encountered. However, several guidelines, which served to operationalize the process somewhat, were followed. For example, if the responses following the additional information were markedly different from the initial response, then the rating was generally at least a 3, because such suggests alternative thinking (this was not a guideline followed in every case due to such factors as social desirability).

8. *Child Behavior Checklist.* This is a 118-item inventory designed to record both perceptions of behavioral problems and social competencies of the adolescent. Norms for behaviors have been developed from large samples (approximately 1300 nonreferred compared to 1300 referred clinical samples) at the National Institute of Mental Health. Variables derived for this study were scales from the adolescent's social competence, school activities, school performance, and two dimensions of behavior problems: internalizing and externalizing.

The largest social competence concern is with the adolescent's behavior with other children. In the section on competence, each parent and adolescent was asked to compare the adolescent to other peers and rate how much time and how well the adolescent did in each category of sports, hobbies, clubs, and chores.

Items characteristic of internalizing dimension include: unhappy, sad, or depressed; withdrawn; nausea, feels sick. Externalizing items include: gets in fights; bragging; hangs around with kids who get into trouble.

9. *Observer Assessment of Abuse.* Several sources are tapped to verify the presence, duration, type, and severity of abuse when possible. This multilevel approach was taken in an attempt to obtain a complete picture of the family's functioning from as many sources as possible as well as to compare the discrepancies among these views.

First, a set of nine sample family descriptions was constructed by Sebes and Ford (Sebes, 1984). Each story was standardized using the same family name and identical first and last sentences, with the two middle sentences being very similar in length and construction. The descriptions differed only in duration and type of abuse and neglect. The stories ranged from 58 to 62 words. These stories were constructed from a review of the literature on abusive families. The stories were presented to several graduate students and professors in the area of abuse, family development, and psychology. These judges were asked to rank order the descriptions according to duration of abuse from longest to shortest.

An Observer Perception form was devised based on Garbarino and Sherman's (1980) Background Questionnaire and Burgess' Observer Perception Format (1978). It contained questions that asked the observers (who were blind to the presence and/or type of abuse) to rate the dwelling as to cleanliness, size, etc., as well as the sincerity of the participants' responses, presence or absence of abuse, target child, type of abuse, severity of abuse, and approximate duration of abuse.

The sources of information from which the above information were obtained are as follows:

1. *Agencies*: Agencies were asked to rate the families on the set of nine family descriptions.
2. *Parents*: Parents were asked to select the family description that best fit or described their family.
3. *Adolescents*: Adolescents were asked to select the family description that best fit theirs.
4. *Observers*: During the interview (and before the parents made their judgment), each observer was asked to match the family to one of the nine sample family descriptions. After the interview, they were asked to rate the family on the Observer Perception Form.

10. Physical Maturation Scale. This is a rating of the stage of puberal development based on observations of three physical characteristics: (1) facial hair and skin condition; (2) body proportion; (3) coordination and posture.

11. Adolescent–Family Inventory of Life Events and Changes (A-FILE). This is used as a measure of family stress perceived by the adolescent. The measure is a 50-item self-report measure of incidents of stress the adolescent has experienced within two time periods: during the immediately preceding year and during the childhood time preceding adolescence. This measure was used as a measure of family stress, perceived by the adolescent and was developed by McCubbin *et al.* (1981). Items were categorized in areas of general transition, sexuality, losses, responsibilities and strains, substance use, and legal conflict. Items include transitions from the family such as "Family moved to a new home" to individual transition, "Teenager began having sexual intercourse." Items were also related to parent–adolescent relationships, "Parent(s) and teenagers have increased arguments over use of car or hours to stay out."

IMPLICATIONS OF THE SYSTEMS PERSPECTIVE

The implications of the theoretical organization of this project are that the family is viewed as a system of interacting roles and individual life courses. The system framework provides a case from which adolescence represents a description of roles and child-rearing practices that formerly showed equilibrium during childhood.

Methodologically, the systems perspective provides a framework within which to incorporate measures of the dynamically interacting components of the system. Analyses of individual family members (mothers, fathers, adolescents) can be conducted in groups or dyads. Discrepancy scores could be derived in comparing judgments from mother–adolescent, father–adolescent, and mother–father perceptions. Finally, analyses can be conducted at the family level to derive correlates of family classifications.

The family systems framework has relevance for intervention issues. If high-risk families can be identified, goals for strengthening positive points and reconstructing weaknesses could be drawn. Finally, intervention could be aimed at the level of most persistent problems in the dynamic system—individual, family, or community. Exemplars of strategic interventions will be included in the following chapters. With this in mind, we can proceed with our efforts to understand troubled youth in troubled families. We turn next to the core issue of assessing a family's risk for maltreatment.

APPENDIX I

Alpha coefficients reported for adolescents (92 male and female undergrads) filling out the scales on maternal versus paternal dominance, of maternal assertiveness and of paternal assertiveness were .68, .49, and .47, respectively (Schwarz and Zuroff, 1979). On the original validation sample test–retest, reliability was found to be .91, and there was .57 correlation between students' and either parents' report.

FACES appears to have a high degree of clinical and empirical validity (Russell, 1979, 1980). The internal consistency (alpha) reliability of the total scores for adaptability and cohesion were .75 and .83, respectively. This measure was based on data computed from a sample of 201 families with a father, mother, and adolescent (Olson et al., 1978).

Seigelman (1965) and MacDonald (1971) reported reliability coefficients for the total scale that range from .70 to .81 and for individual subscales that range from .48 to .82. In addition, Wolk and Brandon (1977) calculated reliability estimates for both normals and runaways for each subscale by parent. These coefficients ranged from a high of .90 to a low of .56. Because it was written for children and adolescents to answer, this measure was also revised so that parents could respond about their own parenting practices.

Interrater reliability was assessed on one-third of the first 135 cases and was 85%. Discrepancies between raters were resolved by mutual agreement.

A Spearman rank order correlation was performed on this data with correlations ranging from .85 to 1.00. Among the in-home observers, reliabilities were calculated to be .73, while the family member ratings of themselves were .48.

Reliability among observers was determined by a cumulative method with an average reliability of .80.

```
┌─────────────────────────────────────────────┐
│ DEFINING HIGH RISK                           │
│                                          5   │
│                                              │
│                                              │
│                                              │
│                                              │
│                              JANET M. SEBES  │
└─────────────────────────────────────────────┘
```

THE ABUSIVE PHENOMENON

Attempts to describe and explain adolescent abuse have benefited from the work done by child abuse researchers. Dissatisfaction with attempts to explain abuse as a function of characteristics of the parent (Wasserman, 1967; Johnson and Morse, 1968; Steele, 1976; Van Stolk, 1972) or child (DeLissovoy, 1979; Friedrich and Boriskin, 1976) or as primarily due to socioeconomic stress factors (Gil, 1970, 1975, 1983; Lystad, 1975) led to an approach that has alternately been called the social interactional (Burgess, 1979), social situational (Parke and Collmer, 1975), or the ecological model (Garbarino, 1977; Belsky, 1978, 1980). The basic tenet of this framework is that maltreatment is multiply determined by forces at work in the individual (ontogenetic development), in the family (microsystem), in the community (exosystem), and in the culture in which the family lives (macrosystem).

In using this approach or framework, then, one would argue that the phenomenon of abuse cannot be understood without assessing the family across all levels. One important qualification to this argument has been offered by Burgess et al. (1981). Concerning the multiply determined nature of abuse, these authors provide evidence that the correlates of abuse are not necessarily theoretically or practically equal to each other. They point to characteristics such as those included in Belsky's (1980) analysis of the microsystem as the most important. For example, based on careful behavioral observation, they report that there are patterns of social interaction that are characteristic of abusive families. These include a lower level of interaction, a less positive more negative quality to the interaction, and a higher likelihood that these negative behaviors, once performed, will be reciprocated. It appears that the initial point of focus for identifying and understanding abusive families might be found at the microsystem level. With only limited solid behavioral evidence such as that provided by Burgess et al. (1981), the question remains—How can we identify families at risk to begin maltreating during adolescence?

Abusive versus Disciplinary Incidents

One major issue in this area involves the distinction between "abusive" incidents and "disciplinary" incidents. For example, parent behaviors that may be acceptable (although not necessarily appropriate) for use with a child (e.g., spanking, a high degree of parental control) may be inappropriate or even abusive when used with a developing adolescent (e.g., control that is too restrictive may result in a decreased capacity to make decisions and to experience age-appropriate developmental dilemmas). Especially when examining the behavior of the adolescent, the problem of distinguishing between discipline and abuse is further complicated if, as Berdie et al. (1977) suggest, others see the adolescent as intentionally escalating the situation. When considering the behavior of the "child," there is much more sympathy than is often given the adolescent. As we stated in Chapter 1, the negative stereotype of the adolescent turns into a dangerous image when dealing with cases of adolescent abuse. Parents may feel more justified in using harsher methods of discipline when the adolescent does something that they consider bad. Thus, even within the family, there may be a changing definition of appropriate discipline (change from calling a behavior abusive to appropriate discipline) with the changing acceptability/ unacceptability of the behavior of the adolescent.

Abuse or maltreatment, rather than being a behavior in isolation, is a part of a continuum of parent–child interactions, of parent "treatment." It seems that most parental behaviors may move up and down on this scale or continuum as a response to many factors including not only the increase in age and developmental status of the child but also the level of transgression. The implicit notion is that perhaps there are some qualities present in at-risk families that do not allow the alteration of parental response to maturation in the child. Before this is pursued, perhaps it would be helpful to look at attempts that have been made to identify those families who may be at-risk.

Measurement

Measurement of risk for maltreatment or even the actual presence of abuse has not been very successful. One important factor is that the examination of child maltreatment using traditional research paradigms is difficult (Starr et al., 1976). Until recently, there has been no reliable, valid, or acceptable system for describing and classifying abusive parental behaviors. Because most of the presently available research and data have not used one overriding system, much of what has been done in the past may suffer from a lack of internal validity. If there is no consistency between studies, then the external validity is limited as well.

Another criticism aimed at abuse research is its post hoc or retrospective approach which identifies and attempts to help families seemingly long after help could be most useful. The largest amount of research has been done with samples obtained from social service agencies or hospitals. Exceptions to this have been samples gathered from newspapers (DeFrancis, 1963), referrals from other sources (Green et al., 1974), and survey procedures (Gil, 1970; Schloesser, 1964). As Egeland and Brunquell (1979) point out, a comparison of these "deviant" populations to normal or other clinical groups generally results in group differences, but these differences tell us little about what factors were important in the development of the pathology. Thus, despite the large amount of information gleaned from retrospective studies using known abusive samples, a most important question goes unanswered—Why do some families in conflict begin to abuse their children during adolescence whereas other similar families do not?

In an effort to counter this problem, more recent attempts have tried to take a more preventive stance. Some of these may be found in the research on "at-risk" families.

An Exosystem Study. One of the broadest efforts to study families at risk was that of Garbarino and Crouter (1978) and Garbarino and Sherman (1980). Their premise was that the likelihood of child maltreatment varies in direct relation to the availability, adequacy, and use made of family supportive resources in the community. This study was based on many research findings including the linking of the role of the neighborhood infrastructure to the dynamics of juvenile delinquency (Devereux, 1960), Collins and Pancoast's (1976) work on "natural neighbors" as helpers/healers in the community, the connections between child abuse and "contemporary social isolation" (Newberger et al., 1977), and finally, the work of Gray et al. (1979), who found child maltreatment and childhood accidents decreased when families identified as "high-risk" for maltreatment were involved in long-term support systems. Garbarino and Crouter's work thus focused on at-risk neighborhoods identified as those with a low level of material and social resources. They argued that the identification of at-risk neighborhoods (with particularly dangerous socioeconomic status and demographic characteristics) could and should be done with an effort to then direct resources and intervention efforts into that area.

Microsystem Studies. A second series of at-risk studies are those that include a set of measures that attempt to capture aspects of family functions and interactions. For example, Egeland and Brunquell (1979) followed 275 high-risk mothers and infants through the child's first year of life. The mothers' status as low socioeconomic status (SES), on welfare, and primiparous were the factors used to consider them at risk. Factors used to differentiate mothers who mistreated their children from those who did not were: the characteristics of the women, infant temperament, mother–infant interaction, and environmental stress. The authors felt that the approach was particularly useful in identifying characteristics or profiles of mothers at high risk to abuse their children.

A second example of studies on high risk families is that done by Kotelchuck (1982) and Newberger et al. (1977). The Family Development Study is a retrospective case control study of pediatric social illness which included child abuse, failure to thrive, accidental injuries, and ingestions. The overall goals of this study were to determine what ecological factors make a child at risk for each of the specific social pediatric illnesses (prediction), and to examine commonalities and differences in the risk factors across the different diagnostic categories (potential misclassification) (Kotelchuck, 1982).

Subjects (N = 201) were all children 4 years old or younger who were hospitalized with a social pediatric diagnosis (not simply abuse cases). These researchers included such a wide range of subjects due to their belief that there may be a common etiology to all the social pediatric illnesses, and that by including all of the children with a social pediatric diagnosis, they were including all potentially abused children. Controls (N = 201) were matched for race, SES, and age of the child. Of the experimental subjects, 48 were child abuse cases, 41 were failure to thrive, 97 were accidental injuries, and 23 were ingestion cases.

Data were collected during 1-hour, in-hospital interviews and included maternal and paternal standardized interviews, a review of the child's medical records, and the child's score on the Vineland Social Maturity Index.

The findings of this study were as follows. Demographic factors did not distinguish experimental families from matched controls, and, contrary to previous findings, the child abuse families were found to be two-parent families of average (N = 4) size with equal representations of males and females. Two powerful groups of child abuse and neglect risk indicators emerged: social isolation and unhappy maternal childhood. Furthermore, child characteristics, whether physical, intellectual, or temperamental, were not very strong risk indicators for abuse or neglect nor was maternal psychiatric status. In sum, they found it very difficult to distinguish among the pediatric social illness families.

A third study that attempted to identify high-risk families (i.e., mothers) was that of the work of Altemeier *et al.* (1979). Using a standardized interview developed by Altemeier, these researchers interviewed approximately 1600 women coming into the Nashville General Hospital to have their babies. They developed a criteria measure and cutoff scores, enabling a classification or ranking of the group in terms of "risk for potential problems." They identified the top 20% as at greatest risk and subsequently followed this group and a random sample from the remaining 80% group for approximately 1 year.

The follow-up study consisted of a home visit by the interviewer prior to the expected date of delivery. During the visit, the Maternal Attitude Scales [a short version of the instrument developed by Cohler *et al.* (1970)] were administered in addition to periodic observations of mother–infant interaction, measures of infant temperament, and indexes of the child's health status.

The results of this study provided some support for the notion that by using maternal interviews, a group of families can be identified who are at risk for child maltreatment. The prenatal interview did identify a group of women among whom were a significant proportion (14%) who later were found to have maltreated their infants. However, this group also contained a larger number of women who did not show any signs of parenting disorders according to the conventional criteria used in the study.

In another report of their research, Vietze *et al.* (1982) showed that it was possible (via regression analyses) to predict child maltreatment from risk status, based on the prenatal interview, infant's birth weight, selected mother–infant interactions, and maternal perception of infant temperament. The most important variable in this prediction was risk status. These authors felt that it is possible to identify high-risk mothers but warned of the dangers of misclassification.

A fourth example of studies on high-risk families is that done by Starr (1974, 1982). The two purposes of his work were to identify variables that differentiated families in which abuse occurs from a matched control sample and to assess the feasibility of developing an instrument to predict abuse. Starr's study is based on his ecological model (Starr, 1978) which stresses the need to evaluate social, familial, and individual factors.

Subjects were 97 families with children 5 years old or younger who had had a report of suspected or actual physical abuse filed by Social Services. Subjects were recruited from among families who had had children admitted to the hospital through the emergency room at the Children's Hospital of Michigan in Detroit. Control group families ($N = 92$) were matched for race, SES, age, and gender of the child and contained children with respiratory or gastrointestinal problems.

Parental measures included four structured interviews (Kotelchuck, 1982), a detailed social isolation questionnaire, Holmes and Rahe's (1967) stress scale, Caldwell's Home Observation for the Measure of the Environment Scale (Caldwell et al., 1968) as well as measures of maternal psychiatric functioning, intelligence, child-rearing attitudes, knowledge of development, and use of disciplinary techniques. Child measures included developmental status, behavior, and child health status.

Results of this study demonstrated that comparing matched abuse and control families evaluated on literature-based questionnaires did not support the well-known causes and correlates of child abuse. Few group differences were found and when found, they generally did not follow a pattern that led to a coherent explanation of child abuse in terms of social, parental, or child variables. Of the 249 variables included, 10 were found to be significant ($p<.01$): (1) Whether the mother had ever been a full-time employee; (2) whether disagreements led to hitting or throwing; (3) the number of different people visited; (4) whether families met with relatives more than once weekly; (5) whether these meetings are often enough or not; (6) whether there is denial of emotional complexity in child rearing; (7) maternal rating of child health; (8) likelihood that low child weight is due to neglect; (9) overall rating of the likelihood of neglect; and (10) child hemoglobin levels (Starr, 1982, p. 129).

Starr concluded his report of research findings by saying that abusive families are more similar to control families than they are different. He identified multiple problem families in both control and abuse groups and felt that both groups were in need of help.

Predictor Instruments. A third set of studies have had as their goal the development of a predictor instrument for the identification of high-risk families and/or individuals. First of these is the work of Bavolek and his colleagues (Bavolek et al., 1979). These researchers developed the Adolescent Parenting Inventory (API) for use with late adolescents. This instrument attempts to identify teens (future parents) who may benefit from parent education, child development courses, etc. Their lack of knowledge about realistic expectations and appropriate parenting practices is thus the indicator of their risk.

Bavolek et al. tested a large number of adolescents in addition to a variety of known abusive adolescents. The conclusions of their study were: (1) That the API is psychometrically sound; (2) in the above study, 12% of the general population of school students sampled had scores that placed them in the at-risk category; (3) institutionalized adolescents with recorded histories of abuse and/or neglect expressed more abusive attitudes toward parenting than noninstitutionalized and nonidentified abused adolescents.

The Michigan Screening Profile of Parenting is another questionnaire developed to identify high-risk individuals. This questionnaire is based on the work of Helfer and Kempe (1968) and Steele (1970). After several permutations based on the results of comparisons of known abusers and others (e.g., medical students' spouses or medical school secretaries) and eventually on a comparison of abusers and nonabusers matched on social class and other variables, the currently used 74-item version has emerged.

In three replication studies with the Michigan Screening Profile of Parenting, Schneider (1982) found that four clusters have consistently been replicated: Relationships with Parents, Expectations of Children, Coping, and Emotional Needs Met (basic trust). The instrument thus assesses both whether there is a background of emotional and physical abuse and whether there still is a feeling of not being loved at the present time.

Schneider goes on to report that only one of the clusters mentioned above seems to have significant predictive value and that is the Emotional Needs Met cluster. She points out that this cluster contains items found to be significant in the studies of others (e.g., Starr, 1982; Kotelchuck, 1982). She noted that of special import was the inconsistency and variability in the responses of abusive parents as compared to controls. Last, and most important, the work of Nicholsen and Schneider (1978), in attempting to distinguish between actually abusing and potentially abusing families, discovered that families in both groups had high Emotional Needs Met scores.

Schneider (1982, p. 158) concludes her many years of research with the following statement:

> While we have been refining this questionnaire and giving it to a variety of different samples over the past twelve years, we still do not know if we have a specific predictive questionnaire for potential child abusers. Our data so far show only that a person's answers are probably related to the presence or absence of some current problems in parenting. What we can say is this: If a person's current perceptions of his or her early childhood and present relationships are seen as negative or inconsistent, further assessment of that person is necessary in order to predict if he or she is at risk for problems in interacting with his or her children. We suspect that such negative or inconsistent perceptions may be related to many different parent–child interaction difficulties, of which child abuse is only one. These are the people Eli Newberger calls "parents in distress" (Newberger et al., 1977). We call them people who have potential for parent–child interaction problems. We no longer feel that we are close to specific predictions of child abuse alone—we are identifying people with a high potential to develop some sort of parent–child interaction problem.

Measurement Critique

Attempts to determine risk for maltreatment, although praised for their preventive focus, have been criticized on several grounds and most often by those who have attempted this research (Kotelchuck, 1982; Newberger et *al.*, 1977; Starr, 1982). Most prominent among these criticisms has been that screening efforts falsely label many families as "high-risk" for abuse when these families in fact are not abusive. This is known as the false–positive or Type II error phenomenon. Many researchers feel that screening efforts often produce more harm than good as those families labeled as at-risk, they argue, may actually go on to become abusive (i.e., a self-fulfilling prophecy). The ethical dilemma is whether the greater danger lies in refraining from labeling a family until it has begun to abuse or in labeling a family prematurely or incorrectly.

In Chapter 1 we established that families in which there is much conflict do not fall into the "normal" range of families during adolescence. The studies reviewed above found several common components to be characteristic of abusive families, but more important, they agree that it is difficult to discriminate between abusing and "problem" families. In light of this consideration as well as the conspicuous absence of any studies that attempt prediction in families with adolescents, the task of the present study begins to take shape as that of identifying problem families with adolescents.

Sampling

When approaching the problem of how to assess adolescent maltreatment, we need to consider two very important findings of the National Incidence Study (NIS) Burgdorff, 1980). The first is that a very high level of adolescents are being abused. The second is that the NIS has indicated that the cases of maltreatment that are reported to Child Protective Services (CPS) represent only a biased and small segment (about one-third) of maltreating families. Many more were found by appealing to sources such as schools, police stations, clergy, etc. This data suggest that family conflict may be reported to many sources, and these reports often lead to revelations of abusive interactions. Knowing that a very high level of problems in the family is not the norm and knowing that these families come to the attention of others than CPS, one begins to get an outline of the methods needed to obtain a sample as well as the approach best suited for studying the sample once obtained.

Thus we decided to use an at-risk methodology—one that takes a probabilistic approach to maltreatment. The main tenet of this approach is the assumption that a group can be identified in which a certain problem will occur with a great enough frequency to warrant more intense examination of a larger sample of people, most of whom may not share the particular problem being studied (Egeland and Brunquell, 1979).

Therefore, to obtain a sample more broadly representative of those potentially at-risk cases, the present study defined the relevant population as a continuum of families including known maltreaters, troubled, and normal families (as described in Chapter 4). Based on the findings of the NIS, the assumption was made that within a representative sample of these troubled and normal families, there would be a group of families that fell along the continuum of parenting from nonabusive (or appropriate parenting) through long-term child abusers. One question still unanswered at this point is "What about the period of adolescence makes a family containing an adolescent become at-risk"?

THE FAMILY SYSTEM IN A DEVELOPMENTAL CONTEXT

To answer such a question, one needs to use a developmental backdrop. It is not just anecdotal evidence of parents that leads us to conclude that adolescents are more at risk for abuse. The NIS, as well as the work of Straus et al. (1980), has left little doubt that there appears to be a curvilinear relationship between abuse and age with increases at early childhood and adolescence. Where the factors that caused infants and young children to be abused are colic, hyperactivity, and/or a frustrated parent's inability to "reason" with them (Straus et al., 1980), the adolescent, in some sense, again becomes a "difficult" child. Nothing pleases her, she needs to consider the opposite side of every coin, and many parents may report that the adolescent no long seems to listen to reason.

During childhood and latency, the role expectations and permissions of family and society are relatively stable both for child and parent. The child's physical characteristics, although rapidly changing, are not those of an adult. The child is dependent upon other family members to manage external dynamics for the family. Whatever the pattern of interactions, one can assume that they are somewhat stable.

Significant changes in family components, or in family contexts, precipitate some disorganization of existing patterns and require some kind of reorganization or incorporation (McCubbin et al., 1980). Upon entering adolescence, children frequently find themselves expected to continue in the role of the child and sometimes to be both child and adult simultaneously. This role strain can and often does lead to aggressive behaviors and conflicts within the family structure.

Discussion of the contribution of the adolescent is not meant to lead one to conclude that the parents do not play a central role. Rather, it is meant to demonstrate that adolescent provocations (which can and are defined very differently by different parents) coupled with a rigid, very strict, but fragile family structure may be the straw that breaks the camel's back (Kadushin and Martin, 1981).

In synthesizing these findings, we begin by noting that the same basic ingredients, though in somewhat different form, may be present in all abusive families regardless of age. What is important is to try to understand why various families did not begin abuse during childhood but instead began abuse during adolescence. Based upon the analysis of family systems presented in Chapter 4 we are lead to consider aspects of the family system experiencing adolescence that affect risk status. It follows from this view that several kinds of factors might be assessed to identify families that may be vulnerable to the onset of adolescent abuse or neglect when that transition begins in a child within the family unit.

1. Assessing *adolescent behaviors* both "normal" and "not-normal" (or delinquent) should be useful in several ways. For one thing, it would indicate the higher baselines where they exist.
2. Assessing the *attitudes* of the parents toward different ways of responding to such adolescent behaviors should also be helpful.
3. Finally, it is important to measure the parents *reported likelihood of performing abusively* given certain adolescent behaviors or family contexts. This, of course, will not give direct evidence that abuse is occurring but instead will indicate those families who have the attitudes and current patterns of functioning that may place them at-risk.

THE DEVELOPMENT OF A PREDICTOR MEASURE

The identification of adolescent problem behavior and the distress it may cause has been approached primarily from two perspectives—one attempts to explore the problem behaviors and distress experienced from the adolescent's perspective (Burke and Weir, 1978; Collins and Harper, 1979; Porteus, 1979) and the other assesses the parents perception of child problems and accompanying feelings (Achenbach and Edelbrock, 1979; Robinson et al., 1977). Because the present study is construing maltreatment as an interactional process, it seemed necessary to use an instrument that measured adolescent behaviors as well as parental reponses. Not being able to identify existing assessment instruments that served this purpose, an instrument was designed for the present study.

Before we go on to describe the actual development of the predictor instrument, several factors that shaped the parameters of the study as well as the design of the questionnaire should be mentioned.

First, it is only very recently that discussions of typical methods of child rearing have reached the point where maltreatment can be identified as a distinct problem (Radbill, 1974). In the much younger literature on adolescent abuse, no equivalent agreement of acceptable treatment of adolescents has been reached. Thus, while the study of child abuse continues to present problems to researchers, adolescent abuse research may be considered even more difficult due to several reasons including the lack of clarity of parental behaviors deemed appropriate for use with a developing adolescent.

A second issue is generated by society's apparent focus on both the elimination of infant and child maltreatment and coinciding, conflicting messages regarding the treatment of youth (Bybee, 1979). Bybee (1979) proposes that this ambivalence in our approach to disciplining youth results, at least in part, from our own confusion as to what constitutes abuse as well as to society's view of the adolescent as a "marginal man" with neither child nor adult status. Thus, while the infant is often seen as a helpless victim, abused adolescents are often seen as somewhat deserving of the treatment they receive. Thus, a particularly important quality of adolescent abuse research, in general, and for our study, in particular, is a focus on the interaction between parent and adolescent, especially the parents' perceptions and responses to adolescent behaviors.

One final parameter of particular importance to the present study is the pervasive use of abusive disciplinary techniques, accompanying social sanctions, and the anxiety, defensiveness, and guilt aroused in caretakers (or teachers, mental health workers, etc.) when one questions their practices or when a child presents the teacher or clergyman with data that make it necessary to file a report. Although every state has mandated abuse-reporting laws, parental discipline reports indicate a 70–90% use of physical punishment sometime during childhood (Clifford, 1959; Erlanger, 1974; Steinmetz and Straus, 1973). When one extends this period to include reports of adolescents, as many as 95% of today's parents have used corporal punishment on their child at some time (Bryan and Freed, 1982). Moreover, 36% of all secondary schools, with the full support of the Supreme Court, report using physical punishment for disciplinary reasons during a typical month (Boesel, 1978).

Thus, the design of the present study, with its broad-based referral system (e.g., clergy, teachers or guidance counselors, protective services), presented a great challenge to research staff. Namely, we had to design instruments sensitive enough to capture indexes of risk for abuse while at the same time be exquisitely aware of the anxiety, potential for defensiveness, and guilt of the reporter or referral source. With these important factors in mind, let us now go on to an explanation of the development of the predictor and criterion measures.

Frequency of Adolescent Normal Behaviors

As several authors indicated, child and adolescent maltreatment by parents appears to be, at least in part, a family interactional problem influenced by the adolescent's behavior (Berdie et al., 1977; Blumberg, 1974; Garbarino and Gilliam, 1980; Patterson and Reid, 1970; Kadushin and Martin, 1981). Due to the wide differences in possible habituation in family patterns, it would seem that varying definitions of provocative or rule-breaking behavior could exist within families. For example, in some families, the performance of typical adolescent behaviors such as wanting more freedom and voicing opinions may be enough to place the family at risk for abuse. Table 5.1 contains a list of adolescent behaviors included in this scale. These behaviors were generated from a review of the literature but more specifically from the work of Adelson (1980), Hindelang *et al.* (1981), and Kempe and Kempe (1978).

Table 5.1. Description and Results of Item Analysis on Scale A

Item no. on AAI	Adolescent behavior subscale	Item-total correlations	
		Mother	Father
Normal behaviors			
5.	Requesting parental approval	.396	.614
6.	Going out with friends	.424	.286
7.	Wanting later curfew	.612	.664
11.	Not doing chores	.687	.557
13.	Voicing opinion on punishment	.715	.617
14.	Coming home crying	.309	.144
15.	Testing limits	.665	.757
17.	Wanting to help in making family decisions	.584	.584
20.	Late for dinner	.610	.558
23.	Coming home crying from date	.473	.569
26.	Carelessness with others' possessions	.585	.698
Not-normal behaviors			
1.	Poor school performance	.472	.373
2.	Truancy	.290	.510
3.	Engaging in "necking," "petting," etc.	.605	.200
4.	Promiscuity	.628	.603
8.	Use of drugs	.284	.630
9.	Soliciting sexual attention	.486	.349
10.	Breaking windows	.259	.213
12.	"Partying" at home unsupervised	.314	.382
16.	Deliberately staying out past curfew	.649	.659
18.	Stealing	.565	.616
19.	Walking around house scantily clad	.337	.435
21.	Overinvolvement in parents' arguments	.345	.510
22.	Physical abuse of siblings	.374	.389
24.	Use of alcohol	.525	.689
25.	Intense arguments with siblings	.349	.412

Frequency of Not-Normal or Delinquent Behaviors

If the frequency of normal adolescent behaviors may be seen as provocative by some parents, the performance of delinquent behaviors could be a potential source of even more family disruption. In fact, the difficult or special child indicated in cases of child abuse may, in adolescence, be described by parents as "aggressive" and "rule-breaking" (Libbey and Bybee, 1979). Kempe and Kempe (1978) emphasize behavioral difficulties of the adolescent (e.g., stealing, academic problems, and running away) as chief correlates of adolescent maltreatment. Table 5.1 includes those behaviors used.

Parental Attitude

This area of measurement included variables concerning the parents' attitudes toward different forms of appropriate and inappropriate parenting practices as well as their perceptions of their approach to child rearing. The broad types of parental behavior were derived from the NIS classification. The types of abusive/neglectful behaviors actually addressed in the questionnaire are listed in Table 5.2.

Because parents are typically the family components responsible for establishing and maintaining some coherence in family interaction patterns, adolescent changes typically pressure them to accept changes in the family patterns. The systems framework suggests that when parents are rigid in their boundaries of acceptable/unacceptable behaviors and show approval of harsh or extreme means of control when these bounds are exceeded, trouble is likely to arise. Thus, one relevant parental characteristic is the parental attitude toward various abusive, neglectful, and appropriate parenting responses to adolescent behaviors.

Perceived Likelihood of Parental Behaviors

This set of variables includes the parents' estimated response when presented with certain adolescent behaviors. If the parents report a high likelihood of acting abusively, then the probability that the family might display maltreating behaviors is expected to be higher than in families without such characteristics.

The rationale for measuring "attitude" and "likelihood" (and, thus, risk) of abuse is as follows. First, the sample was expected to include families varying in their history of maltreatment risk from none to a potentially severe level. To ask parents if they had already maltreated their child would not reveal such diversity. Second, some of the referral sources objected to direct inquiry about maltreatment. Therefore, the present study respected their concern by using terms and methods that would not label or offend families.

Table 5.2. Results of Item Analyses of Scales B and C

		Item-total correlations			
		Mother		Father	
Item no. on AAI	Parental behavior	B	C	B	C
Hands-On Abuse (Physical)					
13.	Approval spanking	.440	.495	.307	.555
24.	Punch with fist	.265	.503	.639	.645
26.	Slap across face	.725	.756	.419	.541
9.	Allowing others to misuse adolescent	.296	.444	.321	.114
19.	Failing to respect privacy of adolescent	.264	.112	.505	.427
Hands-Off Abuse (Verbal)					
1.	Verbal assault	.367	.421	.547	.665
5.	Insult	.445	.472	.435	.486
14.	Insult (psychological)	.589	.288	.516	.660
6.	Inattention to needs	.507	.361	.259	.243
16.	Humiliation	.291	.192	.577	.689
17.	Fostering immaturity	.386	.241	.344	.458
18.	Close confinement	.515	.488	.291	.419
21.	Role reversal	.290	.565	.451	.466
23.	Failure to intervene in emotional problems	.405	.443	.245	.252
25.	Rejection	.521	.525	.377	.523
Neglect					
2.	Educational neglect	.371	.130	.257	.274
3.	Neglect of physical and emotional needs	.317	.786	.322	.335
4.	Physical neglect	.041	.485	.439	.182
8.	Abandonment	.423	.341	.360	.431
10.	Abandonment	.248	.606	.545	.369
12.	Abandonment	.304	.471	.570	.501
20.	Withholding adequate nutrition	.269	−.093	.395	.522
Appropriate Parenting					
7.	Taking away privileges	.443	.889	.378	.444
11.	Taking away privileges	.421	−.093	.543	.512
15.	Taking away privileges	−.094	.889	.701	.751
22.	Time out/apologize	.294	−.214	.062	−.046

The result is a measure reflecting the probability or risk for adolescent abuse. (See Table 5.2.) As we shall see, however, indirect methods were used to assess the actual presence of maltreatment.

Development of the Adolescent Abuse Inventory (AAI). As mentioned in Chapter 4, the AAI was developed to serve the purpose of assessing the frequency of adolescent normal and delinquent behaviors within the past year, parental attitudes toward abusive responses to these adolescent behaviors, and finally the likelihood that the parents would behave in similarly abusive manners. The AAI is a self-report measure (see Appendix I) made up of 26 hypothetical situations to which parents were asked to respond. The hypothetical situations were designed to include a specific type of adolescent behavior to which the parent is reacting in a particular manner. Two separate forms— one for males and one for females—were generated. These were as much alike as possible, with changes in names, pronouns, and slight changes in situations to make them more applicable to the two genders.

After each situation, the parents were asked to respond to three standard question that were tailored slightly to address the specific issues (adolescent and parent behavior) in the situation at hand. The following is an example of a questionnaire item.

John borrowed his parents' tools and paints and did not put them away when finished. Because they were left out, the younger kids got into them and dumped the paints and lost some of the tools. John's parents came in and found this mess and slapped John across the face.

a. *How often has your adolescent been irresponsible like this in the past year?*

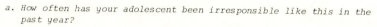

0	1	2	3	4	5	6
never	once	twice	3-5 times	6-10 times	11-20 times	more than 20 times

b. *How would you rate this parent's actions?*

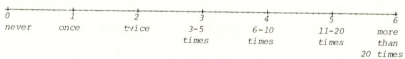

1	2	3	4	5	6	7
very bad	bad	somewhat bad	uncertain	fairly good	good	very good

c. *Under the circumstances described, how likely would you be to behave as this parent did?*

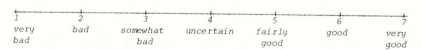

1	2	3	4	5	6	7
would definitely act the same	very likely	likely	uncertain	not likely	very unlikely	would definitely not act the same

Diagram 1

To obtain a measure of the parents' estimate of normal and not-normal or delinquent adolescent behaviors, responses to question "a" on the AAI were summed for mothers and for fathers, respectively. The raw scores were recorded from 0–6 to 1–7 to make values numerically comparable across the scales.

The "b" scale of the AAI was used to measure the parental attitude toward maltreatment. Items on the AAI were grouped into four subscales: Hands-On Abuse (5 items), Hands-Off Abuse (10 items), Neglect (7 items), and Appropriate Parenting (4 items). The raw scores across 22 items were summed for each parent. The scores from the Appropriate Parenting subscale were reversed in direction so they could be meaningfully added to the raw score form the other 22 items, generating a range of possible scores on this subscale of 26–182.

Finally, the "c" scale of the AAI was used to measure the parental likelihood of acting abusively. The subscales and actual subtypes of maltreatment examined were identical to those in question "b," the only difference being the question asked (i.e., Under the circumstances described, how likely would you be to behave as this parent did?). Items within this category were scored by reversing the values of the Likert scales except for those on the Appropriate Parenting items, as these were already scored in the appropriate direction. Once assigned the appropriate values, scores were summed across all 26 items for mothers and fathers, respectively, a procedure that generates scores from 26 to 182. Appendix II discusses the measurement properties of the AAI.

THE DEVELOPMENT OF A CRITERION MEASURE

One ingredient missing in this endeavor, to this point, is a way of classifying families such that the results of the AAI could be evaluated. To determine the classification or categorization of families for the present study, it was necessary to develop a method that would address and include different patterns or constellations of characteristics. Important factors in this assessment would be the duration of the abuse as well as its severity.

Presence/Duration of Maltreatment

Family systems develop habituated patterns of interaction analogous to the habits developed by individuals. Studies of abusive families have indicated that it is helpful to conceive of such habituated family interaction patterns along a continuum from serious maltreatment to positive patterns that do not involve maltreatment (National Center on Child Abuse and Neglect, 1981; Burgess, 1979; Garbarino and Gilliam, 1980; Lourie, 1979). This variable has two interrelated attributes. The first is the kind of family interactional pattern present. The second is how long the interactional pattern has been in existence. Therefore, this variable included both a time reference (duration) and forms of parental treatment/maltreatment, both of which allowed families to be placed along a continuum from probable long-term maltreatment to recent maltreatment to positive parenting.

In the absence of direct observation of a family over a period of years, the above system allows some estimate of family functioning to be given by many "judges" or "raters." In the present study, three in-home interviewers, the three family members interviewed, and one person outside the family (usually the referral source) rated the families.

A set of nine *Family Vignettes* was constructed to provide ratings of family functioning in the least obtrusive manner possible while still allowing a reasonable means of obtaining a self-report of the occurrence and duration of maltreatment (Appendix II). Information on the development and psychometric properties of this measurement instrument can be found in Appendix III. The results presented in Appendix III are encouraging. They indicate that the AAI is a promising direction for research applications.

Administration and scoring were carried out for the observer, mother, father, and adolescent ratings as well as for those of the source outside the family. Each respondent was presented with the randomly shuffled family descriptions. Each judge was given as much time as was needed to choose the vignette that best described the family. As originally derived, any vignette chosen within the 1–3 category placed the family in the long-term child abusive category. Choice of vignettes 5–6 placed the family into the short-term abusive category, and finally, choice of vignettes 7–9 placed the family in the nonabusive category.

An example of a long-term abusive vignette is as follows:

> Mr. and Mrs. Smith live in a small town a few miles from here. There have been arguments in their house for as long as anyone can remember. The kids sometimes got the worst of it, being "yelled at" and "smacked," but sometimes they deserved it. Even though they have some problems, they've always managed to keep the family together.

The following is an example of one of the short-term abusive vignettes:

> Mr. and Mrs. Smith live in a small town a few miles from here. They never had any problems with their children until recently. They've been demanding to do whatever they please lately, and the Smith's have had to get very strict, "grounding" them for weeks at a time. Even though they have some problems, they've always managed to keep the family together.

Finally, this is a sample of a nonabusive vignette:

> Mr. and Mrs. Smith live in a small town a few miles from here. When problems come up in their family, they all sit down and have a "meeting." Now that the kids are getting older, they are given more and more freedom which they seem

to handle well. Even though they have some problems, they've always managed to keep the family together.

OPERATIONALIZING THE TERM HIGH RISK

The AAI is a versatile instrument, and the subscales have, to date, been used in different ways to define high risk (Garbarino et al., 1984). The method chosen for use in this book is described below.

Mothers' and fathers' respective scores on the Parenting Attitude ("b") and Parental Likelihood ("c") scales were summed to give a composite b/c score for each mother and father. Due to the low reliabilities of the Appropriate Parenting subscales, these four items were left out of the summation of the "b" and the "c" scales, leaving a total of 44 items to be summed overall.

Scores of both mothers and fathers on this b/c composite were then submitted to an analysis (Likert), with a cutoff point being generated (as is done by most computer programs assessing reliability and internal consistency indexes for newly developed questionnaires). The high-risk group were thus the top 27% of each parent group. As Table 5.3 indicates, the cutoff score was 103 for mothers and 106 for fathers.

The high-risk group was then composed of families in which at least one parent's score on the b/c composite placed him or her in the highest 27% (i.e., approximately the highest quartile). For the sake of comparison and classification, cutoff points were extended downward at three other quartiles so that all parents' scores could be placed into a category. Thus, the second quartile (i.e., that containing the next 25% of families) ranged from those

Table 5.3. Likert Analyses of AAI Scales and Subscales

AAI scale	AAI subscale	Reliability	
		Mothers	Fathers
a	Normal adolescent behaviors (11 items)	.827	.828
	Not-normal or delinquent adolescent behaviors (15 items)	.749	.771
	Total (26 items)	.877	.881
b	Hands-On Abuse (5 items)	.449	.535
	Hands-Off Abuse (10 items)	.679	.628
	Neglect (7 items)	.339	.594
	Appropriate Parenting (4 items)	.242	.420
	Total (26 items)	.607	.644
c	Hands-On Abuse (5 items)	.601	.580
	Hands-Off Abuse (10 items)	.632	.735
	Neglect (7 items)	.576	.533
	Appropriate Parenting (4 items)	.115	.433
	Total (26 items)	.711	.713

who scored 90 for mothers and 95 for fathers. These were the High–
Medium-Risk Group (2). Those in the third quartile were considered Low–
Medium (3), and those in the fourth quartile were considered Low–Risk (4).
(See Table 5.4.)

Family ratings by the observers using the family vignettes were also
calculated as follows. Each observer selected a rating (1–9) that she or he
thought most accurately characterized the family's functioning. Selection of
a vignette anywhere in the abusive category (1–6) by any one of the three
observers resulted in the family's assignment into the high-risk category (1).
This was done due to the widely noted discrepancies in information
obtained from varying family members resulting in the possibility that only
one of the interviewers may be told or given indications of the family's
problems (Jacobsen, 1971; Larson, 1974; Safilios-Rothschild, 1969). Families for which none of the observers selected an "abusive" vignette (i.e.,
were rated 7–9) were assigned a (2) and placed in the low-risk group. In
Table 5.4, these vignette ratings (or ratings on the criterion measure) are
juxtaposed with the parental risk level as measured by the AAI.

Classifying families by way of parental ratings on the AAI, we have 27
high-risk and 35 low-risk families, with a roughly even split between male
and female adolescents (though this is somewhat less true of the low-risk
group). In comparing the observer ratings on the criterion measure to the
classification of families on the AAI, note that 70% of the high-risk families
were also rated as "abusive" or "at-risk" by the observers, where 26% of the
low-risk families were so classified by observers. This classification of the
families forms the basis for substantive comparisons of high risk versus low
risk. In other analyses, we use the vignette ratings as a basis for comparing
abusive versus nonabusive families.

As mentioned previously, there were many ways in which these scores
could be used to generate risk categories, the above being just one. This
method, although not directly including the adolescent's behavior as measured on the "a" scale of the AAI, measures parental responses to this
behavior (so it is implicit in the measurement). Future analyses of these data
may look at categorizations from slightly different angles to determine the
stability of the results and to add to the richness of the findings.

In Chapter 6 we will look at the characteristics of the families who fall
into the high- and low-risk categories to determine if there are real differences other than scores on the AAI. It will be important to keep in mind the
way in which the families were grouped. Areas of special importance will be
the methods of discipline used, the levels of agreement between parents,
their adolescents, and the observers, the level of life changes, social
networks, and other developmental changes in the family. The hypotheses
presented in Chapter 1 and the family system issues discussed in Chapter 4
guide our efforts.

Table 5.4. Classification of the Families on the AAI

High risk (N = 27)				Low risk (N = 35)			
Rating on vignette[a]	ID no.	M(15)	F(12)	Rating on vignette	ID no.	M(21)	F(14)
1	0034[b]	116[1c]	124[1]	2	0124	95[2]	58[4]
1	0073	107[1]	113[1]	1	0134	98[2]	80[4]
2	0114	119[1]	123[1]	2	0214	101[2]	64
1	0234	125[1]	122[1]	2	0273	96[2]	60[4]
2	0264	104[1]	114[1]	2	0284	90[2]	84[3]
1	0403	125[1]	121[1]	1	0393	96[2]	71[4]
1	0014	—[d]	111[1]	2	0023	89[3]	80[4]
1	0083	108[1]	93[3]	2	0054	86[3]	67[4]
1	0103	50[4]	106[1]	2	0063	75[3]	81[4]
1	0143	58[4]	115[1]	1	0153	87[3]	102[2]
1	0184	102[2]	113[1]	2	0203	80[3]	100[2]
1	0223	103[1]	103[2]	2	0294	78[3]	81[4]
1	0244	120[1]	88[3]	2	0344	75[3]	70[4]
1	0304	120[1]	97[2]	2	0374	88[3]	57[4]
2	0324	100[2]	113[1]	1	0383	86[3]	82[3]
1	0334	120[1]	102[2]	2	0423	71[3]	96[2]
2	0363	75[3]	106[1]	2	0444	89[3]	74[4]
1	0413	118[1]	96[2]	2	0044	69[4]	103[2]
1	0454	93[2]	106[1]	2	0093	69[4]	88[3]
2	0494	85[3]	110[1]	1	0163	70[4]	92[3]
2	0503	98[2]	110[1]	2	0173	58[4]	89[3]
1	0533	103[1]	67[4]	2	0194	74[4]	81[4]
2	0513	87[3]	124[1]	2	0254	70[4]	48[4]
2	0514	107[1]	125[1]	2	0314	66[4]	90[3]
1	0564	69[4]	111[1]	2	0354	48[4]	105[2]
2	0583	91[2]	121[1]	2	0433	61[4]	62[4]
1	0594	100[2]	133[1]	1	0484	51[4]	74[4]
				2	0524	64[4]	66[4]
				2	−0464	79[3]	85[3]
				1	−0473	84[3]	78[4]
				2	−0554	52[4]	98[2]
				1	−0574	67[4]	105[4]
				1	−0603	89[3]	84[3]
				2	−0614	99[2]	74[4]
				2	−0624	92[2]	88[3]

[a]1, high risk for abuse; 2, nonabusive.
[b]Fourth digit of ID no. indicates gender of adolescent. 3, Female; 4, male.
[c]Risk category on AAI: Quartiles

	Mothers	Fathers
1	≥103	≥106
2	≥ 90	≥ 95
3	≤ 89	≥ 94
4	≤ 74	≤ 81

[d]Missing data.

APPENDIX I: ADOLESCENT ABUSE INVENTORY (AAI)

I.D. # _____

Check the appropriate category.

Who is filling this out: Mother _____   Father _____

There is a lot of interest today in the practice of child rearing. Professionals have their way of thinking about good and bad methods, and parents, who raise the children, have their ways. In this questionnaire, we would like to know what you think is appropriate and inappropriate child rearing. To do this we will describe some situations involving parents and their teenagers: ask how often, if ever, situations like these happen in your home, ask you to evaluate the way some parents may act and, finally, ask how you would act.

When answering these questions, please keep in mind that you should be responding with your adolescent son or daughter aged 11–15 in mind. It is also important that you always answer in reference to this same adolescent.

In the following you will find 26 family situations which will describe an adolescent's behavior and the parent's response. After each situation, you will be asked to respond to several questions regarding that situation. Please circle the number and corresponding response which most accurately reflects your feelings, behaviors, and beliefs for each question. Each set of questions (a–d) refers only to the situation which immediately precedes it.

Remember, please do *not* confer with your spouse when filling this form out. Here is a sample item to help familiarize you with the questionnaire format:

Sample: Jerry wanted to go to the opening baseball game very badly. His parents refused to let him go. Jerry went anyway. His parents took his privileges away for 2 weeks.

a. *How often has your adolescent disobeyed your requests?* (Answer as to how often he has done this in the *past year*.)

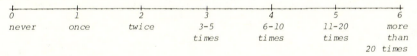

0	1	2	3	4	5	6
never	once	twice	3–5 times	6–10 times	11–20 times	more than 20 times

b. *How would you rate this parent's actions?* (Here actions refers to what the parents have done in response to the adolescent.)

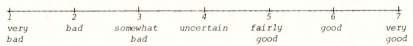

1	2	3	4	5	6	7
very bad	bad	somewhat bad	uncertain	fairly good	good	very good

Someone who answers "1" here would be indicating that they thought the parent's actions were unfair, too harsh and very bad.

Someone who answers "3" is saying that the parent's taking away the privileges was not that great of a response but not too bad.

Someone who answers "5" is saying that the parent's taking away the privileges was an overall good response to the situation.

On the other hand, someone who answers "7" would be showing complete approval of this parent's actions (i.e., taking away Jerry's privileges).

c. *Under the circumstances described, how likely would you be to behave as this parent did?*

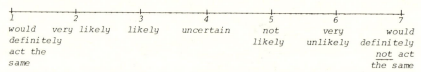

Someone who responds with a "1" is saying they definitely would act as this parent did.

Someone who responds with a "3" is saying they are likely to respond as this parent did.

Someone who responds with a "5" is saying they are not very likely to respond as this parent did.

Someone who responds with a "7" is saying they definitely would *not* respond as this parent did.

d. *What would you prefer to do?* (This gives you a chance to tell us how you would typically respond if your adolescent behaved this way).

1. Jeff came home and plopped his very bad report card in front of his *parent*. While reading the paper his parent said, "With parents like you have, I don't know how you turned out so stupid."

a. *How often has your adolescent had problems with academic performance in the past year?*

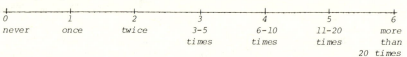

b. *How would you rate this parent's actions?*

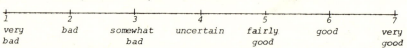

c. *Under the circumstances described, how likely would you be to behave as this parent did?*

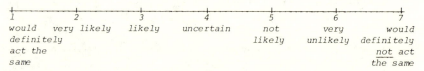

d. *Is there something you would prefer to do rather than what this parent did?*

2. Paul's parents wanted to go on a little trip and could find no one to stay with the smaller children. Paul offered to stay home from school for a few days to watch the kids. His parents agreed to let him do this saying, "You never go to school anyway."

a. *How often has your adolescent offered to stay home from school for several days in the past year?*

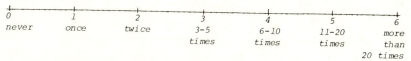

b. *How would you rate this parent's actions?*

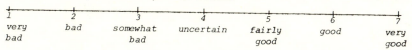

c. *Under the circumstances described, how likely would you be to behave as this parent did?*

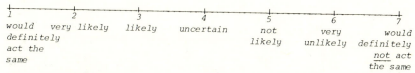

d. *Is there something you would prefer to do rather than what this parent did?*

3. The school called and told Jason's parent that Jason and his "date" were caught acting promiscuously (for example, necking, petting) in the school auditorium during the dance. Jason's parents told the school it was none of their business and hung up. Jason's parents said nothing to him about it.

a. *How often has your adolescent acted promiscuously in the past year?*

b. *How would you rate this parent's actions?*

c. *Under the circumstances described, how likely would you be to behave as this parent did?*

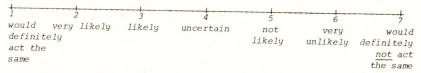

d. *Is there something you would prefer to do rather than what this parent did?*

4. Gordon came home and told his parents he may have gotten his girlfriend pregnant. His parents said, "If you are old enough to know how to get someone pregnant, you're old enough to figure out what to do about it" and refused to help.

a. *How often has your adolescent confronted you with this situation in the past year?*

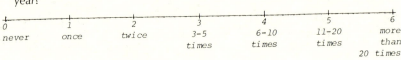

b. *How would you rate this parent's actions?*

c. *Under the circumstances described, how likely would you be to behave as this parent did?*

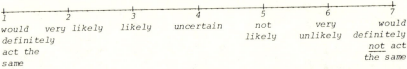

d. *Is there something you would prefer to do rather than what this parent did?*

5. John came home feeling depressed one day and said, "Every time my friends do well on their report card, their parents tell them how good they've done and then give them a treat. Why don't I ever get that—my grades are good?" The parent responded, "You kids are spoiled enough without us making a fuss over every little thing you do."

a. *How often has your adolescent expected rewards for his behavior in the past year?*

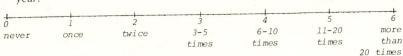

b. *How would you rate this parent's actions?*

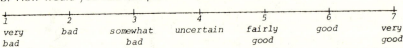

c. *Under the circumstances described, how likely would you be to behave as this parent did?*

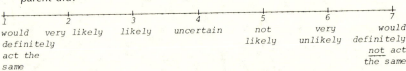

d. *Is there something you would prefer to do rather than what this parent did?*

6. Jerry came home and asked his parents if he could go out to a movie with his friends. Jerry's parents said "absolutely not, you're too young."

a. *How often has your adolescent asked to do more "grown-up" things in the past year?*

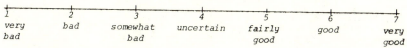

0	1	2	3	4	5	6
never	once	twice	3-5 times	6-10 times	11-20 times	more than 20 times

b. *How would you rate this parent's actions?*

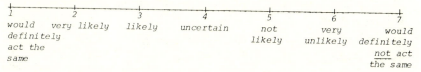

1	2	3	4	5	6	7
very bad	bad	somewhat bad	uncertain	fairly good	good	very good

c. *Under the circumstances described, how likely would you be to behave as this parent did?*

1	2	3	4	5	6	7
would definitely act the same	very likely	likely	uncertain	not likely	very unlikely	would definitely not act the same

d. *Is there something you would prefer to do rather than what this parent did?*

7. George asked his parent on his birthday if he could now stay out until 12:00 with his friends on Friday evenings. His mother replied, "absolutely not, you're still too young." George stomped out of the room and slammed the door. His mother then told him that he could not go out at all this Friday because of his actions.

a. *How often has your adolescent responded to you like this in the past year?*

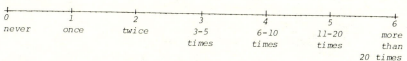

0	1	2	3	4	5	6
never	once	twice	3-5 times	6-10 times	11-20 times	more than 20 times

b. *How would you rate this parent's actions?*

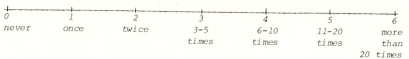

1	2	3	4	5	6	7
very bad	bad	somewhat bad	uncertain	fairly good	good	very good

c. *Under the circumstances described, how likely would you be to behave as this parent did?*

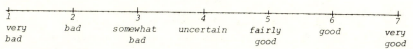

1	2	3	4	5	6	7
would definitely act the same	very likely	likely	uncertain	not likely	very unlikely	would definitely not act the same

d. *Is there something you would prefer to do rather than what this parent did?*

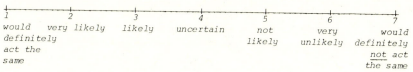

8. Eric came home one evening and appeared to be under the influence of drugs. His parents reprimanded him and he became very angry. He then stormed out of the house, got in a car with a friend, and drove off. Eric's parent said, "Don't worry, he'll sober up and cool off," and they let him go, without knowing where he was going.

a. *How often has your adolescent come home appearing to be under the influence of drugs in the past year?*

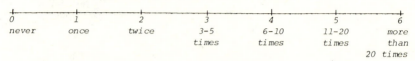

b. *How would you rate this parent's actions?*

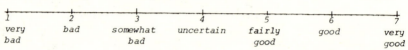

c. Under the circumstances described, how likely would you be to behave as this parent did?

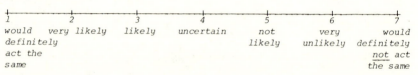

d. *Is there something you would prefer to do rather than what this parent did?*

9. Gregg's mother's friends came over quite frequently. Several of them often told her how handsome Gregg was going to be. They liked to have him sit on their laps and fondle him. Gregg's mother sensed that this wasn't right but said nothing. Gregg soon came to enjoy this very much and began to seek these people out.

a. *How often has your adolescent done something like this in the past year?*

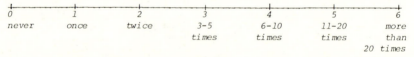

b. *How would you rate this parent's actions?*

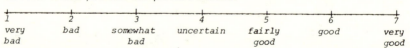

c. Under the circumstances described, how likely would you be to behave as this parent did?

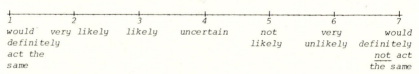

d. *Is there something you would prefer to do rather than what this parent did?*

10. Larry and some friends were caught by the police while breaking some of the windows in the school. They were sent to a juvenile center and their parents were called. Larry's parents refused to come and get him.

a. *How often has your adolescent done something such as breaking a window in the past year?*

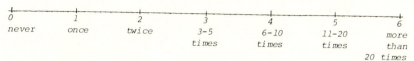

0	1	2	3	4	5	6
never	once	twice	3-5 times	6-10 times	11-20 times	more than 20 times

b. *How would you rate this parent's actions?*

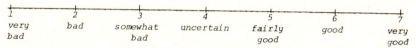

1	2	3	4	5	6	7
very bad	bad	somewhat bad	uncertain	fairly good	good	very good

c. *Under the circumstances described, how likely would you be to behave as this parent did?*

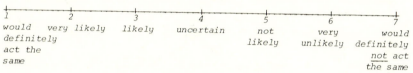

1	2	3	4	5	6	7
would definitely act the same	very likely	likely	uncertain	not likely	very unlikely	would definitely not act the same

d. *Is there something you would prefer to do rather than what this parent did?*

11. Greg did not do his chores one week and his parents told him that because of this he could not use the car this weekend.

a. *How often has your adolescent neglected to do his chores in the past year?*

0	1	2	3	4	5	6
never	once	twice	3-5 times	6-10 times	11-20 times	more than 20 times

b. *How would you rate this parent's actions?*

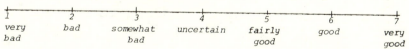

1	2	3	4	5	6	7
very bad	bad	somewhat bad	uncertain	fairly good	good	very good

c. *Under the circumstances described, how likely would you be to behave as this parent did?*

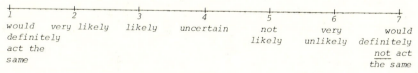

1	2	3	4	5	6	7
would definitely act the same	very likely	likely	uncertain	not likely	very unlikely	would definitely not act the same

d. *Is there something you would prefer to do rather than what this parent did?*

12. Ross's parents want to go away on a trip for a week but don't really want to pay a sitter to watch him. They know he's been hanging around with "a fast crowd" lately. They decide to go away, anyway, and Ross invites several of his "friends" over to "party" with him while they're gone.

a. *How often has your adolescent invited friends over to "party" when you were not at home?*

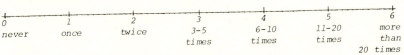

b. *How would you rate this parent's actions?*

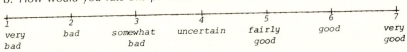

c. *Under the circumstances described, how likely would you be to behave as this parent did?*

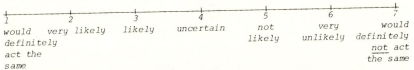

d. *Is there something you would prefer to do rather than what this parent did?*

13. Watching T.V. one night, a show came on where an adolescent who had lied to his parents was given a sound spanking. Joe said "Boy, that's not fair!" The parent watching the show turned and said to his son, "That's the only way to deal with you kids today."

a. *How often has your adolescent taken a position such as this in the past year?*

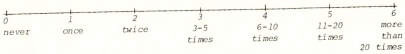

b. *How would you rate this parent's actions?*

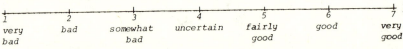

c. *Under the circumstances described, how likely would you be to behave as this parent did?*

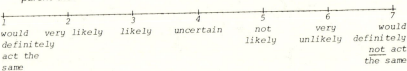

d. *Is there something you would prefer to do rather than what this parent did?*

14. Rich came home from school crying. His parent ignored Rich at first but then told him that only babies cry.

a. *How often has your adolescent come home upset to the point of crying in the past year?*

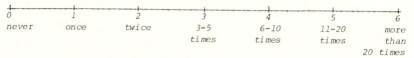

0	1	2	3	4	5	6
never	once	twice	3-5 times	6-10 times	11-20 times	more than 20 times

b. *How would you rate this parent's actions?*

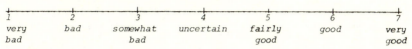

1	2	3	4	5	6	7
very bad	bad	somewhat bad	uncertain	fairly good	good	very good

c. *Under the circumstances described, how likely would you be to behave as this parent did?*

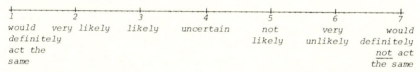

1	2	3	4	5	6	7
would definitely act the same	very likely	likely	uncertain	not likely	very unlikely	would definitely not act the same

d. *Is there something you would prefer to do rather than what this parent did?*

15. Tom's father told him that if he wanted to go out with his friends on Saturday, he'd have to mow the lawn. Tom did *not* mow the lawn but expected his father to let him go out anyway. Tom's father told him, "I'm sorry, Tom, you can't go."

a. *How often has your adolescent gone back on his side of an agreement like this in the past year?*

0	1	2	3	4	5	6
never	once	twice	3-5 times	6-10 times	11-20 times	more than 20 times

b. *How would you rate this parent's actions?*

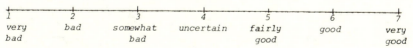

1	2	3	4	5	6	7
very bad	bad	somewhat bad	uncertain	fairly good	good	very good

c. *Under the circumstances described, how likely would you be to behave as this parent did?*

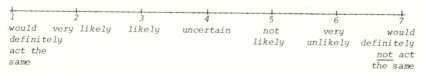

1	2	3	4	5	6	7
would definitely act the same	very likely	likely	uncertain	not likely	very unlikely	would definitely not act the same

d. *Is there something you would prefer to do rather than what this parent did?*

16. David was out past curfew time. His parent came down to the place where he "hung out" with his friends, shoved him toward the door, and said, "It's time to go home."

a. *How often has your adolescent stayed out past curfew in the past year?*

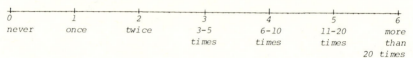

b. *How would you rate this parent's actions?*

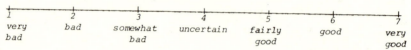

c. *Under the circumstances described, how likely would you be to behave as this parent did?*

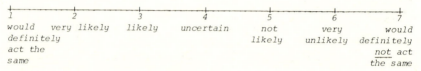

d. *Is there something you would prefer to do rather than what this parent did?*

17. Merv's family was trying to decide where to go on a vacation. Merv was very excited about this and went out and did some "info gathering" of hotels, facilities, mileage, and prices of several different places. At dinner, Merv kept interrupting his parents' discussion, trying to present what he found, and his parent laughed and said, "Children and teens should be seen but not heard."

a. *How often has your adolescent tried to offer suggestions or voice his opinion like this in the past year?*

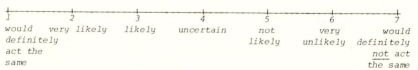

b. *How would you rate this parent's actions?*

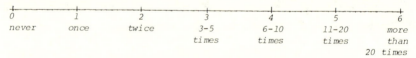

c. *Under the circumstances described, how likely would you be to behave as this parent did?*

d. *Is there something you would prefer to do rather than what this parent did?*

18. Tom really wanted to buy a new radio for himself, but didn't have enough money. He decided to take some of the money his parents had saved. When Tom came home from school that day, his parent asked him if he had taken the money. He replied "no." Furious, Tom's parent told him to go to his room, and would not let him out for two days.

a. *How often has your adolescent taken something that was not his in the past year?*

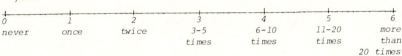

b. *How would you rate this parent's actions?*

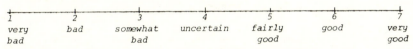

c. *Under the circumstances described, how likely would you be to behave as this parent did?*

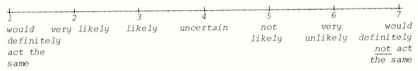

d. *Is there something you would prefer to do rather than what this parent did?*

19. John always walked around the house scantily clad when younger. Noticing that he was starting to mature lately, his mother called him over and persuaded him to show her how much he developed.

a. *How often has your adolescent walked around scantily clad in the past year?*

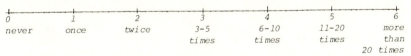

b. *How would you rate this parent's actions?*

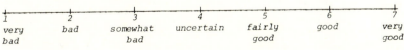

c. *Under the circumstances described, how likely would you be to behave as this parent did?*

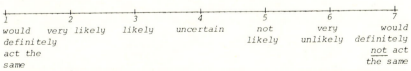

d. *Is there something you would prefer to do rather than what this parent did?*

20. George was consistently late for dinner. His parents told him that if he were late one more time, he couldn't eat dinner for a week.

a. *How often has your adolescent been late for dinner in the past year?*

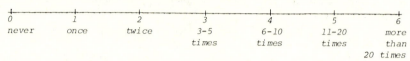

0	1	2	3	4	5	6
never	once	twice	3-5 times	6-10 times	11-20 times	more than 20 times

b. *How would you rate this parent's actions?*

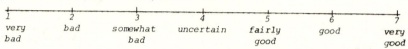

1	2	3	4	5	6	7
very bad	bad	somewhat bad	uncertain	fairly good	good	very good

c. *Under the circumstances described, how likely would you be to behave as this parent did?*

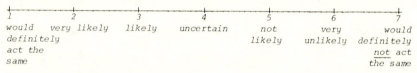

1	2	3	4	5	6	7
would definitely act the same	very likely	likely	uncertain	not likely	very unlikely	would definitely not act the same

d. *Is there something you would prefer to do rather than what this parent did?*

21. Pete was sitting at dinner one evening listening to his parents discussing an issue heatedly. Pete tried to play referee in the argument when his mother came over to him and said, "tell your father he's wrong, don't you think I'm right?" Pete felt confused but continued to try to mediate the argument.

a. *How often has your adolescent tried to play referee in your arguments in the past year?*

0	1	2	3	4	5	6
never	once	twice	3-5 times	6-10 times	11-20 times	more than 20 times

b. *How would you rate this parent's actions?*

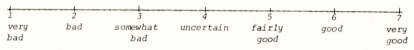

1	2	3	4	5	6	7
very bad	bad	somewhat bad	uncertain	fairly good	good	very good

c. *Under the circumstances described, how likely would you be to behave as this parent did?*

1	2	3	4	5	6	7
would definitely act the same	very likely	likely	uncertain	not likely	very unlikely	would definitely not act the same

d. *Is there something you would prefer to do rather than what this parent did?*

22. Kim was arguing with his brother and eventually pushed him so hard he fell. Kim's father came in and said, "You must learn how to treat your brother better. Please go to your room for one hour and then apologize to him."

a. *How often has your adolescent treated his brothers/sisters like this in the past year?*

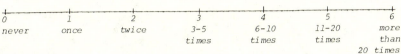

0	1	2	3	4	5	6
never	once	twice	3-5 times	6-10 times	11-20 times	more than 20 times

b. *How would you rate this parent's actions?*

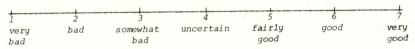

1	2	3	4	5	6	7
very bad	bad	somewhat bad	uncertain	fairly good	good	very good

c. *Under the circumstances described, how likely would you be to behave as this parent did?*

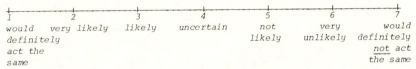

1	2	3	4	5	6	7
would definitely act the same	very likely	likely	uncertain	not likely	very unlikely	would definitely not act the same

d. *Is there something you would prefer to do rather than what this parent did?*

23. Jeff came home sobbing from a date one night. His sister came in and woke his parents up and asked them to come in and talk to Jeff to see what was wrong. The parent said, "Jeff will forget about it quicker if we don't pay any attention to it."

a. *How often has your adolescent came home "upset" like this in the past year?*

0	1	2	3	4	5	6
never	once	twice	3-5 times	6-10 times	11-20 times	more than 20 times

b. *How would you rate this parent's actions?*

1	2	3	4	5	6	7
very bad	bad	somewhat bad	uncertain	fairly good	good	very good

c. *Under the circumstances described, how likely would you be to behave as this parent did?*

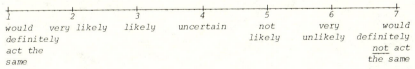

1	2	3	4	5	6	7
would definitely act the same	very likely	likely	uncertain	not likely	very unlikely	would definitely not act the same

d. *Is there something you would prefer to do rather than what this parent did?*

23. Sam came in drunk one night and began to argue with his mother. His father came in just as Sam yelled an obscene remark at his mother and his father then punched him.

a. *How often has your adolescent yelled or made "obscene" remarks to you in the past year?*

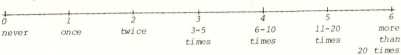

0	1	2	3	4	5	6
never	once	twice	3-5 times	6-10 times	11-20 times	more than 20 times

b. *How would you rate this parent's actions?*

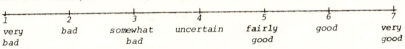

1	2	3	4	5	6	7
very bad	bad	somewhat bad	uncertain	fairly good	good	very good

c. *Under the circumstances described, how likely would you be to behave as this parent did?*

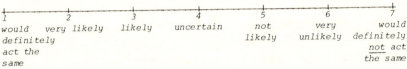

1	2	3	4	5	6	7
would definitely act the same	very likely	likely	uncertain	not likely	very unlikely	would definitely not act the same

d. *Is there something you would prefer to do rather than what this parent did?*

25. Aaron had another terrible argument with his brother and sister. Aaron's parent got so mad that he told Aaron, "I don't even want to be your parent anymore."

a. *How often has your adolescent had arguments with his brothers and sisters in the past year?*

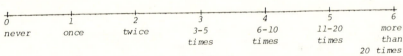

0	1	2	3	4	5	6
never	once	twice	3-5 times	6-10 times	11-20 times	more than 20 times

b. *How would you rate this parent's actions?*

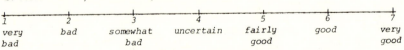

1	2	3	4	5	6	7
very bad	bad	somewhat bad	uncertain	fairly good	good	very good

c. *Under the circumstances described, how likely would you be to behave as this parent did?*

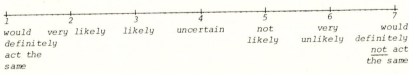

1	2	3	4	5	6	7
would definitely act the same	very likely	likely	uncertain	not likely	very unlikely	would definitely not act the same

d. *Is there something you would prefer to do rather than what this parent did?*

26. John borrowed his parents' tools and paints and did not put them away when finished. Because they were left out, the younger kids got into them and dumped the paints and lost some of the tools. John's parents came in and found this mess and slapped John across the face.

a. *How often has your adolescent been irresponsible like this in the past year?*

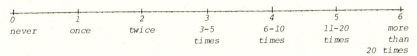

0	1	2	3	4	5	6
never	once	twice	3-5 times	6-10 times	11-20 times	more than 20 times

b. *How would you rate this parent's actions?*

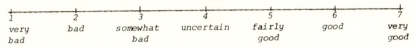

1	2	3	4	5	6	7
very bad	bad	somewhat bad	uncertain	fairly good	good	very good

c. *Under the circumstances described, how likely would you be to behave as this parent did?*

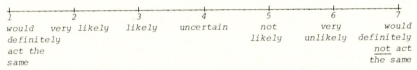

1	2	3	4	5	6	7
would definitely act the same	very likely	likely	uncertain	not likely	very unlikely	would definitely <u>not</u> act the same

d. *Is there something you would prefer to do rather than what this parent did?*

APPENDIX II: DEVELOPMENT AND PSYCHOMETRIC
PROPERTIES OF THE FAMILY VIGNETTES

INSTRUCTIONS

On these cards are sample descriptions of nine families. I'd like you to look at all of them and select the one card or description that best describes (each) (your) (this) family. (Interviewers: hand the cards to the rater—be sure they are shuffled. Record your vignette and their selection on the inside of the folder.)

(Vignettes and instructions were placed on 5 × 8 index cards for purposes of administration. Instructions are read aloud.)

1. Mr. and Mrs. Smith live in a small town a few miles from here. There have been arguments in their house for as long as anyone can remember. The kids sometimes got the worst of it, being "yelled at" and "smacked, but sometimes they deserved it." Even though they have some problems, they've always managed to keep the family together.

2. Mr. and Mrs. Smith live in a small town a few miles from here. Their large family made it rough to make ends meet. The kids were always in the way, and the Smiths had to yell at them a lot to keep things quiet. The kids sometimes felt no one cared about them. Even though they have some problems, they've always managed to keep the family together.

3. Mr. and Mrs. Smith live in a small town a few miles from here. They never had any close friends, and the kids were often absent from school. Sometimes the older kids had to stay and watch the younger ones, but other times their parents just let them stay at home. Even though they have some problems, they've always managed to keep the family together.

4. Mr. and Mrs. Smith live in a small town a few miles from here. They've noticed recently that the children have become "disrespectful," and they've had to slap them across the face several times to remind them that children and teens should be seen but not heard. Even though they have some problems, they've always managed to keep the family together.

5. Mr. and Mrs. Smith live in a small town a few miles from here. They never had any problems with their children until recently. They've been demanding to do whatever they please lately, and the Smith's have had to get very strict and "ground" them for weeks at a time. Even though they have some problems, they've always managed to keep the family together.

6. Mr. and Mrs. Smith live in a small town a few miles from here. Their kids have started to stay out lately way past curfew with a crowd of kids from school. Mr. and Mrs. Smith figured that they should just let them go and that they would learn their own lessons. Even though they have had some problems, they've always managed to keep the family together.

7. Mr. and Mrs. Smith live in a small town a few miles from here. They believe that the kids, now that they're growing up, should be allowed to have some input into making family decisions. Sometimes conflicts arise, but they seem to handle it well. Even though they have some problems, they've always managed to keep the family together.

8. Mr. and Mrs. Smith live in a small town a few miles from here. When problems come up in their family, they all sit down and have a "meeting." Now that the kids are getting older, they are given more and more freedom which they seem to handle well. Even though they have some problems, they've always managed to keep the family together.

9. Mr. and Mrs. Smith live in a small town a few miles from here. They have their ups and downs with the kids, but things always seem to work out. Everyone in the family takes an interest in other family members, and they all have friends who visit frequently. Even though they have some problems, they've always managed to keep the family together.

FAMILY VIGNETTE DEVELOPMENT AND PSYCHOMETRIC PROPERTIES

Each story was standardized using the same family name, identical first and last sentences with the two middle sentences being very similar in length and construction. The descriptions differed only in duration and type of abuse and neglect mentioned. The stories ranged from 58 to 62 words. These vignettes were constructed from a review of the literature on abusive families.

The Family Vignettes were presented to several graduate students (15) and professors (8) in the areas of abuse, family development, and psychology. These judges were asked to rank order the descriptions according to the occurrence and duration of maltreatment, from no maltreatment to maltreatment patterns occurring over an extended period of time. Next, inter-judge reliability was assessed by obtaining a Spearman rank-order correlation on these data with the resulting correlations ranging from .85 to 1.00. The modal correlation was .95.

The psychometric properties of the criterion instrument were then examined in an attempt to establish interviewers' interjudge reliability. Tetrachoric correlations using the ratings of the various judges within the study (the interviewers) at the various times of assessment ranged from .52 to .93. These correlations were calculated based on the interviewers' responses to various hypothetical situations (see example below). These analyses were not done for all interviewers as some only completed one interview. For those assessed, when reliabilities were low (below .80), more intensive training was done. As mentioned previously, this was a difficult process due to the high staff turnover rate.

APPENDIX III: PSYCHOMETRIC PROPERTIES OF THE AAI

To determine the reliability of the scales and subscales of the AAI, a Likert (1932) analysis was performed on the "a," "b," and "c" scales (responses to the "a," "b," and "c" questions) and subscales (i.e., normal adolescent behaviors, hands-on abuse, hands-off abuse). As mentioned previously, the subscales are described in Tables 5.1 and 5.2.

Tables 5.1 and 5.2 also report the adjusted item-total correlations for items on the "a," "b," and "c" subscales. Nunnally (1978) suggests that items on the item-total correlations that fall into the .4 to .6 range are optimal. Table 5.1 reveals that most of the items on scale "a" are quite good. Table 5.2 indicates, however, that some of the "b" and "c" items were not in this range, thus indicating the potential causes for the lower reliabilities of the "b" and "c" subscales.

Using Kohr's (1974) program to analyze scales of the Likert type, Cronbach's coefficient alpha (1951) index of internal consistency was calculated for each scale and subscale. Results of these analyses are in Table 5.3. Overall coefficient alpha reliability for mothers on the "a," "b," and "c" scales were .877, .607, and .711, respectively. For fathers, "a," "b," and "c" scale reliabilities were .881, .644, and .713, respectively. Stratification of the scales into subscales resulted in reliabilities ranging from .115 to .827 for mothers and .420 to .828 for fathers.

Given these preliminary analyses, we drew several conclusions. First, each of the three scales is potentially useful, and it is worth the effort to refine the instrument (Nunnally, 1978). Second, examination of the individual subscales indicates that some are more powerful than others. The subscales on the "a" scale appear to be the most cohesive and reliable. The "b" and "c" subscales for mothers and fathers appear to need further work in the following areas for mothers: attitude toward hands-on abuse, neglect, and appropriate parenting. For fathers, it appears that improvements are needed on the subscales measuring attitude toward and likelihood of performing appropriate parenting. Interestingly, the results also indicate that there are differences in the goodness of items for mothers and fathers and in the type of adolescent behavior that they find provocative. Overall suggestions for the refinement of the AAI may be found elsewhere (Sebes, 1983).

CHARACTERISTICS OF HIGH-RISK FAMILIES: PARENTAL AND ADOLESCENT PERSPECTIVES

JAMES GARBARINO
EDNA GUTTMANN

INTRODUCTION

Now that we have reviewed some general issues concerning how we conceptualize and identify families at risk for adolescent maltreatment, we are ready to examine the families in our study. We do this in light of our efforts to integrate two frameworks, one that focuses on child and parental variables and a second that emphasizes the enduring and transient nature of risk factors.

Caplan and colleagues (1984) found that the main factors related to abuse were child and parent–family variables that could be classified as either precipitating or long-term variables. We can represent them as shown in Table 6.1:

Table 6.1. Caplan's Dimensions of Maltreatment

	Child variables	Parent and family variables
Long-term		
Precipitating		

The child variables include personality and behavior problems, some of which have existed for a long time and others that arise to trigger a specific incident of abuse. The parent and overall family interaction variables

Table 6.2. Cicchetti and Rizley's Model of Maltreatment

	Potentiating factors	Compensatory factors
Enduring factors	Vulnerability	Protection
Transient factors	Challenges	Buffers

include personality and marital problems. These, too, are classified as long-term and precipitative, depending upon their duration.

Cicchetti and Rizley (1981) have proposed another, related model of risk factors for maltreatment. Their main factors lie on the temporal dimension as enduring versus transient and on the "probability of maltreatment" dimension as potentiating versus compensatory. They present the fourfold interaction of these categories at four levels of risk, as we show in Table 6.2.

The potentiating factors increase the probability of maltreatment and constitute vulnerability factors (e.g., child with a difficult temperament, aversive personality characteristics, norms favoring harsh discipline, chronic poverty) or challenges (e.g., family acute stress, physical injury, legal problems, marital problems), depending on their duration. The compensatory factors are either protective factors (e.g., desirable personal characteristics, flexibility, good physical health, social and interpersonal skills) or buffers (e.g., financial savings, social support system), depending on whether they reduce the probability of maltreatment in general or only with regard to a specific incident.

The integration of these two frameworks, when extended by community factors that go beyond the family, may lead to a third framework. This third perspective brings together the two and aids in discriminating child from adolescent maltreatment, as presented in Table 6.3.

When applied separately to children and adolescents, this framework clarifies the differences between child abuse and adolescent maltreatment

Table 6.3. An Integrated Framework of Maltreatment

	Child or adolescent	Parents	Family interaction	Community
Enduring				
Potentiating				
Compensatory				
Precipitating				
Potentiating				
Compensatory				

that have been reviewed in Chapter 1. It highlights that there may be different precipitating events, different compensators, different types of family histories with respect to maltreatment, and different factors that facilitate the abuse.

This framework highlights yet another point, namely, the importance of looking at abuse from the perspective of each family member. Most research on abuse and neglect does not consider all the viewpoints of the family members but rather relies upon a single perspective. Most often parents (mostly mothers) or children are the sources of data. Models of maltreatment derived from that research, as well as others, tend to assume that there is a single description and explanation of the dynamics in each family, while, in fact, each of the family members may have a different view of that dynamics. This is particularly evident in adolescence, where the greater power and autonomy of the teenager can have an independent effect on overall family functioning. Furthermore, understanding these differences in views may clarify the origins of maltreatment in a family, the meaning each participant attaches to specific incidents of abuse or neglect, and the dynamics that sustain it. Thus, rather than searching for some "real" or "true" picture of family functioning, we see it through the eyes of several "beholders."

In the study of 62 high-risk families, as was explained in Chapters 4 and 5, the instruments we used were:

1. Family demographics—this instrument provided socioeconomic and demographic data and helped to assess family resources.

2. Family vignettes—the purpose of using this instrument was to assess the probability of maltreatment in the family (Sebes, 1983).

3. Adolescent Abuse Inventory (AAI)—this inventory aimed at identifying the frequency of the occurrence of a continuum of adolescent behaviors and the degree of abusive attitudes, responses, and actions toward these behaviors that the parents held (Sebes, 1983).

4. FACES—this is a measurement of how family members perceive their family as a social system in terms of its cohesiveness and adaptability (Olson, Russell, and Sprenkle, 1979; Olson, Sprenkle, and Russell, 1979).

5. Child Behavior Checklist—this checklist identified the behavioral problems and competencies of the adolescents (Achenbach, 1978; Achenbach and Edelbrock, 1979).

6. Cornell Parent Behavior Description (CPBD)—this measurement was used to study the perception of each of the family members about the degree of support and discipline that the parents direct toward the adolescent (Devereaux et al., 1969).

7. Interparental Conflict Scale (IPC)—this scale reveals the amount of marital and familial conflict that the adolescent perceives existing in

his/her family in terms of finances, spouse's personal characteristics, child-rearing practices, and joint family activities (Schwarz and Zuroff, 1979).

8. Adolescent–Family Inventory of Life Events and Changes (A–FILE)— this inventory assesses the amount of normative and nonnormative life events and changes by the adolescent, both recently and in the past (McCubbin et al., 1981).

These instruments helped to clarify each family member's view of the enduring and precipitating, potentiating, and compensatory factors involved in risk for maltreatment as shown in Table 6.4.

We will first discuss the factors involved in adolescent maltreatment and then focus on the differences between the adolescents' and the parents' perspectives on it.

THE FACTORS INVOLVED IN ADOLESCENT MALTREATMENT

Overall, 45% of the families were found to be high-risk and 55% low-risk on the basis of their AAI scores. Using the vignette descriptions, 36% were judged to be "high probability for presence of abuse," whereas 64% were classified as "low probability for the presence of abuse." Among the AAI high-risk families, 70% were found to be abusive on the vignettes ("true positives") and 30% nonabusive ("false positives"). Among the AAI low-risk families, about 74% were found to be nonabusive on the vignettes ("true-negatives") and the rest (26%) were abusive ("false-negatives"). In this analysis we focus on the high- versus low-risk comparison (Garbarino et al., 1984), although the abusive and nonabusive comparisons tell the same story (Garbarino, in press). We focus on risk because our broad interest in troubled families goes beyond actual abuse.

As Table 6.5 shows, the high-risk families were not significantly different from the low-risk families on the basis of their socioeconomic characteristics, but they were significantly different in terms of family composition. The high-risk families tended to be larger than the low-risk ones, and parents in the high-risk group reported significantly more remarriages and included one adoptive relationship. Eight of the high-risk families included step-parents (29%), all of them judged to be abusive on the vignettes. Only one of the low-risk families (3%) included a stepparent, and that family was also judged to be abusive.

Moving on to the family and individual dynamics, we find that the high-risk families, in contrast to the low-risk ones, tend to have more problems and to be more stressful, both on the individual level as well as on the family level. The same differences are evident when comparing the families judged to be abusive in contrast to those judged to be nonabusive.

Table 6.4. Instruments Measuring Maltreatment

Instruments	The view of:		Factors related to:				Probability of maltreatment		Temporality	
	Adolescent	Parents	Adolescent	Parents	Family	Community	Potentiating factors	Compensatory factors	Enduring	Precipitating
Family demographics		+	+	+	+	+	+	+	+	+
Family vignettes	+	+			+		+		+	
AAI	+	+	+	+			+		+	
FACES	+	+			+		+	+	+	+
Child behavior checklist		+	+					+		
CPBD	+	+		+			+	+	+	
IPC	+				+		+			+
A-FILE	+		+	+	+				+	+

Table 6.5. Socioeconomic and Demographic Characteristics

Characteristic	High risk (N = 27)	Low risk (N = 35)	
Age of adolescent	13.9	13.9	n.s.
Age of mother	38.2	39.4	n.s.
Age of mother at marriage	22.8	20.8	$p < .10$
Age of father	42.2	41.8	n.s.
Age of father at marriage	28.6	23.0	$p < .05$
Remarriage or adoption (%)	29.0	3.0	$p < .05$
Education			
Mother	13.7	14.7	n.s.
Father	14.8	16.4	n.s.
Hollingshead Index of Status of Occupation			
Paternal	37.2	28.3	n.s.
Maternal	47.6	44.8	n.s.
Paternal employment status (1 = employed; 2 = unemployed)	1.1	1.1	n.s.
Income (4 = $15,000–$20,000; 5 = $20,000–30,000	4.8	4.9	n.s.
Total SES score (scale of 1–5)	3.5	3.3	n.s.
Family size	3.6	2.7	$p < .05$

In the following section, we contrast high- and low-risk families and illustrate these results through family case studies.

Adaptability and Cohesion

The high-risk families tended to be rated higher by all family members on both the cohesion and the adaptability scales of the FACES, so high as to put them near or in the danger zone identified by Olson and his colleagues (developers of FACES). In other words, high-risk families tended to be described as being in the "chaotically enmeshed" category, while low-risk ones were often located in the more functional "flexibly," or "structurally," "connected," or "separated" categories.

Consider the following two families: which illustrate these two scales.

Case Study 6.1
A family with four children. The couple, in their thirties, has been married for 2 years, and the woman is a stepmother to an 11-year-old girl. All the family members perceived their family to be both chaotic and enmeshed. The parents reported having many disagreements between them as well as being dissatisfied with the neighborhood they were living in. Their report is echoed in the girl's report of many conflicts at home surrounding finances, spouse's responsibilities, spouse's personal characteristics, and child-rearing practices. The girl has repeated a grade in school due to her

Table 6.6. Adaptability and Cohesion

FACES scores	High risk (N = 27)	Low risk (N = 35)	
Adaptability (198 = "Chaotic")			
Father's rating	190.3	177.2	$p < .05$
Mother's rating	184.4	178.8	n.s.
Adolescent's rating	198.0	187.4	$p < .05$
Cohesion (270 = "Enmeshed")			
Father's rating	271.5	259.5	$p < .05$
Mother's rating	264.1	260.0	n.s.
Adolescent's rating	265.7	247.7	n.s.

reaction to her parents' divorce and even after that continued to do poorly at school. She has been described as internalizing her problems: being fearful, sad, and withdrawn, often refusing to talk, lost in daydreams, and feeling worthless and unloved. On the other hand, she has also been described as impulsive and disobedient, as one who screams and gets into too many fights, a girl who acts too young and clings to adults, who demands too much attention.

Case Study 6.2
    The couple in their late thirties has been married for 14 years, having two children: an 11-year-old adolescent boy and an 8-year-old daughter. Their family appeared to them as being connected, either flexibly or structurally. They generally reported having a satisfactory marital life. The son was socially competent and did well in school, yet he was described as argumentative, stubborn, immature, and, to some extent, even hyperactive. His father seemed tense and anxious with him, authoritarian and controlling. The mother was quiet and patient and stayed removed from the father–son conflicts. He seems to be rather "typical adolescent": looking down on his father, looking also for his appreciation and never getting it.

Discipline and Support

Results from the Cornell Parent Behavior Description reveal that, in general, parents are seen as being supportive whether the family is a high risk or a low risk, but the degree of support is lower in the high-risk families. Discipline is higher in the high-risk family, which creates a combination of less support and more punishment for high-risk families. Table 6.7 shows the differences on support and discipline between the high- and low-risk families. Again, two families discussed as Case Study 6.3 and 6.4 illustrate these differences.

Case Study 6.3
    A family with seven children, a stepfather, at high-risk, abusive. They are in their late forties, married for 6 years. The youngest child is a 15-year-old boy. His parents are less supportive than the average, yet more disciplinary. The parents reported having many disagreements with each other and having a hard time handling the

Table 6.7. Discipline and Support

	High risk	Low risk	
Support			
Fathers (self-report)	24.7	25.0	n.s.
Fathers (adolescent-report)	21.3	24.3	p < .01
Mothers (self-report)	25.3	25.4	n.s.
Mothers (adolescent-report)	22.7	24.1	n.s.
Discipline			
Fathers (self-report)	15.0	10.0	p < .10
Fathers (adolescent-report)	10.2	8.9	p < .10
Mothers (self-report)	12.0	9.6	p < .01
Mothers (adolescent-report)	10.4	8.9	p < .10

adolescent at home. The adolescent himself reported that his parents had conflicts with regard to children's duties at home, methods of child rearing and obedience. The family members perceived their family as ranging from "disengagement" to "enmeshment" and from "rigidity" to "flexibility" on the FACES. Most of their social support networks did not include each other. Quite a messy family. The adolescent son was a disobedient, impulsive, and cruel person, one who defied his parents to their face, combined with a lonely, sad, shy, withdrawn, and confused person who felt unloved and worthless. It seems that he was involved with some substance abuse, running away, and juvenile probation. Parents who believed in a high degree of discipline, and an adolescent who tried to handle it.

In comparison to this family, a low-risk and nonabusive one:

Case Study 6.4
The son is 14. There is only another child at home. The family members perceived their family as ranging from "disengagement" to "connectedness," and from "rigidity" to "structuredness" on the FACES; yet their view of the parents as being more supportive and a little less disciplinary than the average seems to change several important features of the picture. The parents tended to have conflicts with each other, yet these surrounded issues such as finance and joint family activities. The son participated in advanced classes at school and appeared to be rather competent in what he did. The parents, as well as the boy, mentioned that he argued with them, was impulsive, and talked too much, but no one perceived these as problems. Another "typical adolescent": starting to behave in ways that can challenge parents.

Problem Behavior and Competence

The Achenbach Child Behavior Checklist reveals that, overall, the adolescents from high-risk families have more developmental problems and less competencies than the adolescents from the low-risk families. But this is in the context of a sample drawn largely on the basis of adolescent problems, and, indeed, the overall sample of adolescents stands at about the eighty-

Table 6.8. Problem Behavior and Competence

	High risk	Low risk	
Total internalizing problems			
Fathers	17.7	9.6	$p < .01$
Mothers	18.6	13.4	$p < .05$
Adolescents	25.0	18.1	$p < .05$
Total externalizing problems			
Fathers	23.0	11.9	$p < .01$
Mothers	24.4	12.8	$p < .01$
Adolescents	25.0	15.2	$p < .01$
Social competence scale			
Fathers	18.0	19.7	$p < .10$
Mothers	17.4	19.8	$p < .05$
Adolescents	19.1	20.5	$p < .05$

fifth percentile on national norms. The high-risk adolescents have significantly more internalizing and externalizing problems: They have more somatic complaints and schizoid behaviors, are more immature and uncommunicative, and have more obsessive/compulsive patterns. On the other hand, they tend to be more delinquent, aggressive, cruel, and hyperactive. As behavior problems were negatively correlated with competencies, the low-risk adolescents were found to be more competent in the activities they did at school and socially, in general. Table 6.8 shows the differences between the high- and low-risk families on the Achenbach Child Behavior Checklist.

Two families highlight these comparisons:

Case Study 6.5
A family at high risk and judged to be abusive; the couple are in their thirties. They have one daughter who is 13 years old and had a son who died in an accident several years ago. The family was not very healthy, and the financial situation was also hard. They were "flexibly enmeshed" and highly disciplinary. The girl was perceived by all family members to be highly externalizing and internalizing her problems. She was in the ninety-ninth percentile of somatic complaints and above the ninety-third percentile in terms of being depressed and withdrawn, schizoid and anxious/obsessive. She was also in the ninety-seventh percentile in terms of immaturity, hyperactivity, aggressiveness, and cruelty. She seemed to be too dependent, confused, moody, sad, and lonely but was also self-destructive, used to threaten and attack people, and talked about committing suicide. In terms of competence, she did not have much: She was below average at school, skipped classes, did not get along with other children at school, and was unliked by them. She also did not have hobbies or participate in sports activities, which placed her rather low in terms of social activities and school competencies. The mother and her daughter were close to each other, yet the daughter held the power in the family.

A nonabusive family, at low-risk is a comparison:

Case Study 6.6
The couple are in their late thirties and early forties and also have a 13-year-old daughter. Their health is not very good either, but financially they manage well. The family is rather "structured" and "separated/connected," being high on support and low on discipline. The daughter had hobbies and participated in sports; she got along with other children as well as her parents and brother, and she was above average at school. Overall, she was considered socially competent, although she had several behavior problems. She was rather high in terms of somatic complaints (above the eighty-sixth percentile) but lower in being anxious/obsessive, or depressed and withdrawn. With regard to the externalizing problems, she was mainly aggressive (between forty-fourth and seventy-fourth percentile) but was also, to some extent, delinquent, and cruel, and behaved immaturely. She was fearful and worried but also used to get into fights and tease other children. A rather regular family, with the mother being the reinforcer, parents setting good limits to children's behavior, and an egalitarian marital relationship.

Parental Conflict

The adolescents in the high-risk group perceived much more marital and familial conflict in the realms of finances, spouse's personal characteristics, child-rearing practices, and joint family activities. Although the difference was not statistically significant (there was great variability of scores), it reveals an important distinction between the two groups of adolescents as shown in Table 6.9.

The following two families illustrate this difference:

Case Study 6.7
The couple has been married for 10 years. Both are in their thirties, but for the mother this is her second marriage. The adolescent son, who is 14 years old, is hers, although they have common children too. The boy described his parents as having conflicts over almost anything possible: budgeting and purchasing, spouse's needs and sensitivity, overeating and TV watching, children's duties, manners, and be-haviors, children's fighting and discipline, family plans, and joint recreation. The family was perceived by its members as "chaotically," "enmeshed," or "connected" and by the observers as noisy, messy, and dirty. The son's social support network did not include any member of the family, although he had many friends with whom he used to attack and threaten people, to run away from school, and to cause trouble to the extent of being picked up by the police. The parents were very high on discipline, and the adolescent was around the ninety-ninth percentile of all the externalizing

Table 6.9. Interparental Conflict

	High risk	Low risk
Adolescent report	301.2	193.4

problems, being not much lower on the internalizing ones. He disobeyed his parents completely, stole at home, hit his parents, and ran away, but overall he was very fearful and confused with regard to his messy family.

On the other hand, consider this family with almost no conflict, at low risk, and not abusive.

Case Study 6.8
The couple are in their forties. They have two daughters, who no longer live at home, and an adolescent son who is 11 years old. The family was healthy and financially well-managed. Neither parent had burning concerns, and for both the family was "flexibly connected." They were supportive of the son and provided an average level of discipline. The boy, in turn, got along with other people and did well at school. He was perceived as having social and school competencies and was also engaged in sport and hobby activities. All the family members found him more internalizing than externalizing of his problems, but overall these were not severe. He was mainly immature and hyperactive, "hostile withdrawn," and aggressive. He perceived no conflicts in the family and seemed to develop well.

These two families reveal that one of the major differences between the low- and high-risk families is the level of conflict and overall instability. There seem to be related to the adolescent's behavior as well as to the degree of abuse in a family.

Life Changes

The A-FILE revealed much more recent change in the lives of the high-risk adolescents than it did for the low-risk youth. A second difference was in terms of substance abuse: For a significantly larger number of high-risk adolescents, in comparison to low-risk ones, one of the life changes had to do with beginning involvement with alcohol or drugs. The third difference between the high- and low-risk groups was related to the number of past life changes, but as this difference was nonsignificant, one conclusion might be that recent changes that have occurred due to the adolescence period are more related to being at high risk and under abuse than are the total changes that have occurred in these families' lives. The differences between the low and high risk families, in terms of life changes, are shown in Table 6.10. Consider the following families: In the high-risk group we look first at an abusive family.

Table 6.10. Life Changes

	High risk	Low risk	
Life changes, adolescent report			
Total recent changes	11.1	8.0	$p < .05$
Total past changes	4.5	3.4	n.s
Substance abuse	1.0	0.2	$p < .01$

Case Study 6.9
    The adolescent girl is 16 years old. She had 24 recent changes in her life and 7 in the past. These surround issues such as parental divorce and remarriage, a parent beginning school, suicide attempt in the family, a runaway, starting to have a sexual life, and overall increasing arguments at home between her and her parents. Her life had changed. She said that she was pushed into trying drugs but tried to avoid it. Overall, the family seemed to be concerned about her but was in such a transition that the parents tended to be depressed: Each of them had a different perception of the cohesion and adaptability of the family, they were not always part of each other's social support network, and they had disagreements between them with regard to the girl.
    Within this situation, the girl started being truant, rather low in social competencies, and above the ninety-fourth percentile in terms of all the internalizing and externalizing problems. She became obsessed with thoughts about the changes in the family and its problems and wanted to move away with her boyfriend. She was looking for a different life, perhaps a more stable less conflictual one.

On the other hand, consider this nonabusive, low-risk family.

Case Study 6.10
    The adolescent daughter has experienced two changes in her recent life and none in the past. These changes involved illness in the family and increasing pressures on her to do well at school; rather usual changes in an adolescent's life. The family was enmeshed, its members were to a large extent each other's social support network, and they managed well without having much conflict. The daughter did well at school, got along with other people, and was perceived as very active in terms of activities and home responsibilities. She was competent in these areas. She tended to internalize her problems in terms of being anxious/obsessive and having somatic complaints, but she was also hyperactive, lied, was too loud, and too immature. The father was quiet in this family, letting the mother control it, but they kept the communication within the family open and were able to handle their daughter's beginning adolescence problems.

Cognitive Assessment

    The results do not document any difference in cognitive reasoning as measured by the Peel Assessment.
    As shown in Table 6.11, Peel cognitive scores are virtually the same for members of high- and low-risk families. At least as measured here, cognitive sophistication is not a salient factor in the dynamics of high risk.
    In sum, the comparison between the high-risk and the low-risk adoles-

Table 6.11. Cognitive Assessment

Peel cognitive assessment	High risk	Low risk	
Fathers	3.5	3.6	n.s.
Mothers	3.3	3.4	n.s.
Adolescents	2.7	2.7	n.s.

cents reveals a profile in which high risk is related to being in a chaotic family, with less support and more discipline, having more externalizing and internalizing adolescent problems, being less competent, and having experienced more conflicts at home and recent life changes.

This profile suggests that a combination of the two explanatory models may be in order here. The comparison points to the possibility that maltreatment prevails in families that have some degree of psychopathology and experience family disruption linked to conflicts between the life-course needs of adolescents and parents. Further, it seems that the characteristics of the high-risk families exacerbate each other and pull the family into a vicious cycle of high discipline and low support, more adolescent problem behaviors, more arguments and intrafamilial conflicts, becoming chaotic and thus operating at a higher risk level. The low-risk families seem to suggest that once a family has succeeded in handling one of the categories of adaptability–cohesion, support–discipline, adolescent's problems and competencies, interpersonal conflict or degree of life changes, they are better off as a benign cycle goes to work. The point is that low-risk families appear to contain their troubled adolescents without permitting a pattern of escalating conflict or progressive withdrawal.

In conclusion, it seems that adolescent's, the parents', and the family's characteristics all play a role in the dynamics of high risk, with precipitating factors being stronger than enduring ones. The potentiating factors enhance each other and seem to exclude compensatory factors. Yet when some compensation enters the family, the picture starts to improve. This point offers hope for intervention, as we shall see in Chapter 11.

Having presented a "family profile" of high risk, we can change the level of analysis from the whole high-risk family to its members and look for comparisons among them. What emerges is a difference between the adolescents' and parents' views of the family, of parental support and discipline, and the youth's own problems and competencies.

PARENT–ADOLESCENT DISCREPANCIES IN ANALYZING FAMILY RELATIONS

Previous research reveals significant and important discrepancies between the way adolescents and their parents view each other and the family as a whole (Jessop, 1981). Our results reinforce prior research in this matter. The parents in the high-risk families view their families differently from the way their adolescents do. A review of Tables 6.6–6.10 demonstrates this. The adolescents rate the family higher than their parents on the adaptability scale of the FACES, and their scores for adaptability entered the high-risk category. In other words, they had a tendency to view their family as chaotic. On the Cornell Parental Behavior scale, they rated the parents as

Table 6.12. Discrepancies

Statistically significant discrepancies ($p < .05$) between	High risk (%)	Low risk (%)
Mother–father	5	5
Mother–adolescent	37	21
Father–adolescent	37	21

less supportive and less disciplining than the parents perceived themselves to be. The adolescents also considered themselves to exhibit internalizing and externalizing problems to a larger extent but as being more socially competent than their parents perceived them to be. As Table 6.12 shows, there were more statistically significant parent–adolescent discrepancies in the high-risk families than in the low-risk families (37 versus 21%)—and the same (lower) proportion of significant mother–father discrepancies in both the high- and low-risk groups.

The following examples illustrate such discrepancies in high-risk families.

Case Study 6.11
The adolescent girl is 14 years old. Her mother has been living with her boyfriend for the last 10 years, although all of them reported a highly tense and conflictual relationship. For the daughter, the family seemed chaotic, but her mother and the mother's boyfriend viewed it as flexible and rigid, respectively. The girl has experienced many changes in her recent life, including a suicide attempt, substance abuse, and some contact with juvenile detention. She also perceived many conflicts at home surrounding joint family activities, child-rearing practices, and her mother and the boyfriend's relationship. Overall, a chaotic family. Within such a family, she perceived herself having more problems than both her mother and her mother's boyfriend thought—both internalizing and externalizing these. She rated herself above the ninety-ninth percentile of all the possible categories—being lonely and confused, feeling unloved and worthless, but also attacking people, running away, stealing, and defying her mother and mother's boyfriend. While they perceived her mainly externalizing her problems, she thought she was mainly internalizing them. Thus, they rated her as being higher on cruelty, aggressiveness, delinquency, and hyperactivity, while she thought she had more somatic problems and was being more anxious/obsessive, schizoid, depressed, and withdrawn. Yet, even though they emphasized the externalization of her problems, she thought she was even more externalizing than they did. The girl perceived herself to be highly competent in her activities and more competent at school than her mother and mother's boyfriend thought she was. Overall, as the gap in the family increased and abuse became more severe, she ran away and attempted suicide, promising to run away again any time that she will be abused.

Case Study 6.12
The adolescent boy is 14 years old and in a high-risk family. The family appears highly conflictual, and the son rated it higher on adaptability than his parents did,

although not completely chaotic. He found the parents being much less supportive and disciplinary than they thought they were. Hence, while they thought they were setting limits to his behaviors, he thought he could actually do almost whatever he wanted. The boy perceived himself to be internalizing and externalizing his problems more than his parents thought he was. He was more obsessive/compulsive, and schizoid but also more hostile, withdrawn, and delinquent. He perceived having more problems at school, including getting in trouble there, as well as being self-destructive, nervous, suspicious, and unliked by other children. Overall, a nonabusive family, but at high risk, having large discrepancies between the parents' and the adolescent's view of it.

These two families illustrate the differences that prevail between parents and their adolescents. The first example shows the differences that exist in terms of family adaptability and the adolescent's problems and competencies, while the second one exemplifies the differences in terms of parental support and discipline as well as the adolescent's problems. They reveal that in the high-risk families, the adolescent's view is more extreme than the parents' view. To the adolescent, the family appears more chaotic, less disciplinary, and less supportive; much more problematic. The adolescents' views of themselves were also more extreme than their parents' view of them. On the one hand, they perceived themselves higher on having problems, both internalizing and externalizing. A common picture was that the parents saw the adolescent as mainly externalizing his/her problems, whereas the adolescent felt that he/she was more internalizing. This suggests that the parents focused on the nonnormative visible behaviors, whereas the adolescent was more concerned with less visible behaviors but, perhaps, more disturbing ones. Yet, overall, the adolescents presented a picture in which the parents did not fully comprehend the extent and quality of their problems. On the other hand, the adolescents also viewed themselves as being more competent than their parents reported. This suggests an even greater parent–adolescent gap from the adolescents' viewpoint: The parents not only misinterpreted their adolescent's problems, but they also devalued their competencies. From the parents' viewpoints, adolescents may seem unrealistic in terms of their self-perception: They have an unrealistic appreciation of their competencies and an exaggerated view of their problems. Thus, underlying the visible gap, revealed by the instruments of this study, may be a gap between the adolescent perception that they are misunderstood by the parents and the parental view that adolescents have unrealistic self-perceptions.

In conclusion, we found disagreements between high-risk parents and their adolescents with regard to family relationships and personality characteristics. As mentioned earlier, this conclusion is consistent with previous studies that also found parent–adolescent disagreement. They found that the more subjective and intrafamily an issue was, the greater the disagreement about it (Hess and Torney, 1965; Jessop, 1981; Kandel *et al.*, 1968; Kohn and Carroll, 1960; Larson, 1974; Niemi, 1974). This disagreement was even more profound when adolescents and their parents were asked about family transactions and relationships. In these studies, as well as in ours, the parents provided a more idealized picture of the family than did their sons and daughters. Perhaps the adolescents give a more accurate picture, since they are less concerned with social desirability. Indeed, Sebes (1983) found that adolescents scored lower on the social desirability subscale of FACES than did their parents (and high-risk families showed a nonsignificant tendency to score lower than did low-risk families). She also found that adolescent reports were more in accord with "objective" assessments of the family.

Another explanation of the idealized picture given by the parents in comparison to what the adolescents describe is that adolescents see their families as being more problematic as a consequence of their own transitional stage in life.

This study may suggest another hypothesis, namely, that the more a family is at high risk the larger will be the discrepancies between parents and adolescents with regard to family and personality matters. These discrepancies, in turn, enhance the level of risk of the family, since conflicts and arguments take place where no mutual agreement exists.

Conclusions

In this chapter, we examined high-risk adolescents and their families, with an emphasis upon the correlates of maltreatment. Perhaps we can bring the total picture into sharper focus by considering four specific families. Each represents one of the four combinations of risk and actual presence of maltreatment shown below in Table 6.13.

FAMILY TYPES

The probable presence of maltreatment can be illustrated by the four family types presented below.

Table 6.13. Four Family Types

Risk: (AAI score)	Probable presence of maltreatment	
	Present	Absent
High	The Johnson family	The Washington family
Low	The Vernon family	The Roberts family

The Johnson Family: High-Risk/Abusive

The mother is 38 years old, and she married when she was 18 years old. Her education is 12 years (GED), and she is working at a school cafeteria. The father is 41 years old, his education is 10 years, and he is a carpenter. The couple has seven children, all of them still living at home—their ages are 20, 18, 17, 16, 14, 13, and 12. The target adolescent is the 16-year-old girl. She is in tenth grade and was evaluated to be in her postapex period of development.

Both parents said that the health and financial situation at home were not too good, and both felt that they did not have enough time for recreation. The mother spent 35% of her time with the children, 35% with her husband, 20% with the husband and children, and 10% alone. The husband spent 80% of his time with the children and his wife, 15% with his wife, and 5% alone. Both were concerned with having too many disagreements with each other. The mother was also worried about the 16-year-old girl being out of control at home and having problems at school. The father was worried about the family income, his wish to change jobs, the fact that he was depressed, and the adolescent's problems at school (including truancy). Both of them described the family as being "enmeshed" on the FACES, but whereas the father saw it as "chaotic," the mother's view was "structured." For the girl, the family appeared as "flexibly separated." The mother's social support network was 64% kin, and the father's was 86% kin, although excluding his wife and children. The girl's social support network was 42% kin.

All the family reported that the adolescent was doing well in sports and home responsibilities, but she did not have hobbies. All of them said she had lots of friends whom she used to meet many times during the week. The mother said she got along with her parents, brothers, sisters, and other children, but not with herself. The father, on the other hand, said she did not get along with her brothers and sisters but did get along well with herself, and the girl herself said she got along with everybody, except for her parents. Her parents said she was below average at school, whereas she perceived herself as being average. All of them said that she skipped school, which was a problem. The mother said she was defiant with teachers, did not pay attention in classes or do her homework, that she acted out in classes, and that she talked back to teachers. The father said she used vulgar language at school, got into fights, and had a generally poor attitude toward school.

Along with these school problems, the parents and she herself reported the girl as hyperactive, argumentative, cruel, that she got into many fights, had bad friends, was impulsive, lied, screamed, was nervous, had temper tantrums, was too loud, and was suspicious. They also said she was fearful and worried, was secretive, had daydreams, and suffered from psychosomatic pains. They all indicated she was using drugs and drinking alcohol. The parents added to this that she was obsessed with sex and boys, demanded too much attention, and felt unloved. They said she was disobedient, confused, jealous, and often refused to talk. The mother said the girl was afraid to stay alone, was shy, moody, and cried a lot. The father said she was too dependent, acted too young, was lonely, afraid of school, felt worthless and unliked, but also destroyed others' things, threatened and attacked people, and used to steal at home. The girl focused also on her fears of school and snakes, on her nightmares, unhappiness, moods, truancy, substance abuse, and being destructive.

She was rated by the Achenbach Child Behavior Checklist as highly externalizing and internalizing by all family members.

Mother's assessment	Father's assessment	Daughter's assessment
Internalizing		
99.4 Schizoid	99.6 Somatic	99.9 Schizoid
98.8 Somatic	complaints	99.2 Depressed
complaints	98.5 Anxious	withdrawal
98.4 Depressed	obsessive	98.3 Somatic
withdrawal	98.3 Schizoid	complaints
97 Anxious	90 Depressed	98 Anxious
obsessive	withdrawal	obsessive
Sum of	Sum of	Sum of
internalizing 32	internalizing 30	internalizing 31
Externalizing		
98 Delinquent	99.9 Delinquent	99.9 Delinquent
97 Aggressive	99.9 Cruel	99 Cruel
96 Cruel	99.9 Aggressive	98.3 Immature
96 Immature	98.3 Immature	hyperactive
hyperactive	hyperactive	93 Aggressive
Sum of	Sum of	Sum of
externalizing 30	externalizing 54	externalizing 35

In terms of the adolescent's competencies, she evaluated herself the highest on school and activities' competency, while the father found her the most socially competent:

	Mother	Father	Daughter
Activities	2	2	6
Social competence	14	42	28
School competence	2	2	12

The parents perceived themselves to be highly supportive and disciplinary, whereas the girl thought they were much lower on both dimensions:

	Self-rating by:		Rating by daughter of:	
	Mother	Father	Mother	Father
Support	27	22	15	14
Discipline	16	18	12	10

The girl has experienced 15 recent changes in her life and 5 in the past. These surround changes in jobs, schools, illness, increasing arguments at home, a sister becoming pregnant, using drugs and alcohol, and being suspended from school. The conflicts she perceived at home were about income, punctuality, children's duties and fights, and children's language. Her parents shared decision making about finances and joint family activities, but decisions with regard to the children were the mother's territory.

The observers found the mother and daughter sincere, but not the father. The family was found to be highly neglective, with moderate emotional abuse and developmentally damaging behaviors. Physical abuse was low. The daughter appeared as pleasant and cooperative but the whole family as "struggling." The father was concerned with the daughter's problems at school, especially her drinking and use of drugs. He had little contact with his daughters. The mother was very worried about her daughter. Overall, there appeared to be high sibling cohesion with low parent–child or marital cohesion.

In sum, the family was mainly found as neglecting. It was evaluated as being at high risk and abusive.

AAI: Mother 125	Vignette: Mother 9	Interviewer 2
Father 121	Father 5	Interviewer 5
	Daughter 7	Interviewer 6

The Washington Family: High-Risk/Nonabusive

The mother is 37 years old and she married when she was 17 years old. She has completed 11 years of education, and she is employed as a manager of a school cafeteria. The father is the same age, also has 11 years of education, and is self-employed as a carpenter. The couple has three sons aged 20, 19, and 12. The youngest child is in his early pubertal stage of development and is in seventh grade. The oldest son does not live at home.

Both parents said that the health situation was not working very well in their family. The father thought that the financial situation was also bad, but his wife did not. She had enough time for recreation—40% of her time was spent with the children and husband, 30% alone, 20% with her husband, and 10% with her children. The husband did not have enough time for recreation and spent 35% of his time with his wife, 30% with the children, 30% with the children and wife together, and 10% alone. The mother's main concern was that she was tense, while the father was worried over his wife's health, the son's situation at school, and the fact that he did not have enough work. Both parents, as well as the son, found their family "enmeshed" on the FACES, but for the mother it was also "chaotic," for the father "structured," and for the boy "flexible." The mother's social support network did not include her husband or children and was composed of 20% kin; the father's was 58% kin and the son's 27% kin.

All the family reported the son to be doing well in terms of sports, sports organizations, hobbies, and home responsibilities. The adolescent himself said that he was doing very well in sports. They also said that he got along with other children, himself, his parents, and his brothers. The mother thought he was getting along very well with other children and his parents, while the father and the son said that his brothers were those with whom he got along very well.

He was average at school with no problems there, except for perhaps "talking," which has ended as the father said. All of them said that he used to argue, had trouble concentrating, talked too much, and was fearful. The parents mentioned that he was lonely and jealous, with the mother's addition that he was too dependent and felt too much guilt, had daydreams, felt unloved, was stubborn, moody, worried, and had friends who had contact with the police. The father's additional point was that he felt no guilt, had temper tantrums, and was unliked by other children. The son said that he was disobedient, had friends who got into trouble, was impulsive, and acted against his parents' orders. He said that he acted too young, was lonely and confused, demanded too much attention, felt unloved and worthless, was secretive, shy, withdrawn, and overall did not like other people. Overall, the mother and the son saw him as internalizing, whereas the father thought he was more externalizing. (See the Achenbach Child Behavior Checklist below.)

Mother's assessment	Father's assessment	Son's assessment
Internalizing		
98 Schizoid	81 Somatic	99 Somatic
95 Immature	complaints	complaints
95 Somatic	72 Schizoid	95 Schizoid
complaints	60 Obsessive	95 Immature
73 Obsessive	compulsive	94 Communicative
compulsive		91 Obsessive
73 Communicative		compulsive
Sum of	Sum of	Sum of
internalizing 15	internalizing 4	internalizing 26

Externalizing

84 Hostile withdrawal 71 Aggressive 54 Hyperactive	74 Hostile withdrawal 70 Hyperactive 67 Aggressive	98 Hostile withdrawal 94 Hyperactive 86 Delinquent 72 Aggressive
Sum of externalizing 8	Sum of externalizing 8	Sum of externalizing 13

In terms of the adolescent's competencies, he evaluated himself the highest on activities and school competencies, while his father saw his strengths in social competencies.

	Mother	Father	Son
Activities	44	50	95
Social competence	16	45	28
School competence	26	58	63

The adolescent's and parents' perceptions of support and discipline in their family were rather similar.

	Self-rating by:		Rating by son of:	
	Mother	Father	Mother	Father
Support	22	20	21	21
Discipline	12	9	11	10

The adolescent has experienced six recent changes in his life and four in the past. These involved parental new job, school change, death and illness, and increased pressure to do well at school. The conflicts at home surrounded transportation of family members, children's duties, punctuality, and obedience. He perceived his parents to make decisions separately, depending upon the issue.

The observers saw the father as dominant in the family but treated the adolescent fairly. All of them were found to be sincere, having extremely low emotional and physical abuse and neglectivity at all.

The family was found to be at high risk but not abusive.

AAI: Mother 104 Father 114	Vignette: Mother 8 Father 8 Son 9	Interviewer 7 Interviewer 8 Interviewer 7

The Vernon Family: Low-Risk/Abusive

The mother is 35 years old, and she married when she was 18. Her education is high school, and she is currently employed as a lighting consultant, on a part-time basis. The father is 36 years old, he has a high school education, too, and is a plumber. According to the wife, he was unemployed for 6 weeks, but he said that he was working. The couple has a 16-year-old daughter who is at her late pubertal period of development. The daughter's boyfriend (who is 17 years old) lives with them.

The parents said that the health situation was not good for the family, but financially, they managed just fine. Both complained of having too little time for recreation. The wife spends 45% of her time with the child and her husband, 20% of it with the husband, 20% with the daughter, and 15% alone. The father spends 30% of his time each with his daughter, his wife, and his wife and daughter together, and he spends 10% of his time alone. The wife's main concerns are that she tends to be depressed and tense, she wants to change jobs, and has disagreements with her husband. The husband's main concern is the disagreements with his wife. For both of them, the family appears as "flexible" on the FACES, but while the mother sees it also as "disengaged," the father views it as "connected." For her, the social support network is 36% kin, while his is 63% kin. For the adolescent, the family appeared as "structured connected" on the FACES, and her social support network is 33% kin.

Both parents, and the adolescent herself, evaluated her as doing well in her sports, hobbies, and home responsibilities. All of them indicated that she has 2–3 friends, but while the mother said that they met once or twice a week, the father said that they met a lot, and the girl said that it varied. The mother said that she got along well with others, while both the father and the daughter indicated that she got along very well with others. All of them said that she was above average at school and participated in an accelerated enrichment class. The mother noted that there were some problems at school, but she did not specify them. The father and the daughter mentioned no school problems.

All the family said that the daughter used to argue and to demand too much attention. Also, she was disobedient and impulsive, on the one hand, and fearful, teased, unliked by other children, secretive, stubborn, and worrying, on the other hand. All of them indicated that she used to be overweight and clumsy. The parents added that she had obsessions with boys and sex, lacked guilt, and hung around with both older and younger kids. The mother's additional focus was on loneliness, perfectionism, night-mares, being jealous, moody, and cruel, and on hanging around with kids who get into trouble, being nervous, and having temper tantrums. The father's additional focus was that his daughter was confused, daydreamed, was afraid that she would do something bad, that she felt unloved and worthless, heard things, lied, stole at home, and was suspicious. The girl added that she was hyperactive, self-destructive to the extent that she deliberately harmed herself, attempted suicide, talked of killing herself, had daydreams and nightmares, feared she would do something bad, had temper tantrums, and was too much preoccupied with sex. She also noted that she heard her name called when she knew nobody was around. (See Achenbach Child Behavior Checklist.)

Mother's assessment	Father's assessment	Daughter's assessment
Internalizing		
98.3 Somatic complaints	97 Depressed withdrawal	98.8 Schizoid
93 Anxious obsessive	90 Schizoid	98.3 Depressed withdrawal
91 Schizoid	90 Anxious obsessive	98 Anxious obsessive
88 Depressed withdrawal		95 Somatic complaints
Sum of internalizing 20	Sum of internalizing 20	Sum of internalizing 28
Externalizing		
96 Cruel	98 Cruel	98.3 Cruel
95 Immature hyperactive	97 Immature hyperactive	97 Immature hyperactive
94 Delinquent	94 Delinquent	93 Aggressive
84 Aggressive	94 Aggressive	90 Delinquent
Sum of externalizing 17	Sum of externalizing 24	Sum of externalizing 24

In terms of the adolescent's competencies, she rated herself always higher than her mother did but to some extent similarly to the way her father rated her:

	Mother	Father	Daughter
Activities	42	52	52
Social competence	28	55	62
School competence	16	99.9	62

The girl evaluated the parents as less supportive than they thought they were but almost the same with regard to discipline:

	Self-rating by:		Rating by daughter of:	
	Mother	Father	Mother	Father
Support	23	29	19	23
Discipline	10	12	13	11

The adolescent has experienced 15 recent changes in her life and 7 in the past around such issues as parents changing jobs, illnesses, the discovery of emotional problems, alcohol in the family, attempted suicide, starting sexual intercourse, and increasing arguments at home. The main conflicts at home were around the transportation of family members, overeating, obedience, tolerating child's behavior, child's duties and sexual behavior, her friends, and her home responsibilities. The parents were viewed by her as making most of their decisions together, with the mother deciding on the rest.

The adolescent was observed as sincere, but not so the parents. The mother was identified as controlling the family and the father as controlling what he says, to a large extent. The daughter was described as clumsy and as one whose self-esteem had increased that year. The father was found to have had a drinking problem, which seems to have cleared up, and there were hints of sexual abuse and/or pregnancy.

The family was found to have a moderately high degree of developmentally damaging behaviors and an extremely low to low degree of emotional and physical abuse and neglect.

Overall, it was rated as abusive but in low risk:

AAI: Mother 70	Vignette: Mother 1	Interviewer 1
Father 92	Father 7	Interviewer 7
	Daughter 9	Interviewer 8

The Roberts Family: Low-Risk/Nonabusive

The mother is 46 years old, married when she was 25, and has a master's degree in computer sciences. She is employed part-time as a computer programmer/consultant. The father is 48 years old, has a Ph.D. in mechanical engineering, and is a college professor. For both parents, this is their second marriage, and they have two daughters: The older is 17 years old, and the target adolescent is 15 years old, in the tenth grade, and was assessed to be in her postapex period of development.

Both parents said that the health and financial situations were fine in the family. The mother had enough time for recreation, whereas the father felt that he had too little time. The mother shared 20% of her time with the children, 5% of it with her children from her previous marriage, and 20% of it alone. The father spent 50% of his time alone, 40% with his wife, and 10% with the children. Both did not have many concerns but reported having problems with the 15-year-old daughter. The mother also reported being depressed and wishing to change jobs.

The parents said that their daughter was above average in sports, sport organizations, hobbies, and home responsibilities. She was also above average in most subject matters at school. They said that she had almost no friends, and that she did not get along with other children, and hardly with her sister. However, she got along with her parents and very well with herself. The mother added that she was in honors class in math, English, and history, but that occasionally she got too upset over an academic problem. This problem started 4 years ago and still exists. The father did not find any school problems.

The adolescent said that she was doing well in sports and hobbies and very well in her home responsibilities. She reported having many friends, whom she met many times during the week. She perceived herself, too, as getting along with other children, not getting along with her sister, but getting along very well with her parents and herself. She reported being above average at school and having no school problems at all.

All the family said that the daughter used to be argumentative, disobedient, impulsive, and refused to talk and defied her parents to their faces. Also, she was portrayed as having daydreams, being jealous, secretive, shy, stubborn, moody, sad, and worrying and feeling that she had to be perfect and that she was worthless. The parents added that she was withdrawn, liked to be alone, and was unliked by other children. The mother focused also on that she acted too young and too dependent, was obsessed with school and sports, was afraid of social situations, was nervous, insensitive, and lacked empathy. The father's additional focus was that the girl was obsessed with being perfect, demanded too much attention but felt unloved, and that others were out to get her, that she feared she would do something bad, and that she did not like other people. The girl felt, in addition to the feelings about her that she shared with her parents, that she was upset, experienced too much guilt, and could hardly concentrate, but that on the other hand, she disobeyed her parents a lot and wanted their praise.

In terms of the Achenbach Child Behavior Checklist, all the family saw her more internalizing than externalizing:

Mother's assessment	Father's assessment	Daughter's assessment
Internalizing		
99.7 Depressed withdrawal	99.9 Depressed withdrawal	90 Depressed withdrawal
95 Anxious obsessive	98.3 Anxious obsessive	90 Anxious obsessive
91 Schizoid	77 Schizoid	76 Schizoid
Sum of internalizing 23	Sum of internalizing 30	Sum of internalizing 15
Externalizing		
96 Immature hyperactive	96 Cruel	91 Delinquent
91 Delinquent	91 Delinquent	75 Immature hyperactive
88 Cruel	86 Aggressive	72 Aggressive
78 Aggressive	81 Immature hyperactive	
Sum of externalizing 15	Sum of externalizing 17	Sum of externalizing 11

In terms of the adolescent's competence, she evaluated herself much higher than did her parents:

	Mother	Father	Daughter
Activities	54	44	91
Social competence	7	0.1	88
School competence	15	60	99.1

Within the family, the mother evaluated it as "rigidly separated" on the FACES, the father as "structured engaged," and the daughter as "flexibly separated." The mother's social support network was 55% kin, while the father's was only 38% kin, and the daughter's 21%. The daughter also evaluated her parents as being less supportive than they thought they were and her father as less disciplinary:

	Self-rating by:		Rating by daughter of:	
	Mother	Father	Mother	Father
Support	25	24	21	20
Discipline	8	7	8	4

The daughter has experienced seven life changes recently and four in the past, which were around issues such as job change, new school, divorce, increasing arguments at home, and drugs and alcohol. She reported that the conflicts between her parents surrounded spouse's friends, insensitivity, duties of children, tolerance of children, and joint family activities. The mother made most of the decisions, especially those concerning the children, while the father participated in decisions about family activities.

The observers found the father and daughter to be sincere, but not so the mother. The relationships between the mother and the daughter were described as distanced and polite, and the mother's requests of her daughter were in the form of orders. The father looked arrogant and snotty, but he was cooperative and had nice and warm relationships with his daughter. The observers found the family to have both very low emotional abuse and developmentally damaging behaviors.

Overall, the family was rated in low risk and not abusive:

AAI: Mother	80	Vignette: Mother	7	Interviewer	7
Father	100	Father	7	Interviewer	7
		Daughter	9	Interviewer	8

Conclusion

It seems that family, parent, and adolescent variables, perhaps also some community variables, are all interrelated and influence the dynamics and outcomes in high-risk families. Also, transient or precipitating factors, perhaps the very onset of adolescence itself, appear to play a significant role in the level of risk and actual occurrence of abuse. Further, potentiating factors seem to maintain or even enhance each other to the extent that they exclude compensating factors from playing a role in such families. In other words, once a family becomes high risk and abusive, this tends to maintain or accelerate itself as the adolescent becomes more problematic and intrafamily relationships become more tense and conflictual. These families are characterized by psychopathology, problem behaviors, and malfunctioning relationships as well as instability and uncertainty related to simultaneous adolescence and midlife transitions. Their skills for coping with these life transitions are limited, and unless there is an active effort to insert compensatory factors into the picture, high risk is maintained and eventually translates into actual maltreatment.

These high-risk families are characterized by a disagreement between parents and their adolescents concerning family relationships and the nature and degree of the adolescent's problems. The discrepancy seems to maintain or even increase the level of risk and abuse. Each side cannot see the family situation from the viewpoint of the other and feels that its side is completely misunderstood by the other side. Thus, the existence of the parent–adolescent discrepancy in family and personality perception is another potentiating factor. It maintains or enhances both the instability related to the joint life transitions and the psychopathological events.

In sum, these are families where high risk correlates with parent–adolescent discrepancy to maintain or even increase the level of risk and abuse. It seems that to change the picture, we must initiate an active effort to decrease these discrepancies or to insert some other adolescent, parent, family, or community compensatory factor. We will return to this in Chapter 11 when we discuss intervention. Our next task, however, is to explore the issues of social competence, problem behavior, and family structure in greater depth. These are the issues in Part III.

CHALLENGES TO ADOLESCENT DEVELOPMENT

III

In these four chapters we take a closer look at selected aspects of individual development and family functioning. In Chapter 7 we review what is known about the development of social competence and its relevance to adolescent functioning. We then take a look at how family risk factors relate to adolescent social competence as measured in our study. This leads us to Chapter 8 in which we examine the origins of problem behavior in adolescence. Adolescents in high-risk families are likely to bring to fruition patterns of problem behavior initiated in childhood. We see some evidence of this in our families.

Chapter 9 examines the social psychology of economic stress in high-risk families. Although income alone is not a salient factor in adolescent maltreatment, it appears that experiencing psychological stress associated with unsatisfactory economic conditions and allocation of family resources does play a role. In Chapter 10 we explore a special issue, the degree to which adolescents in step-families are at special risk. Our concern is with the factors that mediate between the challenges of dealing with adolescence and the special cultural and social psychological features of step-families.

```
┌─────────────────────────────────────────────────────┐
│                                                   ╎   │
╎ SOCIAL COMPETENCE                                 ╎   │
╎ IN ADOLESCENCE                                    ╎   │
╎                                          7        ╎   │
╎                                                   ╎   │
╎                                                   ╎   │
╎                                                   ╎   │
╎                                                   ╎   │
╎                                                   ╎   │
╎                                                   ╎   │
╎                                                   ╎   │
╎                           AARON T. EBATA          ╎   │
└─────────────────────────────────────────────────────┘
```

INTRODUCTION

As discussed in the preceding chapters, adolescence has been stereotypically viewed as a chaotic, "tumultuous" period. Although recent studies have tempered and modified this view (e.g., Douvan and Adelson, 1966; Offer and Offer, 1975; Garbarino and Kelley, Chapter 1 this volume), much more attention has been paid to the *problems* of adolescence—to destructive behavior or maladjusted individuals rather than to well-adjusted, fully functioning youth. Clearly, the majority of adolescents do well in social, academic, and peer-related endeavors, despite what may be "normative" mood variations and problems (Larson *et al.*, 1980; Rutter *et al.*, 1976).

We can think of the range and variability in "normal" and "dysfunctional" patterns of development as part of a continuum of adjustment and psychological well-being that are *developmental outcomes*, or products of growth and socialization. We can evaluate these outcomes in a variety of ways, including: (1) the acquisition of developmentally appropriate behavior; (2) by success in meeting the demands and expectations of relevant social contexts; (3) by the possession of individual characteristics, attributes, or behaviors that are socially valued and/or relevant for adaptive functioning in relevant social contexts; and (4) by the presence or absence of psychopathological symptoms.

Traditionally, psychologists have focused on *mal*adjustment and have

151

considered "mental health" as freedom from aberrant, dysfunctional, or pathological symptoms. More recently, however, a greater focus has turned to examining the degree to which an individual functions *successfully* in the world and on the skills and abilities necessary for competent functioning.

The concept of *competence* is especially important in studying and working with "high-risk" youth, where there is reason to believe that optimal growth (or positive developmental outcomes) is threatened. A focus on competence requires moving beyond just the consideration of individual characteristics and symptoms to an analysis of how these symptoms and characteristics interact with environmental conditions to determine the quality of adaptive functioning. It also requires us to consider the need to examine competence at multiple levels of analysis, the importance of underlying developmental processes, how environmental conditions influence the development of these processes and their behavioral manifestations, and how individuals can influence the social context in ways that will affect their own further development.

COMPETENCE AND SOCIAL ADAPTATION

There have been numerous attempts to define the concept of *social competence* and to identify its component parts (e.g., Anderson and Messick, 1974; Zigler and Trickett, 1978). While many definitions have been proposed, the term's most general use has come to mean *effective functioning in relevant environments*. As such, it connotes some level of "adjustment," "adaptation," and "mental health." In its broadest use, it implies a general, overall level of functioning and adjustment across the major domains of life. Sundberg *et al.* (1978), for example, define competence as "personal characteristics (knowledge, skills, and attitudes) which lead to achievements having adaptive payoffs in significant environments" (p. 196). There have been several different approaches to competence that have appeared in the literature. These approaches can be categorized as "bag of virtues," "maturity oriented," "interpersonal success," and "level of functioning" (Garbarino and Ebata, 1985).

The *bag of virtues* approaches (Kohlberg and Mayer, 1972) attempt to specify the set of traits that characterize a healthy, functioning person. Foote and Cottrell (1955), for example, say that competence is synonymous with being able to marshal one's resources to achieve one's desired outcomes or goals. This defines competence as simply having what it takes (the means) to get what one wants (the ends). And, it says there is a set of traits that promotes this: health (optimal use of physical resources); intelligence (ability to organize and mobilize resources); empathy (ability to predict the feelings of others); autonomy (a stable, positive sense of self); judgment (ability to estimate and evaluate alternatives); creativity (the capacity for innovation and the ability to evoke new roles in the self and other). Anderson and Messick (1974) go so far as to list 29 characteristics representing social competence.

Some have tried to link competence to socialization and development by invoking the concept of *maturity*. Maturity here means a full flowering of all that a person can be, biologically, psychologically, and socially. Heath (1977) is in this tradition when he views maturity as a "determinant of generalized competence" involving a set of universal traits. These traits include: "ability to anticipate consequences; calm, clear thinking; fulfilling potential; ordered; predictable; purposeful; realistic; reflective; strong willed; and unshakable" (p. 204). Greenberger and Sorenson (1974) define the link between competence and maturity as the integration of a subjective sense of worth, behavior that facilitates interpersonal contacts, and being in tune with the society at large. Buhler (1969) offers the same message.

While a person may need particular skills, abilities, or characteristics to function successfully in different environments, some theorists feel that an important part of competence is *believing* that one is competent, *wanting* to affect the environment, and *feeling* good about doing so successfully. Having an internal sense of competence or "drive for mastery" means an individual *wants* to be competent and is intrinsically motivated to engage the environment (Harter, 1978; White, 1959).

Some have come to use the term *competence* specifically for successful *interpersonal* functioning, for developing the necessary skills that lead to positive personal and social outcomes. Most of the research dealing with the development of social competence in children and adolescents focuses on some aspect of interpersonal relations (individual friendships or acceptance by the group). Ford (1982), for example, defines social competence in adolescence as the "attainment of relevant social goals in specified contexts, using appropriate means and resulting in positive developmental outcomes" (p. 323), while O'Malley (1977) considers it to be "productive and mutually satisfying interactions between a child and peers or adults" that "attain personal goals of the child" and are received in either a benign or positive manner (p. 29).

According to Weinstein (1969), the stability and functioning of any social system depends on individuals being able to "effectively pursue their personal goals" and be "successful in achieving personal purposes." Although a social system may define expectations for the performance of roles, everyday living requires negotiating with others who may have opposing motives or purposes in order to establish a pattern in which most people's basic needs get met. To participate in society, people must be able to control the responses of others. Therefore, the acquisition of skills needed to engage in these negotiations is central to the socialization process.

Defining interpersonal competence as "the skills and abilities allowing an individual to shape the response he gets from others," Weinstein has outlined three major components of this ability. The first characteristic on Weinstein's list is *empathy* or what others have called *role-taking*. It is the ability to accurately "take the role of the other" and to be able to accurately predict consequences that one's actions will have on the perceptions of the other. The second component is the availability of "a large and varied repertoire of lines of action" or *interpersonal tactics*. This implies that an individual needs to have a wide range of alternative behaviors from which to choose, such as being assertive in one setting and accommodating in another. Finally, an individual must have the *interpersonal resources* to be capable of employing effective tactics in situations where they are appropriate. These resources are personal orientations or traits that may predispose an individual toward displaying or inhibiting particular kinds of behaviors, such as patience and courage. The particular strategy an individual uses in an interpersonal situation would depend on these intrapersonal resources and would characterize an *interpersonal style*.

Greenberger and Sorensen (1974) have proposed that "the capacity to interact effectively with others" is an essential component of "psychosocial maturity." In order to be *interpersonally adequate*, an individual must develop:

1. *Communication skills*: the ability to convey and receive messages (in which empathy plays an important part)
2. *Enlightened trust*: learning whom to trust and under what conditions, including recognition of individual and situational factors in making judgments of trustworthiness
3. *Knowledge of roles*: an awareness of social conventions and the understanding of role requirements relevant to interpersonal functioning

The importance of good interpersonal relationships for personal satisfaction and social stability seems obvious. Several theorists (including Hartup, 1978; Sullivan, 1953; Youniss, 1980) have argued that good peer relations, particularly during adolescence, are essential for healthy psychological development. Research supports this view. Several studies show that poor peer relations not only relate to poor mental health but are also related to problems such as delinquent behavior (Roff *et al.*, 1972), poor school achievement (Westman *et al.*, 1967), and various forms of mental illness and personality and behavior disorders (Cowen *et al.*, 1973; Kohlberg *et al.*, 1972; Roff, 1972; Roff and Sells, 1968; Roff *et al.*, 1972; Watt, 1978).

The *level of functioning* approaches emphasize the situation-specific aspects of competence and argue against generalized definitions. For example, McClelland (1973) argues that intelligence (IQ) testing (assessing general intellectual ability) tells us little about how well people are doing and will do in the specific situations they face in their lives. Each situation has its own agenda. Success in the classroom makes different demands from success in the video arcade, for example. Having said that, however, McClelland does indicate some behaviors and characteristics that *often* seem important if one is going to function well in life's situations. These are patience, the setting of moderate goals (neither unrealistically low nor high), effective communication skills, and a general resilience in the face of frustration or adversity (*ego strength*). The overriding point in McClelland's view is adequate functioning in real life situations rather than general "intelligence" or "intellectual development." Competence, in this approach, involves social adaptation.

Thus, most perspectives on competence differ in terms of whether the focus is on *outcomes* ("indicators" of competence), on the skills, attributes, or personal characteristics that lead to successful outcomes (the "components" of competence), or both. For an adolescent, these outcomes might include having friends, doing adequately in school, getting along with family members, or having interests and participating in activities. At the same time, however, the attainment of these outcomes often requires certain attributes, skills, and behaviors that reflect basic capacities and underlying developmental processes and may be goals or desirable attributes in and of themselves. Social competence in this case may also mean intelligence, assertiveness, or high self-esteem. The term *competence* is often used to refer to either (or both) the ends as well as the means, but the focus in most cases is on *positive* outcomes and adaptive responses: on the kinds of personal characteristics and supporting environments that predict positive outcomes.

The theme running through all of these definitions is *adaptiveness* or functioning in situations in a way that is both beneficial (or at least not harmful) to one's development and not detrimental to others in the environment. In conceptualizing competence as an integrative *developmental* construct, Waters and Sroufe (1983) define competence as an "ability to generate and coordinate flexible, adaptive responses to demands and to generate and capitalize on opportunities in the environment" (p. 80). The competent individual, then, is one who can "make use of environmental and personal resources to achieve a good developmental outcome." Assessment of competence, or "adaptive capacity" in this view, should focus on success in addressing developmentally relevant issues and tasks. During adolescence, relationships with peers, functioning at school, and involvement in hobbies, interests, and activities seem to be relevant areas of study.

This developmental perspective on adaptation has certain implications for our understanding of the role that the social environment has in the development of competence.

First, it establishes competence as a "goal" of socialization and development. We are (or at least should be) moving adolescents toward fully competent adulthood. They need to *be* good at something to *feel* good about themselves and to be good citizens (and workers, and eventually, perhaps, good parents). This gives us goals, and thus standards, with which to evaluate the performance of institutions and individuals that assume responsibility for the well-being and nurturance of youth.

Second, this perspective emphasizes positive capacities rather than simply describes the absence of negative characteristics, deviance, or pathology. Some individuals function competently despite these handicaps. Third, our definition recognizes that different social environments—as defined by social class, ethnicity, or culture—encourage and reward different things and thus establish different kinds of competence. This is evident in the work of those who study the diversity of socialization among groups that differ on the basis of culture and ethnicity (Laosa, 1979; Ogbu, 1981), social class (Kohn, 1977), or gender (Chodorow, 1978; Gilligan, 1982). But it also asks us to consider how different social environments for adolescents relate to each other. Are they separate but equal? Is one dominant over another? The answers have significant implications for assessing competence in adolescence.

Settings characterized by economic deprivation, cultural aggression, racism, or psychopathology pose one of the challenging issues facing us—the issue of what is *normal* development and competence. Can we use the same criteria in defining and evaluating competence in these settings? Some say yes. They argue that all adolescents need to learn certain basic skills and how to get along in the mainstream culture. Others argue that we must understand people in terms of their specific experiences. Ogbu (1981), for example, says that the "ghetto theory of success" reflects the demands and resources of certain socioeconomic conditions. A competent youth in such a situation is one who can function within that setting, regardless of its deviance with respect to the rest of the society.

Another issue challenging the meaning of competence is found in the development of children and youth who overcome earlier difficulties as they grow up and seem to function successfully despite adverse conditions—for example, having psychologically disturbed or abusive parents (Garmezy, 1977). These resilient or *stress-resistant* youth call into question our assumptions about how the environment nurtures development. Although some have attributed their success to superior constitutions or a *self-righting tendency*, they often are found to have some less than obvious social resources to draw upon for psychological support (Goldberg, 1977; Sameroff and Chandler, 1975). For example, longitudinal research by Werner and Smith (1982) found that both personal and social factors were important in whether children categorized as "at high risk for behavior disorders" actually showed those problems at 18 years of age. In general:

> The invulnerable child developed a strong early attachment and autonomy during the preschool years, mastered competencies in childhood, and had a sense of some control over life events during adolescence. The home environment had at least one stable caregiver (a parent, sibling, or grandparent) who was supportive but not over protective and fostered the child's growing autonomy (Ulrey, 1981, p. 37).

These special cases (deviant settings and stress resistance) demonstrate the importance of two general principles: (1) Human beings strive to meet some universal needs but do so in ways that are culturally diverse and society specific; and (2) human beings are notable for their resilience and adaptability. Competence is based on the striving to meet personal and cultural goals, goals that have a basis in the very nature of the human organism. In a nurturing environment, the competent youth thrives; in a hostile environment, the competent youth adapts in order to survive. Thriving and surviving translate into environmental terms as the human ecology of developmental opportunity and risk and the development of social competence is the crucial outcome.

The assessment of social competence is important for several reasons. First, social adaptation (e.g., behavior and performance in school and relationships with peers) may be indicators of underlying developmental processes or problems. Psychopathological symptoms often do not appear until later in adolescence, and there is evidence that competence is an important indicator of future functioning (Garmezy, 1975 and in press). Second, competence is an indicator of an interaction between the child and the environment. Assessments of competence may illustrate the quality of social opportunities and experiences in relevant contexts that may promote or hinder the individual's further development. Finally, a child's competence in one setting may influence how others, particularly parents, perceive and treat the child.

THE DEVELOPMENT OF COMPETENCE

We have said that competence can be considered the goal of socialization and development. Whether and how the individual acquires specific competencies and whether individuals are seen as competent members of society depends on an interplay of personal and environmental factors.

From conception onward, biological and genetic factors play a critically important role in development. Genetic characteristics can put a child "at risk" for impaired development by preventing a child from developing required competencies. Mental and physical handicaps, congenital health disorders, physical attributes and appearance, and temperament all fall into this category.

Although these factors may have direct influence on the acquisition of social competence, they commonly exert their influence through the social environment, particularly by affecting how other people treat the individual. Thus, for example, mentally or physically handicapped adolescents could be at risk for impaired social development if they are not able to elicit the kinds of responses from peers and adults that would establish the kind of secure nurturing attachment they need (Ulrey, 1981).

Some researchers consider individual differences in style of behavior (*temperament*) as an adaptive response that has genetic origins and historical implications for the development of adaptive cultural modes of child rearing (Freedman, 1974; Super, 1981). Several authors (e.g., Thomas and Chess, 1977b) suggest that individual differences in temperament are associated with differences in functioning. It is not so much that individuals with one particular temperament are more competent than individuals with other temperaments. Rather, outcomes in development and the influence of temperament lie in the "fit" between the individual and the demands of significant environments such as family and school (Lerner et al., 1982). This highlights the principle of assessing individual social competence in terms of specific situations rather than in general terms.

Parenting and Competence

Garbarino and Kelly (this volume, Chap. 1) have argued that some families with adolescents can be considered "at risk" for developing or already engaging in destructive parent–child relationships, and that these relationships can have a negative effect on developmental outcomes for the adolescent. There is considerable evidence that certain parental practices put the child "at risk" for less than optimal development. On one extreme, physical abuse or severe neglect during childhood can threaten the physical health and well-being of children. This type of treatment can have cognitive and emotional consequences as well. More often, however, parental behavior is more subtle and effects not so clear cut.

In viewing empirical studies of the effects of different styles of child rearing, Rollins and Thomas (1979, p. 348) conclude that: "Socially competent behavior of children, that is, behavior that is valued in society as desirable and has instrumental utility, is positively correlated with parental support, power of same sex parent, inductive control attempts, and the importance of such socially competent behavior to parents; it is negatively correlated with coercive attempts of parents." Aggression and antisocial behavior, on the other hand, are related to less support and more coercion.

These inferences have been largely unidirectional—from parent to child—but it is clear that influences may be *reciprocal* (Bell and Harper, 1977). A child who is well behaved and does well in school is easy to support and praise; one who is easily distracted and has difficulty controlling his or her impulses and activity level may "require" more control and discipline. Several studies show strong relationships between family functioning and child behavior problems, but the direction of causality is ambiguous. Mash (1984) has noted that an association between child problems and family characteristics can be interpreted in a variety of ways. According to Bell (1964), family characteristics can be considered as an etiological factor underlying a child's problem, a response to some characteristic of the child or a "secondary" reaction of a child's behavior that was a product of earlier family functioning. Although early work emphasized that role of the family as a causal factor in the development of behavior problems, recent work suggests that problem children have effects on parents, and that parents respond in certain ways to problem behavior (Heatherington and Martin, 1979; Mash, 1984; Patterson, 1982). Not only can parenting influence the development of individual characteristics (such as behavior problems) and accomplishments, these characteristics can also influence parenting. Aggressive children may require ever-escalating attempts at parental control that may result in a "cycle of coercion."

The remainder of the chapter will use data from the Family Interaction Project to illustrate (1) the relationship between behavior problems and social competence as measured by academic performance, involvement in activities, and relationships with others; and (2) the relationship between parenting behavior and competence. While the cross-sectional nature of the study precludes conclusions about cause and effect, the results can be integrated with previous findings to illustrate the importance of assessing social competence and its implications for intervention and further study.

COMPETENCE, BEHAVIOR PROBLEMS, AND PARENTING

Measures

We discussed the measures used to assess competence, behavior problems, and parenting in earlier chapters. We review them here briefly.

Social Competence. Social competence was assessed using the Social Competence Scale of the Child Behavior Checklist (Achenbach and Edelbrock, 1981). Parents were asked to specify the kinds of sports, activities, and organizations that their child participated in and to rate the quantity and

Challenges to Adolescent Development

quality of their child's involvement relative to other children their age. Information was also gathered on jobs and chores, friendships, relationship to parents and siblings, and school performance. Three subscale scores are derived from this measure (Activities, Social, School) as well as a total competence score. The scale indicators are presented in Table 7.1.

Generally, these scales show relatively high agreement between parents and yield stable results when administered on two different occasions (test–retest reliabilities range between .68 and .93). Achenbach and Edelbrock (1981) reported significant differences in social competence scores between clinically referred children and demographically matched non-referred children, with clinical status accounting for 39% of the variance in

Table 7.1. Competence Scale of the Child
Behavior Checklist[a]

Activities scale (0–12)
  I. Sports
    A. Number of sports
    B. Participation in sports
    C. Skill in sports
  II. Nonsport activities
    A. Number of nonsport activities
    B. Participation in activities
    C. Skill in activities
  III. Jobs and chores
    A. Number of jobs
    B. Job performance

Social Scale (0–12)
  IV. Membership in organizations
    A. Number of organizations
    B. Participation in organizations
  V. Friends
    A. Number of friends
    B. Contact with friends
  VI. Behavior with others and alone
    A. Behavior with siblings
    B. Behavior with other children
    C. Behavior with parents
    D. Plays and works by self

School Scale (0–6)
  VII. School performance
    A. Academic performance
    B. Special class placement
    C. Grade repeated
    D. Other school problems

---

[a]Total competence score ranges from 0 to 30.

social competence. More detailed information on scoring, reliability, and validity can be found in the Manual (Achenbach and Edelbrock, 1983) and in a monograph by Achenbach and Edelbrock (1981).

Behavior Problems. The Behavior Problems Scale of the Child Behavior Checklist was used to assess behavior problems that the target child might have exhibited. This 113-item instrument (detailed in Chapter 8) results in a profile of nine "narrow-band" problems scores (eight for boys) and two "broad-band" scores: *internalizing problems,* which includes problems traditionally considered as "neurotic" or "overcontrolling" behavior (i.e., depression, somatic complaints); and *externalizing problems,* which includes "acting out" or "undercontrolling" types of behaviors (i.e., aggression, delinquency, hyperactivity). A total problems score is also calculated.

Parenting. Previous research has reported that high support and low coercion relate to social competence. This was assessed by parents' and adolescents' perceptions of parenting on the *Cornell Parent Behavior Inventory* (CPBI) (Devereaux et al., 1969) which assessed two dimensions of parenting behavior, *support* and *discipline.* Parents were instructed to indicate how they behaved toward their children by responding to 11 questions on a 7-point scale. In addition, adolescents were asked to rate their mothers' and fathers' behaviors using an identical parallel form.

The combined score of the B and C scales of the *Adolescent Abuse Inventory* (AAI) (see Chapter 5), which was completed by each parent, was used as an indicator of potential for developmentally damaging parenting behavior, with higher scores indicating greater risk for abuse.

Analysis

The analyses used were selected to address two basic questions. First, what is the relationship between overall behavior problems and competent functioning? Second, how is competence related to how parents treat adolescents? Two analytic strategies were used to determine the relationship between social competence, parenting, and behavior problems. First, an analysis of variance (ANOVA) approach was used to see if there were differences in problems and parenting in families of children of various levels of competence. In order to use the family as the unit of analysis, these variables were analyzed by sex of adolescent, three levels of competence, and sex of parent.[1]

Second, multiple regression was used to determine the relative influence of parenting and behavior problems on competence. These procedures were also used to determine the effects that competence and problems had on parental support, discipline, and risk for abuse.

[1]Sex of parent was used as a repeated measures factor.

Competence Scores

An average competence score was calculated for each adolescent by taking the mean of both mothers and fathers scores on each of the subscales and the total score.[2] These average competence scores were used in all subsequent analyses. For analysis of variance procedures, a new variable *level of competence* was created by considering those below the twenty-fifth percentile of the sample distribution of total competence scores as "low competence," those between the twenty-fifth and seventy-fifth percentile as "average," and those above the seventy-fifth percentile as "high competence." Separate cutoff points were determined for boys and girls, so competence was determined relative to each subjects' gender group.[3] Mean competence scores and cutoff points are displayed in Table 7.2.

We will present the results as follows. First, we will examine the relationship between competence and behavior problems. Next, we will show the relationship between competence and parenting from the perspectives of *both* parents and adolescents.

Table 7.2. Mean Average Competence Scores for Boys and Girls by Level of Competence

Level of competence	Girls[a]	Boys[b]
Low	14.16 (1.62)[c]	14.67 (1.57)
Average	19.10 (1.57)	19.87 (1.31)
High	22.78 (1.33)	22.99 (0.72)

[a]$N = 27$.
[b]$N = 34$.
[c]Standard deviations are in parentheses.

[2]In order to determine whether there were differences between parents in how they rated their children on social competence, subscale and total competence scores were analyzed using a 2 (sex of adolescent) x 2 (sex of parent) repeated-measures analysis of variance, with sex of parent as the within-group factor. No significant main or interaction effects were found, indicating that mothers and fathers did not differ in how they rated their children, and that boys and girls received comparable competence scores. Correlations between mothers' and fathers' ratings for competence ranged from .21 to .78, with correlations for the total score at .58 for girls and .49 for boys.

[3]The cutoff scores used to classify "low competence" for this study (boys < 16.5, girls < 17.8) are comparable to cutoff points recommended by Achenbach and Edelbrock (1983) to describe children in the "clinical range" (at or below the tenth percentile for their age and sex group).

RESULTS

The Relationship between Competence and Behavior Problems

Parents' perceptions of behavior problems exhibited by the child were represented by three scores from the Child Behavior Checklist: internalizing problems, externalizing problems, and total problems. Table 7.3 presents the correlations beween social competence and behavior problems. Greater number of problems are related to lower social competence scores, with the strength of the relationship for girls larger than for boys and correlations with fathers' perceptions of problems greater than correlations with mothers' perceptions of problems.

A series of analyses showed that the number of problems parents reported were different depending on how competent they perceived their children to be.[4] Parents of less competent children report significantly more internalizing, externalizing, and total problems for their children than parents of average or highly competent children. Table 7.4 shows that the effect is particularly evident for externalizing problems, where parents of less competent children report three times as many problems as parents of highly competent children. The mean number of total problems for the least

Table 7.3. Correlations between Average Competence Ratings and Behavior Problems[a]

Behavior problem	Girls	Boys	Total
Internalizing			
Mothers	−.43		−.26
Fathers	−.62	−.39	−.49
Externalizing			
Mothers	−.65	−.47	−.49
Fathers	−.75	−.59	−.67
Total			
Mothers	−.63	−.32	−.47
Fathers	−.72	−.62	−.67

[a]Only r's significant at $p < .05$ are presented.

[4]Repeated-measures ANOVA's showed significant level of competence effects for internalizing problems ($F[2,54] = 8.99, p = < .001$), externalizing problems ($F[2,54] = 28.06, p < .0001$), and total number of problems ($F[1,54] = 24.73, p < .001$). There were no other significant main or interaction effects. Multivariate statistics were also calculated for logically related groups of dependent variables, but given the small sample size and exploratory nature of the study, priority was given to the univariate approach. In general, except for parents' perceptions of their own parenting, all other sets of univariate ANOVA's were also multivariately significant.

Table 7.4. Mean Ratings on Perceptions of Behavior Problems by Child's Level of Competence[a]

Parent reports of behavior problems	Level of competence			F
	Low	Average	High	
Internalizing	27.17 (10.49)	13.48 (11.45)	10.12 (7.42)	8.99***
Externalizing	31.60 (15.15)	14.19 (8.36)	8.42 (6.73)	28.06***
Total	59.33 (24.17)	29.70 (14.75)	20.07 (9.10)	24.72***

[a]Numbers in parentheses indicate standard deviations.
*$p < .05$ **$p < .01$ ***$p < .001$.

competent children (59.33) is well above the ninetieth percentile cutoff point (38) suggested by Achenbach and Edelbrock (1983) as being in the "clinical" range.

While the previous analyses illustrate *group* differences, the relationship between competence and problems for *individuals* can be more clearly illustrated by classifying subjects by level of competence and severity of behavior problems. Those subjects with internalizing problem scores above the seventy-fifth percentile (for their gender group, as rated by mother[5]) were classified as "high internal," while those below the seventy-fifth percentile were considered "normal." The procedure was repeated for externalizing problems. This cross-classification of subjects is presented in the top half of Table 7.5.

Although there is tendency for less competent children having more internalizing problems than average or highly competent children, this difference was not statistically significant. The relationship between competence and *externalizing* problems, however, is strong and clear. A majority of the less competent children (73%) were also "high externals." Only 9% of the average competence children exhibited externalizing problems, and *none* of the highly competent children scored above the seventy-fifth percentile on external problems.

These numbers may be somewhat misleading, however, as some adolescents were high on *both* internalizing and externalizing problems, while others were high on one or the other. The lower portion of Table 7.5 presents a reclassification of subjects by competence and *combined* internalizing and externalizing problems. Those falling in the "normal" range of problems are primarily of average or high competence, or conversely very few of those who are average or highly competent also show behavior problems. Those with problems, however, tend to be less competent, especially those with *externalizing* problems. All of the high externals and

[5]Classification by type of behavior problems using fathers' scores was comparable.

Table 7.5. Cross-Tabulation of Subjects by Level of Competence and Severity of Behavior Problems[a]

| | Level of competence | | | |
Problem classification	Low	Average	High	χ^2
Internalizing				
High	7 (46.67)	5 (15.63)	2 (14.29)	5.77
Normal	8 (53.33)	27 (84.38)	12 (85.71)	
Externalizing				
High	11 (73.33)	3 (9.38)	0 (0.00)	28.41*
Normal	4 (26.67)	29 (90.63)	14 (100.00)	
Combined problems				
High internal and external	6 (40.00)	3 (9.38)	0 (0.00)	32.82*
High internal only	1 (6.67)	2 (6.25)	2 (14.29)	
High external only	5 (33.33)	0 (0.00)	0 (0.00)	
Normal	3 (70.00)	27 (84.38)	12 (85.71)	

[a]Numbers in parentheses indicate column percentages. Scores higher than 75% of the sample based on mother's report (separately for boys and girls).
*$p < .001$.

six of the nine who were high on both internalizing *and* externalizing problems were low competence children. Of the five adolescents who are "high internalizers," only one is of low competence.

The Relationship between Competence and Parenting

In the results that follow, no differences were found between mothers and fathers in how they rated their children, nor were there differences between how sons and daughters were rated.[6]

Parent Perceptions. Parents are slightly more supportive of girls than boys. However, parents of low, average, and high competence children report being equally supportive in dealing with their children. Parents of low competence children report using greater discipline, however, than parents of average or highly competent children. The direction of the AAI scores parallel those of the discipline scale but were not statistically significant. These results are summarized in Table 7.6.

In general, less competent children receive more discipline, but they also exhibit more behavioral problems than average or high competence children. Given the relationship between discipline, problems, and com-

[6]Parenting variables were analyzed within 2 (sex of adolescent) × 3 (level of competence) × 2 (sex of parent) repeated-measures ANOVA's. There were no significant main effects for sex of adolescent (sex of adolescent effect for support was marginally significant (F[1,54] = 3.77, $p < .06$). There were no significant two- or three-way interactions.

Table 7.6. Mean Ratings on Perceptions of Parenting by Level of Child's Competence[a]

| | Level of competence | | | |
	Low	Average	High	F
Parent reports				
Support	25.00 (3.83)	26.16 (3.09	25.00 (2.11)	0.03
Discipline	11.75 (2.99)	10.61 (2.60)	9.57 (2.11)	4.11*
AAI B and C	96.79 (22.18)	89.61 (19.59)	84.25 (13.56)	2.10
Adolescents reports				
Support	20.90 (4.52)	23.89 (3.43)	25.00 (3.42)	5.78**
Discipline	11.37 (3.42)	9.50 (2.70)	8.54 (2.84)	5.44**

[a]Numbers in parentheses indicate standard deviations.
*$p < .05$ **$p < .01$ ***$p < .001$.

petence, it may be likely that discipline is not related to lack of competence per se but to the presence of behavior problems, which tend to occur more often in less competent children. When the total number of behavior problems is controlled, the differences in discipline by level of competence are no longer significant.

Adolescent Perceptions. Previous analyses showed that parents of less competent children report using discipline more often than parents of average or highly competent children. Reports from their children confirm this relationship (Table 7.6). Less competent children report receiving more discipline than average and highly competent children. Less competent children, however, also report less support than average and highly competent children. As in the parent reports, however, these effects are no longer significant when controlling the total number of self-reported behavior problems.

Parent Predictors of Competence. The relative influence of parenting and behavior problems on competence was assessed by entering both mothers' and fathers' scores on support, discipline, AAI, internalizing problems, and externalizing problems into a stepwise regression model. Given the correlations between mothers and fathers ratings and the goal of keeping the *family* as the unit of analysis, this strategy was used to determine the best predictors of competence within families from the parents' perspective. The greatest prediction was obtained with four father variables accounting for 52% of the variance in competence scores. Higher competence was related to greater father support, less discipline, and fewer internalizing and externalizing problems as reported by the father. None of the mother's ratings added significantly to the variance accounted for by the father ratings.

To examine parenting as a response to characteristics of adolescents, a series of stepwise multiple regression models were run separately for mothers' and fathers' ratings of support, discipline, and risk for abuse using total competence and problems scores as predictors. Fathers' support was predicted by both problems and competence, while neither predictor entered the equation for mothers. Both fathers' and mothers' reports of discipline were predicted by problems only. Risk for abuse as measured by the AAI was predicted by problems for fathers and low competence for mothers.

Summary

The following picture emerges from these data. Those who do well in school, who participate in sports and other activities, and who get along well with others are perceived by parents as being relatively free of problems and receive less discipline from them. Those who do poorly in school, who are less active, and have poorer relationships with others also have additional behavior problems and receive more restrictive and controlling parenting.

For mothers and fathers, parental discipline is related to behavior problems. Risk for abuse, however, while being predicted by problems for fathers, is predicted by low competence for mothers. Support from fathers is best predicted from both problems and competence, but mothers' support was unrelated to either support or competence.

DISCUSSION

The results show that behavior problems (or "symptoms") and competence (or "social adaptation") can be considered as two sides of the same coin ("mental health" or "adjustment"), and that parenting behaviors perceived by both parents and children are related to these different aspects of adjustment.

The presence of externalizing behavior problems is related to lower competence, which is related to less support (as reported by the adolescent) and greater discipline (as reported by both parents and adolescents). These parenting tendencies seem to be related not to the lack of competence per se but more to the parents' perceptions of their child's problems.

The finding that adolescents who are high on externalizing problems or high on externalizing *and* internalizing problems are the least competent and that they receive more discipline and less support are consistent with findings that these types of children are at greater risk for later adjustment problems.

A growing number of studies have shown that externalizing behavior problems (including aggressive and antisocial behavior) show greater stability and predictability to other adjustment problems than do internalizing behavior problems (Kohlberg et al., 1972; Loeber, 1982; Robins, 1966; 1979; Rolf, 1972). Those who exhibit extremes in both internalizing and externalizing behaviors, however, seem to be at greatest risk for a variety of adjustment problems, including schizophrenia. John et al. (1982), for example, found that subjects diagnosed as schizophrenics were described by teachers 10 years earlier as being isolated, withdrawn, socially inept, and were also more likely to be rated as being more aggressive, disturbing in class, and persisting in reactions when upset or excited.

Ledingham and her colleagues (1984) are conducting a prospective longitudinal study of children who have been identified by their peers as being highly aggressive (A), highly withdrawn (W), and highly aggressive and withdrawn (AW). Teacher ratings on the Devereaux Elementary School Behavior Rating Scale showed both A and AW groups higher on classroom disturbance, impatience, disrespectful–defiant behavior, and external blame. The AW group, however, received the most deviant scores from established norms on 10 of the 14 scales and was rated as the most externally reliant, most inattentive–withdrawn, and unable to change from one activity to another. Mother ratings also show the AW group higher on distractability, poor self-care, pathological use of senses, and need for adult contact. In general, the data characterizes the AW child as immature, having attentional difficulties, and being unpopular with peers.

A 3-year follow-up (Ledingham and Schwartzman, 1983) showed differential academic success among the target groups, with the AW children doing the most poorly. Only 52% of the AW children were in regular classes at the expected grade level, compared to 59% of the aggressive children, 75% of the withdrawn children, and 83% of the controls. AW children also suffer more multiple setbacks, with 12% failing a grade and being placed in a special class (as compared to 7% of the A children, 2% of the withdrawn, and none of the controls).

While it is tempting to assume that nonoptimal parenting "caused" these developmental outcomes, it is possible that parental behavior is a response to problem behavior and poor functioning that may have roots in delayed or deficient developmental processes (e.g., attention, impulse control) that might have organic or biological bases. More than likely, the relationship between parenting, behavior problems, and less than competent functioning is a system that has developed through "transactional" processes of mutual influences and changes that serve to maintain each component (Sameroff, 1975).

The triad of maladjustment (behavior problems, competence, and parenting behavior) has implications both for the assessment of and intervention with high-risk children. First, adjustment must be thought of not merely in terms of presence or absence of symptoms but on the basis of how effectively the child functions in relevant social contexts. Poor adaptation may be due not only to the presence of problem behavior but also to the lack of or deficiency in other skills or developmental processes that prevent them from behaving appropriately and effectively or from acquiring these skills and behaviors. They are put (and put themselves) into situations where developing these skills is very unlikely.

Assessment, therefore, must target not merely the presence or absence of problems but also the degree to which children adapt not only to relevant contexts but also the presence or absence of skills, characteristics, and abilities that allow them to meet environmental demands and challenges. An emphasis on assessing social adaptation is also important in that it gives an indication not only of the kinds of resources and opportunities that are available to the child that may promote development of skills but also to stresses and obstacles that may hinder or prohibit the development of these skills (or encourage the development of behaviors that are less desirable yet may be "adaptive" given the particular situation).

Inferences about the predictability of future adjustment based on assessments of problems and competence, therefore, must take into consideration several relevant findings from previous research:

1. Externalizing behavior (particularly when it is extreme, has had a long history, and occurs in multiple settings) is a better predictor of a wide array of adjustment problems and is more stable than internalizing problems.

2. Adaptational problems are better predictors of later adaptational problems *and* symptomatic behavior than symptom behaviors are of later behaviors or adaptational difficulties. Children who should be considered at-risk are those who exhibit extremes in symptomatic behavior *and* who have adaptational difficulties, particularly if these problems have been longstanding.

3. While adaptational problems may be due to symptomatic behavior, they may also signal developmental and behavioral *deficits* that the child has not yet acquired.

4. Children with problem behavior and/or adaptational difficulties often live in situations that maintain problematic interactions or hinder the development of appropriate behaviors and skills.

Adolescence is an important time in the development and demonstration of competence. It calls forth both the desire to function successfully in the world and the need to feel good about that ability. Often deficits that were only potential in childhood become real in adolescence, when demands for socially desirable characteristics and skills increase markedly in school and the world of work. With some skills and confidence as a foundation, the adolescent will be ready to develop further skills that may be important during his/her adult years.

Adolescence is a time when individuals begin to influence the course of their own development to an unprecedented degree (Lerner and Busch-Rossnagel, 1981). Adolescents have increased opportunity to select particular environments and situations and in many cases are able to arrange the quality of their experiences. What they have arranged can influence the course of their growth. This is both the promise and the danger of adolescence. Their appearance and behavior stimulates those around them to treat them in certain ways, ways that may be different from when they were children as their image changes with their bodies. An "ugly duckling" may blossom into a swan, whereas an attractive child may become an unattractive teenager. In addition to selecting roles, adolescents are assigned to roles and duties and are expected to act in adult-like ways in making decisions and taking responsibility for their actions. Thus, adolescents must now confront directly a set of stresses and resources from which they might have been shielded previously. Beyond just being influenced by these forces, adolescents can make something out of these risks and opportunities. This highlights the cost of social incompetence: missed opportunities for enhanced present and future development.

Intervention efforts, therefore, may require not only the treatment or control of problematic behavior that less competent children have but also the development of inadequate or deficient skills and abilities that will enable youngsters to create and take advantage of developmental opportunities. While these changes in individual behavior may influence family functioning, they may also require restructuring family interaction patterns and other environmental conditions (e.g., classroom) to be more conducive to the development of adaptive capacities. In any case, our analyses certainly tell us that the key to understanding adolescent adjustment and family relationships lies in our understanding of problem behavior. With this in mind, we turn to Chapter 8, a more detailed examination of behavior problems and adolescent psychopathology.

BEHAVIOR PROBLEMS IN ADOLESCENCE

8

TERESA M. COONEY

In Chapter 1, we discussed the problems encountered when describing characteristics of "normal" adolescence. These problems bear some consequence for this chapter since our view of "pathology" is that it represents a condition marked by abnormality in some structure or process. This chapter will address behaviors commonly observed in adolescents that are considered problematic by individuals who come into contact with them. Some behaviors discussed here are considered deviant because they are not prevalent in the majority of the adolescent population. Others are viewed as deviant because they conflict with societal expectations, despite their widespread prevalence among adolescents. We avoid some common technical classifications (such as the American Psychiatric Association's classification scheme—the Diagnostic Statistical Manual [DSM-III categories]) in the present discussion because the methods necessary to arrive at these diagnoses are not always available to those in contact with adolescents. Rather, we discuss problems in the manner in which observers in the adolescent's environment view them. We favor this approach since the expectations of the adolescent's environment define normal and abnormal behavior; and the tolerance level of that environment is what determines whether the behavior is considered problematic enough to require intervention (Ross, 1980). Also, these are the data usually available to the practitioner.

Before identifying those behavior problems commonly associated with

171

adolescence, it is important to consider the context of adolescents' everyday experiences. Adolescence is generally viewed as a transitional period bridging childhood and adulthood (Hopkins, 1983). Biological changes, primarily in the form of sexual maturation, mark the onset of this period (Petersen and Taylor, 1980) which eventually calls for changes in the adolescent's psychological development and social behavior. These alterations, with their swift onset and demands for adjustment, make the period of adolescence one of extreme vulnerability (Hopkins, 1983).

In serving as a bridge between childhood and adulthood, adolescence fails to operate clearly under the norms or values of either period. Parents often expect their adolescents to assume more responsibility and independence, yet when adolescents wish to express their independence in setting their own curfews or wearing outlandish clothes, their parents often intervene and set restraints on their behavior. Covington (1982) suggests that the lack of clear behavioral norms in adolescence partially explains the prevalence of problems observed during this period. While the values and behaviors of childhood are no longer accepted as appropriate, the values and roles expected of adults are not totally permissible either, creating a double-bind for individuals in this age group.

The social structure of adolescence may add to the problems these youth experience. A report published in the early 1970s (Coleman and Associates, 1974) suggests that modern work-family patterns and education forms restrict teenagers' contact with other age groups. Through age-graded schools, teens not only are cut off from contact and responsibility for younger children but also are kept from the labor force where exposure to adult role models would be possible. One consequence of age-segregation of this type has been the emergence of the peer group as one of the major sources of socialization for young people (Bronfenbrenner, 1970). While the role of the peer group in the socialization process is valuable in some respects, it does not provide the necessary guidance for development of other roles, such as those in the family and work settings. The strong influence of peers over the influence of family will be discussed later with regard to behavior problems, such as substance abuse. This issue will pose questions regarding the need for greater balance between peer and familial contact and influences in adolescence.

THE ROLE OF THE FAMILY IN NORMAL
AND ABNORMAL DEVELOPMENT

The role of the family in children's lives usually changes when offspring reach adolescence. The adolescent, while developing a greater sense of self, experiences strong pulls away from parental control and protection (Konopka, 1980), in search of an identity apart from the family (Turner, 1970).

Conflict and tension frequently arise, since adolescents' emerging needs for independence are not accompanied by an equivalent weakening of the parent–child ties on the part of the parents (Turner, 1970). Parents may view their child's emancipation as rejection of the home (Thornburg, 1975). In response to their adolescents' push for autonomy, parents may attempt to prevent additional loss of control by resorting to increased authoritarian discipline. At a time when adolescents are clarifying values, seeking new, more important social roles, and experiencing a greater capacity for activity, the restraints induced by such discipline may interfere with their socioemotional development (Konopka, 1980). Therefore, the period of adolescence demands increased sensitivity on the part of parents to the needs of their offspring. It is critical that parents recognize and respect the needs their adolescents have for increased exploration outside the home and their desire for greater independence. Yet, parents also must be alert and prepared to provide any supportive guidance and concern their offspring may seek during resurgences of earlier needs for parental identification and dependence (Turner, 1970). Being parent to an adolescent is a very challenging task in most circumstances.

Understanding the social context in which adolescents live—the dynamics of their educational, social, and familial environments—provides added insight to our understanding of the behavior problems they exhibit and the coping strategies they employ in dealing with their problems (Phillips, 1968). We must keep these factors in mind as we proceed to identify the onset and meaning of these behavior problems.

THE ONSET OF ADOLESCENT BEHAVIOR PROBLEMS

The presence of psychopathology in adult populations has been related positively to the occurrence of both positive and negative life events (Myers et al., 1974). Thus, for example, a change of residence or obtaining a new job, regardless of whether or not it was desired, may be stress-inducing.

Adolescence is a time of change and involves a quickening of the pace of life events. The many new physical, psychological, and social experiences common to individuals during this stage may explain the high rates of problems adolescents encounter. Coddington's work (1972a, b) verifies the extreme levels of life events experienced in adolescence. The curve depicting life events rises gradually from age 2 to 12. It then accelerates and peaks around the ages 15 to 17.

The multiplicity of biological and social changes confronting adolescents may create new demands that have the potential for triggering off many new behavior problems. For example, recent research has shown that multiple school transitions in adolescence negatively affect adolescent functioning (Schulenberg et al., in preparation).

The problems experienced in adolescence might not all be new ones, however. Problems observed in adolescence may be altered manifestations of problems that were present in childhood. Polansky et al. (1981) provide one example of behavior transformations of this type. They note that neglected children, who in childhood are characterized by withdrawal and other types of introvertive behavior, often "turn mean" (p. 135) in adolescence. Polansky and his colleagues attribute these altered behaviors to a reorganization of psychological defenses in adolescence for dealing with the world.

Due to the character of behavior and mood in adolescence, there is the risk that early signs of disorder and problems may be dismissed as predictable changes of "normal" adolescence (Weiner, 1970). Thornburg (1975) believes that many extreme behaviors adolescents display are self-controlled signals used to alert parents to take notice of their changing needs and rights for new treatment. We will address this idea later with regard to specific behavior problems such as delinquency and suicide.

BEHAVIOR PROBLEMS

Classification

The specific behavior problems common to children are found to vary by age (Eaton et al., 1966) and sex of the child (Achenbach, 1966; Achenbach and Edelbrock, 1978, 1979). Thus, for example, hyperactive behavior is more common in childhood, while delinquent behavior is more common in adolescence; boys are more likely to display discipline problems in school, and girls are more likely to experience somatic problems and phobias. Those interested in typology have developed norms that reflect these differences.

In developing taxonomies of behavior problems, researchers have benefitted widely from the use of the factor analytic technique. This statistical method is used to reduce a large number of items—in this case problem behaviors—into clusters or classes of interrelated behaviors. The work of Achenbach (1966) and Achenbach and Edelbrock (1978, 1979) has successfully employed this technique in deriving a typology of behavior problems for children aged 4–16. The majority of behavior problems cited in their checklist is classed into two basic types: externalizing or internalizing. Externalizing behaviors represent problems in the conduct of relations between individuals and their environment. A typical item for the externalizing scale inquires about a child's "cruelty, bullying or meanness to others." Internalizing behaviors, on the other hand, represent personality-type problems where the disturbance is manifest more within the individual. Describing a child as being "nervous, high-strung or tense" would indicate problem behavior points on the internalizing scale.

Although the two dimensions represent extremely different styles of "problems," individuals scoring high on one type commonly score high on the other. Edelbrock (personal communication, January 1983) reports correlations of .40–.45 for the two scales (16–20% of the variance is shared by the two scores) yet points out that the moderate correlation does not indicate redundancy in the problem types. Rather, Edelbrock considers children's propensity for behavior problems to have a general dimension in which more specific domains of externalizing and internalizing problems exist. Analogous to this, he explains, are the verbal and performance areas of the more general intelligence test. Although the two dimensions represent specific patterning of intelligence abilities, they are highly related because they are both part of a general intellectual ability. Similarly, external and internal behaviors are specific patterns of a general dimension of problem behavior.

Another explanation for the relationship between the two types of behaviors is derived from a psychodynamic interpretation of behavior problems. Marohn et al. (1980) propose that delinquent behavior (an externalizing problem) is an effort by adolescents to provoke parental response when they are experiencing internal conflicts. These researchers believe internal problems and deficiencies are externalized in delinquent acts due to adolescents' inability to express feelings of anger, sadness, depression, etc. In this perspective, where externalizing problems serve as a behavioral release of internal stress, an increase in the latter should predict a similar increase in the former.

Classification as a Predictor

Attempts have been made to determine childhood indexes for predicting behavior problems in later life. The use of adolescent behavior ratings in the prediction of troubled behavior in adulthood has been highly effective (Gersten et al., 1976; Garmezy et al., 1979). Garmezy et al. (1979) classified children as internalizers and externalizers and then followed them through to adolescence where they observed their behavioral outcomes. Adolescents who had been classed as externalizers in childhood were overrepresented in the group of school dropouts, performed lower academically, and were the source of more disciplinary problems in school than were the internalizers. M. Shea's (1972) dissertation work at the University of Minnesota also demonstrates that the occurrence of internalizing and externalizing behavior in adolescence accurately predicts the prevalence of problems experienced up to 30 years later in adulthood. Individuals categorized as externalizers in adolescence experience more difficulties in adulthood than those labeled "internalizers." In adulthood, externalizing adolescents experienced high frequencies of unemployment, more time spent in mental health care facilities and correctional institutions, higher divorce rates, more emotional distress, lower average occupational levels, and greater SES decline than internalizers and controls. These results are consistent with other findings (Robins, 1966, 1972; Masterson, 1972). All suggest that the prevalence of externalizing problems (e.g., antisocial behavior) is more predictive of adult disturbances than is the prevalence of internalizing problems.

Other studies focusing on peer relations have associated various adult adjustment problems with peer problems during childhood (Roff et al., 1972; Cowen et al., 1973). Children's negative, aversive behaviors may create problems with peer relations. Recent work (Bierman and Furman, 1984) has revealed that training children in conversation skills and providing group experiences for them may increase their chances of peer acceptance and improve their self-perceptions. Through early detection and treatment of behavior and peer problems in childhood, many adult problems may be prevented.

Prevalence of Behavior Problems

The types of behavior considered problematic differ throughout childhood. In a cross-sectional study of students in grades 1–12, teachers reported age differences in problem behaviors (Eaton et al., 1966). Younger children often exhibited difficulty with classroom attentiveness and work habits. They were more likely to be careless and were prone to lying and vandalism. Youth in grades 7–9, however, were more likely to manifest disruptive behaviors, generally in the form of interruptions, smartness, restlessness, and disorderliness in the classroom. For students in senior high, problems were more likely to involve misconduct outside the school, with acts such as smoking, drinking, unexcused absences, and illicit sexual activity being the most frequently cited problems. These problems appear to have some indirect influence on students' school functioning, since teachers and school officials were aware of them. The objectivity of the teachers' reports should be cautiously accepted, however. There was no report of the reliability of their observations. The teachers' expectations of student behavior might have biased their reports, leading them to report these findings even in their absence.

Achenbach and Edelbrock (1981) collected data on the prevalence of behavior problems in 1300 children aged 4–16 who were being seen in 28 mental health facilities. Their examination revealed a peak in behavior problems for boys around ages 8–9, followed by a steady decline in the total number of problems through their teen years. However, behavior problem scores peaked for girls around age 12 or 13, before undergoing a steady drop thereafter. Although Achenbach and Edelbrock reported reductions in the number of overall problems throughout the teen years, there were specific problems that increased in likelihood as the age of the group increased. While the number of externalizing behavior problems was likely to decrease with age, internalizing problems were more common in older children. This finding is consistent with others that report an increased number of diagnoses of depression for children as they progress through the 10- to 19-year-old age period (Weiner, 1980). The increase in internalizing behavior problems in adolescence may be related to the level of cognitive development adolescent children have achieved. Until adolescence, their ability to introspect and reflect on and ponder internal feelings has been limited. The reduction of externalizing behavior problems in adolescents may also provide one reason why externalizers are prone to more problems in adulthood. It may be that their deviancy is increasingly out of line with the behavior of their peers as they age.

Gender Differences

Differences between males and females have been reported not only in the number of problems observed (Eaton et al., 1966; Werry and Quay, 1971) but also in the types of problems typically associated with each sex. Boys are referred for clinical intervention and reportedly exhibit higher levels of behavior problems than girls (Gove and Herb, 1974). The differences, however, must be considered in light of the type of behavior problems that predominate in boys. Boys qualify as externalizers 2:1 compared to girls (Achenbach, 1966) and as such are displaying more problems of the type that are open to observation by others and likely to motivate adult intervention (e.g., delinquent acts). Girls outnumber boys 2:1 as internalizers (Achenbach, 1966), experiencing more internal conflicts, such as depression, which are not so readily observed by others like parents and teachers who are generally responsible for clinic referral.

Another explanation, though, takes us back to the earlier discussion of environmental tolerance. As Miller et al. (1971) point out, acts that are commonly stereotyped "boy's behavior" may create greater overt disturbance in the environment, be it school or home. Therefore, the likelihood of boys being referred to treatment is greater. Eme (1979), in a review of gender differences in psychopathology, points out that male deviance has a lower annoyance threshold than female deviance. Studies he reviews suggest that the principle indicator for childhood referral is parental reaction rather than severity of disturbance.

Whatever explanation one accepts (and a combination of them is quite possibly the true state of affairs), it is of interest to note that these sex differences are maintained into adulthood. Men in the adult clinical population are more likely to exhibit conduct-type problems than women, while there is a greater tendency for the latter to be diagnosed with personality problems (Phillips, 1968).

Common Behavior Problems

Depression and Alienation. The occurrence of depression increases throughout adolescence, although prevalence rates escalate from only 1.5 to 4.5% for the population, ages 10 and 17, respectively. Some (Weiner, 1980) claim that with increased age, sex differences markedly increase. Weiner (1980) cites statistics that at ages 10–14, males and females have similar rates—between 1.5 and 2.0% for both sexes. By ages 18–19, however, the rate for females has climbed to over 10%, with the males' rate staying around 3–4%. Yet, Kaplan *et al.* (1984) find no gender differences in rates of depressive symptomatology. Although it is unclear whether marked gender differences exist, many people have suggested reasons for a higher incidence of female depression and problems in adolescence. They suggest that adolescent girls are aware that they are moving into an adult role that is valued less by society (Gove and Herb, 1974) and that their role in adolescence and adulthood is more ambiguous than males (Douvan and Adelson, 1966).

Official rates of depression in adolescence create the impression that the problem is not prevalent during this period. Mental health workers, however, challenge these reports, claiming that a discrepancy exists between observed levels and actual rates in the population. They provide two arguments for the underestimation of the problem. First, depressive behaviors are likely to be ignored in adolescents because of the assumption that adolescents are prone to transient moods. Rather than being viewed as symptoms of depressive problems, certain behaviors may be misunderstood as age-related patterns of normal behavior that will not persist. Second, Glaser (1967) suggests that adult indicators of depression may provide inaccurate measures of depression in children and adolescents. Therefore, the absence of certain behaviors that are considered "signs of depression in adults" should not imply that depression is not a widespread problem for adolescents. In addition, Weiner (1980) believes that the escalated activity level common in adolescents may lead them to forego even thinking about how they feel, thus masking depressive affect even more.

One popular model of depression (Beck, 1970, 1974) links its existence to cognitive orientations that emphasize negative views of oneself, the world, and the future. These negatively toned conceptions of self and surroundings were uncovered in the three depressive subgroups identified by Mezzich and Mezzich (1979). They observed that the depressed sample was either restless and feeling unhappy with the world, was feeling socially frustrated, as if they had been abandoned, or was acting in self-depreciating ways with feelings such as guilt and low confidence. The greater propensity for depression in females was also evident in their study of 212, 12 to 18 year olds in a clinical setting. Forty-six adolescents comprised their depressive subgroup. Of these, 78% were females and 22% males.

The work of Craighead and his associates (1978; Craighead *et al.* 1981) has also identified this attributional style of depressed adolescents. Depressed adolescents seem to attribute failures to general personal factors that may lead to feelings similar to learned helplessness.

Since depressed adolescents commonly maintain negative views of themselves and the outside world, it is not surprising that depression is generally linked to alienation and withdrawal from their surroundings. A study of 96 college students linked alienation in these youth to extreme forms of parental control in their childhoods. Individuals who were raised in homes where parents encouraged autonomy scored lower on measures of alienation. It was suggested that the more alienated individuals were more likely to have controlling parents who had raised them with a narrow view of values and norms. Consequently, these individuals have difficulties coping with a society that reflects broader views. Alienation in their case is viewed as a means of retreating from a society in which they do not fit (DeMan, 1982). This finding may be useful later as we examine data from the Family Interaction Project.

Suicide. Commonly linked to alienation and depression is the act of suicide and suicide attempts (Corder, Page, and Corder, 1974). Extreme increases in rates of teenage suicide in the last two decades have stimulated widespread concern not only for this problem but with those symptoms linked to it. Suicide rates have increased 300% for individuals in the 15- to 24-year-old age group (Klagsbrun, 1981) in the last 20 years. The rate for males rose from 6.4 per 100,000 in 1957 to 21.8 in 1977. Female rates maintained their subordinate position to males' yet still rose from 1.8 in 1957 to 5.3 in 1977. Although adolescents comprise only 6% of the total number of suicides (Corder, Shorr, and Corder, 1974), suicide represents the third leading cause of death in teenagers (Vital Statistics of the United States, 1979).

Adolescent suicide attempts represent 12% of the attempts made by the total population. Yet, their rates of actual committed suicides represent only 6% of those suicides committed by the entire population (Weiner, 1982). This discrepancy between attempts and successes has led some to believe that threats of suicide need not be taken seriously, since for many teens they appear to be ploys for attention and help. While Klagsbrun (1981) acknowledges that, indeed, teenagers frequently resort to suicide attempts as a means of communicating a need for attention and help, they still indicate serious problems. Several studies show that repeated suicidal behavior is common for suicide attempters (Barter et al., 1968; McIntyre et al., 1977). Klagsbrun (1981) cites the fact that for four of every five people who commit suicide, there has been at least one and usually more previous attempts at suicide. Similarly, Otto (1971) revealed that 67% of 1700 suicide attempters studied had died of self-inflicted means 15 years after their first suicide attempts. The first couple of years following a suicide attempt appear to be the greatest time of risk for actual suicide (Dahlgren, 1977).

While females are more likely than males to attempt suicide (three times the rate of male attempts), males are three times more likely to actually commit suicide. This difference is frequently attributed to the suicide methods males and females use; methods such as guns and hanging, more commonly used by males, are more frequently fatal than pills and gas, which females are more likely to employ. Gender differences in the ratio of successful suicides for males and females have decreased over the last decade, however (Klagsbrun, 1981). Some relate recent trends in gender differences to the changing roles of females in society. As females take on more typically masculine roles, they may start employing means of self-destruction that have been previously considered male methods rather than the passive methods they have generally used. As pointed out, the former methods are more likely to result in death. On the other hand, the changes in sex differentials for suicide completion in the past decade may also be the result of increased pressures and frustrations in females as they assume high-status and high-pressure roles that were previously confined to males (Klagsbrun, 1981).

The problems of suicide and attempted suicide have surely reached a point that demands immediate attention. In order to deal successfully with the problem of suicide, it must be approached in a preventive manner, with special attention paid to early danger signals. Research has shown that suicide attempts among early adolescents are more likely to be related to problems in the parent–child relationship, whereas circumstances outside the family more often influence attempts in later adolescents (Triolo et al., 1984). Also, depression has been identified as the most prominent psychological characteristic associated with teenage suicide (Weiner, 1975). These factors suggest that early intervention with those problems that indirectly affect suicide attempts and, in the long run, suicide rates in adolescence must be considered. It may be necessary to approach intervention from several directions, focusing on factors either within or beyond the family, dependent on the age of the child.

Substance Use and Abuse. Substance use—used here to refer to the use of alcohol, cigarettes, and drugs—represents a class of behaviors considered deviant or problematic, although over one-half of high school youth have tried such substances, at least once, by their senior year (Johnston, 1973; Bachman, et al., 1980). Alcohol is the most frequently tried substance, with 90% of students having tried it once, while cigarettes (70%) and marijuana (over 50%) rank second and third, respectively, with regard to overall experimentation (Bachman et al., 1980). Although males more frequently report heavy drinking and drunkenness (Demone and Wechsler, 1976), gender differences in substance use have largely disappeared over the past few years (Demone and Wechsler, 1976).

The extensiveness of substance use has spurred researchers to search for antecedents and consequences of consumption. Due to the scarcity of longitudinal work in the area, however, most merely have uncovered correlates of alcohol and drug use, at best. Young teens who drink frequently have been found to score lower on measures of self-concept (Butler, 1982), and heavy alcohol use has also been related to devaluation of school achievement, both among high school (Milman and Su, 1973; Adler and Kandel, 1982) and college students (Moos et al., 1976).

One of the few longitudinal studies of substance use and abuse employed a wide array of independent variables in the examination of substance use in 705 students from a black ghetto community (Ensminger et al., 1982). By obtaining ratings of the students' school behavior 10 years earlier (in grade 1), the researchers were able to link a wide variety of personality characteristics in childhood to patterns of substance use in adolescence. Behavior characteristics observed in grade 1 were more highly predictive of later substance use for males than females. For males, aggressive behavior combined with shyness, in grade 1, correlated most strongly with heavy substance use as a teen. This did not hold for females. However, school preparedness in grade 1, or what can be considered precocity, was positively related to higher levels of substance use in high school students of both sexes.

In addition to personality correlates, the study also related peer, school, and family factors to substance use. While weak family bonds were the best predictors of higher levels of substance use (except for cigarettes) for females, strong peer bonds carried the most influence in higher levels of substance use for males. Similar results have also been reported in a recent study (Brook et al., 1984) of fathers and daughters where marijuana use by the child was negatively associated with the amount of time father and daughter spent together. Father–daughter relationships were less child-centered for marijuana users than nonusers. As far as school bonds, Ensminger et al. (1982) found that they predicted similarly for both sexes, as youth with weak school bonds were four times as likely to be heavy marijuana users than their peers with strong school ties. A problem in directionality of these relationships remains, however, since longitudinal data of bondedness to peers, family, and school were never obtained. Thus, it is unclear whether the substance use in high school preceded or followed the existing patterns of bondedness to family, peers, and school.

The role of family and peer factors in substance use has been studied cross-culturally as well. Adler and Kandel (1982) present results that show that substance use in the United States has its strongest links to peer influence. The strength of this relationship is unmatched in any of the other countries they studied. This may mean that the peer culture in the United States is a more powerful source of socialization than even the family at certain points in development.

What appears to be close to a "normative" pattern for progression of substance use has emerged for teens (Kandel and Faust, 1975). A highly predictable pattern involves the start of use through drinking of beer and wine, followed by progression to hard liquor and/or cigarettes, next to marijuana, and then for some the use of hard drugs. Use of the latter is never approached by the majority (80%) of teens, however (Kandel and Faust, 1975). Furthermore, while levels of drug experimentation are high, according to Bachman et al. (1980), habitual use is not the mode. Individuals who use drugs on occasion for recreational purposes are more similar to nonusers than to abusers. This is an important point, one that helps us understand other situations in which psychologically "normal" adolescents engage in socially abnormal behavior.

Delinquent Behavior. Delinquent behavior exemplifies one form of externalizing behavior problems commonly associated with youth. Although delinquent behaviors are considered legal offenses committed by individuals under age 18 (Law Enforcement Assistance Administration, 1974), acts may be classed as such even when apprehension by authorities does not occur (Hopkins, 1983). Since about 90% of acts fall into the latter part of this definition (Empey and Erickson, 1966), official statistics understate the problem of adolescent delinquency. This trend becomes apparent when one considers adolescents' behavioral self-reports. Particularly for behaviors such as truancy, reckless driving, speeding, substance use, and shoplifting, rates are high, with at least one-half of males and approximately one-third of females reporting experience with such behaviors at least once (Kratcoski and Kratcoski, 1975). In addition to misrepresenting the level of the problem of delinquency, official prevalence statistics may create misconceptions regarding the common profile of delinquents. Because of biasing in reporting and arrests, the impression has been created that minorities and persons from lower socioeconomic statuses are more frequently involved in juvenile crime (Gold and Reimer, 1975). Hindelang et al. (1979) argue, however, that the differences in self-reports and official reports are due to different definitions of delinquent behavior being employed in the data gathering procedures. Official reports are said to emphasize more serious offenses. Hindelang *et al.* also add that SES is not the critical factor in the differential rates of delinquency that have been reported. Rather, they see ethnic background as a critical variable, and this is often linked to economic status in our society.

Previous statistics also reveal gender differences in the frequency of delinquent behavior. Males are repeatedly found to exhibit higher rates of delinquent behavior (Hopkins, 1983). Yet, the Uniform Crime Reports for the United States (1975) published in recent years have documented a decrease in gender differences for juvenile crime, as female arrests have more than tripled and male arrests have only doubled between 1960 and 1975. These rates have risen much faster for youth than for the adult population, of both sexes, however.

Attempts to discover antecedents of delinquent behavior have had marginal success. The expense and time required to conduct longitudinal work has led most researchers to concentrate instead on correlates of delinquency, such as below-average IQ levels (Hirschi and Hindelang, 1977); lower SES levels (particularly in urban settings) (Erickson and Empey, 1965; Empey and Erickson, 1966); negative attitudes toward school and less school involvement (Kulka *et al.*, 1982); and lower educational attainment (Bachman *et al.*, 1978).

Yet, a 17-year longitudinal study conducted by Glueck and Glueck (1968) in Boston has uncovered some interesting outcomes related to adolescent delinquency. Using a sample of 500 institutionalized delinquent 14-year-old boys and 500 matched control subjects, the Gluecks collected an extensive range of information regarding background and school variables. Their data revealed that parental and family factors were the strongest predictors of the sample's delinquent–nondelinquent classification. In their sample, delinquent adolescents were more likely to come from broken homes than nondelinquents (Glueck and Glueck, 1959). While broken homes are repeatedly associated with a greater incidence of delinquency in adolescents, there are those (McCord *et al.*, 1962) who argue that it is not family structure (intact versus broken) that determines delinquency but rather other factors that are generally associated with broken homes. Similarly, Griffin and Griffin (1978) note the relationship of factors such as parental tension and rejection, financial problems, and discipline to the occurrence of delinquent behavior. From the perspective of McCord *et al.* (1962), the prevalence of such factors would predict higher rates of delinquency, even if found in intact families. And, broken families that can avoid such problems can probably escape greater likelihood of delinquency in their children. Bachman (1970) claims that it is the quality of the parent–child relationship that best predicts delinquent behavior. Thus, it can be suggested that adolescents from broken homes may fare as well as those from intact families, as far as avoiding delinquent behavior, provided positive parent–child relations are maintained. Here, as elsewhere, it is the process more than the structure of adolescent experience that affects the course of development.

Long-term prognoses of delinquent youth have revealed interesting outcomes for establishing their own families. The Gluecks (1968) found that delinquent adolescents, 17 years later at age 31, were more likely than nondelinquents to have been involved in early, unstable, short-lived marriages themselves as adults. Similarly, the work of others (Bachman *et al.*, 1978) suggests a relationship between higher levels of aggressive behavior in junior high school and a greater likelihood of early marriage and parenthood.

Although studies seem to indicate that delinquents have many common family characteristics, it is critical to recognize that these predictors are most appropriately applied to groups of young people rather than being used to make a prognosis for the life of any specific child (Ross, 1980). This further caution from Ross (p. 133) is also of value: "Delinquency is a function of a complex interaction of factors," and it is unlikely that any one condition, like father absence, the "broken home," poverty, or erratic discipline is a direct cause of delinquency.

THE FAMILY INTERACTION PROJECT

This final section will be devoted to examining the various aspects of problem behavior and its correlates in the Family Interaction Project (FIP) data.

Prevalence of Problems

Achenbach and Edelbrock's (1983) criteria for categorization of internalizing and externalizing types was used for the primary classification. The classification scheme first requires that the adolescent score above a T-score of 63 on either the Externalizing or Internalizing scale to be included in the respective category. In addition, the adolescent classified as an externalizer must have an externalizing score at least 10 points greater than his/her internalizing score. Similarly, the internalizer must score 10 points higher on the internalizing scale than on the externalizing scale. Six boys and six girls were classed as externalizers by these criteria, while only one male qualified as an internalizer. Because observers from the adolescents' environments referred them to the study, this tendency toward externality was not surprising. Certainly, externalizing adolescents would more frequently be identified as "problem children" by important others in their environment, since that is the type of behavior that is most noticeable. Similarly, we would not expect extreme pathology from this group due to its nonclinical nature.

Gender differences within the sample were nonexistent with regard to the mean levels of behavior problems. There were trends, however, toward females having more behavior problems on both the internalizing and externalizing scales and on the total number of behavior problems, according to the mothers' reports. Age differences also did not emerge when comparing the adolescents on mean number of externalizing and internalizing problems as well as on subscale scores. In part, this lack of significant effects of gender and age may be attributed to the small N's that result when dividing the sample into subgroups by age and sex. The sample size requires extreme mean differences for significance.

The relationship between internalizing and externalizing problems was exceptionally high within this sample. Where Edelbrock (personal communication, January 1983) reported a value of $r = .4$ on the average for several other investigations, the values obtained here were $r = .59$ and $r = .72$ for females and males, respectively, based on their mothers' reports. Considering that few subjects emerged as "pure" externalizers or internalizers, these high correlations are to be expected. Furthermore, adolescents' own reports of their internalizing and externalizing behavior problems are even more highly correlated, ($r = .83$, $p < .0001$) which may indicate that a general dimension does exist with regard to problem behavior. Or as Marohn and colleagues (1980) suggest, externalizing problems may in fact be another way of manifesting internal dilemmas.

Life Events

The FIP employed the A-File as its measure of life events. As mentioned above, the occurrence of life events has been closely associated with symptomatology (Myers et al., 1974). Within this sample, a similar relationship emerges between behavior problems and life events, particularly with regard to more recent life events. Correlations reach .59 between externalizing problems and life events and .34 for life events and internalizing problems. These correlations are particularly strong for females, with correlations reaching .66 and .62 between recent life events and externalizing and internalizing behaviors, respectively. In addition, females also show significant positive relationships between problems of both types and past life events ($r = .56$ for externalizing and .40 for internalizing behaviors). The strength of these relationships for females relative to males may signify greater vulnerability of females to stressful events. The significant relationship of behavior problems and past events may also indicate that females experience more prolonged reactions to life stressors than males. An additional factor that may be at work in these gender differences relating to life events is age. The females in the sample are approximately .5 year older than the males. Coddington's (1972a, b) work reveals a steady rise in life events throughout the teen years, so females may be ahead of males in these experiences, by age as well as relative biological maturation.

Some caution must be exercised, however, in interpreting these significant correlations due to the characteristics of the two instruments. The A-File is composed of six subscales representing different life events' domains. These six subscales are: transitions, sexuality, losses, responsibilities and strains, substance use, and legal conflict. The problem encountered when dealing with these two scales is that some of the behaviors considered by Achenbach and Edelbrock as problems, such as running away from home, are also included as life events on the A-File. The overlapping of items with the behavior problem measure is greatest on the responsibilities and strain scale. Correlations between scores on the two scales for females are $r = .55$ and $r = .57$ for externalizing and internalizing problems, respectively. Males' scores behave differently, with only the externalizing scale significantly correlating with the responsibilities and strains subscale ($r = .43$). For both males and females, however, the responsibilities and strains subscale is the most strongly related with the behavior problems measure of all the subscales on the A-File. The overlap leads to a cautious conclusion that the relationship that does exist between the two constructs of life events and behavior problems is probably not so strong as the correlations suggest. But it does highlight one of the ways in which adolescence is a high-risk period in the life course: Stress, change and normativeness are tied together tightly.

Parent Characteristics

Much of the discussion in part of this chapter emphasized the role of social context in adolescent development and the relationship between peer and family factors and problem behavior. Chapter 7 discusses peer relations. Here we will focus on family, specifically parenting, factors. In examining their effect, however, it is critical to begin by considering both parents and the relationship of their parenting behaviors. It is important to consider the possibility that the two parents' behaviors may interact. Also, each parents' behaviors must be considered alongside other behaviors in their repertoire. For example, the parent who uses moderate to severe discipline in an environment balanced with warm and supportive affection certainly should be viewed differently from the one who uses the same level of discipline in a cold, nonaffective atmosphere. Also, the particular behaviors of one parent may buffer or exacerbate those of the other. A major shortcoming in much of the parenting literature is the neglect of studying both parents. Trying to predict children's behavior based on information from only one parent's behaviors surely leaves many unanswered questions.

Therefore, to begin to relate parenting to problem behavior of the sample adolescents, we first consider the relationship between the two behaviors of interest—discipline and support—and their presence in the parenting repertoires of the mothers and fathers. For both mothers and fathers, separately, a negative relationship exists between support and discipline; however, only the correlation of $r = -.33$ for mothers' scores reaches significance. For fathers, although there is a similar trend, support and discipline are not significantly related. An extremely high correlation of $r = .65$ ($p < .0001$) is produced by comparing mothers' and fathers' support levels. A similar relationship exists for their corresponding levels of discipline ($r = .52$, $p < .0001$). Therefore, from the adolescents' perspectives, mothers' and fathers' parenting on these two dimensions is highly predictive of each other. And finally, there is no significant relationship between mothers' support and fathers' discipline or fathers' support and mothers' discipline. Clearly, these adolescents do not see one parent "making up for" the behavior of the other. A comparison of these correlations for high- and low-risk parents results in very similar relationships as for the total group. The only difference between the two groups is the relationship between mother's support and father's discipline. In the high-risk group, increased discipline by the father is accompanied by decreased support from the mother. The fact that mother's support and father's discipline are not so intricately related in low-risk families may be one reason that they are categorized as such.

Problem behaviors do relate in some ways to parents' discipline and support. For both mothers and fathers, the level of adolescent externalizing problems is highly related ($r = .48$ and $.45, p < .003$, respectively) to the use of discipline. Mothers' discipline levels are similarly related to internalizing problems as well. Fathers may concentrate their actions in relation to externalizing behaviors because of their obvious nature. This would make sense since fathers' communications with their children are thought to be less direct than mothers' (Turner, 1970), and internalizing problems are often not highly visible, requiring more direct communication for awareness. Mothers' support, on the other hand, is negatively related to only externalizing behavior problems.

Parents' propensity for abusive relationships with their adolescents also is highly related to levels of support and discipline. However, this relationship behaves differently for mothers and fathers. High levels of discipline are strong predictors of risk for abuse in mothers; however, for fathers, low levels of support appear to be the critical determinant of abusive tendencies.

It is clear that behavior problems, particularly externalizing ones, are related to discipline and support and also that support and discipline are related to risk for abuse. But, how do behavior problems relate to the likelihood of abuse and, furthermore, with all of these factors so closely linked, what best predicts risk for abuse classification? First, both internalizing and externalizing problems are associated with higher levels of risk for abuse. However, only the latter type reaches significance. Employing t-tests to examine the difference in group means for adolescents from high- and low-risk families, adolescents in the former exhibit significantly more total behavior problems and externalizing behaviors. A discriminant function analysis was performed to determine which of the factors—discipline and support for each parent and externalizing and internalizing problems—most clearly distinguishes categorization of families into high and low risk for abuse. This analysis revealed that using externalizing problems and fathers' support levels provides the best prediction of the family's classification into high- and low-risk categories. Using these variables, 70% of the families are correctly classed into the same high- and low-risk groups as they were using the AAI scores. This result is consistent with the general hypotheses that adolescent abuse (in contrast to child abuse) is more overtly and directly related to problem behavior of the "victim," and that fathers are at special risk to become abusive to their adolescent(s). This finding also suggests that more than a single predictor variable must be considered in examining family interaction. The interplay between fathers' support and adolescents' externalizing problems appears critical. Obviously, a single-predictor variable would have been insufficient in our search for "family" factors related to the likelihood of adolescent abuse. Certainly, these two significant indicators point to the validity of risk for abuse as a family problem.

Family Consensus

When dealing with multiple reports on the same measure, it is always difficult to determine which family member's report to use in analyses. In addition to getting at issues of validity and reliability, however, examination of family member agreement on particular measures may provide insight into certain aspects of family functioning. A closer look at mother–adolescent and father–adolescent agreement on occurrence of behavior problems illustrates this point.

Table 8.1 reports the percentage of behavior problem items on which adolescents agreed with their parents jointly and with each parent separately. These data suggest three main conclusions:

1. In all cases, there is more agreement between family members on the presence of externalizing behavior problems. This is to be expected since they are more obtrusive in the environment. Internalizing problems are more

Table 8.1. Mean Percentage of Agreement on Adolescent's Behavior Problems

	Dyad: Adolescent and	Percentage agreement
High risk		
Internalizing	Mother	47.33
	Father	44.82
	Both parents	32.48
Externalizing	Mother	60.78
	Father	57.90
	Both parents	47.74
Low risk		
Internalizing	Mother	40.62
	Father	34.11
	Both parents	20.72
Externalizing	Mother	43.62
	Father	43.88
	Both parents	27.55

likely to go unnoticed by individuals in the environment, thus adolescents would be more in tune with their internal problems and their parents would be less familiar with them than other problems.

2. Mothers and their children are more likely to be in agreement with regard to the presence of problems than are fathers and their adolescent offspring. This result may reflect greater involvement and awareness on the part of mothers in the lives of their children than of fathers. Bienvenu (1969), in fact, reports that adolescents claim to discuss personal problems with their mothers more than their fathers. Certainly, more open communication may account for greater agreement.

3. There is greater agreement, at every level of reporting, in high-risk families than in low-risk families. Initially, this finding contradicts notions that abusive families are disorganized, chaotic, and lacking in communication. However, findings of several studies can be adapted to explain these results. Alexander (1973) reports that clinical, problem-ridden families display a higher ratio of negative affect and defensive communications to positive affect and supportive communications than nonclinical families. The data herein may reflect the tendency of high-risk families to discuss and dwell on their adolescents' behavior problems. The more adolescents hear about negative aspects of their behavior, the more likely they may be to agree with these conceptions and, possibly, even to fulfill them. In contrast, low-risk families may focus more on positive interactions. Discussion of problem behavior may be infrequent; therefore, the opportunity to share views on the subject and to reach greater agreement is less likely.

Burgess and his associates (1981) also found higher rates of negative interaction, both verbal and nonverbal, in abusing families. Conveyance of disapproval and dislike for actions of others was more likely in these families as well. This further supports the view that problem behavior (at any level) is complained about more often in abusive families and thus increases likelihood of consensus between parents and adolescents. One could even propose that open discussion of this type could promote self-fulfilling behavior. A recent study of 14 to 18 year olds revealed that the more criticism teenagers perceive from their parents for specific behaviors, the more likely they are to view themselves that way (Harris and Howard, 1984). In addition, those teenagers who report high levels of parental criticism accompanied by parental rejection are also the ones to score lowest (most negatively) on the self-image measure. This finding is illustrative of Cooley's (1909) "looking-glass-self" and may explain why adolescents of high-risk families see themselves more like their parents' reports than do their age-mates in low-risk families. One possibility is that adolescents in high-risk families may alter their behavior to fit their parents' negative perceptions of them so that a cycle develops in which problem behavior reinforces parents' negative beliefs, which in turn stimulate more problem behavior.

CONCLUSION

This chapter has addressed some of the difficulties adolescence can present for chidren and their parents. Adolescence can be a stressful period, marked by many biological and social changes, which may produce vulnerabilities for young people. Most adolescents, however, are able to adjust to this period without experiencing major, long-term problems. Therefore, a chapter such as this deals with problems experienced by only a small minority of adolescents. Still, we cannot dismiss the importance of these problems: When they occur, they can be devastating for the entire family, and they frequently have long-term consequences for the adolescent. As such, adolescent problems cannot be brushed aside with the hope that the child will "grow out of them." Teachers, parents, and others who come in contact with adolescents must be aware of the problems that may develop in order that early detection and treatment can occur. This may be the best preventive measure we can take for protecting against troubled adulthood.

SOCIOECONOMIC STRESS AND FAMILY FUNCTIONING IN ADOLESCENCE

9

JOAN I. VONDRA

FAMILY RELATIONS IN A SOCIOECONOMIC CONTEXT

In this chapter, we turn our attention to the family economy and the relation of the family to economic systems. We know that economic resources and their use play a critical role in differentiating among families. Blue-ribbon panels repeatedly have cited deficient economic resources as the principal culprit in subjecting American families to excessive stress and children to developmental risk (see National Academy of Sciences, 1976). The role of economic impoverishment and low socioeconomic status in affecting the well being of infants and young children is well established. Less clear is the role these forces play in the lives of adolescents—where financial needs are greater (it costs more to support an adolescent), but alternative financial resources are often more numerous (e.g., the adolescent's own earnings and the relative freedom of parents to seek income without "childcare" costs or responsibilities). All this reinforces our view that we need to proceed with an examination of the socioeconomic context of parent–adolescent relations.

An Ecological Approach to Family Functioning

The goal of this chapter is to do more than simply examine the impact of the socioeconomic setting on modern families. Rather, it is to illuminate more clearly the *processes* by which social and economic conditions exert

191

their impact. Knowing, for example, that choice of discipline strategy and level of verbal stimulation differentiate low-income youth from their middle- or upper-class counterparts tells us nothing about *why* this should be so and *how* it is that socioeconomic factors are related to such measures of competence and performance. Our goal, in other words, is to understand not only effects but also mechanisms of influence. Consequently, we see the need to adopt a more dynamic perspective than one that considers only single-source, single-direction, single-target influences; we need to think about the interaction of effects between individuals and their circumstances. Indeed, it was this awareness that prompted social scientists to turn to an ecological approach to human development in the first place. This perspective focuses on the interplay between person and environment, encouraging us to note how characteristics of the environment (for example, the sense of community and safety in a neighborhood) may influence the persons living in it (for example, parental attitudes about peer contact) who, in turn, may have important effects on the environment (support and participation by parents in youth groups and activities), or vice versa. It is this dynamic view of the changing relations between persons and the environment in which they live that guides the analyses we pursue here.

Our further goal, then, is to use an ecological approach to understand better both the constructs and the processes that act potentially as causal links between socioeconomic conditions and a variety of parenting outcomes. To accomplish this, data from the Family Interaction Project (FIP) are examined in terms of the nature and direction of relationships between: (1) socioeconomic resources; (2) perceived job and family economic role stress; and (3) the continuum from competent to maladaptive parenting, identified in earlier chapters.

Qualitative Differences in Parenting

One may view the goal of child rearing as the socialization of children and adolescents into concerned, competent, psychologically healthy, and productive members of society. Successful or competent parenting then implies *adaptive* parenting—child-rearing practices that are conducive not only to a youngster's own well being but also to his or her progressive adaptation into the larger society. Importantly, a youth who is later able to function effectively as an adult member of society is more likely to secure for him or herself the material, social, and psychological resources required for personal and, eventually, family well being. Consequently, qualitative differences in parenting may have important socioeconomic as well as developmental repercussions not only for the immediate generation but even for future generations.

Given this scenario, parental behavior that jeopardizes the development of children may be considered dysfunctional or *maladaptive* in so far as children are not provided the necessary nurturance and guidance to ensure personal well being and effective socialization into competent adulthood. A considerable literature on the abuse of children and adolescents implicates as maladaptive, in this sense, parental practices encompassing the broadest range of behavior—from excessive restriction to flagrant neglect, from extreme punitiveness to emotional abuse. In sum, any substantial degree of insensitivity to a youth's physical, social, or emotional needs represents a threat to development, both as an individual and as a member of larger social organizations—schools, churches, communities, etc.

The Determinants and Correlates of Child Maltreatment

We have discussed already the multiple spheres of influence that contribute to destructive parent–youth relationships. Here, we will emphasize the situational factors that provide a context for maladaptive family functioning. Numerous studies have implicated the role of adverse family economics and inadequate social supports as causal elements in the etiology of child maltreatment (see Siegal, 1982). The relationships between these conditions and abusive or neglectful outcomes support the claim that rates of child maltreatment can serve as "social indicators of the quality of life for families" (Garbarino and Crouter, 1978). We can think of child maltreatment as a symptom of family stresses resulting from adverse socioeconomic conditions—adverse in that family members are experiencing these conditions as being in some way deficient in meeting their needs. Siegal (1982) goes so far as to say that "perhaps there is no better single example of the importance of studying the socioeconomic conditions underlying parent–child relations than child abuse" (p. 16).

The fundamental contribution that socioeconomic factors make to parenting outcomes is illustrated further by studies relating social class, occupational status and unemployment, and social network support to observed and/or self-reported differences in the quality of nonabusive parenting. Among the differences in parenting are sensitivity to, support for, or discipline of children, competence and/or confidence in the parental role, and attitudes about child rearing. Indeed, Belsky (1984) integrates these data in support of his hypothesis that the information on parenting gleaned from child abuse studies is directly relevant to "normal" variations in parenting attitudes and practices. If this is the case, factors implicated in the etiology of maltreatment, including socioeconomic stresses and supports, should contribute in a similar fashion to variations in parenting across the entire spectrum of parental differences. Furthermore, the underlying process of influence should be consistent, despite specific individual or situational strengths and deficits.

Socioeconomic status (SES) has a relatively long and well-documented history as a summary or marker variable used as a basis for identifying differences in parenting styles, child-rearing attitudes, parent–child relations, and developmental outcomes for children (e.g., Hess and Shipman, 1965; Lewis and Wilson, 1972). As some have pointed out, however, social class represents only a far-removed ("distal") determinant of parenting, and there is, as yet, little understanding of the actual processes that relate the two. Does SES have its impact primarily through material resources (finances, services, leisure time, etc.), through its impact on parental well being (physical health, self-esteem, self-confidence), through parental values and expectations (suggesting a role for parents' own experiences growing up), or through some other, as yet unspecified, causal pathway?

Although many researchers offered hypotheses about the nature of these processes (e.g., Gecas, 1979), there are few empirical efforts aimed at examining them systematically. Nevertheless, social class and individual socioeconomic factors have been linked repeatedly with a broad spectrum of parenting qualities and competencies. It is these relationships that doubtless account, at least in part, for the differential developmental prognoses for children of differing socioeconomic status. Indeed, as noted earlier, two major studies (by the National Academy of Sciences and the Carnegie Foundation) independently concluded that "inadequate economic resources are the central villain in undermining adequacy of families as a context for child development" (p. 22).

Qualifying the Maltreatment Data: The Victim's Age

It is important to qualify many of the findings relating socioeconomic factors and extremes of dysfunctional parenting (i.e., abuse) by making a distinction between the outcomes that occur among infants or young children and those that occur among preteens or adolescents. In examining the data of the National Study of the Incidence and Severity of Child Abuse and Neglect (1982), it is immediately apparent that a substantial proportion, approximately 47%, of all "child" abuse cases documented in the study involved youngsters aged 12 to 17 years old. This is in marked contrast to the 17% who were 5 years old or younger. It also represents a prevalence rate that is *greater* than the percentage of teenagers found in the general population of children and youth (38%). In contrast, abuse of very young children occurs at rates *below* their representation in the general youth population (28%). More important, families in which adolescent abuse occurs differ systematically, both in demographic characteristics and in the type of maltreatment perpetrated, from those in which younger children are abused (Garbarino and Gilliam, 1980; Olson and Holmes, 1983). Several of these differences are described below.

Probably as a consequence of age, life stage, and experience, the small subset of parents who mistreat only their adolescents (i.e., *not* the long-term abusers who continue to mistreat during adolescence the offspring who were mistreated during childhood) are more likely than those who mistreat younger children to be married and a stepparent, to have a higher level of education, to have full-time employment (regardless of gender) and, not surprisingly in light of these findings, to have a larger income (American Humane Association, 1977).

Unfortunately, it is not possible to determine from these data whether such social and demographic characteristics help to identify a unique (causal) pattern of maltreatment (true "adolescent abuse") or whether all families with adolescents are simply more likely to exhibit this socioeconomic differences—a plausible consequence of attaining this more advanced family "life stage." In the absence of comparable national figures for the entire population of families with and without adolescents, it is more reasonable to assume that among parents perpetrating strictly adolescent maltreatment, relative age and experience are responsible for differences in marital and occupational status as well as education and income level. This extreme of maladaptive parenting may still stem from socioeconomic factors that *relative to other families with adolescents,* are viewed as inadequate.

There is, however, some separate evidence to support the notion that adolescent maltreatment describes a somewhat distinct subclass of abuse. Although physical abuse in general remains constant or decreases with the age of the victim, "dangerous" forms of physical abuse (including "beating up" or use of a gun or knife) bear a U-shaped relationship with age (Straus *et al.*, 1980). Sexual abuse is also more characteristic of teenagers, particularly females. Sexual abuse of girls peaks just prior to or during early adolescence, and the majority of perpetrators (at all ages) are fathers or stepfathers. This helps to explain the increased proportion of paternal (versus maternal) violence that also marks adolescent abuse (Finkelhor, 1979).

Incestuous fathers appear especially to deviate from the typical pattern of child abusers: "Of the three patterns of incest . . . identified, the one that includes the majority (80%) of fathers has no hint of mental illness about it. These men are often upstanding citizens with higher than average levels of education and income" (Garbarino and Gilliam, 1980, p. 155). It is far from clear, at present, to what extent sexual abuse shares features in common with either physical abuse or neglect. To the degree that its etiology, its parental and familial correlates, and/or its consequences may differ substantially from other forms of maltreatment, it could account for some of the discrepancies in demographic data on adolescent versus child maltreatment.

Another consideration is raised by Straus and his colleagues (1980), who point out that physical abuse is more likely among younger (infants and preschoolers) and older (adolescents) children. They cite this curvilinear ("U-shaped") incidence of physical abuse across age as evidence of the role of child characteristics in very early and very late (i.e., adolescence) childhood.

> The fact that preschoolers and older teenage children share in the risk of being abused is very important. Many parents and social scientists have felt that the abuse of young children was the result of their parents' frustration in dealing with them. . . . Many parents of children in their late teens bemoan the fact that their children "no longer listen to reason." Thus we find that children too young to reason with and older teenagers, who refuse to be reasoned with, are both vulnerable to the same resolution of the conflict—violence (p. 71).

The contribution of the adolescent does not, however, imply that the other determinants of parental functioning are not operating in concert to precipitate a violent or negligent conclusion. Indeed, exacerbation of an already stressful situation by "provocative" adolescent behavior may be the catalyst for maltreatment. This is amply demonstrated in Kadushin and Martin's (1981) case analysis of child and adolescent abuse.

By integrating these findings, we can see a continuum of influences, each of which may contribute to dysfunctional or maladaptive parenting, but in a pattern that changes as the "child" grows up. The underlying assumption is that the same pattern of effects governs all styles of parenting—competent or otherwise—at any given age. However, it is assumed that this pattern exhibits systematic change over the course of time as children mature. Therefore, a single set of individual (e.g., gender, temperament, "acting out" behavior) and demographic characteristics (e.g., SES, family size) would play a role at all ages for the entire continuum of parental style, but single factors would vary systematically in their relative contribution across age. For example, the role of "child" characteristics seems to be of greatest importance before youngsters reach shool age or after they reach adolescence, although there is certainly some role, albeit smaller, when children are of elementary school age.

Such an argument suggests that there should be some generality of findings on the etiology of maltreatment across all ages. Factors that have a role at one age should also have a role when children are either younger or older. The relative importance of these identified factors, however, will depend upon the developmental level of the child, the maturity of the parents, and the life stage of the family.

THE MODEL OF EFFECTS

The adequate investigation of parenting from a primarily economic ecological perspective requires the use of a framework that can integrate the many relevant factors into a coherent and meaningful scheme. Such a scheme is provided by Moen *et al.* (1981) in the framework they proposed for exploring the processes by which macrolevel economic changes (i.e., changes on the level of government and other major social institutions) have their impact on family functioning. Their approach involves a series of progressive shifts in focus, from the level of social, economic, and political institutions to single families, to the individuals within that family, and finally, back to the level of family functioning again. The framework is diagrammed in Fig. 9.1.

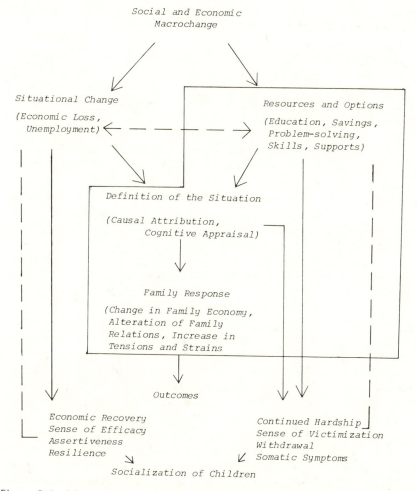

Figure 9.1. Moen, Kain, and Elder's (1981) model for the process of socio-economic influences on the family.

This ecological framework consists of six independent but interrelated sets of factors: (1) Social and economic macrochange; (2) situational change; (3) resources and options; (4) definition of the situation; (5) family response; and (6) outcomes (culminating in the socialization of children). For the purposes of this discussion, only that portion of the framework dealing with more static individual and family variables, that is, categories three through five (set off in Fig. 9.1), will be addressed.

In constructing this framework, Moen and her colleagues aimed at greater understanding of relationships found in research between socioeconomic conditions and family functioning by mapping out likely *processes of influence*. Although the model expressly examines the impact of major social and familial economic *changes*, we assume here that the same pattern of relations characterize more static or unchanging socioeconomic influences. Thus, rather than emphasizing the dynamics of resource availability and family adaptations and responses during a period of parental unemployment (i.e., situational change), the focus in the present analysis is on the dynamics of parental reactions to the current pattern of resources and perceived stresses.

One of the salient features that the model brings to the topic in question is an emphasis on "the role of adaptive responses as mediating linkages between economic realities and their consequences for children" (p. 9). These responses are indicated by the categories of definition of the situation and family response. Clearly, subjective assessments by the individual or the family of events or circumstances impinging on family functioning are considered to be instrumental in determining both the parental reactions and, ultimately, the family outcome.

It is hardly necessary to argue the fact that individuals perceive, react, and respond to similar or even identical environmental conditions in quite different, idiosyncratic ways. W. I. Thomas' (Thomas and Thomas, 1928) oft-quoted observation that "if men define situations as real, they are real in their consequences" bears testimony to the importance of this subjectivity. The literature on locus of control serves as one example of the widespread implications that differing perspectives have for individual functioning. When one feels that events and circumstances are beyond personal control, attitudes and actions, including those of a parent, are altered (Bugental et al., 1980; Mondell and Tyler, 1981). Similarly, the impact of socioeconomic hardship—an "incomplete" education, a low-status job, a deficient income, poor health, an overdemanding schedule—is postulated in the Moen et al. model to undermine parenting through the subjective stress it creates.

This characteristic of the framework has major implications for an understanding of the more immediate ("proximal") determinants of parental functioning. More specifically, whereas resources and options are seen to exert a direct effect on both the definition of the situation and family outcomes, their effect on the family response (i.e., parenting) is mediated by individual and/or family perceptions and assessments (i.e., the subjective manner in which parents or family define their circumstances. In consequence, a mere enumeration of the social and economic conditions that confront parents during the child-rearing years is insufficient for predicting qualitative differences in parenting. Beyond the immediate contribution of parental psychological resources and child characteristics are the subjective interpretations and reactions of parents toward the role of their environment as a supportive or stressful context for parenting.

Evidence for the Model

Scattered data attest to such a higher order effect in both abusive and nonabusive parenting outcomes. Garbarino and Crouter (1978) cite preliminary results from a pilot study by Bronfenbrenner suggesting a relationship between *perceived* stresses and supports and, among other things, parental attitudes toward their children and the overall level of conflict in the home (family response classifications). From their own data concerning parental perceptions about the supportive role of neighborhoods, the same authors go on to describe perceptions as "potentially important factors to consider in studying the human ecology of child maltreatment" (p. 610). Sociographic areas comparable in terms of social and economic structure and resources deviated from expected rates of child maltreatment as a function of the positive affect expressed about life in that area (Garbarino and Sherman, 1980).

In a study by Colletta (1979), maternal restrictiveness and punitiveness were correlated with reports of overall support from spouse, kin, and friends in three distinct socioeconomic family contexts—low- and moderate-income single parents and two-parent households. Crnic and his colleagues (1983) clarified the relationship between support/stress and parenting by presenting evidence that, again, satisfaction with the support received from "intimate" social contacts (spouse, relatives, and close friends), rather than more objective measures of amount or quality of support received, predicted child-rearing attitudes, and affective responding in mother–infant interactions. In confirmation of the pathway between socioeconomic resources and parental responses diagrammed in the Moen et al. framework, Crnic et al. concluded that: "It may well be that the perceived satisfaction with support available is as crucial . . . [as] the presence of support per se" (p. 4).

Within the realm of employment, further confirmation of the mediational role of subjective factors is provided. Child-rearing attitudes and practices can be predicted from both paternal (Kemper and Reichler, 1976) and maternal (Yarrow et al., 1962) satisfaction with employment. Yarrow et al. asserted that:

> Mothers' employment status is not related to childrearing characteristics. The data, however, support the hypothesis that mothers' fulfillments or frustrations in non-mother roles are related to childrearing. When mothers' motivations regarding working are taken into account, the non-working mothers who are dissatisfied with not working (who want to work, but out of a feeling of "duty" do not work) show the greatest problems in childrearing (p. 137).

Their "problems" encompass: control of their children, parental confidence, satisfaction with the parent–child relationship, and summary scores of parental "adequacy."

Pleck (1981) reported employed wives' satisfaction with their husbands' participation in housework/childcare to have a substantially greater correlation with their individual and/or family adjustment than the actual labor contribution made by husbands. Similarly, Straus and his colleagues (1980) cite husbands' dissatisfaction with the family's standard of living to be one of the nine best predictors of child abuse by mothers. It is noteworthy that no other strictly economic variable (i.e., income or unemployment) was a strong enough predictor, in and of itself, to be included on this list.

From a small but intensive examination of work influences on family life, Piotrkowski (1979) elucidated three separate carryover effects of work: positive or negative "spillover" and energy deficit. She then went on to make a "convincing argument that work experience is brought into the family via the worker-parent's emotional state, which partially determines the person's availability to family members, especially children" (Bronfenbrenner and Crouter, 1982, p. 65). This allusion to intervening individual variables can be elaborated on briefly but meaningfully in the context of parental psychological resources.

The evidence summarized suggests that individual reactions to objective socioeconomic conditions mediate the amount of stress experienced. One could surmise, therefore, that there exist parental or familial psychological characteristics that act to exacerbate or ameliorate the occurrence of such stress. In fact, several investigators have incorporated into their studies of parenting a construct labelled "coping style."

Mondell and Tyler (1981) include in their definition of the competent parent, "an active, planful, invested coping style including high initiative, goal-setting, forbearance, and a capacity to build from both success and failure" (pp. 73–74). Olson et al. (1978) describe a comparable family characteristic, termed "family adaptability," which they assess through a parental self-report scale. Common to both constructs is the capacity to adapt to and thus to cope with whatever opportunities and/or adversities are encountered in daily life. Such a quality would likely facilitate functioning in any context, although its effects would be most apparent when social or economic conditions challenge personal efficacy.

Some substantiation of this is provided in a study by Colletta and Gregg (1981) investigating the relationship between social support and stress. These researchers discerned an association between coping style (use of direct action as a method of coping) and support reportedly received from spouse, relatives, and friends. Their data attest to the likelihood that this type of characteristic serves as a personal resource for parents, perhaps prompting them to seek out and utilize social resources within the family and within the community. Certainly, it might be expected to influence how parents interpret circumstances or events and how they respond to them.

To complete this consideration of subjective perceptions, we need only concede a point made by Kadushin and Martin (1981) in their analysis of the role child behavior plays as a catalyst for abusive parenting:

> To do further justice to the complexity of the problem, it should be recognized that the child's behavior is objectively neutral. It is the *parents' perception* of the behavior, and their attitude toward the behavior, which define it, for them, as aversive or not, and which then determines their feelings in response (pp. 255–256, emphasis added).

Subjective interpretations apparently mediate more than one of the pathways between parenting and its proximal determinants. Certainly, it is evident that there is an important role for subjective experience in the causal sequence linking the socioeconomic context with abusive and nonabusive parenting. Whether or not Moen et al.'s (1981) framework will help to elucidate this role remains to be tested.

Application of the Model

In order to explore in depth the socioeconomic ecology of parenting as it is assessed by ratings of competent or maladaptive parental practices, the Family Interaction Project data set was examined from the perspective of Moen et al.'s (1981) framework. In the following paragraphs, we specify the particular variables used to represent each of the three relevant categories in the framework: (1) resources and options; (2) definition of the situation; and (3) family response.

Resources and Options. These are defined by Moen and her colleagues as the economic, social, and psychological resources that each family (or family member) brings to the situation. Examples include education, savings, problem-solving skills, and emotional and instrumental supports. For the purpose of our analyses, and on the basis of previous research, this

category was composed initially of the following socioeconomic characteristics demonstrated or hypothesized to be related to parenting—competent
or dysfunctional: (a) parental education; (b) parental occupational status; (c)
family income (per capita); (d) physical health; (e) social network strength;
and (f) family adaptability.

Definition of the Situation. This aspect of the framework addresses the
"causal attributions" or "cognitive appraisals" that family members make in
experiencing their social and economic circumstances. We must note here
that any comprehensive examination of the role that economic factors play
in the ecology and etiology of parental functioning should take into account
the economy of the home as well as that of the marketplace. Economic role
behavior and family role behavior, linked closely across home and work
place (Bronfenbrenner and Crouter, 1982; Engerman, 1978; Pleck, 1981)
are presumably even more tightly interwoven across different home activities, including parenting. This implies subjective assessment of both work
life and home life for a complete "definition" of the economic situation.

Pertinent to this discussion are results that suggest that such factors as
socioeconomic demands on the mother *at home* and at work (Garbarino,
1976), perceived assistance in childcare (Zur-Spiro and Longfellow, 1981),
maternal satisfaction with husband's housework/childcare role (Pleck,
1981), the division of labor across work places (Straus *et al.*, 1980), and the
division of power within the family (Allen and Straus, 1979) are influential
contributors to family adjustment, family violence, and/or the quality of
parenting.

Considerations of the home economy can also be applied, in reverse, to
underscore the potential importance of nonlabor activities in the home for
quality of parenting. Given the large and growing proportion of dual-earning
parents, it is reasonable to expect that socioeconomic demands exert some
of their impact through the leisure time available to parents and family. Van
Meter and Agronow (1982) point out that: "If the non-work aspects of life
are regarded as potential forces in alleviating accumulated stress, then the
curtailment of these roles may be seen as further frustrating, hence, possibly
stressful" (p. 131). As a result, both parent–child relations and parenting per
se may suffer when leisure time spent with children is restricted inordinately
or is used as double time for accomplishing necessary household tasks.
Quantity *and* quality of time spent with one's children are likely to be
impaired when the personal resources of parents are taxed by the dual
demands of job and home.

As indicated from this discussion, the economic "situation" ought to
encompass the work places of both home and job (if outside the home). To
this end, definition of the situation consisted here of: (1) Economic family
role satisfaction; and (2) job role satisfaction. In turn, each was further

subdivided into two classes of attitudes/responses, partly as a function of the availability of detailed information from the data set. Economic family role satisfaction was assessed as (a) satisfaction with household assistance and the division of labor; and (b) satisfaction with family/leisure time. Job role satisfaction was conceptualized as (a) satisfaction with the family income; and (b) satisfaction with work. It was reasoned that these variables would act in a complementary fashion to convey an adequate and reasonably accurate portrait of how family members perceive their socioeconomic circumstances.

Family Response. Examples that Moen *et al.* (1981) used to illustrate this category included changes in the family economy, alteration of family relations, and an increase in tensions and strains. Strain originating from economic factors may be expressed in the marital relationship as well as the parent–child relationship, the latter being both a direct and indirect outcome of parenting practices. Child abuse, in particular, was cited as one potential response to perceived economic difficulties: "Whether expressed through contentiousness in marriage or along other paths, economic pressures qualify as a paramount factor in child abuse" (p. 31). Although the authors note the ambiguity in the causal direction of this relationship—"It is not clear whether the behavior of abusive parents (indirectly) causes or is caused by worklife instability" (p. 31)—their conviction of an important link between socioeconomic stresses on the family and the incidence of child abuse is apparent.

The decision to use qualitative differences in the "adaptiveness" of parenting as the family response is then particularly apt. Since the original study was designed as an investigation of adolescent maltreatment, the range in assessments of parental behavior covers the broadest continuum—from perceived competence to suspected abuse. The design of the study appears, for the most part, to complement this model empirically. However, it is important to be aware that the focus in Moen *et al.*'s framework is on economic changes, so that sudden unemployment, rather than chronically low socioeconomic status or specific day-to-day resource impoverishment, receives greater attention and plays a more significant role in their scheme. Nevertheless, as pointed out previously, it is hypothesized here that the same *process of influence* operates to some extent in both cases. Figure 9.2 portrays the structural model that results from the incorporation of all elements relevant to the present analysis.

Limitations in Using the Model

Theoretical limitations in the use and operationalization of this framework must be acknowledged. Of primary importance is recognition of

Resources and Options

Maternal Education
Paternal Occupational Status
Per Capita Family Income
Family Health
Social Network Strength
Family Adaptability

↓

Definition of the Situation

| *Economic Family Role* | *Job Role* |
| *Satisfaction* | *Satisfaction* |

Division of Labor	*Income Satisfaction*
Adolescent Help	*Work Satisfaction*
Family/Leisure Time	

↓

Family Response

Continuum of Maladaptive Parenting

Figure 9.2. Empirical operationalization of the structural relations defined in the Moen, Kain, and Elder model (1981).

the fact that socioeconomic correlates represent only one subset of factors thought to have an impact on parenting in general and the incidence of child maltreatment in particular. Other factors, for instance those classified loosely under the rubric of parental ontogenetic development (Burgess, 1980), would include psychological characteristics of the parents, their attitudes toward child rearing, and their own history of nurturance or deprivation during childhood.

Similarly, research (Kadushin and Martin, 1981; see also Burgess, 1979) indicates that characteristics of the children themselves may place them at risk for maltreatment. Examples include prematurity, physical or mental handicap, "acting out," or simply being fussy and difficult to manage. These same characteristics seem likely to influence all styles of parenting, regardless of the relative position on the continuum of caretaking quality.

Related to this issue is the problem of possible third variable explanations responsible for correlations between economic factors and parenting outcomes. Although there are as yet no data relating parental or familial problem-solving skills to child maltreatment, the possibility that social competence—as a parent, as a spouse, or even a worker—may mediate or perhaps underlie the interrelationships between ecological factors and abusive parenting has been noted (Garbarino, 1977; Richardson et al., 1983). A lack of social competence could prompt both economic difficulties through poor work relations, impoverished social networks through poor social relations, and dysfunctional parenting through problems (now exacerbated) in the role of caregiver. However, to the extent that social and economic conditions created, in part, by the parents themselves would still have important feedback effects on these parents and, therefore, would continue to influence parenting (in extreme cases, maltreatment), there remains important value in the analyses described here. This value derives from the effort to begin charting potential pathways—both direct effects and effects mediated by subjective experiences of stress—to link the more global (and "distal") impact of socioeconomic resources with the quality of parental functioning. Understanding the *processes* by which ecological factors influence family functioning must inevitably remain a valuable endeavor.

Hypotheses

The general purpose of the analyses described here is to begin exploring the processes that relate and/or mediate socioeconomic status and parenting. This goal is realized through the use of a revised and adapted version of Moen et al.'s framework, linking socioeconomic circumstances—or the economic ecology of families—to a continuum of parenting quality. It is essential, nevertheless, to formulate more focused hypotheses concerning specific relationships within the framework. Hence, on the basis of conceptual and empirical work on this topic, it was hypothesized that:

1. A variety of socioeconomic resources and options, while not necessarily interrelated, would directly influence how individual and family members perceive and experience their economic roles and circumstances within the family context. Resources and options (e.g., occupational status, family income, health, and social network strength) were hypothesized to exhibit a direct, positive relationship to the definition of the situation.

2. How positively family members experience their individual and familial economic situation was hypothesized, in turn, to bear an inverse relationship to the family response (i.e., the degree to which parenting was judged to be maladaptive to development). Economic family role satisfaction and job role satisfaction, however, need not show a strong interrelationship.

3. In addition to this mediated relationship, resources and options would further influence parental functioning through a direct, albeit more modest, association that is independent of the stress or support perceived by parents.

Providing an example of one possible family situation may aid in conceptualizing the interplay between each of the three relevant categories in the framework.

> Conceive of a family with poorly educated parents ($-$) who have a low, although not poverty-level income ($-$). The father is a blue-collar worker ($-$), the mother a housewife. Although the mother is dissatisfied with both the family income ($-$) and her status as a housewife (-), she is currently seeking some sort of low-status paid employment to supplement their income now that two of the three children are in school. She is pleased by both her husband's and children's (particularly the eldest's) efforts to contribute their share in the housework ($+$).
>
> As a result, in part, of their assistance, this mother has often had the opportunity to enjoy leisure time with her family or numerous friends ($+$). It is therefore not surprising that she sees her family as generally close-knit ($+$), despite inevitable quarrels between the children and occasional outbursts from her husband after a particularly draining work day.
>
> She has, however, often found the cramped living quarters where she spends much of her work and family time very irritating and has recently experienced an increase in arguments with her husband ($-$), who does not see the necessity of her search for employment outside the home—among other reasons, because they would have to pay a neighbor to care for their youngest child.
>
> Although this mother has always believed in the maxim "spare the rod and spoil the child," she finds herself more impatient with them recently and punishing them more harshly for minor infractions ($-$).

This example illustrates how socioeconomic conditions that are, in the balance, somewhat negative for this family might contribute to an outcome that would be rated as poor quality or mildly abusive parenting.

It could be conjectured, in this case, that gainful employment for the wife might stimulate positive perceptions about her (new) job role ($+$), eventually leading to a decline in parental arguments ($+$) as she finds herself with a higher threshold for family tensions and able to supplement family finances ($+$). In turn, her increased tolerance of the children's misbehavior might result in fewer and milder instances of physical punishment ($+$).

On the other hand, spiraling tension between this mother and her husband and children ($-$) and less time to devote to her friends ($-$), when she finds her manual labor job far more exhausting than she had anticipated ($-$), could escalate harsh disciplinary actions into a severely abusive situation ($-$).

METHODS

Sixty of the families participating in the Family Interaction Project, described in earlier chapters, provided data for the analyses described here. Both male ($N = 32$) and female ($N = 28$) preadolescents were included in these analyses, as were intact ($N = 51$) and stepfamilies ($N = 9$). There is evidence to indicate that a step relationship between parent and child may be at particular risk for becoming abusive (see Burgess and Garbarino, 1983; Daly and Wilson, 1981). However, the economic emphasis of this investigation did not warrant exclusion of these families for what are primarily psychosocial differences. Economic hardship is *not* an identifying characteristic of stepfamilies.

For the present investigation, the unit of analysis was the individual family member—more specifically, the mother. Due to the subjective component of the framework (i.e., the definition of the situation), employing the family as the unit of analysis would have introduced complicated averaging or discrepancy techniques for combining individual data that were deemed beyond the scope of this inquiry and problematic in interpretation.

Mothers were selected as the target subjects for a number of reasons. In the first place, research has demonstrated repeatedly a parental sex difference in rates of child maltreatment. Mothers are significantly more likely than fathers to be the perpetrators of abuse (Straus *et al.*, 1980), almost certainly because they also tend to have primary responsibility for the care of their children. Patterson's (1980) work indicates not only that mothers engage in the highest frequency of interactions with their children, but also receive the highest number of negative or aversive behaviors directed toward them.

Although this pattern is reversed during the adolescent years, the change appears to be a consequence of the rapid increase in cases of sexual maltreatment by fathers, rather than a decrease in abusive encounters between mothers and children. The fact that mothers are still charged with the greater proportion of care for their (now) adolescent offspring allows ample opportunity to practice whatever quality of parenting mothers have adopted.

The primary role that mothers continue to play in the lives of their young teenagers provides a second rationale for employing mothers as the unit of analysis, since they, in the traditional sense, continue to represent "family." Finally, the current trend for women to join the labor force offers a valuable opportunity to examine maternal (paid) employment within this economic framework as a potential ecological contrast to exclusive (unpaid) work in the home. Needless to say, a similar analysis for fathers, allowing comparisons across gender, could serve as a particularly meaningful contrast study.

Terms and Transformations

The measures described here are those providing the data for the present analysis. Description of measures will proceed according to the category and construct being examined. However, before embarking on a detailed explanation of how the constructs were operationalized, it would be helpful to distinguish the various levels of data classification used here.

At the broadest level of classification are the three theoretical *categories* of the Moen *et al.* model: resources and options, definition of the situation, and family response. Each contains one or more *factors* or variables, including variables that have been summed arithmetically. Thus, resources and options include factors of income, health, and social network but also SES (a combination variable). Many of these factors, in turn, consist of two or more (questionnaire) *items*. In the case of mother's satisfaction with her job role, the factor of work satisfaction is a summary score formed from two items on the demographics questionnaire. In the following section, the individual items chosen to represent each of the relevant factors are outlined in detail.

To allow analysis of relationships between continuous and categorical variables, all ordinal data were transformed to a uniform scale ranging from 1 (indicating a definite stress) to 9 (indicating a definite support). As a consequence of this procedure, item values could be summed within categories to obtain single, comparable factor scores in which each item was weighted equally. This sum then represents the extent to which the factor is considered a stress (low score) or support (high score) for individual or family functioning.

In addition, to conduct analyses between categories (e.g., resources and options, definition of the situation), variables that exhibited significant patterns of interrelationship were standardized and summed to create single combination scores. SES, described in detail later, represents one such combination score. Having clarified these several points, let us consider how each construct was operationalized.

Category and Factor Measures

Resources and Options. Education (highest grade attained in school) and occupational status (designated as white collar or blue collar in accordance with the Hollingshead Scale, 1967) are two of the three traditional characteristics used to classify families according to SES. Since a large proportion of mothers were not employed outside the home and since occupational status traditionally represents the status of *paternal* employment, the father's occupation was used as the sole basis for determining occupational status. In contrast, *maternal* education was considered the more relevant measure of parental formal schooling, for one reason because paternal occupation would automatically tend to reflect father's education. More importantly, maternal attitudes and maternal perceptions, presumably influenced more by maternal than paternal education, were the focus of the study.

Family income, family health, and (maternal) social network strength were derived from the *Family Interview Questionnaire*, described in earlier chapters. Reports of family income were divided by the number of family members to provide measures of per capita income, used in all analyses. Social network strength was evaluated in terms of size and "interconnectedness" (i.e., the percentage of members who know and are known to each other). These two characteristics have been identified as potentially important factors in the provision of support by the social network (Hirsch, 1979; Mitchell and Trickett, 1980). Having a greater number of friends, kin, and co-workers who have contact, not only with oneself, but also with each other, may increase the social and psychological functions of that network.

Finally, family adaptability was assessed by the Adaptability Scale from the *Family Adaptability and Cohesion Scales* (FACES) (Olson *et al.*, 1978). It should be noted here and elsewhere that unless otherwise specified, all questionnaires and interviews were those completed by the mother.

Definition of the Situation. Three items from the Roles subscale of the FACES were used to measure satisfaction with the division of labor. These items are as follows:

FACES
31. No one in our family seems to be able to keep track of what their duties are.
69. In our family, everyone shares responsibilities.
87. It seems as if males and females never do the same chores in our family.

In addition, two items from the Schwartz–Getter *Interparental Conflict Scale* (Schwartz and Zuroff, 1979) were used separately to complete both this measure of satisfaction with the division of labor and that of satisfaction with help from the adolescent (described below). This scale is an assessment by the adolescent of the frequency of parental arguments on a variety of topics.

Obviously, these are not measures of maternal satisfaction per se. They do provide some indication, however, of *parental* dissatisfaction (either mother's or father's) with the current contribution of household labor made by the adolescent. In this sense, they do tap theoretically relevant aspects of the definition of the situation, although the inconsistency of the viewpoint (paternal versus maternal) makes strictly maternal interpretations difficult. The two relevant items are:

IPC
32. (Conflicts about) spouse's degree of involvement with the children (used in the factor of division of labor).
22. (Conflicts about) children's duties and responsibilities (used in the factor of adolescent help).

A single item from the *Child Behavior Profile* (Achenbach, 1979) served in conjunction with the IPC item (no. 22) to define satisfaction with adolescent help. The pertinent item appears below:

Child Behavior Profile
IV. Please list any jobs or chores your child has . . . compared to other children of the same age. *How well does he/she carry them out?*

Qualitative rating of the adolescent's assistance (below average, average, or above average) was then combined with conflicts over children's duties and responsibilities as the measure of maternal satisfaction. Responses on all of the above items were transformed to the uniform scale described earlier and summed appropriately to create the two factors of satisfaction with the division of labor and satisfaction with adolescent help.

Family/leisure time was measured by responses on two items of the Demographics Interview. These are listed below:

Demographics
3.01 How much time do you feel you have to do things you would like to do?
3.05 Overall rating: Taking everything into account, how would you rate your chances to enjoy things together?

Responses were already scaled from 1 to 9 and therefore simply summed to create the time factor.

Job-Role Satisfaction. A single scalar item from the Demographics assessed income satisfaction. The item was worded as follows:

Demographics
4.03 Overall rating: In general, how would you rate the money situation?

Work satisfaction, the final component of the definition of the situation, was measured by two items from the Demographics Interview, again in terms of a transformed and summed score. The score consisted of the following items:

Demographics
9E. (Indicate how often you) got so tense at work that you "blew up."
9F. (Indicate how often you) wanted to change jobs.

Family Response. Judgments about the degree to which a given family was characterized by competent versus maladaptive parenting were based on two separate measures—vignette and abuse ratings. The advantage of using the vignettes was the fact that they were completed by multiple sources: each of the three family members as well as the three observers (see Appendix I).

Vignettes were collapsed into three general categories—high-quality, low-quality, and abusive parenting—on the basis of family and interviewer response agreement and subjective evaluations of meaningful distinctions between characterizations of parenting. Vignettes no. 7, no. 8, and no. 9 represent high-quality parenting—parenting that appears highly supportive of child and adolescent well-being and that, simultaneously, is viewed as conducive to future adaptation through its promotion of psychological health and social competence. Vignettes no. 2, no. 5, and no. 6 were selected to represent more marginal, "low-quality" parenting—parenting that, if not actively abusive, is nevertheless maladaptive to some degree due primarily to an inappropriate amount of parental control (either too excessive or too permissive). Vignettes no. 1, no. 3, and no. 4, on the other hand, represent more unambiguously maladaptive, and even abusive, parental practices— creation of a home environment in which children and adolescents are confronted with continual argument or criticism, with frequent or harsh punishment, or with parental neglect.

Although the three "maladaptive parenting" vignettes were carefully phrased to avoid being outrightly abusive descriptions, relative to the other vignettes, the kind of parenting they portray is quite clear. For reasons of social desirability, it was felt that more explicitly abusive characterizations should be avoided. Nonetheless, in each of these vignettes, the implication is one of parents who not only refrain from promoting the well-being of youth but who also actively undermine present or future competency through overt or covert psychological denigration. "You are a bad person always in need of punishment," "Your views and opinions aren't worth my respect," and "You aren't worth my concern" are some of the underlying sentiments designed to be captured by these descriptions. The threat that each of these represents for the well functioning of children, of youth, and of future adults is obvious.

Primary emphasis in terms of vignette classification was on those choices made by adolescents and by interviewers. Whereas parents might be heavily influenced by social desirability in making their selection, adolescents were thought to be less so, with "less to lose" by frankness in their (confidential) responses to the interviewer. On an anecdotal level, this seemed to be the case, for abusive encounters between parent and adolescent were occasionally reported by the adolescent but, at best, only alluded to by parents. This was the situation for one family in which the father served time in prison for the sexual mistreatment of his daughter (reported by this teenager) but referred only to the period of internment rather than the cause for internment; and in another, where questionable discipline strategies described as "strict" by parents were detailed only by the adolescent. For this reason, adolescent and interviewer choices were given equal weighting before summing to obtain the global vignette rating.

The second global rating (Appendix II) consists of three qualitatively distinct scales of abusive parenting: (1) emotional abuse—exemplified by humiliation, extreme inconsistency, "put downs," parental withdrawal of love; (2) physical abuse—examples of which include hitting, slapping, punching, striking with an object, and (3) developmentally damaging behaviors—including extreme restrictiveness, continuing to treat the developing adolescent as a child, extreme parental control, and other related behaviors. Since these abuse ratings were already on a uniform scale, they were simply summed across scales and across observers to obtain the general rating of abuse.

Limitations of Measurement

It is quite clear that the majority of measures comprising the present investigation are of uncertain reliability and validity. Use of individual or, at best, small subsets of items from various instruments precludes knowledge about psychometric quality of the data. Although this is unfortunate, it does not automatically invalidate the data. In some respects, combinations of items from a variety of instruments represent a more conservative test of the hypotheses, since different response sets or differential interpretations elicited by independent instruments would tend to minimize meaningful relationships of the kind outlined here between items from separate instruments. To whatever extent possible, reliability checks were conducted and variables that failed to demonstrate consistency were eliminated from analyses.

Validity issues naturally were also of concern. In general, however, the use of a model to provide relatively specific information about the nature and direction of a pattern of relationships that should obtain is one condition working to combat conclusions based on spurious relationships. Chance associations between two or more sets of items due to factors *not* relevant in this analysis should not tend to hold up when broader conceptualizations are examined.

It must be emphasized that strictly correlational data such as these do not imply causality. Agreement between empirical patterns of relations and theoretical constructions of the phenomenon are necessary but not sufficient evidence for the validity of the model. Causal relations are demonstrated only through manipulation of relevant, and control of irrelevant, variables designated as such by a model. As a matter of fact, even within the framework, there is some provision made for the possibility of reciprocal effects (e.g., outcomes are equipped with a feedback loop to resources and options).

The correlational analyses described here, however, elucidate the direction for future research—what questions will be asked and how they will be phrased—by suggesting relationships and/or effects that have only been alluded to up until now. They will also furnish the basis for beginning to examine the empirical and heuristic value of the framework proposed by Moen et al. (1981) as a means for linking the socioeconomic ecology of families, their subjective perceptions of the situation, and the outcomes that transpire. The successful implementation of this model would represent a significant advance in the current understanding of the ecological process culminating in dysfunctional or maladaptive versus competent patterns of child rearing.

ANALYSIS AND RESULTS

Category Construction

To whatever extent possible, variables considered for inclusion in any category of the model were assessed in terms of their reliability and validity. Since the first category, resources and options, is conceptualized as the objective social and economic conditions in which family life is embedded, the psychometric property of greatest importance for variables belonging to this category is reliability of measurement. Whenever feasible, comparison of maternal and paternal responses regarding each of the factors of interest provided some indication of the reliability of these data.

Variables with moderate to strong agreement between parents included information about mothers' jobs (type of job and hours worked) and family income. There was little agreement between parental reports of the number of family illnesses experienced since the birth of the adolescent. This is not surprising, given the well-documented inaccuracy of long-term retrospective data. It may also be a consequence of the fact that mothers were reported, by and large, to have provided primary care for nonhospitalized child illnesses. It is likely that recall is, in part, a function of personal involvement at the time of illness. For this reason, maternal reports were selected as the most accurate estimates of family illness for the purpose of analysis.

Two factors were eliminated from analyses due to psychometric weaknesses. These were the FACES Family Adaptability Scale and maternal social network strength. Parental agreement about family adaptability was quite modest ($r = 0.27$, $p < .05$), indicating that it was not an especially objective assessment of the construct. Social network strength exhibited few meaningful relationships to any factors within the same category or to the family response outcome measures. The poor associative and predictive value of this variable does not by any means imply that the construct of social network is unimportant within this model. Rather, it suggests that the relatively undifferentiated measure of social network "strength" as the size and "interconnectedness" of the network does not effectively capture the network's role here as a support or a stress for parenting. More detailed inquiry into the emotional or instrumental role of network members and maternal satisfaction with this role might well prove a meaningful variable within the model.

Interrelations between those variables retained in the category of resources and options identified a common "socioeconomic status" factor consisting of maternal education, paternal occupational status, and per capita family income. These related variables were combined consequently to form a single SES factor. In final analyses, then, two factors represented the category of resources and options: socioeconomic status and family health.

A brief aside regarding parental education—what we expected to find and what we actually did find—merits attention here. A number of studies have tended to support the proposition that the less education parents have, the more likely they are to maltreat their children (Egeland and Brunnquell, 1979; Garbarino, 1976). Straus and his colleagues (1980), on the other hand, discovered a curvilinear relationship, with a moderate amount of education (completion of high school) most highly associated with both spouse and child abuse. The least violence was reported among parents who had not completed grammar school or who had some college education. These researchers argue that attainment of the average educational level—completion of some or all of high school—does not provide Americans with a proportionate advantage in the labor market. This factor may create frustration and stress for such parents who "still find themselves cut off from high status, well-paying professional jobs" (Straus et al., 1980, p. 147).

Data from Garbarino and Sherman's (1980) analysis of abuse across neighborhoods bears further testimony to this hypothesized effect. "High-" and "low-risk" abusive neighborhoods, matched for socioeconomic status and ethnicity, differed in the expected direction as a function of education and occupation. Areas at high risk for abuse had a lower percentage of individuals in "professional/managerial" occupations but *more* high school graduates. These data certainly suggest that a curvilinear relationship should be observed in a parenting study with a wide range of parental school achievement.

The expected relationship was not, in fact, found in the present investigation, although it may well be an accurate portrait of parental effects. Due to the unusually high level of education among mothers in this sample, only the upper portion of the education-parenting curve is relevant here. Some or all of high school was the *lowest* level of formal education reported by these mothers, and in no case was grade school the terminal educational achievement. Hence, the finding that a grade school (versus high school) education results in lower levels of maladaptive parenting was beyond the demographic confines of the study. Instead, education and parenting were related in the manner defined by the upper portion of the curve; that is, the higher the educational attainment of mothers, the lower was the rating of maladaptive parenting ($r = 0.32$, $p < .05$).

Definition of the Situation. Of the two subcategories that comprise the definition of the situation—job and economic family role satisfaction—the latter proved more robust in its operationalization. Contributing items showed some nonzero associations, and the factors they represented were related within the category.

Among the three factors comprising economic family role satisfaction, evaluations of adolescent help and division of labor were positively and reliably correlated. Consequently, the two were standardized and summed to create a more general factor of family assistance. The factor of family/leisure time, although not related to either of these variables, was correlated with mothers' desire to change the division of duties with their husbands. For all subsequent analyses, then, the subcategory of economic family role satisfaction was operationalized as two factors: a four-item measure of family assistance and a two-item measure of family/leisure time.

In contrast, only three items were utilized initially to create the job role satisfaction factors. Unfortunately, there was not only a lack of agreement between maternal ratings of job and income satisfaction, but the former variable appeared to be singularly unilluminating in its relationships both within and beyond the category of definition of the situation. As was the case with the social network measure, ineffective operationalization rather than theoretical weakness might have been responsible for its failure to function within the empirical model. In view of a variety of internal and external validity problems, the factor of work satisfaction was also eliminated from analyses. Thus, the three items originally representing the category of job satisfaction were reduced to a single rating of satisfaction with the family income.

Family Response. Both the abuse rating scales and the family vignettes have been described in earlier chapters. Initially, abuse scales and vignette classifications were considered separately as potential outcome measures for the present analyses. However, upon examination, these proved to be highly related and to exhibit similar patterns of relationships with the measure used to assess validity, as well as in a number of preliminary analyses. Consequently, the two were combined by standardizing and summing abuse and vignette scores to form a single rating of maladaptive parenting.

Interrater reliability was moderate (ranging from 0.43 to 0.60 on the abuse scales and 0.43 to 0.49 on the vignette classifications, depending on the family member interviewed). Validity was examined by relating both family response measures with two scales from the *Cornell Parent Behavior Description* (Devereux et al., 1969; Devereux et al., 1962). Both the abuse and vignette ratings correlated significantly and in the expected direction with the discipline scale. On the other hand, only the abuse rating reliably predicted scores on the support scale. Nevertheless, these results are in keeping with the nature of the parental ratings, which were designed to tap potentially injurious parenting rather than the degree of competency, sensitivity, and warmth exhibited by parents.

In sum, despite the fact that both outcome measures rely on the subjective judgments of interviewers and adolescents, there is some degree of reliability and validity inherent in each. Together they represent a fairly comprehensive, if subjective, portrait of parenting that appears to a greater or lesser degree at risk for thwarting the developmental competence of young adolescents.

Assessing the Model

Categorical Relationships. Factors derived from the model were entered into two multiple regressions. In both cases, the combined rating of maladaptive parenting (i.e., the abuse and vignette ratings) was the variable we were trying to predict. Factors in the first regression were entered in the causal sequence indicated by the model. Thus, socioeconomic status, family health, (satisfaction with) family assistance, family/leisure time, and income satisfaction were entered in that order. Results are summarized in Table 9.1. As can be seen from this table, our efforts to predict ratings of maladaptive

Table 9.1. Socioeconomic Correlates of Maladaptive Parenting in 60 Families Containing an Adolescent

Correlate	Maladaptive parenting
1. Socioeconomic status	$r = 0.32$
2. 1 + family health	$R = 0.37$
3. 1 + 2 + family assistance	$R = 0.56$
4. 1 + 2 + 3 + family/leisure time	$R = 0.74$
5. 1 + 2 + 3 + 4 + income satisfaction	$R = 0.74$

Table 9.2. Socioeconomic Correlates of Maladaptive Parenting in 60 Families Containing an Adolescent Beginning with Subjective Variables

Correlate	Maladaptive parenting
1. Family assistance	$r = 0.50$
2. 1 + family/leisure time	$R = 0.70$
3. 1 + 2 + income satisfaction	$R = 0.71$
4. 1 + 2 + 3 + socioeconomic status	$R = 0.73$
5. 1 + 2 + 3 + 4 + family health	$R = 0.74$

behavior were quite effective ($R = -0.74$). More importantly, the factors of SES, family assistance, and family/leisure time each made significant contributions to the prediction, with the factor of family health making a marginal contribution. Only income satisfaction, the last variable added to the equation, was not noticeably related to the outcome measure, once all the other variables had been controlled.

Importantly, when we first control for the effects of family assistance, family/leisure time, and income satisfaction, (definition of the situation factors) we find that neither socioeconomic status nor family health (resources and options) are helpful in our efforts to predict maladaptive parenting. Consistent with the previous results, income satisfaction remains largely irrelevant in our prediction. These findings are apparent from the second regression, the results of which appear in Table 9.2.

In terms of Moen *et al.*'s model, we see that by controlling for factors representing the definition of the situation, the resources and options that had seemed helpful in predicting parenting become essentially meaningless. In other words, resources and options appear to have their impact on the quality of parenting practiced *indirectly*, through their influence on how parents perceive their socioeconomic circumstances. The empirical results we obtain therefore support the model of causal influence that Moen and her colleagues proposed.

Simple, follow-up analyses provided us with some good ideas to explain why income satisfaction offered so little help and family health offered us more help than we expected in predicting maladaptive parenting. In the first case, we found that income satisfaction was significantly related to our family/leisure time factor. Because we always used the family/leisure time factor first as a predictor, there was little information that income satisfaction could add afterward. A possible explanation for the relationship between these two factors may rest in parental efforts to improve the family income. Parents (either mothers or fathers) who are dissatisfied with their income may spend longer or more intensive hours trying to advance in their occupation or working at extra employment. Obviously, this would infringe on time spent in family and leisure activities, more than it would on time spent carrying out routine household chores. Furthermore, dissatisfaction with income may act as a psychological stress that interferes with enjoyment of leisure activities.

We find it interesting that family health appears to bear some relationship to parenting (through definition of the situation factors) above and beyond its relationship to socioeconomic status. It seems probable that numerous health problems in the family would tend to be experienced as burdensome to household functioning and a drain on maternal energy (recall that mothers are the primary caregivers during family illness). The well-developed relationship between physical and/or mental handicap in children and their likelihood of being maltreated may be a relevant observation in this regard. Frequent family illness, particularly among children, may elicit less than optimal parenting behaviors. More detailed inquiry into the source of illness (i.e., the family member) and the nature of the health problems would probably provide some clue as to how family health has its impact.

Deviant Case Analysis. Figure 9.3 illustrates the distribution of actual parenting ratings received around the ratings that would be predicted using the data on resources and options and definition of the situation. Notice that a subset of families (indicated in the figure) deviate more than the others from the parenting ratings that we would predict knowing about their socioeconomic situation. In an effort to explain this deviation, we compared individual cases on a variety of potentially meaningful factors. Families whose actual parenting scores were substantially higher or lower from the scores we would predict were *not* systematically deviant on most of the measures we used to compare them. Whether the characteristic was family size, adolescent gender, mother's age at marriage, maternal social network strength, frequency of parental arguments, or number of adolescent behavior problems, there was no immediate pattern that might explain these discrepant scores.

One interesting pattern did, however, emerge. This pattern was related to the work status of mothers. Only 1 of the 7 mothers (14%) whose families scored unexpectedly *high* on maladaptive parenting worked part-time (30 hours or less per week). In contrast, 8 of the 10 mothers (80%) whose families scored *lower* than expected on maladaptive parenting were employed part-time. This same pattern of part-time employment held up when we considered the 12 most discrepant families in each direction (higher or lower than predicted parenting scores). Mothers from families rated unexpectedly high on maladaptive parenting either worked full-time (31 or more hours per week) or did not work outside the home. Mothers from

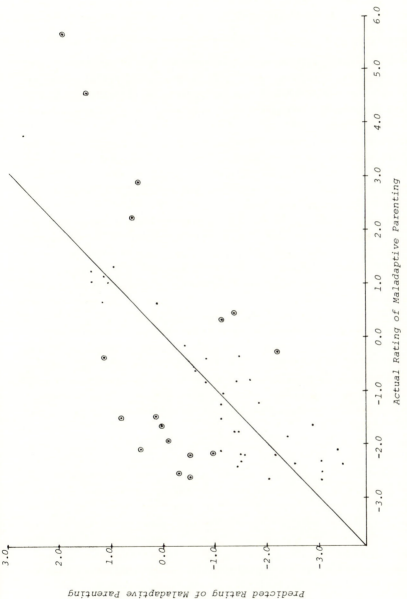

Figure 9.3. Actual and predicted ratings of maladaptive parenting in 53 families, based on the multiple regression equation of socioeconomic correlates (see Table 9.3). Dot, family rating; circled dot, discrepant family rating.

219

families rated unexpectedly low on maladaptive parenting, in contrast, almost invariably worked in a part-time capacity outside the home.

It seems, then, that employment status of mothers is a relevant factor not considered up to this point with respect to the model of the determinants of parenting. This finding certainly brings to mind the literature on familial effects of maternal employment. Indeed, it offers further, although limited, confirmation of the common observation that part-time maternal employment is the most beneficial employment status for the children and adolescents involved, particularly when those youngsters are male (see Bronfenbrenner and Crouter, 1982).

To pursue further the issues related to maternal employment, all families were classified into one of four groups, depending upon maternal employment status. Findings from this additional analysis and discussion of their implications for both these families and for the model as a whole are presented in the following section.

Contrasting Families by Mother's Employment. Families were classified into the four employment groups on the basis of the number of hours per week mothers worked in paid or voluntary employment outside the home. Divisions between groups represent natural breaks in the continuous distribution of hours mothers worked—spanning a range from 0 to 84 hours (in the case of one mother who worked in a family business). The nonemployed group consisted of 13 mothers who worked exclusively in nonpaid household labor. The low part-time group ($N = 14$) worked between 1 and 20 hours per week, the high part-time group ($N = 12$) worked between 21 and 30 hours, and the full-time group ($N = 21$) worked a minimum of 31 hours per week. Because there seemed to be no differences relevant to the model being used between families in which mothers worked as volunteers versus as wage-earners, these two groups were merged (in the low part-time category).

Group sample sizes were too low and variability too great in the parenting ratings to find significant differences between the employment groups with respect to scores on maladaptive parenting. However, there are a number of interesting relationships that distinguish these groups with respect to the factors examined in the model of effects. Rather than enumerating the several significant and many insignificant relationships, we feel that a brief descriptive paragraph on each group probably best captures the real and inferred dynamics distinguishing these employment groups.

No outside employment group (0 hours) ($N = 13$). These are somewhat larger families in which mothers are not employed but are still, typically college-educated. There are, in general, more family health problems reported, possibly due to the larger family size. Fathers' white-collar jobs have further to stretch financially, and the higher *all* components of socioeconomic status, the considerably more they are seen to help out at home.

Adolescents are considered more helpful when their mothers are better educated. Family assistance and family/leisure time are very highly correlated with the adaptiveness of parenting (the strongest relationships across all groups) and both factors are, on the average, rated highest by these mothers.

Ratings of parenting in these families are "middle of the road" relative to the other employment groups, with greater variability. There may well be more punishment noted due to the greater number of (young) children in these families.

Low part-time employment group (1–20 hours) (N = 14). White-collar, relatively well-paid fathers in this group are viewed as slightly more helpful when socioeconomic status is higher, particularly the family income. Adolescents, especially, are perceived to be more helpful when fathers' income and mothers' education are higher. Mothers do some work outside the home in a very obvious part-time capacity (sometimes simply a few hours per week of volunteer work) and, in general, they rate their families' help and leisure time quite highly. However, neither family assistance nor family/leisure time is significantly related to maladaptive parenting. Family health, instead, appears to play the important role here.

Maladaptive parenting ratings are lowest of all in this group, with less variability. Even when we control for perceived family assistance and family/leisure time, the higher the socioeconomic status, the less maladaptive the parenting. Thus, there seems to be a direct role for SES as an influence on parenting.

High part-time employment group (21–30 hours)(N = 12). There is a more even distribution of white- and blue-collar fathers in this employment group. Although mothers work closer to full-time hours, their education is slightly lower than that of mothers in other subgroups. On the other hand, health, family cohesion, and the marital relationship are described in better than average terms. Both family assistance and family/leisure time tend to be rated lower than in other work-status groups. Adolescents' help is largely unrelated to SES, whereas perceptions of fathers' contributions actually decrease with higher SES. This may be, after all, a preferable state of affairs, since their perceived assistance surprisingly predicts more maladaptive parenting. It is possible that mothers in this group are working out of economic necessity, and that the more their jobs monopolize their time and energy, the more fathers are forced to contribute to household labor (although maternal ratings suggest that fathers do not help enough). Thus, fathers' assistance may be more indicative of either overworked or role-conflicted mothers, not mothers who feel satisfied with the family roles.

Parenting is second-best, following the shorter part-time employment group, although these two groups look very different in background.

Full-time paid employment group (31–84 hours)(N = 21). Smaller, two-income families with full-time employed and relatively well-educated mothers comprise this group. The more advanced mother's education and the higher father's work status, the superior the rating of his assistance. However, the higher his status and the more money entering the household, the *poorer* the rating of the adolescent's contribution. With these opposing forces at work, socioeconomic status does not show a reliable relationship to family assistance. At the same time, however, family assistance and family/leisure time are both strongly predictive of less maladaptive parenting, perhaps partly because both appear to be somewhat lacking for these families. Here, too, is the one place where income satisfaction is also predictive of less maladaptive parenting.

Marital and familial arguments are more common among these families, and parenting is poorest, although there is much variability.

The Meaning of Part-Time Employment. It is quite obvious from the descriptions given here that these work status groups represent quite distinct sets of families, with different resources and options, different perceptions of the socioeconomic situation, and quite variable responses to each in terms of the adaptiveness of parental practices. Since the purpose of this study is not to compare maternal employment status but to understand how social and economic circumstances affect parenting, inferential statistical analyses were not conducted on these data. Instead, data were used to provide some notion of the different ways and different degrees in which resources and options, definition of the situation, and family responses might be interrelated. The contrast, for instance, between what appear to be economically well-off, low part-time families and more middle and lower middle class, high part-time families is considerable. In the one (low part-time), patterns of relationships seem generally to support the model used here. In the other (high part-time), an absence of predicted associations with parenting, and even reversals in some relationships, clearly set this group apart as somewhat unique in this sample, a conclusion supported by its demographic profile (see group descriptions).

In Table 9.3, we trace important factor relationships within each maternal employment group. By far, the greatest conformity to the Moen *et al.* model is exhibited by data collected from nonpaid mothers who spend their working hours in the home. Ironically, data on those mothers working full-time in paid employment also exhibit relationships that, by and large, agree with the pattern predicted by the model.

In contrast, there is only modest agreement with the model in the data collected from low part-time employed mothers and almost none in the data from families whose mothers work in more extensive part-time employment. Importantly, these latter two groups are also those receiving the lowest average ratings for maladaptive parenting (i.e., the highest quality parent-

Table 9.3. Selected Factor Relationships Exhibiting Discrepancies Across Maternal Employment Groups

		Maternal employment groups			
Factor relationships		Group No. 1 (no out- side work N = 13)	Group No. 2 (low part-time N = 14)	Group No. 3 (high part-time N = 12)	Group No. 4 (full time N = 21)
SES	Family assistance	0.79**	0.56*	−0.21	0.11
SES	Family/leisure time	0.39	−0.09	0.21	0.02
Family assistance	Maladaptive parenting	0.76**	0.23	0.20	0.63**
Leisure time	Maladaptive parenting	0.78**	0.24	0.21	0.61**
Health	Maladaptive parenting	0.38	0.72**	0.33	0.06

*p < .05.
**p < .01.

ing). Conclusions about the special benefits for parenting attached to the part-time work status of mothers would seem to depend upon an understanding of this situation.

From a more methodological viewpoint, we might suppose that the failure of these part-time employment groups to conform to the model is, in part, due to the nature of the parenting measure. The rating employed in this study assesses not so much parental competency as parental inadequacy. If the families of part-time employed mothers do, in fact, exhibit more adaptive parenting, then a measure of parental competency is likely to be a more discriminating outcome measure for picking up what may be relatively subtle differences in the quality of parenting practiced in these families.

There are other, equally plausible, hypotheses for the patterns exhibited by the different work-status groups—hypotheses that may coexist with methodological explanations. Primary among these is one focusing on the role of definition of the situation factors. It is noteworthy that family and job role factors play the greatest part among families with mothers who work full-time in the home or full-time in paid employment.

Mothers who have primary responsibility for household functioning to the exclusion of regular employment outside the home are likely to place considerable emphasis on the home labor participation they perceive among family members. Daily work life for these mothers requires pre-occupation with home and family, since home is both haven and sole work place for these individuals. When this is the case, family members assume more prominence in their roles as co-workers as well as kin, and their contribution to a smooth-running household has a correspondingly dual impact. Leisure time, too, is important for these mothers, who experience a more narrowly defined sphere of activities. Recreation with, versus services for, spouse and children represents a major flux in the day-to-day pattern of home activities. Notably, for this group only, family/leisure time is strongly related to perceived family assistance. Involvement in home life by family members may therefore be the more general construct being tapped for this set of families. Given the paramount role that home life presumably plays for these mothers, perceived involvement of family members would seem to be a psychological factor of great import to mothers. Family involvement may be interpreted by these mothers as recognition for the endless services they provide within the home.

It is easy to see that instrumental roles of family members would be important for full-time wage-earning mothers as well—for different reasons. Responsibility for household functioning may often become a ponderous burden on top of a full-time commitment to outside employment. For practical rather than purely interpersonal reasons, family household labor contributions would be integral to efficient household functioning. Mothers have no choice but to rely on the assistance of family members to get all the jobs done at home. One would also expect these mothers to place a high value on the amount of leisure time available—the chance to "enjoy things together as a family," as the Demographics Questionnaire phrases it. For both groups of families, division of labor and leisure time would represent salient issues in the day-to-day functioning of mothers.

Among mothers working part-time, this need not be so. For those working the fewest hours (i.e., 20 hours per week or less), employment may furnish the chance to diminish (although certainly not abolish) reliance on family for the psychological support that household assistance and family time together represent. The opportunity to interact regularly with others in the context of jointly carrying out services, to get away from home on a regular basis and interrupt the mundane schedule of household labor, to gain tangible reward for labor (gratitude for voluntary services, wages for paid services), and perhaps most importantly, to gain a sense of accomplishment for two jobs well done, may all be keys to greater emotional independence from home and family. Self-esteem is no longer exclusively bound up in the family setting, so the psychological support of family involvement no longer dominates the socioeconomic origins of dysfunctional parenting.

The process is perhaps only slightly different for mothers working in a high part-time capacity. These mothers probably are employed out of economic necessity—family income tends to be lower than that of all but the single-earner families, and paternal occupation is lowest in status. Maternal occupation—ranging from self-employment to secretary, from cafeteria worker to store clerk—suggests initiative on the part of mothers to supplement the family income by whatever means possible. This implies acquisition of a job but not a career. Furthermore, we should recall that household help from fathers *decreases* with SES, according to mothers, and is *positively* related to maladaptive parenting, but that family cohesion, the marital relationship, and health are all *highest* relative to other work-status groups. A tentative explanation rests in the personal efficacy that these mothers acquire by performing two essential roles simultaneously—not only providing a substantial portion of the family income but also carrying out all the duties and responsibilities of full-time motherhood. Because their hours of paid employment are not so extensive as those of a full-time wage-earner, family assistance may not have the same instrumental value that it has for mothers employed full time. At the same time, the commitment to a second job, with all that it entails both socially and psychologically, may continue to serve an important socioemotional function. In this way, we again hypothesize that part-time employment reduces the role of family assistance and family/leisure time in predicting maladaptive parenting.

Understanding and Expanding the Model

The many disparities revealed between the various work-status subgroups are persuasive testimony for the inclusion of maternal employment as a broad organizing factor within the category of definition of the situation. How mothers will respond to socioeconomic conditions—both subjectively (in terms of satisfaction and stress) and objectively (in terms of observable parental behavior)—is closely related to their involvement in the extrafamilial labor force. In addition, the potential importance of such factors as job investment and its counterpart, maternal role investment, illustrates some of the difficulty in selecting factors of relevance in any given practical application of the Moen *et al.* model.

As a qualification to this discussion, we should point out that definition of the situation factors assessed or implicated here are certainly not the only ones of theoretical and empirical relevance to this or any comparable ecological model of parenting. Although we expect that all resources and options must, eventually, be linked to parental functioning through more immediate, "proximal" factors, it is *not* expected that these will consist entirely of the sorts of socioeconomic factors described in this model as the definition of the situation. By including other relevant factors such as marital satisfaction, child-rearing attitudes, and expectations that are specific to individual children, we might find ourselves able to predict maladaptive parenting even more effectively.

The potential importance of other contributing factors is illustrated by the role of adolescent behavior problems. As measured by the *Achenbach* (described in earlier chapters), the undercontrolled, "externalizing" misbehavior of adolescents that mothers reported related both to lower perceived family assistance, less family/leisure time, *and* to more maladaptive parenting. Importantly, though, both the definition of the situation factors (family assistance and family/leisure time) remained meaningful, although less powerful, as predictors of parenting even after using the *Achenbach* data.

These results indicate that the effects of adolescent misbehavior do not supercede other familial influences that may shape maternal perceptions of and satisfaction with household assistance and family time. Neither do they wash out the possible effects of these latter subjective factors on observed parenting. Although provocative behavior on the part of the adolescent certainly contributes to lower evaluations by mothers of their socioeconomic situation, as well as to maladaptive parenting, it is not wholly responsible for the associations between them. Again, this finding adds credibility to the validity and utility of the Moen *et al.* framework as a *socioeconomic* model of parenting.

Methodological and Theoretical Limitations

The flexibility in the Moen *et al.* model makes it a convenient framework for use in adapting theory to available data but makes it a difficult model to assess reliably and validly. The opportunity to interpret and operationalize each of the categories of the model in quite different ways suggests that extensive use of the model could yield as many different patterns of results as there are applications of the model. To be of real empirical value, some consensus needs to be reached regarding its operationalization.

The flexibility inherent in this model permitted its application in the present analysis, which focused on a very circumscribed portion of the model and addressed only maladaptive parental behavior. However, parenting is multiply determined. Belsky and Vondra (in press) categorize the determinants of parenting—and of maltreatment—into three general classes: (1) parental psychological resources; (2) child characteristics; and (3) contextual sources of stress and support. It is clear that our application of Moen *et al.*'s model does not by any means assess the contributions of all or even any one complete category of parental determinants. As illustrated by our analysis of the role of adolescent behavior problems (i.e., "child characteristics"), there is much excluded in the model we employed. Nevertheless, it does provide what seems to be a valuable method of relating characteristics belonging to the third category—contextual sources of stress and support—to observed differences in the adaptiveness of parental behavior. Despite its conceptual and methodological limitations, there is much suggested here that warrants extended empirical inquiry.

Certainly, we must recognize a large number of empirical limitations in the current analysis. Factor measures are of questionable reliability and validity, the measure of parenting is not consistent with other measures in its unit of analysis (i.e., it is an evaluation of general parenting in a given family versus ratings specific to maternal behavior), the maternal employment groups are too small to permit more than conjecture about discerned differences, and there is considerable restriction in the kinds of data gathered that could be incorporated after the fact into a test of the Moen et al. model.

The fact that predicted and often provocative findings have been documented despite these multiple problems may, in itself, be testimony to the heuristic and explanatory value of the model. The ultimate test, of course, is replication of these results through a comparable study employing a database specifically designed to assess the constructs, relationships, and patterns described in the model.

CONCLUSIONS

A Phenomenological View of the Determinants of Parenting

Previous research on the determinants of parenting and the origins of child abuse have tended to dichotomize objective and subjective influences on parenting. The common approach is to examine "objective," situational causes by focusing on the social and economic circumstances providing the background for parenting. Subjective measures designed to tap individual values and perceptions are typically reserved for more "organismic" (person) influences such as child-rearing attitudes and expectations. If there is but one conclusion of this analysis, it is the vital importance of developing and maintaining a phenomenological view of the determinants of parenting, considering the impact of objective events on subjective experience. More significant than the occupational status of father, the educational attainment of mother, and the income or health of the family are the *subjective reactions* parents have to the more immediate (economic) conditions of home and family life that these broader socioeconomic indicators only help to create.

Although there are, no doubt, other "proximal" socioeconomic factors besides maternal rating of family assistance, of family/leisure time, and of satisfaction with the family income, that are equally or more relevant to parental maladaptiveness, even these somewhat arbitrary social and economic characteristics of family life, *as they are defined by parents*, have considerable power in predicting ratings of dysfunctional parenting. If a mother relies on her family's affective or instrumental support for maintaining optimal or even adequate household functioning, then her perception that this support is absent or insufficient is likely to influence her own functioning in that household, the foremost activity of which is child rearing. Even when the relationship between objective resources and options available to the family and the parenting that takes place within that family appears a direct one (i.e., not related through definition of the situation factors), it is likely that there are numerous subjective perceptions and interpretations mediating the relationship but simply not identified in the empirical model used here. So long as the subjective reality of perception and reaction is characterized by inadequacy and negativity, the behavioral response is likely to be one of similar inadequacy, even when objective conditions may predict near "normal" functioning.

Within the methodological and theoretical confines of this analysis there still exist innumerable lessons having to do with the determinants of parenting—lessons embodied in, but not restricted to, the model proposed by Moen *et al*. These lessons are ecological in nature; they instruct us to look beyond explanations that rely solely on organismic (person) causes or environmental influences. They instruct us to bridge the deceptive dichotomy between person and environment, to consider the interplay between the two that uniquely defines the *experience* of the individual. Only when there is awareness of individual experience will there be knowledge about the most immediate influences on the behavior and functioning of the individual and of the family.

Implications for Intervention

Once we recognize the powerful role of subjective perception as a window into parental behavior, we have a vital tool for improving our efforts to help families in need. We see direct applications of a model like that of Moen *et al*. for three related aspects of intervention: identification, service delivery, and progress assessment.

With respect to the first aspect, identification, we can speak about service distribution. Although widescale improvement in parental functioning depends upon resources and supports for all families, particularly those operating without the supports generally recognized as important for the well-being of families, it is the families who feel the inadequacy of their situation that are most in need of help. As we have seen here, it is the families who find objective resources lacking and their own efforts inadequate to deal with the resulting hardship who are most at risk for maladaptive patterns of parenting. In other words, the demand for supportive services is greatest among families whose objective needs are exacerbated by their own perception of internal (familial) and external (resource) inadequacy. Given that parents expect both more (financial and household assistance) and less (dependent, demanding behavior) from their adolescents, we can expect to find a greater role for adolescents in effecting such a sense of internal socioeconomic inadequacy.

If the focus of our intervention is on treatment or prevention for those considered to be "at risk" for later dysfunction (as opposed to enhancement for all families), then we would do well to develop indexes of risk that include information on both objective circumstances and subjective perceptions. From a phenomenological perspective, it is understandable that poor income and a low-status job should be less effective predictors of problems in parenting than reported *enjoyment* of leisure time together and *satisfaction* with help around the house. We act in accordance with the reality that we perceive. We cannot presume to know how someone will behave unless we can acquire some understanding of how that person thinks and feels. The very label, "human services," indicates the importance of taking human subjectivity into account. As humans, we create, perceive, and respond to our own reality, a reality that differs from individual to individual, and family to family.

The model we have described and data we have presented to support it argue that families in similar socioeconomic circumstances are not alike in their responses—overt and covert—to social and economic circumstances. Whereas one family may work together to cope with adversity, another family may reel beneath environmental pressure and find itself slipping out of control. Whereas one family perceives and draws upon internal and external resources, another family perceives and condemns the powerlessness of its members to effect change. These differences have important implications for the second aspect of intervention—service delivery. Providing resources and services to the first family may bolster its own efforts to cope. Providing resources to the second family without increasing its awareness of the role its own members play as catalysts for change may foster helpless dependency and resource mismanagement. As any therapist would argue, the key to improvement is personal responsibility for improvement through a sense of personal self-efficacy. (Bandura, 1977).

If families perceive themselves as inadequate to cope effectively with their circumstances, it is unlikely that a short-term relief from hardship will evoke long-term strides in family functioning. When families have been identified, then, as viewing themselves to be helpless or inadequate to cope, it is essential that the thrust of services is on helping the family gain the means and conviction to marshall its own forces for change and adaptation.

Suggesting, as we do, that subjective perceptions should serve to guide selection for and delivery of services to families, it is natural that we should also support their use as a barometer for improvement within the family system. Families that continue, over the course of intervention, to view their socioeconomic situation as a stressful one—due to resource impoverishment, family role inadequacy, or a combination of both—are unlikely to demonstrate improved parental functioning by the time intervention would normally be terminated. The absence of psychological change at this level would alert professionals to the need for extended services or alternative intervention strategies. Dissatisfaction with the support or experiences within and beyond the family would act, therefore, as a marker for pressures that continue to undermine the quality of parenting practiced. Again the key to more powerful effects is subjective experience rather than objective circumstances. No matter how job status, income level, and household assistance vary, unless there is a corresponding change in how each appears to the parent(s), their supportive function for that parent remains untapped. On the other hand, stable changes in parental perceptions would represent inroads into the problem that could be effectively translated into improvements in parenting.

Just as we can learn from individual differences in responses to socioeconomic conditions, so we can learn from individual differences in responses to programs of intervention. With the knowledge gained, we can devise richer conceptual models and more effective applications of them. These are, after all, the goals of applied research. In the area of parenting, they are goals only just becoming realized; in an area as crucial as parenting, they are goals demanding our best efforts for children and youth.

APPENDIX I:
FAMILY VIGNETTES USED TO RATE
THE RISK FOR ADOLESCENT MALTREATMENT
Vignette No. 1

Mr. and Mrs. Smith live in a small town a few miles from here. There have always been arguments in their house for as long as anyone can remember. The kids sometimes got the worst of it, being "yelled at" or "smacked," but sometimes they deserved it. Even though they have some problems, they've always managed to keep the family together.

Vignette No. 2

Mr. and Mrs. Smith live in a small town a few miles from here. Their large family made it rough to make ends meet. The kids were always in the way and the Smiths had to yell at them a lot to keep things quiet. The kids sometimes felt no one cared about them. Even though they have some problems, they've always managed to keep the family together.

Vignette No. 3

Mr. and Mrs. Smith live in a small town a few miles from here. They never had any close friends and the kids were often absent from school. Sometimes the older kids had to stay and watch the younger ones, but other times their parents just let them stay at home. Even though they have some problems, they've always managed to keep the family together.

Vignette No. 4

Mr. and Mrs. Smith live in a small town a few miles from here. They've noticed recently that the children have become "disrespectful," and they've had to slap them across the face several times to remind them that children and teens should be seen but not heard. Even though they have some problems, they've always managed to keep the family together.

Vignette No. 5

Mr. and Mrs. Smith live in a small town a few miles from here. They never had any problems with their children until recently. They've been demanding to do whatever they please lately and the Smiths have had to get very strict and "ground" them for weeks at a time. Even though they have some problems, they've always managed to keep the family together.

Vignette No. 6

Mr. and Mrs. Smith live in a small town a few miles from here. Their kids have started to stay out lately way past curfew with a crowd of kids from school. Mr. and Mrs. Smith figured that they should just let them go and that they would learn their own lessons. Even though they have some problems, they've always managed to keep the family together.

Vignette No. 7

Mr. and Mrs. Smith live in a small town a few miles from here. They believe that the kids, now that they're growing up, should be allowed to have some input into making family decisions. Sometimes conflicts arise, but they seem to handle it well. Even though they have some problems, they've always managed to keep the family together.

Vignette No. 8

Mr. and Mrs. Smith live in a small town a few miles from here. When problems come up in their family they all sit down and have a "meeting." Now that the kids are getting older, they are given more and more freedom which they seem to handle well. Even though they have some problems, they've always managed to keep the family together.

Vignette No. 9

Mr. and Mrs. Smith live in a small town a few miles from here. They have their ups and downs with the kids but things always seem to work out. Everyone in the family takes an interest in other family members and they all have friends who visit frequently. Even though they have some problems, they've always managed to keep the family together.

APPENDIX II:
ABUSE SCALES USED TO RATE
THE RISK FOR ADOLESCENT MALTREATMENT

Scale No. 1: Physical Abuse
(i.e., hitting, slapping, punching, striking with an object, etc.)

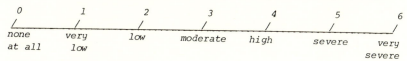

Scale No. 2: Emotional Abuse
(i.e., humiliation, extreme inconsistency, "put downs," parental withdrawal of love, etc.)

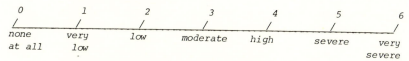

Scale No. 3: Developmentally Damaging Behaviors
(i.e., extreme restrictiveness, continuing to treat the developing adolescent as a child, extreme parental control, etc.)

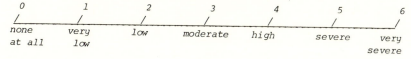

ADOLESCENTS IN
STEPFAMILIES

10

JAMES W. MIKESELL
JAMES GARBARINO

INTRODUCTION

Most of the current writing on destructive family relationships focuses on factors within a traditional family unit, that is, two married adults (first marriage) with their own children. This is understandable because the traditional nuclear family is still normatively and statistically the predominant family unit within our society. With increasing rates of divorce and remarriage over the past decade, however, the "reconstituted" or stepfamily has become significantly more prevalent, so much so that it has become one of the major family types. This has led many professionals as well as stepfamily members to pose questions about the nature of stepfamily functioning.

Despite a good deal of discussion of stepfamilies, there have been very few substantive empirical studies about how adolescents function within them. Moreover, those that have been conducted are, in many ways, contradictory. From the standpoint of destructive family relations, this is an area of research that seems to warrant considerable investigation for two reasons. First, adolescence is a time of multiple transitions. Many of these transitions can be difficult and trying for both the adolescent and the family as a whole. Acknowledging the challenging nature of these transitions has led to researchable questions about how the special circumstances of the stepfamily influence these transitions. Second, discussion of stepfamilies as a social problem and public issue (Espinoza and Newman, 1979) motivates attention to empirical realities. Stepfamilies have also faced transitions that in all likelihood were difficult and trying, at least at some point. Stepfamilies are formed in the wake of one of two stressful events—after a divorce or death of a parent. The current interest in life stress and support thus contributes to the motivation to study stepfamily formation and functioning.

Adolescents within a stepfamily, then, would seem to create a unique situation where both of these transition issues might compound, causing even greater challenges to family and individual functioning. While this is hypothetical, it nonetheless points out that there is reason to pursue this issue. A better understanding of stepfamilies with adolescents would not only shed more light on questions pertaining to the stepfamily but would also contribute to a more comprehensive view of problems faced by the adolescent.

This chapter provides a basis for understanding the adolescent in the stepfamily. We pursue four strategies for accomplishing this mission. First, we present a general overview of important background information about stepfamilies. This will provide the foundation for a more in-depth understanding about stepfamilies in the context of North American society. In pursuit of this goal, we consider demographic information about stepfamilies, we define how a stepfamily differs from a traditional nuclear family, and we outline some historical connotations typically associated with the stepfamily and how this may affect stepfamilies today.

Second, we discuss how to conceptualize the special nature of stepfamily functioning. This will establish a framework that permits a description of adolescents in stepfamilies and explores how the step situation may present them with opportunities for development as well as risks to their functioning.

Third, we compare the risk for abuse of adolescents in both stepfamilies and traditional nuclear families. Previous research suggests specific hypotheses about the risk for abuse inherent in the opportunities and risks facing the adolescent in the stepfamily. We use results from these analyses to highlight these risks.

Finally, we offer some conclusions about differences between adolescents in stepfamilies and traditional nuclear families. This includes a discussion of the significance of our findings to the planning and evaluating of research and human services aimed at stepfamilies and their special role in adolescent maltreatment.

DEMOGRAPHICS OF STEPFAMILIES

As mentioned previously, the number of stepfamilies is on the rise. While the exact number of stepfamilies is not known, a good estimate from the late 1970s indicates that about 10.2% of the families in the United States are stepfamilies (Glick, 1979). The actual amount is certainly higher because:

(1) the 10.2% estimated by Glick (1979) includes only those stepfamilies with children under the age of 18 years old; (2) the estimate does not include stepfamilies headed by natural father and stepmother (Glick, 1980). This figure may account for 5 to 10% of all stepchildren (Glick, 1980).

Based on population projections and divorce rates, Glick (1979) also estimated that the number of stepchildren under the age of 18 will increase to approximately 11% of the total number of children by 1990.

DEFINITION OF STEPFAMILIES

A stepfamily is defined as a family in which one or both of the adults have children from a previous marriage (Espinoza and Newman, 1979). A traditional nuclear family, on the other hand, is defined as a family in which both adults are the genetic parents of the children in the household. Thus, a stepfamily is not the same as an adopting family (of course, a stepparent may elect to adopt his or her stepchildren in some circumstances). In the case of regular adoption, neither of the parents is the genetic parent of the child.

Thus, stepfamilies can take on many forms. For example, one type of stepfamily includes a stepfather who has never been married before and has only one stepchild (brought into the marriage by the child's mother). A more complex form involves two adults who have been married before and who both bring with them one or more children into the second marriage. Most analyses do not pursue the nuances of such subcategories, but rather focus upon the fact that a step relationship exists within a particular family household. It is this critical distinction that serves to differentiate the stepfamily from what we might call the "biological" family (for want of a better term). The stepfamily brings together an adult with a child who has no biological link with that adult but does have such a link with that adult's spouse.

HISTORICAL OVERVIEW AND IMPLICATIONS

The assumption underlying most discussions of stepfamilies is that this type of family operates in ways that differentiate it from the biological family. In order to examine this assumption more closely, we would do well to review the many connotations historically and stereotypically linked with the stepfamily. Much of what we already "know" about stepfamilies has been learned from less than reliable sources, including fairy tales and folklore (Jacobson, 1979; Pfleger, 1947; Schulman, 1972). Thus, an overview of these historical issues should help us identify any preexisting conceptions that may cloud our analysis of stepfamilies.

The prefix "step-" originated from the Middle English word "steop," meaning "to bereave." At first, this term was used to describe orphan children, but was later applied to those who were related to their "parents" by remarriage (Webster, 1978). This association with bereavement or death does make historical sense. In past centuries, and even decades, remarriage was the result of the death of one of the original spouses in a marriage. Divorce and subsequent remarriage was quite rare (indeed was and still is prohibited in some church laws).

It is possible that the negative undertones implicit in the use of the prefix "step-" continue. There are many reasons for this. Step relations have been at the brunt of many unpleasant stories, novels, fairy tales, and folklore. The cruel or wicked stepmother theme is dominant in these stories (which made demographic sense in an earlier era when women died in childbirth often enough to make remarriage by widowers the most common route to step relations). For example, in *Cinderella*, *Snow White*, *Hansel and Gretel*, *The Six Swans*, and other fairy tales, the hostile and evil stepmother plots against her poor, innocent stepchild. Even adult fiction contains this theme—to wit *East of Eden*, by John Steinbeck, which depicts strained and hostile feelings between the stepmother and stepchildren. Such negative images of stepfamilies are not limited to Western literature and culture. African mythology and Hawaiian and Polynesian folklore also contain many examples (Pfleger, 1947).

Although it seems reasonable to consider that folklore and fiction is at least a gross indicator of past attitudes and behaviors toward step relations, the actual impact this literature has on our present attitudes and beliefs toward stepfamilies is undetermined. Furthermore, the proposition that we even think differently about stepfamilies from the way we do about traditional nuclear families is an empirical question that merits investigation. Fortunately, there is some research available to shed some light on this question. A study by Ganong and Coleman (1979) examined responses (predominantly by females) to a series of adjectives describing natural fathers, natural mothers, stepfathers, and stepmothers. This use of the "semantic differential" scale showed that natural mothers and fathers were considered much more positively than were stepfathers and stepmothers. The authors concluded that the "step-" prefix is pejorative, and that members of our society still possess negative stereotypes toward stepfamilies.

Although the study by Ganong and Coleman (1979) indicated that popular, stereotyped attitudes toward stepfamilies may still be negative, this does not preclude researchers from investigating the functioning of these families. Our task it to consider the conditions under which the challenges and risks of the step relationship operate to produce problems for children and parents. As researchers and practitioners, we must be aware that biases embedded in our society's attitudes toward step relationships may affect specific hypotheses we develop and carry into our research. We must always be open to the idea that we are creating differences *a priori* simply by our assumptions about the nature of the stepfamily. Such self-fulfilling prophecy may be at work in the attitudes and behavior of stepfamily members as well, of course, for they too have been enculturated in the negative stereotype of step relationships. As we shall see later in this chapter, this attribution may play a role in the difficulties some of these families experience.

THE SPECIAL NATURE OF STEPFAMILIES

Despite the fact that stepfamilies comprise a significant segment of the population, they are still considered a nontraditional or even nonnormative family form (Macklin, 1980). Along with the label of "nontraditional," however, is a set of assumptions about the manner in which these families behave. More specifically, stepfamilies are often thought to be challenged in unique ways that pose risks to their members (Duberman, 1975; Espinoza and Newman, 1979; Visher and Visher, 1979). Remembering, however, the caveat stated earlier about potential biases in studying stepfamilies, we must provide clearer propositions about those characteristics that can create risk for stepfamily relations. Conversely, special circumstances available in the stepfamily may give rise to opportunities for growth and enhancement, and we must be alert to these as well. The assimilation of new family members can be a source of care and support. Indeed, it is the expectation of such benefits that often motivates remarriage and subsequent reconstitution of families. Sorting out risks from opportunities requires an integrated model of stepfamily functions.

There have been several attempts to describe the factors or stages relevant to stepfamilies (Espinoza and Newman, 1979; Kleinman et al., 1979; Mills, 1984; Nelson and Nelson, 1982; Papernow, 1984; Schulman, 1981; Walker and Messinger, 1979). None of these models really provides an in-depth view of the interrelatedness of many of the issues thought to be operating in stepfamilies. However, collectively they do provide a comprehensive list of these factors and stages. We should point out however, that we present this model to provide a basis for reflecting those factors already identified in the literature as being specific issues confronting stepfamilies. As such, it is intended more as a heuristic device than a highly developed theoretical model.

Existing efforts to conceptualize the stepfamily generally address issues that fall within one of the following four domains: structural reorganization; emotional strain; role performance; and, resource shortage. Structural reorganization of family units into a stepfamily is a developmental challenge to stepfamily members as the new family unit forms. Emotional strain arises from the feelings of guilt, grief, and anger associated with forming the new family and dismantling the old. Role performance, particularly in the stepparenting role, constitutes a third domain. Stepparents have little in the way of cultural guidance to fall back upon. Finally, stepfamilies may experience a shortage of resources that would enhance the operation and maintenance of the stepfamily. Examples of these resources include social supports, kin networks, and money. Each of these may suffer in the transition from the old to the new family.

Structural Components

A change in family structure affects "those factors that contribute to the sense of identity differentiating the members of one group from another" (Walker and Messinger, 1979). Changing the family structure or redefining the family "boundaries" can precipitate adjustment problems for stepfamily members (Schulman, 1981). This derives from the confusion and disruption that takes place any time there is a change in family composition or relationships. A stepfamily makes special demands, demands more complex than the challenge of a new baby. In a stepfamily, each member has a personal history and often a set of additional if not competing loyalties and roles (e.g., to a parent from a previous marriage).

Forming a stepfamily may disrupt established interaction and communication patterns or communication between parent and child (Nelson and Nelson, 1982). The introduction of new members makes it likely that members of the "old" family will not have so much time to spend with each other as part of the "new" family. Children and adolescents may not be capable of understanding these changes and may resent the new relationships that precipitate them.

A related issue involves the alliances that form in stepfamilies. The people in the family who share a common history (i.e., a mother and her own daughter, genetically related siblings) tend to align themselves against the stepparents or stepchildren (Schulman, 1981). Such alliances will occur until more trust in the presence of a step relation develops and the reorganization in the stepfamily takes place.

One final issue is territoriality (Bernard, 1956; Schulman, 1972). Because reconstituted families usually settle in a house that some of the members lived in prior to the remarriage, often there are problems on deciding on what kind of "space" to give one another as well as who has certain rights to particular materials not previously shared (rooms in the house, toys, etc.). Until reformation of the boundaries of the family takes place, problems in issues of territory and space are likely to occur.

Emotional Components

Some of the special emotional issues involved in stepfamilies revolve around grief over the loss of previous family members, guilt about being part of a new family, idealization of past members, and myths or fantasies about stepfamilies that cause anxiety (Duberman, 1975; Fast and Cain, 1966; Maddox, 1975; Papernow, 1984; Schulman, 1972; Visher and Visher, 1979).

Frequently, the remarriage and subsequent beginning of stepfamily formation churn up negative feelings in the participants (Maddox, 1975). Sometimes, especially in the case of children, these feelings are superimposed on feelings of grief over the loss of the mother or father. This is especially true when a parent remarries soon after the death of another parent. Thus, grief and sorrow over the loss of one parent can serve as emotional interference with the transition into the stepfamily. Maddox (1975) points out that the remarriage of one of the parents may create feelings of guilt in the children about loyalty to the other parent (Visher and Visher, 1979). These feelings of guilt may cause the child to reject the stepparent as a substitute for his or her natural parent, for to accept the new parent figure appears to constitute disloyalty.

Another issue related to the emotional adjustment of stepfamilies centers on myths and fantasies about step relationships (Jacobson, 1979; Ganong and Coleman, 1979; Pfleger, 1947; Schulman, 1972; Smith, 1953). Here we see the influences of cultural stereotypes on family functioning. While myths and fantasies are not emotions per se, the impact they may have on stepfamily members may account for a good deal of the emotional upheaval experienced (Papernow, 1984). Many of the writings on the problems with myths seem to highlight those that are experienced by stepparents. Examples of these are the myth of the "wicked" stepmother (e.g., Pfleger, 1947) and the myth of "instant love" (Duberman, 1975). While these myths are more specific to the role of the stepparent, they are commonly associated with underlying anxiety and guilt some stepparents seem to have. When combined with the feelings that stepchildren themselves may experience, the feelings can contribute to the creation of a negative emotional climate in the stepfamily.

Role-Related Components

Stepfamily members, especially the stepparents, face difficulties in defining and accepting their role (Fast and Cain, 1966; Giles-Sims, 1984; Kompara, 1980; Nelson and Nelson, 1982; Visher and Visher, 1978a). There is little guidance on what to expect and demand of step relations, particularly stepparent–child relations. Stepparents act as replacements or "surrogates" for the absent natural parent, but their role is ill-defined (Kompara, 1980). There are no reliable models or definitions which the stepparent can follow (Fast and Cain, 1966; Giles-Sims, 1984; Messinger, 1976). The lack of institutionalized norms for stepparenting contributes to a sense of role ambiguity (Cherlin, 1978). Consequently, many stepparents report difficulties in performing stepparenting tasks (Messinger, 1976; Visher and Visher, 1978a).

Perhaps as a function of the ambiguity and difficulty in role-related behavior, stepparents are not so active in parenting behavior. Moreover, they may not be held accountable by their spouse for not being so active (Giles-Sims, 1984). This discrepancy between the stepparents expectations that they follow in a parenting role and that they are not so active or sanctioned for lack of participation suggests that there may be conflict centered on the stepparent role (if the stepparent wants to participate in parental activities but is not encouraged to do so, etc.). Thus, questions about the role of the stepparent appear to be a special concern for stepfamilies.

Resource Components

Resources here refer to people or materials available that provide assistance and serve to enhance the functioning of the stepfamily. Resources include money, kin networks, and social support systems (Clingempeel, 1981; Duberman, 1975; Maddox, 1975; Nelson and Nelson, 1982; Richardson and Pfeiffenberger, 1983; Visher and Visher, 1979). The general premise is that a shortage (or, as will be pointed out in the case of kin networks, an abundance) will be likely to serve as a stressor to the stepfamily.

One of the more obvious resources is money. It is generally acknowledged that the lack of adequate financial means serves as a source of strain for any type of family. What is especially important to stepfamilies, however, is that frequently the money has to be distributed in many more ways than would generally take place in a traditional nuclear family. Stepfamilies often are faced with issues of child support for nonresident as well as resident children from a previous marriage (Espinoza and Newman, 1979). In addition, as in the case of territoriality discussed earlier, there are frequently problems related to who controls the money and how it is spent (Espinoza and Newman, 1979). Thus, when one considers the multiple external influences on the functioning of a stepfamily, the issue of finances is of obvious importance.

Another resource is kin networks. Clearly, many stepfamilies could have an extensive network of cousins, aunts, uncles, and grandparents. Many authors have argued that the size of the kin network is hard to manage for the stepfamily. Moreover, the large number of significant others may serve more to interfere in the operation than to enhance it (Duberman, 1975; Maddox, 1975).

A study by Clingenpeel (1981) sheds even more light on this issue. As hypothesized, marital quality in "complex" stepfamilies (those with a high degree of kin) was lower than those stepfamilies with a moderate amount of kin complexity but no worse than those stepfamilies with a smaller kin network. This result suggests that some support from relatives is helpful to the stepfamily, but that too much can in fact serve as a strain (at least on the marriage). Thus, it does appear that relatives can serve as a resource to the stepfamily when in moderation, but that too many or too few may hinder aspects of stepfamily functioning.

Finally, there is the issue of whether or not stepfamilies have access to appropriate nonfamilial social support systems (Richardson and Pfeiffenberger, 1983). Although there have been some associations founded to deal with the concerns of stepfamilies,[1] most of these are on a national level, and local resources and support groups are still uncommon. A lack of resources at the community level may serve to feed feelings of isolation and frustration experienced by some stepfamilies.

OPPORTUNITIES AND RISKS TO ADOLESCENTS IN STEPFAMILIES

Our discussion has centered on factors thought to relate to the functioning of the stepfamily as a whole. The purpose of this review is to provide a framework or context in which to understand adolescents in stepfamilies. Our focus, thus far, has been the special challenges and risks associated with step relations. We should remember that stepfamilies may offer some special opportunities particularly useful to adolescents.

In addition, in order that we reach a more in-depth understanding of the adolescent in the stepfamily, it is necessary to describe what the adolescent is contributing in terms of characteristics that impinge on the stepfamily as a whole. This will be useful in helping to understand that the adolescent, in part, shapes his or her own behavior, and it is not just a matter of the stepfamily determining the behavior of the adolescent.

The notion of adolescence as a time of inherent transition and developmental change contributes to the understanding of the functioning within the stepfamily. The stepfamily also faces changes and adjustments that may pose threats to the functioning of its members. Thus, the adolescent in a stepfamily may pose special risks not typically found in traditional nuclear families.

---

[1]The following are organizations that have been established to help meet the needs of stepfamilies: The Stepfamily Foundation, Inc., 333 West End Avenue, New York, NY 10023 and The Stepfamily Association of America, Inc., 900 Welch Road, Suite 400, Palo Alto, CA 94304.

Opportunities

There is a considerable body of research to suggest that adolescents in stepfamilies are at no greater risk than adolescents in nuclear families (Bohannon and Yahraes, 1979; Burchinal, 1964; Wilson et al., 1975). Thus, adolescents in stepfamilies may be offered the same opportunities for development. The most obvious benefit to an adolescent is that there is a "replacement" of the parent no longer in the home. Frequently, the loss of that parent is a traumatic experience, with which the adolescent may find it difficult to cope. A subsequent remarriage may offer a more positive outlook, a sense of family cohesion, and financial resources not available previously. In fact, some have suggested that, especially in the case of remarriage after divorce, those persons frequently take steps to ensure a more positive environment for the family (Wilson et al., 1975). Thus, one must consider that family reconstitution can present the adolescent with a more stable environment and would be beneficial to his or her development.

In addition, the adolescent in the stepfamily may experience increased autonomy that contributes to greater self-esteem and maturity. For example, an adolescent may have to share in the responsibility for child care when there is only one parent, but when another adult is brought into the family, there can be relief for some of these responsibilities and an opportunity to experience the fullness of adolescence (Johnson, 1980).

There have been a considerable number of studies to demonstrate that adolescents in stepfamilies are no different from adolescents in traditional nuclear families. For example, it has been shown that adolescents in stepfamilies are no less happy with their lives, have the same amount of self-esteem, are no different in personality characteristics, and generally function at the same level as other adolescents (Bohannon and Yahraes, 1979; Burchinal, 1964; Wilson et al., 1975). Others indicate no differences between adolescents in stepfamilies and adolescents in traditional nuclear families in school performance and activities (Bohannon and Yahraes, 1979; Burchinal, 1964; Nye, 1957; Perry and Pfuhl, 1963) and no differences in delinquency and drug use (Blechman et al., 1977; Nye, 1957; Perry and Pfuhl, 1963).

Moreover, it appears that stepfathers are beneficial to adolescent males in terms of cognitive development and performance (Chapman, 1977; Santrock, 1972). It is argued that the presence of a stepfather attenuates the loss of the natural father. Interestingly, this outcome does not appear to take place for adolescent *females* in stepfather families (Chapman, 1977; Santrock, 1972), a finding that supports the view that a stepfather can serve as a role model to an adolescent male and influence him in a positive manner.

Risks

It may seem a bit awkward to present a number of findings showing no differences between adolescents in stepfamilies and adolescents in tradition-al nuclear families and then turn around and discuss how adolescents in stepfamilies may be at risk. In fact, those that have reported positive effects of stepfamilies on adolescents suggest that such an examination may simply be a continued attempt by the scientific community to perpetuate preexist-ing biases about stepfamilies when there are, in fact, no differences between stepfamilies and traditional nuclear families (Bohannon and Yahraes, 1979). The fact is, however, that there *are* many contradictions in the literature about the well being of the adolescent in the stepfamily, and that to assume that any bias is unidirectional (that is, biased against stepfamilies) would be scientifically irresponsible. While it is true that many of the con-ceptualizations of stepfamily functioning utilize a deficit–comparison model (Ganong and Coleman, 1979), this does not in itself negate the validity of the results of such studies. Unfortunately, there is simply no clear picture of how an adolescent functions in the stepfamily, and, until there is, issues of risk must be objectively explored.

In contrast to those results previously cited as positive to the adolescent in the stepfamily, there has also been a substantial body of literature that indicates that the adolescent in the stepfamily does not function so well as the adolescent in a traditional nuclear family. Some studies report that adolescents in stepfamilies have lower self-esteem and mental health, more psychosomatic complaints (Rosenberg, 1965), lower adjustment and satis-faction with their family situation (Bowerman and Irish, 1962; Perkins and Kahan, 1979), and difficulties with discipline and divided loyalty (Lutz, 1983; Strother, 1981). Other research reports that adolescents in stepfami-lies experience greater degrees of stress (Colvin et al., 1981), and that this stress *increases* rather than decreases with the passage of time (Strother, 1981). Halperin and Smith (1983) have also reported that stepchildren (aged 10–12 years) perceive both their natural fathers and stepfathers more negatively than do children in traditional nuclear families.

These results provide a reasonable basis for asking whether adolescents in stepfamilies may be at greater risk than adolescents in traditional nuclear families. Given the contradictory nature of these studies, however, it is difficult to make direct comparisons and state whether or not adolescents in stepfamilies do in fact face greater risks. When one contemplates some of the research reported on issues that are considered to make stepfamilies special or unique (e.g., role ambiguity with stepparents), however, we can make a case that the risk to the adolescent in the stepfamily is real, particularly in the case of adolescents who are themselves already exhibiting behavioral problems.

Perhaps the most compelling argument for risk to the adolescent in a stepfamily lies in results of research on abuse. Numerous studies indicate that the incidence of child and adolescent abuse in the stepfamily is higher than in traditional nuclear families (Burgess, 1978; Daly and Wilson, 1981; Gil, 1970; Giles-Sims and Finkelhor, 1984; Wilson and Daly, 1984; Wilson et al., 1980). Stepfamilies seem to exhibit a greater number of behaviors that are thought to be predictive of actual abuse (Burgess, 1979; Garbarino et al., 1984; Kimball et al., 1980; Lightcap, Kurland, and Burgess, 1982; Martin and Walters, 1982).

It is not unlikely that those factors thought to place adolescents in the stepfamily at risk (problems with discipline and conflict with their parents, familial issues, etc.) are related in some way to the risk of abuse. One task in trying to explain risk for abuse to adolescents in stepfamilies is to identify some of these factors.

In order to do so, it is not enough to compare stepfamilies and traditional nuclear families on whatever variables happen to be available and then make inferences about where differences may lie. Such an exercise merely invites the construction of a set of assumptions that may, in fact, be capitalizing on spurious relationships. Moreover, cost–benefit considerations must be made when randomly comparing different variables without hypotheses about relationships of those variables. Rather, it would be more useful to examine the risk for abuse of adolescents in stepfamilies within a framework that is based, at least to some extent, on empirical validation. Such a framework can provide a means of employing hypothesis testing about the nature of adolescent functioning in the stepfamily.

The general framework generated earlier can serve as a conceptual basis for such an examination. The set of four domains thought to describe ways in which stepfamilies are unique is a useful model for assessing the issue of abuse in stepfamilies. If stepfamilies do in fact face greater risks for abuse of adolescents, the issues of family restructuring, emotional climate, role performance, and social support can highlight how these risk factors manifest themselves. In addition, measurement of variables mentioned as risks to an adolescent in stepfamilies (i.e., problems with discipline, higher stress) can also prove useful when examining abusive relationships in the stepfamily. Thus, research on abuse in stepfamilies would encompass many factors of stepfamily behavior and, hence, be multivariate rather than univariate.

RISK FOR ABUSE IN STEPFAMILIES: RESULTS OF THE FAMILY INTERACTION PROJECT

For the present analyses, we used measures described in an earlier chapter.

Research Hypotheses

Given the general framework presented previously and the nature of the measurement instruments used, we can identify a number of hypotheses about the risk for abuse of adolescents in stepfamilies. Even though this framework is descriptive rather than explanatory, it is, at least, based upon previous empirical findings. Thus, a multivariate examination of the risk for abuse in stepfamilies becomes possible.

Utilizing the domains and factors mentioned previously, specific hypotheses about the nature of destructive relationships in stepfamilies can be broadened. Therefore, rather than simply examining risk between family types, particular characteristics thought to be germaine to the functioning of stepfamilies (i.e., role ambiguity, family structure) can also be compared using risk (as measured by the AAI) and family type (stepfamily or nuclear family) as independent variables. Although the percentage of stepfamilies in this study (13%) is basically comparable to the population at large (10–11%), the number of stepfamilies used in this study was somewhat low ($N = 8$) for purposes of statistical analyses. Thus, when interpreting the results, one should keep this in mind.

The hypotheses, based upon issues typically addressed in the stepfamily literature as being pertinent to the efficacy of stepfamily functioning, are as follows:

1. Demographic factors, as defined by family income, educational level of parents, and housing characteristics (house size, house and yard upkeep, etc.), will be no different between stepfamilies and traditional nuclear families. In order to compare these families on other variables related to their functioning, it is necessary to make sure there is no systematic variation in demographic characteristics.

2. Adolescents in stepfamilies are at greater risk for abuse than adolescents in traditional nuclear families. Risk (as measured by the AAI) is defined as parental attitude toward maltreatment and the likelihood that they would act in abusive ways.

3. It is also hypothesized that the ability of the stepfamily to organize, adapt, and control its functioning will be lower in adolescents and parents in stepfamilies than in adolescents and parents in traditional nuclear families. The ability to perform these functions is defined by the FACES subscale of adaptability.

4. In addition, disciplinary issues, as defined by the Cornell Parent Behavior Checklist will be more problematic in stepfamilies than in traditional nuclear families.

5. Parenting behavior, defined by adolescent responses to the Interparental Conflict Scale will be more conflictual in stepfamilies than traditional nuclear families.

6. Adolescents in stepfamilies will experience greater stress and lower degrees of personal competence than adolescents in traditional nuclear families. Stress and competence are defined by the Achenbach Child Behavior Checklist.

Results

The results of these hypotheses, generally speaking, indicate that adolescents in stepfamilies do face greater risks for abuse than adolescents in traditional nuclear families. These results, however, are not without contradictions (see Table 10.1 for an overview of the results). As expected, stepfamilies and traditional nuclear families did not differ on demographic characteristics.

The comparison of risk for abuse (as measured by the AAI) between family types was highly significant [$X^2(1,58) = 7.46$, $p < .01$]. Thus, the claim made by previous researchers that stepfamilies are at greater risk for abuse is supported with this data as well. Specific areas of family functioning that yielded significant differences (after removing the effects of risk) between the stepfamilies and the nuclear families were the adaptability subscale of the FACES for the adolescents [$F(1,54) = 4.13$, $p < .05$] and the Cornell Parent Behavior Description scores for both adolescents [$F(1,54) = 4.42$, $p < .05$] and parents [$F(1,51) = 4.00$, $p < .05$]. It seems, then, that adolescents in stepfamilies may experience difficulty in adapting to reformation of the family and also have problems with child-rearing practices. Parents in stepfamilies also seem to experience problems in child-rearing activities.

The number of stepfamilies ($N = 8$) is very small for conventional statistical comparisons. As a result, very large apparent differences may not reach the necessary level of statistical significance. This is clearly a problem in Table 10.1. For example, the difference in reported interparental conflict appears to be quite large (453.81 for the stepfamilies versus 227.66 for the nuclear families). The large variation in scores and small number of stepfamilies prevents this difference from reaching normal criteria for establishing statistical significance, however. We observe the same phenomenon when we examine the Achenbach Child Behavior Checklist results. Adolescents and parents from stepfamilies report less competence and more problems than do their counterparts from nuclear families. For example, adolescent reports of competence for stepfamilies are 17.50 versus 20.53 for nuclear families. Parents report a similar picture (34.55 for stepfamilies versus 38.73 for nuclear families). For the measure of internalizing problems, stepfamilies report much higher levels (for adolescent reports 31.25 versus 19.32; for parental reports 35.50 versus 28.02). The same pattern is evident for externalizing problems (adolescent reports 28.50 versus 18.04;

Table 10.1. Comparisons of Adolescents in Step and Nuclear Families

Variables	Step families (M = 8) X̄	SD	Nuclear families (N = 54) X̄	SD	p<
Demographic					
income					
(4=$15–20,000;					
5=$20–25,000)					
Father	4.63	1.51	4.97	1.51	n.s.
Mother	4.25	1.16	4.91	1.23	n.s.
Education (years)					
Father	14.13	3.80	15.76	3.74	n.s.
Mother	12.75	1.16	14.42	2.48	n.s.
Housing					
No. of rooms	7.75	3.50	8.91	3.47	n.s.
Cleanliness	6.43	4.15	4.55	2.00	n.s.
Yard upkeep	5.42	2.57	4.23	1.66	n.s.
Neighbor's upkeep	5.00	1.41	4.65	2.99	n.s.
Risk (AAI): % High risk	88%	.35	58%	.48	<.01
FACES					
adaptability					
Adolescent	208.25	23.64	189.12	16.00	<.05
Parents	380.75	35.64	361.87	25.00	n.s.
Cornell PBD					
Adolescent	76.13	8.30	71.12	8.12	<.05
Parents	80.75	5.23	76.95	5.60	<.05
Interparental					
Conflict (IPC)	453.81	432.77	227.66	250.57	n.s.
Achenbach CBCL					
Adolescent					
Competence	17.50	2.60	20.53	3.31	n.s.
Internalizing	31.25	19.02	19.32	11.12	n.s.
Externalizing	28.50	18.60	18.04	11.72	n.s.
Parents					
Competence	34.55	6.06	38.73	6.55	n.s.
Internalizing	35.50	15.39	28.02	17.48	n.s.
Externalizing	52.25	30.51	30.67	21.58	n.s.

parental reports 52.25 versus 30.67). All these apparently large differences do not reach conventional levels of statistical reliability, however, and we must await future research with larger samples to verify the trends we observe here.

Conclusions

Overall, these data provide further support to the notion that stepfamilies face greater risk for abuse than do traditional nuclear families. Such findings have been consistent and, thus far, uncontested. More research on this issue, however, is certainly needed before we can claim unequivocally that stepfamilies are in fact at greater risk for abuse.

How this risk may be manifested according to other factors of stepfamily functioning is less clear. It seems adolescents and parents in stepfamilies perceive greater difficulties with child rearing. The adolescents tend to see their parent and stepparent as having a greater degree of conflict and less agreement over what those child-rearing practices should be than do adolescents in nuclear families.

Moreover, if adolescents in stepfamilies experience difficulties in family reorganization and maintenance in addition to child-rearing practices, it would seem tenable to expect that these adolescents would also experience more problem behaviors and be less socially competent. The trend (albeit statistically uncertain) is in this direction. Thus, there is support for the hypothesis that adolescents in stepfamilies are at greater risk for abuse than adolescents in nuclear families, and these adolescents see child rearing and family reorganization as difficult. There are still unanswered questions about other areas of stepfamily functioning that need to be addressed. The process linking stepfamilies to abuse remains unclear.

DISCUSSION AND RECOMMENDATIONS

While our overview of those factors thought to relate to stepfamily functioning and its relationship to the risk of abuse of adolescents in stepfamilies was provocative and challenging, it did not provide the clear distinctions between stepfamilies and traditional nuclear families we need to have. Of course, this does not mean that such relationships do not exist. Rather, it seems more likely that reliance on a description of these factors without any real propositions about the interrelation of these factors diluted any substantive findings of differences between family types for the risk of abuse.

Thus, more elaborate conceptualizations of stepfamily functioning are needed if we are to better understand how these families behave. Simply comparing different variables without attempting to explain how they may be interrelated is bound to lead to conflicting results. Such is the case in the stepfamily literature.

Related to the issues of building conceptual frameworks on stepfamily functioning, there is a need for more elaborate methodological approaches to stepfamily research (Clingempeel et al., 1984). Simply relying on self-reports does not capitalize on different kinds of information that one can receive about interactions and behaviors within the stepfamily. If a more complete understanding of stepfamilies is to be reached, more time and energy must be expended in order to achieve this end.

In addition, if one conceptualizes stepfamily formation as a transitional change, it is necessary to chronicle how such change occurs. That is, longitudinal analysis of stepfamily formation and subsequent functioning must be documented—a need we did not address in the results presented here. One consistently nagging problem in stepfamily research is that stepfamilies are compared to traditional nuclear families, as if the nuclear family is the standard by which to make comparisons. It is rarely taken into account that these families may systematically differ as a function of time since reconstitution. Thus, it becomes especially important to identify different types of stepfamilies.

In sum, stepfamily research is beginning to demonstrate the level of sophistication necessary to address the basic questions that have faced researchers for a number of years. Many areas of stepfamily functioning have been identified as being different from nuclear families. These factors have been thought by many to place stepfamily members at risk for problems in their functioning. The example of risk of abuse to adolescents in stepfamilies highlighted in this chapter is one such case. In order to demonstrate more definitively how these risks are manifested, more strenuous research endeavors must be put forth. Our failure to demonstrate the pathways for this effect is a challenge for future research.

THE PROSPECTS FOR TROUBLED YOUTH AND TROUBLED FAMILIES

IV

In this concluding section we consider the prospects for troubled youth and troubled families. What will become of troubled youth as they move through adolescence. Can troubled families learn to function more effectively? Chapter 11 explores a wide range of intervention models relevant to troubled youth and their families. It critiques these approaches to intervention on the basis of their consistency with the developmental needs of adolescents and the realistically expectable capacities of parents. Chapter 12 reviews the available evidence on the consequences of maltreatment. It then considers the prospects for the families in our study and offers some hypotheses about how high- vs. low-risk families will adapt to troubled youth.

```
┌─────────────────────────────────────────────────┐
│                                                  │
│ PROSPECTS FOR                                    │
│ INTERVENTION WITH                                │
│ TROUBLED YOUTH            11                      │
│ AND TROUBLED                                     │
│ FAMILIES                                         │
│                                                  │
│                                                  │
│                                                  │
│                                                  │
│                                                  │
│                        LOUISE GUERNEY            │
└─────────────────────────────────────────────────┘
```

In the preceding chapters, we have explored the sources of risk and stress present in the lives of troubled youth and their often troubled families. What are our options in responding? What interventions have been undertaken? Are other interventions possible and needed? What problems exist in creating and implementing effective interventions? We now turn to a discussion of these topics.

INTERVENTIONS CURRENTLY EMPLOYED

When the declared goal of intervention is the removal of maltreatment toward youth, the most predictable treatment target will be the parents. We will discuss the validity of this strategy later in this chapter. Whether or not the strategy is consistent with our views on the etiology of maltreatment in families, the fact is that parents are perceived as the obvious choice. They are the perpetrators; they have the legal responsibility for their children and they are relatively accessible. We should recognize the advancement that the targeting of parents represents. Until we began to respond to the revelation that adolescent acting out, depression, and suicide are frequently associated with abusive parenting, we directed our intervention efforts only at the youths. We must appreciate that the targeting of parents moves us away from the view that youth alone are responsible for their plight. Unfortunately, juvenile offenders are still treated frequently as though a principle had been publicly stated that, "You are entitled to protection from abuse as long as you don't act out in response to it. Once you act out, you are no longer treated as a victim but as an offender." (Chapter 2 of this volume relates to this issue.)

Problems in Working with Parents

We face a number of problems in directing the major interventions toward the parents of youthful abuse victims. First, since adolescent abuse is as likely to occur in higher income families as it is in low-income families (see Chapter 1), designated agencies are in a delicate position to carry out interventions. Agency workers are readily intimidated by the status of higher income families and can tend to deal with these feelings by identifying with the parents against the youths (Sugg, 1981). This can turn the casework goal toward "correcting" the youth rather than redirecting the parents. Second, the youngsters themselves often play a part in covering up the abuse, particularly in families respected in the community. They do not wish any more than the parents to expose the family to public scrutiny. These youth suffer not only abuse but shame and guilt about being part of such a family and frequently a feeling that they have been the cause of the situation, whether or not they truly have contributed. In such instances, help to parents cannot be offered unless they themselves seek it. This is more likely to be the case when the parents have not been abusive prior to adolescence, and they can recognize that things have gotten out of hand in the family (Sugg, 1981). Sometimes they will seek help for other problems, more readily admissible, and the abuse problems will emerge.

Since the likelihood of needed interventions actually taking place is limited with parents as the only target group, supplemental interventions with youths as the target should, and have been, developed. Discussion of those will follow in a separate section.

INTERVENTION STRATEGIES WITH PARENTS

Since parents who abuse are frequently not identified as such, it is probably safe to say that any kind of intervention appropriate for application with families or parents of adolescents has been utilized to reduce family conflict having an abuse component. Intervention in many instances is undertaken in response to the acting out of the adolescent abuse victim. Clinical depression and/or suicide attempts of the adolescent also account for involvement in intervention. In the process of intervention, the abuse may be uncovered. This is a signal to interventionists that a new goal of abuse removal should replace or be added to the initial goals. It is critical to the success of the abuse intervention that the parents and youngster also accept the goal of substituting other responses for the counterproductive, abusing ones. Currently, most professionals offering such interventions are "mandated reporters" and could inform the parents that the professional would be required to report abuse to the protective service agency. How most professionals handle this matter is not known. Unless the state's law leaves no choice, the professional is faced with a troublesome confidentiality problem. The professional may consider this "blackmailing" clients into treatment. However, this stance can also serve to motivate the family to tackle the abuse problem in a serious way, facing more realistically the factors involved in their youngster's unacceptable behaviors.

In addition to attempting to redirect the goals and processes through therapy, professionals often suggest that families seek other types of services, such as parent support groups and parenting skills programs. Goals of these programs are not abuse removal but rather positive parenting.

While a great variety of interventions exist, only the largest cities offer a full array. Interventions provided for parents will be a function of the availability of therapies in the community rather than their expected efficacy for the families. Realistically, comparative efficacy of therapies rarely can be a consideration because of the limited range of services offered. Child protective service agencies, with an official government charge to protect children and youth against abuse, will recommend that treatment be given. While the agencies themselves, generally without resources to offer extensive treatments, provide a limited number of direct services to families with adolescent maltreatment, they do monitor the progress of treatment recommended to the families. The agencies sometimes make treatment a contingency for family maintenance or reunion.

PROFESSIONAL STRATEGIES

Official Agency Treatments

Placement. A common strategy employed by professionals officially charged with working with identified abusive parents is placing the youth outside the family in foster care or a small group home. This strategy is fraught with the potential for creating many problems, along with its obvious result of removing the youngster from the abusing parents. Most cases are not so extreme as to require separation of this type for more than a "cooling off" period or the time needed for the agency to assess danger to the youth and the potential for working with parents. Many times, separation is not used at all upon initial referral. Agencies will attempt first to engage the parents in some form of treatment for the abuse and accompanying problems (e.g., alcoholism or mental illness) in the parents. Placement follows only if treatment fails or is resisted by the parents.

Contracts. A simple step that appears to be effective in some cases is a contract arranged by the official agency for parents and youngster to fulfill. Sometimes the agency also participates in the contract by offering to respond in specified ways (e.g., reducing the number of times checks are made on youngster and/or parents by agency staff). For the parents and youngster, the contract spells out expected behaviors for which compliance is sought by the respective participants. The youth will be expected to be at home by a certain time, for example. Of course, parents would be expected to comply to a demand for no abuse. However, should the youngster fail to comply, and the parents become abusive in retaliation, the fact of abuse would be considered more primary than the youngster's noncompliance. In such an instance, referral for services for the youth as well as the parents would be in order.

Table 11.1 represents the types of strategies used for eliminating adolescent maltreatment. The table is based on one developed to conceptualize helping strategies of all kinds for all purposes by Whittaker in the book, *Social Support Networks: Informal Helping in the Human Services*, by Whittaker, Garbarino and associates (1983). Continued discussion of strategies in this chapter will be organized largely around the categories laid out in Table 11.1.

Treatment for Parents as Individuals

Direct services from the child protection agency are frequently limited to the contract strategy described above, in addition to placement, of course. Referrals are made for more extensive parent therapy to community professionals who agree to provide services for the (generally low) fees paid by the agency. Sometimes the agency specifies a treatment deemed necessary, but more commonly the professionals offer what *they* believe to be appropriate based on their diagnostic and therapeutic persuasions.

Methods included in this section on individual approaches frequently would be used with two parents at the same time. Nonetheless, the treatments would still be considered as "individual" for our classification purposes, because they remain focused on the dynamics of each individual parent, even when the therapy is directed toward parent–child interactions. Family *system* dynamics are not considered, and/or the youngster is not present in person at the treatment sessions or in any way directly a participant in the procedures. If either of the latter features are included, the treatment is classified as a family approach.

Treating Personal Problems of the Parents. Frequently, a therapist will determine that the parent(s) are suffering from an emotional or behavior

Table 11.1. Adolescent Maltreatment Intervention Strategies and Examples[a]

	Treatment		Prevention	
	Parents	Youth	Parents	Youth
Professional				
Individual	Psychotherapy Parent skill training Stress and anger management Placement	Placement Anger management Social skills training	Parent education and skills training	Education for parenthood Exploring childhood
Multiple	Marital counseling Family therapy Contract	Contract Network therapy	Values clarification	Values clarification
Nonprofessional				
Individual	Hot-lines	Youth-staffed hot-lines	Crisis lines	Peer counseling Youth phonelines
Multiple	Parents Anonymous Toughlove for Parents Alcoholics Anonymous	Toughlove for Kids Parents Anonymous Peer support groups	Neighborhood coalition Parenting education Parent support groups Stepparent programs	Alcohol and drug prevention programs Separation and divorce support groups

[a]Based upon Whittaker et al., 1983.

disorder from which the abusive behavior stems. Alcoholism is implicated in many neglecting parents, for example (Wolock and Horowitz, 1984). There are many disorders that could be primary, with abusive behaviors considered secondary. There exists a plethora of treatment strategies for most. Any traditional psychotherapy approach could be selected. Therefore, descriptions of treatments will not be included here. What is important to remember is that the therapist has opted for a direct assault on a personal problem of the parent, based on the premise that it causes the abuse and its cure will result in stopping the abuse. Or, the therapist believes that without working on the problem diagnosed as primary, efforts to deal directly with the abusive behavior will be futile.

Treatment for Parents Directed to Antecedents of Abusive Behaviors. With or without arriving at a diagnosis of a primary problem within the parent(s), many therapists would seek first to deal directly with the abusing behavior per se. This strategy is based on the therapists' assumption that problems residing in the parents are important but less immediately and directly relevant to the treatment goal of abuse removal.

Treatment would be directed toward behaviors in the parents that are antecedents to abusive behavior. Common among these would be problems with stress, anger, or assertion. Depending on their therapeutic convictions, therapists would choose one of those problem areas upon which to focus. They would need to make a choice at this juncture and decide whether it would be more useful to orient the treatment toward the problem as it occurs in all contexts or only in relation to the parent-child context.

The next section will examine some examples of the two types of strategies that are directed to the abusive behaviors.

Stress Management Approaches. There is a growing body of evidence that demonstrates that high levels of stress precede acts of violence, in both domestic and other group situations (Feindler, 1981; Meichenbaum and Cameron, 1981; Rosenberg and Repucci, 1983). While these are not specifically connected with *adolescent* maltreatment, they are representative enough of the dynamics of stress and interpersonal relationships and/or child maltreatment to suggest that parallels would be extremely appropriate. The Rosenberg and Repucci study (1983) isolated stress from another generally hypothesized contributing factor—that of negative attributions to children by abusing parents—and found that only stress accounted for the differences between abusing and other unskilled but nonabusing mothers. It would suggest that these parents are experiencing demands that are beyond their coping capacities. Some of the stressors of the parents studied by Rosenberg and Repucci (1983) might have been ones beyond the power of any psychosocial intervention (e.g., the death of a family member or a major physical problem of the parent). Nonetheless, the "Efficacy Principle" would dictate that methods now well established by clinicians for teaching such parents how to manage personal stress would be the most useful approach. For many, it is likely that this is not only the most feasible strategy but also the treatment of choice. The effectiveness of stress management programs with many subgroups of American society in relation to a myriad of symptoms is very impressive (e.g., Meichenbaum and Cameron, 1981; Novaco, 1979).

Anger Management. Because of high levels of stress associated with the frustration of wishes, goals, plans or the like, and/or poor self-control, some persons have a low threshold for tolerating impulses to strike out verbally and/or physically. Attempts to sensitize adults to this process as it occurs, so that it can become a conscious and therefore controllable one, have been very successful in reducing expressed aggression. In addition, programs generally include the teaching of alternative methods of releasing angry feelings that are more socially acceptable (Novaco, 1979).

Instruction in relaxation methods and stress-controlling procedures has been shown to be effective in promoting more positive feelings toward young children (Egan, 1983). Such methods should also be effective with parents of adolescents since the same goals of positive control of parents' feelings and youngsters' behaviors would be sought.

Assertiveness Training. Despite what might appear to be a contradiction, some abusive persons have been found to be less assertive than desirable. Such persons vacillate between inhibiting and suppressing feelings—mild annoyance, disappointment, etc.—and excessive unleashing of them in aggressive form (Waldo et al., 1983). Learning to operate at the midlevel of "assertiveness" permits expression of feelings at the time experienced in a manner that does not violate social norms. Thus, the need to become excessive in expression to relieve the tensions of pent-up negative feelings is eliminated. Relationships become more satisfying to such individuals because they do not feel misunderstood and put-upon when they can assert their personal needs.

Successful programs have been reported for training parents to become more assertive both as individuals and in the context of the parent–child relationship (Canter, 1982).

Child Management. Yet a third parent strategy is to try to deal with parents' child-management techniques. With this approach, the implicit assumption is that the abuse is a result of a child-control technique gone awry. Child-management techniques are a direct attempt to alter the interactions between parent and child and to replace aversive forms of control with more benign means to achieve child compliance (Egan, 1983).

Therapists choosing child-management approaches conceptualize the problem as entrapment in a "cycle of punishment" for both parent and youngster. Parents are seduced into thinking that their punitive behaviors are genuinely effective over the long run because these often bring about a quick, "cheaply achieved" cessation to unwanted behaviors. In other words, parents are reinforced for inappropriate management measures. The youngsters, conversely, are reinforced for their inappropriate behaviors by the parental punitive responses, unless these are more than balanced by positive behaviors. If the latter is not the case, and it is presumed not to be where patterns of continued abuse exist, the cycle continues to be reenacted and escalates. The frequency of negative responses increases as youngster and parent alike continue to be reinforced reciprocally by them (Sawicki and Brown, 1981).

The major therapeutic task would be conceived as changing the contingencies for reinforcement in order to replace the cycle of punishment with one of reinforcement for genuinely appropriate behaviors. Feelings toward their children have been demonstrated to change positively in parents as a result of such treatment (Egan, 1983). Even though the children were on average preadolescents in the Egan study (1983), the laws of learning operate at all ages. Expectations are that parallel empirical results could be achieved with adolescents. Certainly, there are an ample number of case studies with youngsters of all ages to demonstrate the clinical effectiveness of these direct approaches to changing behaviors around control issues (e.g., Patterson, 1984). Furthermore, the method has the advantage of addressing expectations as well because the behavioral therapist decides with parents which contingencies should be changed. In so doing, the therapist would have the opportunity to help parents separate realistic from unrealistic behaviors for reinforcement and extinction.

Professional Family/Couple Therapy Approaches

As Garbarino and Vondra point out (1983a), any intervention that involves the parents and includes treatment plans for the youngster should permit input from the youngster as well. Those parent and adolescent therapy and family therapy models that provide full participation on the part of the youngsters are promising vehicles. Here we consider some of the better known approaches, whether or not they have reported success specifically with identified abusive families. This choice has been made because of the probability that the therapies have been employed successfully with families that were unrecognized as abusers by themselves or the therapists. Thus, it is likely that they *have* achieved many successes with abusing families. Moreover, the therapies to be described contain elements deemed to be important in changing family abusive behaviors. We believe that treatments to be described here would have even greater promise if the problem were out in the open from the start.

Conventional Family Therapies

Structural Family Therapy. Probably the best known of the family therapies is Structural Family Therapy (Minuchin and Fishman, 1981). This method focuses on the way in which power is "structured" in the family. Children are frequently identified as parenting their parents and siblings in place of the parents. Restructuring the power becomes the therapist's task in order to create a more realistic fulfillment of the various family roles. All the children of the family are included in most of the sessions, but the parent(s) can be seen alone for some sessions. Attention to any subsystem of the family to the exclusion of the others can be used as a strategy at any time, if the therapist sees this as advisable.

No other conventional family therapies will be singled out for attention here. The important thing to remember is that in all, the entire family system is considered, with focus on subsystems as they become most relevant. Stepparents and grandparents can be incorporated for all or part of the treatment. The problem is shared by the whole family, and the input of the whole family is valued. The interdependence of each individual and subsystem to each other and to the whole family system is respected. No one is deemed more responsible for the family's plight than others. In the solution of a specific problem component, the responsibility may be placed on someone. However, all are expected to contribute to the problem solution and to support changes in those member(s) made responsible for change. Feedback and nurturance are developed in the family as well as being contributed by the therapist.

Conventional Parent Therapy or Counseling for Couples

As with Family Therapy, the approaches are many. Again, few empirical treatment comparisons or even outcome studies exist. If couple therapy is offered to an abusive or at-risk family, the problem would be considered a manifestation of a conflict in the parents or the adolescent would have had to have been unavailable (left home or refuses to attend). By whatever method of working with couples the therapist or counselor prefers, the parents would be guided toward relevant family issues. (The difference between *therapy* and *counseling* is not significant here. The use of the two terms is to indicate that both therapy and counseling professionals treat such problems. Their methods usually would not differ along any disciplinary lines.)

Even when the adolescent is not included, the focus of the couples' approach could be on the youngster, nonetheless. The professional would counsel the couple on how to relate to the youngster and could use any combination of the techniques already described in individual therapy. Very frequently, a basic marital conflict will emerge. In such instances, the therapist attempts to involve the parents in marital therapy. The rationale here is that dissatisfaction or conflict in the marriage have resulted in displacement of hostility or affection to youngsters. Such spillovers presumably can be corrected by verbal and/or behavioral therapies that redirect emotional expression in constructive ways. This approach would be particularly relevant in relation to sexual abuse, where displaced feelings presumably result in destructive family role behaviors (Sugg, 1982).

Skills Training Approaches for Couples and Families for Therapeutic Purposes

Of all the multiple member approaches to problems involving family members, the most research on outcomes and processes has been done on the skills-training approaches. The effectiveness of these methods to bring about change on both affective and power (control) dimensions of family functioning has been established (Goldstein, 1973; B. Guerney, 1983; Jacobson, 1977).

Instead of focusing on family deficits and teasing out the causes and "cures" for them, the skills approaches use learning technology to teach the behaviors that members need for appropriate family functioning. These have been identified repeatedly (e.g., in studies by the National Institute of Drug Abuse [Gelb, 1984]) as those of communication, negotiation or mediation— in short, problem-solving techniques. Some skills approaches are focused only on overt personal and interpersonal behaviors (e.g., Stuart, 1980) whereas others also include a focus on underlying feelings and how to express and accept those as well (e.g., B. Guerney, 1977).

In Guerney's Relationship Enhancement methods, several models have been developed to address the whole family or family subsystems (e.g., the marital dyad). When adolescents are included in the treatment, they have an equal voice with their parent(s) in all the arrangements, skills-training exercises, judgments of outcomes, and expressions of feelings. These inputs reduce the power differentials that are generally a major issue in distressed parent–parent–adolescent relationships. Trust and affection can emerge when the helplessness and despair behind power abuse can be understood by family members. What follows is acceptance that these abuses are inappropriate expressions of frustration in the relationships. The skills learned allow the family members to use new positive behaviors to replace the destructive ones and to implement their new understanding of family power problems (Guerney et al., 1981).

Group Therapy with Family Systems or Subsystems

The Relationship Enhancement (RE) Therapy (B. Guerney, 1983) approach often places together small families (no more than four members—one or two parents and/or one parent and three children) together to form a group. Most typically, a cross-family group is composed of a single parent and one or two adolescents with another single parent and her one or two children. The exposure to another family(ies) adds an additional dimension (social support) to the already powerful skills approaches. These families generally provide each other with nurturance. The RE process encourages family members from the same family to provide feedback to each other in skillful ways. The same process is extended so that cross-family feedback and cross subsystem feedback is possible (e.g., teenagers from one family to teens from the other). Social norms thus can be dealt with on a broader basis. While two or more families dealing with abuse have not been placed together in this format, the prospects for success would appear high if the method were applied to this population. (For further descriptions of the RE approaches, see B. Guerney, 1977, 1983.)

TREATMENTS FOR YOUTH

This section is last in order to emphasize the position taken in this chapter that treatment for youth should not be the first strategy followed. While the problem of adolescent maltreatment cannot be considered a problem of the youth alone, strategies to assist youngsters in managing themselves in ways that do not provoke the wrath of adults also have a place in the intervention arena. By learning how to raise their own thresholds for expressing defiance, anger, and feelings of adult persecution, adolescents are able to decrease negative responses from adults. Programs for managing anger have been demonstrated to be useful with youngsters who act out at home and school (Feindler et al., 1980; Novaco, 1979; Varcoe, 1983). Another program of demonstrated value for reducing antisocial behaviors of adolescents is *Skillstreaming the Adolescent* (Goldstein et al., 1980). This structured learning approach provides training in several pro-social skills known to be the antitheses to trouble-generating behaviors (e.g., positive ways of handling teasing, accusations, and aggressive impulses). These programs consist of systematic methods for building up a repertoire of positive behaviors that displace, as well as control, the negative behaviors.

The unique approach of Network Therapy should be mentioned here because of its goal of providing psychosocial and practical support to adolescent cases, even though the youngster remains the "identified patient." The goal of the Network Therapy (Speck and Attneave, 1973; Schoenfeld, 1984) technique is to convene the adolescent and his/her family's network and direct its resources toward helping the adolescent. Included are relatives, friends, clergy, teachers, neighbors, and others who have any relationship to family members. "This usually mobilizes support in the adolescent and tends to bring the network members closer to one another" (Schoenfeld, 1984, p. 95) and alleviates the isolation that families in crisis often experience. Schoenfeld (1984) observes further that adolescents' conflicts are often intergenerational, with the youth and his/her peers on one side and parents and their peers on the other. Less involved network members (e.g., clergy, neighbors) often can provide the "vehicle for a breakthrough."

NONPROFESSIONAL SERVICES FOR PARENTS

Nonprofessional services are frequently utilized with at-risk or abusing parents. These tend to be of the community support genre. Patterned on the classic Alcoholics Anonymous (AA) Model, the most well known of this type, is Parents Anonymous (PA) (Lieber, 1983), which also now operates on a national basis. Parents Anonymous targets not only admitted or even adjudicated abusers but also parents who are concerned that they might become abusive to their children of any age. Thus, it performs a preventive as well as a treatment function. With abusive parents of younger children, the PA "parents supporting parents" model has been shown to be as effective as clinical interventions. With many impulse control problems, the strategy of peers helping peers has been demonstrated to be equally or more effective than professional approaches (Cohn, 1979). Control of one's impulses to strike out at *others* as opposed to using *self*-destructive behaviors such as drinking does pose additional problems, however. Nonetheless, the principles of mutual or peer support, namely, nurturance, feedback, and peer monitoring, with equity and reciprocity among the members, seem to be effective (Garbarino, 1980b).

It is encouraging that some professionals organize support groups for their clients with control problems as an adjunct to the individual or family professional therapy they provide. Some professionals encourage the groups to operate without their sustained input. Others prefer to be present with the group serving as an on-site consultant, if not some sort of facilitator (Lattimer, 1984).

One of the most positive features of the mutual support group is its capacity for operating almost completely free of professional consultation. Many professionals have spearheaded the formation of groups in their communities for any one to attend, irrespective of ties to the practice of the professional. Some community mental health and other agencies have initiated groups as well. Here we see a unique cooperation between professional and lay persons with professionals fully supportive, even responsible in some cases, for its development, a strategy called for by Garbarino (1979) and others (Lenrow and Burch, 1981).

A community support program of a different type introduces a new philosophy into the management of adolescents. It is a support program for parents called TOUGHLOVE, which is conducted by parents and for parents of acting-out youth, some with very severe problems. TOUGHLOVE takes the position that the parents have not been "tough" enough, that is, made demands for compliance and enforced consequences for noncompliance that were consistent and aversive enough to help youngsters respect parental rights and authority. The originators and leaders of this movement, Phyllis and David York (York et al., 1983) are no doubt correct in their judgment that much acting out by some adolescents has its origin in parental inconsistency and abandonment of authority. They contend that this void is filled by peers who support each other in antisocial behaviors. It is questionable if they are correct in their further assumption that all of the acting-out youngsters have perceived themselves as valued, respected children of their parents. The program urges parents to seek help "to make the children comply to parents' rules." It does not urge parents to seek help with enforcement of rules that are mutually respectful of the child as well as the parent. The Yorks provide nothing in the way of data as to how many youngsters have improved under this system, even though local groups are being formed across the continent under their guidance. They contend that it does help youngsters become functioning family members and provide some case examples supporting their contention. Mostly they press the idea that the parents feel greatly bolstered by their membership in TOUGHLOVE because of the mutual support aspects. The Yorks have published *Toughlove for Kids* (York and York, 1983) that is intended to be used for support groups for youth that can be set up to parallel their parents groups.

PREVENTION STRATEGIES

Prevention Strategies with Parents

Parent Education. Less clinical than the skills-training programs described above, educational approaches can be effective for preventing and reducing problems (e.g., Brownstone and Dye, 1975). Typically, these are nonprescriptive programs, prepared for use with any parents who wish to avail themselves of the courses. Frequently, agency staff become parent trainers and conduct the programs in a group format. However, they may be used with individual parents as well. Most of the programs provide important information about adolescent or child development and concepts about relating to and managing children. Most have experiential components as well; frequently audio tapes are provided. Some have skills-practice components. Such programs had not been developed originally for parents at high risk for abuse. However, the assumption is made in offering them that improved parenting will help with generic parent-child problems of any sort. Gratifyingly, the assumption has been supported by empirical evaluation of program effects. Best known among these programs are *Parent Effectiveness Training* (PET) (Gordon, 1975); *Systematic Training in Effective Parenting* (STEP) (Dinkmeyer and McKay, 1976); *The Art of Parenting* (Wagonseller et al., 1978); *Valuing in the Family* (Brayer and Cleary, 1974).

Many community agencies, churches, and continuing education programs include one or more programs geared to parents of adolescents. The number of published programs is impressive. They represent three respected, yet distinct, approaches to human development—Rogerian (Rogers, 1951), Social Reinforcement (Bandura, 1973), Adlerian (Dreikers and Soltz, 1964), and various combinations of these. Comparative effectiveness for preventing problems or even teaching parental behaviors is not available for programs for parents of adolescents. Regardless of this, the face validity and intuitive appeal of knowing something about how to parent has been sufficient to institutionalize parent education. Is it likely that any negative consequences could come of offering courses based on theories of demonstrated validity about individual and interpersonal development? Hardly. Therefore, as in the case of public school education, which was not known to be effective at the time of its inception, professionals, paraprofessionals, nonprofessionals, parents, and policymakers have become advocates for parent education. Unfortunately, it is not so widespread as public education nor so compulsory, but the breakthrough in thinking necessary to support the concept has been made. Further refinements should follow.

Parent Education for Parents at Risk. What does at risk mean in the context of parent education? It implies simply that the life circumstances or individual characteristics of either parent and/or child are known to be associated with parent and/or child problems. For example, many stepparents of adolescents are at risk for relationship and child-management problems when faced with troubled youth. Other parents of adolescents known to be at risk are single parents, parents whose life circumstances (their health or jobs) prevent optimal support from others, and those with unsatisfactory marriages. At-risk youngsters are those who must shoulder adult responsibilities, those who live in isolation, and those with health or academic problems. Many interventionists advocate parent education for all such parents *before* problems have developed or at least when they are just starting. For example, many community agencies schedule regular programs for new stepparents or even whole stepfamilies so that the new relationships and responsibilities can be explored and misperceptions corrected.

Support Groups for At-Risk Parents

Community organizations of lay persons have been created by individuals in at-risk situations. Recognizing their special burdens, they have united to educate and support each other. Parents Without Partners is one such group with many local branches. Stepparents' organizations (e.g., Stepparent Association of America, Inc.) along with associations for foster parents and parents with adopted children are available in many communities in recognition of the added complexity to family relationships when parenting must be shared with biologically unrelated adults acting in new parental roles.

The empirical evidence that such educational and support activities make a genuine difference in reducing family problems is not yet available. We know already, however, that parents report that they experience the benefits that are usually derived from participation in support groups (L. Guerney and Wolfgang, 1981). Support groups have been demonstrated to enrich individual participants' lives (Whittaker et al., 1983). It is expected that research now being conducted will confirm that these parent programs also benefit families.

Community Networking for Problem Prevention. A model that has been used in a limited number of middle-class communities for the purpose of introducing some social control over adolescents is the Parent Network (Simpkinson and Redmond, 1982). Parents form mutual parenting networks that arrive at guidelines for community-wide "conduct standards" for youth. The teens can be included to help negotiate these norms. Once consensus has been reached, parents in the network abide by it in enforcing rules for their youngsters. Furthermore, they attempt to disseminate these norms to the entire community. Schools may also be part of the community consensus. The expected and achieved result is that clarity and consistency about expected behaviors of the youngsters on the part of all in the community will prevent confusion and conflict. Drinking and other high-risk behaviors can be controlled. Organization and maintenance of these community networks is a task that only the most perseverant and dedicated can accomplish. The rewards are apparently great when they do (Simpkinson and Redmond, 1982). With rapidly changing social conditions resulting in different social environments for virtually every cohort, this approach establishes an anchorpoint for everyone concerned. Community guidelines assist parent and youngster alike in keeping their behaviors within accept-able boundaries. A sense of control over the social environment can provide security and reduce the anxiety and anger that can arise when standards and support for them are uncertain.

Support Strategies for Youth

In this section, we will describe services targeted to youths as individuals. These services are primarily supportive and frequently at the preventive level. Unlike individual *treatment* for youth which requires an identity as a "certified" victim or offender, support services place no external classifica-tion demands on the consumer of the service. The premise of support/preventive services is that individuals are the best judge of whether they require the service and are free to approach the service providers. Support service providers generally do not offer treatment as well but refer clients to those who do and try to support them in carrying through the referral. Frequently, support services are out-reach in nature, making special, some-times very innovative, efforts to reach potential consumers of the service. This measure sends an important message to sensitive youths: "This service is really meant to be used—see how readily available it is." Fees for the services are low or nonexistent. Services may be received in many instances without parental knowledge or approval. The importance of this feature is critical for youngsters who would be afraid of family reactions to their seeking help.

The services described here will be listed in order of decreasing formality and increasing accessibility to youth.

Peer-"Counseling" Programs

Many schools and church groups train selected adolescents in their institutions in listening or helping skills so that their peers in need of support may have ready access to help. The goal is to be friendly and provide advice for further help if it appears appropriate. Confidentiality is assured. The basic premise is that adolescents, like adults, will more readily seek support from nonprofessional peers. Generally, these programs are supervised by pro-fessionals. The programs have had a history of uneven success. The model of "peer in the image of professional" failed to work in a large high school, despite excellent training and much effort to advertise the low risk of using the service to students. In an analysis of the failure, the conviction de-veloped that the peers sitting in offices and "standing in for counselors" presented even a greater barrier than going to a professional. Students seemed to be less sure about possible outcomes than they were with professional counselors whose roles and relationships to the school and family were well understood (Peterman, 1974, personal communication).

In contrast, a program that permits the peer "counselors" to circulate freely among the other students in the course of their natural school day is working very well in several schools in Maryland and southern Pennsylvania. Training and supervision features of the program are similar to the unsuccessful one (Rocks, 1984, personal communication). The hypothesis developed on the basis of these results is that students will more readily avail themselves of a peer support service if access to the peer providers is simplified, natural, and informal. The latter model more closely resembles the informal approaches made to natural helpers in the community.

Indirectly, any service set up for youth activities (e.g., YMCAs and recreation centers) fulfills the same goal. Caring, youth-oriented contacts are genuine, informal resources for youth. Unfortunately, some abuse-prone families deny such opportunities to their children, preferring them to live in isolation, insulated from supportive segments of the community.

Formal Support Programs for At-Risk Youth

Organizations set up for adults frequently develop parallel programs for teens that contain all of the features of adult support programs. Parents Anonymous has embarked upon a campaign to create "Kids Groups" to parallel their parents groups. Such groups are functioning in more than 50 communities (Lieber, 1983). There are youth programs for foster children annexed to local foster parent organizations, and for the learning disabled, with local chapters of the American Association of Citizens with Learning Disabilities (AACLD). Chartered at the national level are the youth organizations of Alcoholics Anonymous—Alateen—and International Youth Council, affiliated with Parents Without Partners.

Local schools and mental health centers conduct programs for children and youth who are experiencing major changes in their family structures (e.g., separation, divorce, and the acquisition of stepparents). One successful model conducted in the school for youth is *Changing Families* (Sheridan, 1980, 1981).

Phone Services for Youth

While extremely helpful and clearly of benefit to youths in circumstances that are known to place them at risk for abuse, the participant programs do require an acceptance by the youth, and in most instances the parents that support activities are appropriate. While in no way pejorative, labels are necessary nonetheless for youngsters to participate in the more formal programs. Labeling does bring with it at least a minimal degree of intrusiveness on the youngster's and family's privacy.

For the youth or family that cannot deal with even this minimal amount of public acknowledgment of their personal or family difficulties, the telephone service is ideal. It is nonintrusive, absolutely anonymous, and totally within the control of the caller. Only services oriented to the most extreme cases (e.g., suicide lines) have the capability and legal right to try to trace calls, and then only when the life of a caller is imperiled. Despite the limitations of phone services, they fill many service gaps. An additional one is their relatively low cost, which permits them to operate 24 hours a day when services from formal agencies and informal helpers, even friends, are frequently unavailable. The natural response to use the telephone by troubled persons is revealed by the tendency, particularly of young people, to call all-night disc jockeys and talk shows to divulge their problems.

Some youth lines are staffed by other youth under the supervision of trained adults, usually professional counselors. Comparisons of the services offered by youth versus adults in relation to the seriousness of calls, referrals made, and other such issues are not available. All of these services have the goal of providing support and making referrals only if the youngsters are interested. They are not designed for emergencies, although they are ready for them. Being there to deal with feelings, provide feedback, and assist in coping really classifies them as "warm" rather than "hot" lines.

A related service springing up around the country involves phone services for latchkey children and youth. While the emphasis of these lines is on the after-school hours, when millions of children are known to be unsupervised on a daily basis, unsupervised youngsters are vulnerable at any hour. The goal of 24-hour service would seem appropriate. This approach enjoys wide acceptance by children and youth—10% of callers in one community are 13 or older (L. Guerney and Moore, 1983)—in towns and cities all over the country.

Drug and Alcohol Abuse Prevention

These programs are directed to young as well as teenaged children. They are aimed at developing ego-strength, enhancing decision-making skills, and clarifying values. Participation in such programs can prevent youth from becoming involved in substance abuse. Youthful drunkenness and drug use spark aggression in some parents, prompting harsh psychological and physical responses. Parents whose personal psychology would not ordinarily generate abusive responses can become so frustrated with their offending teenagers that they strike out in rage and in the hope of restoring some control.

Programs for Adolescent Parents

These young parents, primarily mothers, are not at high risk for abuse from their parents unless they live at home. However, they are at high risk for abusing their own children (DeLissovoy, 1973). Their immaturity, frequent discord in their own families of origin, their loss of a reference group in many instances when they become different from their schoolmates, tend to create vulnerability to the stress of the parenting role. Fortunately, in recent years more is being done for these youngsters to try to help them stay in the mainstream and to facilitate their entry into supportive helping networks, both formal and informal. Parent education is offered in a supportive climate for the young parents.

FUTURE PROSPECTS FOR INTERVENTION

A reading of the array of services that exist for parents and adolescents that deals with factors related to maltreatment could lead to a sense that much is being done for families to both prevent and treat. In fact, many of the services mentioned are not available in all communities, are underfunded or funded on a yearly basis only, and are underutilized by the target groups to the extent needed for sufficient impact (Rosenberg et al., 1979).

The programs described represent many strategies, some proven and some only promising or merely worth noting. Which are effective and which are not? Where are the biggest gaps in meeting family needs? Where do we need to go? Where is it feasible to go, in light of the realities with which interventionists must live?

Effectiveness of Interventions

Asking for the most return for the investment requires studies of the comparative effects of implementing the various strategies. The complexity of meaningful evaluations across approaches with comparable populations makes it very difficult to answer the important questions. Experts from the National Institute for Drug and Alcohol agree that communication skills and skills in establishing rules and expectations are needed for successful family functioning (Gelb, 1984). Studies of the incidence of abuse in various neighborhoods reveal that there is differential vulnerability as a function of neighborhood features (Garbarino and Sherman, 1980). The use of community support strategies is highly successful in the area of impulse control as well as in secondary problem prevention (Lenrow and Burch, 1981). Certain groups (e.g., stepparents and adolescent parents) are known to be particularly vulnerable to maltreatment. Treatment is available only after damage has been done and is very expensive. These few facts that have been established point to a need for a shift to strategies at the prevention level.

Looking back from the time that a problem is revealed in a family to the earliest inception of factors that operated to create and to maintain the problem, we can see that prevention applied at the broadest and most distant level from the current problem might have had some impact on preventing the family from moving up the ladder to more severe dysfunction. For example, a youngster who is hyperactive because of a neurological impairment can create havoc in a family that is vulnerable to control difficulties, and as we saw in Chapter 8, many abused youth evidence developmental problems. Once early control difficulties are revealed (usually because of problems of some sort in the child), preventive efforts can be used to contain the problem from becoming permanent and extreme. Looking back, we can see that the control shortcomings could have been addressed preventively by teaching the parents skills and providing them with supports. Looking back further to the most basic kind of prevention effort that would have had positive effects for such a family, we can recognize that eliminating negative factors in the family's social and economic infrastructure would have reduced the parents' control vulnerability. Finally, moving back yet another step, prevention of the neurological problem in the unborn or newborn child would have been prevention of the ultimate variety.

There is really no reason to delay prevention work until it has been determined at which of the prevention levels intervention will be most productive. Prevention of abnormal dysfunction at any of the levels would create a decrease in problems at the next level.

In speaking of preventing problems, it is more stimulating to innovation to conceptualize the preventing of problems as the promoting of positive qualities and behaviors. Preventing negative consequences of parental stress would be viewed as promoting the highest and best known parental functioning. With an eye toward that goal, it is relatively easy to see where action should be taken. Strengthening the social and economic infrastructure is beyond the scope of the behavioral scientist, as is basic action for promoting the healthy intrauterine neurological development of infants. However, public health promotion for prenatal care for mothers and neonatal care for them and their infants would be efforts well within the scope of community-oriented behavioral interventionists. Immediate measures of success could be developed in terms of the numbers of persons availing themselves of the health-promotion services. Years later, statistics on birth defects or problems in thriving compared to those of the pre-health-promotion era, could demonstrate whether or not the desired effects had been obtained. All that is further required to do these kinds of positive promotion is the "will" to do so.

"Will," in this context, translates to the enduring pursuit of methods that will promote healthy functioning by all those with access to public and private resources. Endless studies to define what health is and means to individuals are not necessary to begin work. Examining any one problem area can readily lead to recognizing major dysfunction. Asking what is the opposite to the dysfunction quickly yields the major features of healthy functioning. Achieving these features becomes the interventionist's goal, and the objective becomes the identification of the best means to reach the goal. For example, it is known by employers, mothers, and most of the community-at-large, that normal stress can become distress when mothers at work are worried about their children at home, particularly when the latter are alone. Concern over children is a major impediment to good work performance (Crouter, 1984). The goal, then, becomes promoting means to support and control children so that mothers will know that their health and safety is assured (in as much as that is ever possible). We could develop after-school programs with many options to suit family needs. We could educate to facilitate mothers' coping with their dual roles. Women could, upon entering the work place, be given orientation programs to their double roles as workers and parents by women who have successfully managed both.

Whenever an additional role is added for *any* individual—a man becoming a father, for example—orientation should be given as a part of community and/or work-place services. The Employee Assistance Programs, now so popular and so beneficial to worker and employee alike, can provide people with knowledge of what to expect of their new roles, suggestions for coping, practicing skills for doing so, and means of receiving additional help if needed.

Realities for the Interventionist

While all of the knowledge to implement strategies such as the one described above for working parents is presently available, the "will" required for such programs on the part of the relevant actors is not currently present. This is the case with most interventions that are not direct treatment, although the Employee Assistance Programs are seen as providing the means for a great breakthrough in thinking about prevention by promoting positive functioning. For employers who have such programs, the monies saved in reduced absenteeism and the reduction of habit-control problems such as alcoholism (Salade, 1984) provide hard evidence that prevention strategies really work.

In the interim, in making choices about where and how to intervene in relation to major problems, the interventionist is probably going to have the greatest success in meeting all of the demands made of intervention by the community if the intervention devised can be both treatment and prevention. By this we mean that it can help deal with everyday problems experienced by participants but at the same time have the effect of preventing further problems. An example of an intervention with these dual properties, pertinent to maltreatment of adolescents, is the parenting-skills course that teaches parents how to deal with their preadolescent children. The parent education strategy both for remedial and prevention purposes has become accepted and of proven efficacy (Coufal and Brock, 1979; L. Guerney, 1983). Since the skills of communication and healthy means of asserting parental control are actually generic, they could be taught at any age prior to adolescence. However, keeping in mind the need to program when motivation to learn is highest, it would be most appropriate to time the training to coincide with heightening parental anxiety about dealing with adolescents (i.e., immediately prior to the teen years). These programs can be offered relatively inexpensively, frequently, and targeted to special or broad populations as needed.

Neighborhood Parent Education. Carrying the parent education strategy back another step toward a more basic level of prevention, the development of "neighborhood parent educators" would seem quite feasible, as soon as the "will" for it develops. Such an approach would be both preventive and remedial, low in cost, provide local social support and control, and be readily available. Natural helpers in neighborhoods could be identified (realistically those neighborhoods at high risk for maltreatment problems would need to be in the first wave). They would be given training in parenting principles, helping principles, and advocacy strategies. Sensitivity about overprofessionalizing natural helpers is now widespread, so training could be conducted that would preserve the appeal of the natural helper to the community (Gottlieb, 1981). The neighborhood parent educators would make it their business to offer programs to new parents and parents entering new stages of child rearing (e.g., school-age and adolescence). Programs could be conducted in homes or a neutral community setting, preferably with groups, but also with individual families if they are unwilling to join groups. The neighborhood worker could take responsibility for latchkey children in the area and offer coping-skills training and support programs for youngsters who are at risk on any dimension. In areas of high population density, a worker could be responsible for a housing development, block, or other meaningful unit. Professional consultants could be available on a regular basis to the neighborhood workers.

Officially, that is to funders, other agencies, etc., the neighborhood parent educator's overarching goal would be "quality control" of parenting. In the neighborhood, the worker would serve as a family advocate. The title should reflect that conceptualization of the role. "Family aide" or "family advocate" would be possibilities. The critical task would be to serve as friend to the families, calling on them when they arrive in the neighborhood and when they leave, giving them the name and location of their next neighborhood's educator, visiting when a new baby arrives, when a child is starting school, is ill, etc. Unlike the family visitors proposed by Kempe (1976), families would not be required to relate to them. These workers would have their hands on the pulses of the neighborhood's parents and be available for positive purposes as well as when help was needed. The essence of natural helping is that helpers are known to be of positive value on an ongoing basis. Thus, community members turn to them when in need because of their histories as well as their availability. The "Family Advocate" would be a more informal and accessible version of the "neighborhood wise man" (woman) to whom communities have turned when necessary since tribal days.

The Level of Intervention

Strategies such as the neighborhood parent-advocate approach designed to provide support and social control in given neighborhoods still address the problem of maltreatment prevention only on a per family basis. In the same way that a neurological impairment will occur in a predictable number of infants if genetic, prenatal, birth, and neonatal conditions are not optimal, maltreatment may occur in a predictable number of families when social conditions are less than optimal. Since the social conditions of given families are derived from the larger social system, we are only ameliorating when we prevent or correct maltreatment on a family basis. In the words of David Gil, one of the pioneers in the study of family violence, "one ought to avoid the illusion that ameliorative measures, designed specifically to reduce suffering, can also eliminate the sources of violence and abuse from the fabric of society (Gil, 1983, p. 306).

If strategies are to go beyond the mere containment of problem behaviors, decisions must be made about system levels at which to intervene. Clearly, these decisions will be based on beliefs about the causes of the problem. If one believes that conditions of the family, community, or society at large are responsible, one will not be content to deal only with problematic or at-risk individuals. Believing that unemployment is a major causal factor in setting off abusive responses in individuals with histories that make them susceptible, one could very sensibly decide to invest money into programs that provide employment. If one believes that susceptible individuals who become unemployed will not abuse if they are given emotional support in some way from the community, one could plan support interventions as opposed to trying to find jobs. This, of course, would not be so basic a correction. However, it is more manageable and more within the scope of possibility than supplying jobs to all of the unemployed. Interventions at the higher levels (i.e., those aimed at the macro-and exosystems) are much more difficult to implement because they involve more people and more resources. Rarely can we undertake these efforts on more than a demonstration basis without massive political mobilizations.

As a result of these practical principles constricting interventions, we tend to intervene first at the level of victim and perpetrator, an approach that virtually no one will oppose. We are more likely to move on to a more basic level sooner rather than later if costs of the individual strategies are high. Reducing the use of foster care is an example of an effort to cut costs, not only for reasons of the child's best interest, but because of the staggering price of placement as a solution to family instability or inadequacy (Hubbell, 1981). Current good casework practice demands work with the natural family before children are removed, a more basic intervention strategy.

Another example of the process described above has occurred in relation to adolescent maltreatment. In the past, youth were the recipients of intervention if trouble existed in the family. Many professionals were uncomfortable with that tactic because of their awareness that factors at the family level contributed heavily to and even caused problems in the youngster. However, before anything could change, methods for working at least with minimal effectiveness with families first had to be devised. Second, the public at large—professionals, government officials, and community leaders—had to agree that the cost was too high for the minimal effectiveness achieved in focusing interventions only on youth. Third, evidence had to be accepted that youths could in fact frequently be victims in families and deserved help in dealing with families that mistreated them.

What are conscientious interventionists to do when they are aware that afflicted individuals are reflecting problems in other larger systems, and further know that changing the structure or function of the larger system is slow, uneven, and much less manageable and consensual than working at the individual level? Analogously, what do physicians do about diseases that are environmentally induced? For example, they refuse to treat malaria victims until all of breeding places of mosquitoes have been eradicated? No, instead they call for the intermediate step of reducing the number of mosquitoes, through extensive spraying. Certainly, it is more likely to be perceived as within the purses and imaginations of most people to settle upon the spraying approach. The "Principle of Efficacy" is generally at least implicitly applied in arriving at these kinds of intervention decisions. What is the lowest level at which intervention can be undertaken that will result in a visible difference in the relevant phenomenon at a reasonable cost and time?

In the case of maltreatment, factors are implicated at all levels from the individual parents up to and including the societal level (Belsky, 1980). Most parents are not abusers, even though most have been exposed to similar values and many to similar environmental stresses as those who do abuse. Clearly, there are legitimate areas for intervention at the individual parent level, a level at which interventions can realistically be planned and implemented with expected effectiveness. Considering all of the issues of concern to the interventionist, it becomes apparent that it is at the level of the individual parent(s) that interventions must be focused at this time. It is important to remember that policymakers and interventionists do not believe that they are "removing swamps" when directing interventions toward parents. At most, they are "spraying" and perhaps no more than attempting to reduce the severity of the "disease" symptoms. There is still an enormous need to get at the underpinnings of the abuse of children and youth by addressing *additional* interventions to the attitudes, values, and functioning of society as a whole that spawn the conditions that mediate the abuse of our children and youth.

These practical issues are disconcerting to interventionists. None wants to wittingly or unwittingly contribute to the prolongation of any problem by addressing interventions to only the most available and visible components. Nonetheless, we must direct efforts where it is most possible until the social climate supports problem solving of a more basic and enduring nature.

APPENDIX I: AN INTERVENTION CASE STUDY: THE FIP INTERVENTION PROGRAM

RATIONALE FOR THE INTERVENTION PROGRAM

Parents are the target of choice for intervention at this stage of development in the field of adolescent and child maltreatment as we have seen earlier in this chapter. Educational approaches seem most appropriate when the target group of parents are at risk for maltreatment as opposed to actually abusive. When low-risk parents are also to be included in an intervention plan, no treatment goal is really appropriate. The emphasis more appropriately should be on information and skills that would be of value to both groups of parents. Both high- and low-risk parents can benefit from programming for the enrichment of parent–adolescent relationships and positive adolescent management alternatives.

For the FIP intervention case study, both high- and low-risk families were of interest. Project personnel were vitally concerned with education for high-risk families but also believed that low-risk families would be interested as well. Our response was to offer the opportunity for parent education to all parents at the time of their participation in the interviews. For reasons to be explained later in this section, there appeared to be advantages to including both high- and low-risk families in the same program. The goal was increased use of positive behaviors by parents and children. To this end, the programs described in the next section were piloted. We will also include some more specific principles of intervention programming not previously discussed and show how they were applied in this FIP case study.

Issues in Recruitment

Unlike traditional clinical interventions, psychoeducational programs (e.g., parent education) usually must use out-reach efforts to recruit the desired participants. Even when a program has been designed to address the needs of a particular clinical group (e.g., abusing parents), unless the program is compulsory, vigorous efforts must be made to direct participants to the program. Participants need to understand the purpose of the program and relate it to needs *they* perceive as desirable to address.

Impersonal invitations to all members of a target group (e.g., via posters) to enroll in a program are generally not enough. While educational in nature, the topics in psychoeducational programs are personal and relatively intrusive, and perhaps threatening—not quite the same as enrolling in a computer course.

One step that interventionists have found helpful is to seek the support of mediating or liaison persons (L. Guerney, 1977; Rosenberg et al., 1979).

These mediating individuals, generally known to intended participants in relation to some other service (e.g., teacher, case worker) assist in clarifying the value of the program, encouraging participation, and offering prompts about mechanics of enrollment. Incentives for enrolling also help. Baby sitting, transportation support, and recognition awards often are effective along with the more usual financial ones. More about incentives will be discussed under "Attendance" later in this chapter.

FIP Program. Mediators in our program were the research team members who interviewed families. At the time of the interviews, they informed parents that participants in the research project would be offered a parent-education course after all interviews had been completed. Researchers offered information and encouragement about the course. Even though the interval between interviews and the course was long in some instances, contact between project personnel and parents frequently continued, not only for research reasons, but also because parents inquired about the program or other nonresearch family issues. Interviewing teams had established rapport and credibility with the families, helping to overcome "natural" resistance to participation in a course so personal as one on parenting. Project personnel had laid the original groundwork, making it easier to approach parents at course time.

Personalized letters were sent to each family with postcards to be returned indicating the best nights and locations for class attendance. Since our parents lived in many communities, a location was to be chosen that was central for the largest number who were willing to attend.

Parents were also asked if they would be interested in bringing along their project-aged children to a parallel program for adolescents. The primary purpose of this request was to provide support for parents for child care. However, we were also genuinely interested in the children's participation, both for its possible value for them and for their parents should the children make any positive gains as a result of participation. The final recruitment step was a phone call notifying families of the night and location. No distinction was made in recruitment between high- and low-risk parents. The plan was to mix the families in any way that their own response to the program arrangements would dictate. Issues about "mixing" group members will be discussed later. Nineteen parents representing 14 individual families agreed to participate. Total response represented about 27% of project families. Eight of the families planned to bring one or more children.

Choice of a Site for Group Meetings

Sensitivity to the psychological significance of the site at which programs are offered can be a factor in program success (Abidin, 1980). The location can be a barrier of a subtle nature to some parents. Parents are not so likely to attend if the site is distant, complicated to reach (e.g., parking difficulties), in a threatening neighborhood, or in a building that has negative connotations. Mental health centers, child welfare agencies, and schools are sometimes avoided because they elicit negative emotional responses for certain participants. A school might be considered a neutral site to middle- and upper-income families, but to the economically and/or educationally disadvantaged, a school can represent years of negative experiences.

FIP Program. For some rural families, the University is a threatening place. For the site for the FIP program, we were fortunate to have access to a small "homey," noninstitutional-looking building on the periphery of the Pennsylvania State University campus, right off a main street, with parking available. From past experience, we knew this location was more acceptable to many rural families than other campus locations.

Attendance

Attendance at noncompulsory parent-education classes is notoriously erratic, if not actually poor (Rosenberg et al., 1979). Therefore, it was decided that an incentive for attendance should be piloted. The following scheme was introduced.

Each parent received a coupon each week upon attendance at the class. A family with two parents attending thus received double coupons. Each of these coupons was deposited in a coupon box from which would be drawn on the last night a coupon for an "Attendance Prize." While there was a risk that someone who attended less frequently would win, everyone understood that the more coupons earned the greater the chance for winning. The prize was $75. This amount seemed large enough to serve as an incentive to overcome the typical difficulties experienced in getting to classes of this type. The children were also offered an attendance prize via an attendance coupon drawing on the last night. This prize was $25.

The results with the use of these attendance incentives were very encouraging. Multiplying the maximum number of participants (19) by the seven classes results in 133 possible attendances. Actually there were 114 attendances or an unusually high 85% (see L. Guerney, 1977).

Issues in Grouping

The customary practice when assembling parent-education or support groups is to place together parents who are at risk on a similar dimension (e.g., single parents, divorcing parents) or whose children are at risk in relation to specific handicaps (e.g., parents of children with asthma). This homogeneous approach to grouping is based on the conviction that content is more critical than process in problem solving. People with asthma of course do not have the same problems as people with arthritis. But do they not both share the common goal of needing to learn how to reduce stress and to simplify their lives to facilitate their at least somewhat limited functioning? If one examines the *processes* that different types of persons need to solve problems, it is possible to identify many processes that can be translated into teachable skills.

The author disputes the need to separate parents into discrete groups for parent training. Basic parenting skills are generic to all parents in a common culture. Moreover, groups sharing only content often reach dead ends. There are a limited number of complaints and methods for dealing with them for any category of parents. On the other hand, all parents, regardless of their category, can relate to positive skills. If they are particularly deficient, they should gain the most (Weiss, 1973). If they are already applying knowledge and skills, as many low-risk parents are expected to be doing, they would experience a validation of their parenting and receive much rewarding feedback from leaders. Finally, the more functional parents also serve a modeling function for less competent parents in the group. This phenomenon of higher functioning persons teaching and supporting the less able is the basis for the gains demonstrated in support groups (Killilea, 1976). It is not a one-way street, however. The "Helper/Therapy" principle demonstrated by Riessman (1965) operates to provide help to those who serve as therapists as well as vice versa.

Of course, the unique needs of specific parents must be identified and examined in relation to program components. Modules must be included with content specific to the identified needs of the target parents. For example, a program aimed at or containing a number of single parents must address issues of relevance to them. Not doing so would leave them feeling unconsidered. On the other hand, the generic parenting skills are required for dealing with situations common to all parent-child interactions. Use of examples for discussion and skills practice that are relevant to the specific situations of parents is an excellent way to meet their needs and at the same time release the programmers from the homogeneous grouping restriction.

The FIP Grouping. The author, who served as both program developer and parent group leader, made a decision at the outset that the high- and low-risk FIP parents would not be separated. Aside from having the strong convictions about grouping discussed above, the author was aware that volunteers for the parent training might not fall conveniently into groups of appropriate size. With absences and attrition, a parent group really should have at least eight members at the time of its inception. Thus, four or five members can be expected to attend on a regular basis, the bare minimum for viable group functioning.

Issues in the Content of the Parenting Course

What should be the content of a parent education program designed to address the needs of both high- and low-risk parents? What needs are peculiar to the two respective subgroups and how should these be addressed? For this programmer, there was no question that the skills approach was the one to take. Evidence exists that skills approaches are most productive in changing behavior as well as increasing knowledge or positive feelings about the parent and children (Coufal, 1982; Egan, 1983; Guerney and Wolfgang, 1981; O'Dell, 1979). The skills approach requires that parents be given information about more general principles followed by demonstrations and modeling of preferred behaviors implementing the principles. These leader activities must be followed by practice by the parents in use of skills and application of the principles demonstrated and taught. Homework must be included to promote transfer and generalization to home settings.

Note, however, that the skills approach is really only a method of teaching. Any kind of content can be adapted to a skills approach as long as behaviors appropriate to social roles or status can be taught. What should be the specific content then of the FIP Parent Program?

Lack of empathy and of positive communications with their children have been cited on the part of high-risk and abusive parents (e.g., Burgess and Conger, 1978; Gray, 1978). Empirical evidence is strong on the value of teaching empathy and other positive communication skills to generate more positive parental attitudes toward children (Egan, 1983; Guerney and Wolfgang, 1981; Wolfe, 1984) as well as enhancing family, peer, and professional relationships (Carkhuff, 1969; Feshbach, 1983; L. Guerney, 1976).

Therefore, empathy was stressed as the basic communication skill (see Table 11.A1 for an outline of the FIP Pilot Parenting Program). The eight skills taught were adapted for the special needs of adolescents and their parents from the generic *Parenting*, a skills-training program developed by the author (L. Guerney, 1980). *Parenting* contains five basic skills and one complex integrative skill for discriminating the appropriate application of the basic skills to meet parental goals. The program can be adapted to meet special parenting needs, and adaptations have been empirically evaluated as effective for parents of newborns (Schellenbach, 1979) and foster parents (L. Guerney, 1977).

The course is conceptualized as having two major thrusts, both considered essential to the promotion of parent/child relationships. The first part is directed toward the affective dimensions of relationships, with empathy as the key skill. The second part addresses the control (or power or influence) dimension endeavoring to teach parents many discipline alternatives. For the FIP parents, seven control skills were included (e.g., contracting). Two

Table 11.A1. Outline of the FIP Parenting Program

Session I	Overview of program What to Expect of your Adolescent
Session II	Adolescent–parent relations What are the issues?
Session III	Listening and speaking to increase communication Practice in the use of communication skills
Session IV	Strategies for problem solving Establishing goals Structuring for success Reinforcement
Session V	Setting limits and deciding consequences
Session VI	Cooperative problem solving and contracts
Session VII	Putting it all together—How each lesson builds from the last

informational lessons were also included: realistic expectations and relationship issues for adolescents.

Principles of Leadership

Of necessity, parenting-skills programs must be task oriented. The scheduled content makes the classes proactive, reducing opportunity for parents to introduce their problems and reactions to them from the leader and/or other members. Time for discussions, therefore, must be built in so that parents' needs to recite problems and commiserate with other parents are satisfied. The leader must be ever watchful to be sure that these discussions do not consume too much of the group time. However, these exchanges are an important element in building rapport and mutual support among group members. While skills learning and practice palces greater demand on parents, the skills components are the most effective in promoting behavior change (Coufal and Brock, 1982; O'Dell, 1973). Discussions provide catharsis and social support which are less effective in promoting new behaviors.

The leader must model warmth, genuineness, empathy, and positive reinforcement for the parents—all goal behaviors associated with the parenting skills. Feedback from parents indicates that they are sensitive to and appreciative of these qualities of the leader (Guerney and Wolfgang, 1981). Positive reinforcement for appropriate responses is critical to participation and learning. Group members acquire these behaviors from the leaders and employ them in the group, which provides them with acceptable means to show caring and to exercise social control over each other.

The leader should also avoid preconceptions about parent abilities or deficits and potential. Thus, possibilities are minimized that biased expectations about learning will enter into the leaders' response to group members. Case workers conducting parent groups confess that they must deal with negative attitudes toward parents with chronic difficulties.

It is probably preferable, although there is no empirical evidence to support this known to the author, that leaders be *un*acquainted with parents' histories if they are to conduct classes with goals of behavior change. It is probably wise to assume that the phenomenon of expectation limiting progress described by Rosenthal and Jacobson (1968) in relation to teachers of children, could operate with adult educators of high-risk groups. While Rosenthal's work has been challenged, enthusiasm and conviction on the part of leaders toward adults' learning ability has been demonstrated to be important to success (Cheavens, 1958).

FIP Leadership. In order to be certain that there were no preconceptions on her part that might influence the quality of parent responses, the leader requested project staff not to tell her until classes were finished into which risk categories the participants were classified. The other principles of leadership described above also were carefully followed.

THE FIP CHILDREN'S GROUP PROGRAM

This too was a pilot effort. The program was intended to parallel the parents' program and promote the communication, relationship-building, and problem-solving skills in the youngsters. High- and low-risk children were combined. Leaders were uninformed until the program was over about the risk status of the youngsters. See Table 11.A2 for the outline of the children's program. Leaders were two male graduate students, with some intervention experience with youngsters.

A total of 12 youngsters attended the sessions. However, despite the attendance award, the children were not nearly so regular in attendance as their parents. Illness, homework, or other competing activities were the reasons given. Classes averaged six children per session, with only two attending every session. Children were in all cases dependent on parents for transportation and permission to attend.

The target age group was youngsters between 10 and 15. However, children aged 7–13 were brought along by their parents. Permission to do so had been requested during the recruitment phase so that group leaders were aware in advance that program content might need to cover a wider range of ages.

Table 11.A2. Skills Training for Adolescents and Preadolescents

Duration:	7 classes (1.5–2 hours)
Trainees:	Approximately 6 per session
Ages:	10–15
Purposes:	Increase communication and relationship skills.
	Provide styles of interaction that are alternatives to aggression, withdrawal, and immaturity.

Basic presentational mode (two experienced male leaders):

    Modeling (discussion of skills and examples with inappropriate and appropriate manners of responding)

    Role playing

    Feedback

    Transfer of training (real-life situations and homework)

Class topics:		
	First class:	Introduction/communication and relationships
	Focus:	Introduction, ground rules, overview of program, discussion of adolescent development (problem-oriented), discussion of the importance of communication and relationships, discussion of basic reinforcement, role-plays of class issues.
	Second class:	Knowing and expressing feelings
	Focus:	Understanding what you are feeling, attributing events to feelings, rights and responsibilities for feelings, knowing when to express feelings (strategic interactions), skills in communication (effective and ineffective ways), consequences of communication, assertiveness, role-plays of class issues.
	Third class:	Listening
	Focus:	Reflective listening skills, anticipating others' feelings, consequences and benefits of listening, role-plays of class issues.
	Fourth class:	Parents and families
	Focus:	Communication skills applied to parental and family issues, parental expectations, sibling difficulties, dealing with specific problems (e.g., anger, limits).
	Fifth class:	Friends and school
	Focus:	Communication and self-awareness skills applied to friendship and school issues, peer groups, boyfriend/girlfriend, loneliness, teachers, grades, parent–peers–school interactions, vocational decisions, drugs.
	Sixth class:	Group activity (local video games establishment was visited, by child choice)
	Seventh class:	Review of skills, practice, evolution of the program by trainees

Issues in Evaluation

It is the practice of the author to use only formative evaluation procedures in the piloting of a program. Revisions are made more readily if the program is considered in process. Furthermore, outcome measures are premature when "kinks" have yet to be worked out of the program. Outcome measures could be invalid if the intervention process did not proceed as conceptualized. If a pilot effort suggests that only limited changes are needed for continued use of the program, outcome measures are employed for the second use of a program.

Irrespective of the stage of program development, one must always gather feedback from program participants about their perceptions of the program. Information about individual components is especially important in the earlier stages of program development. Participant ratings of the comparative value for them of the components are especially useful.

FIP Parent Program Feedback

This was a pilot program with an unusual membership constellation. While the *Parenting* program had been proven successful with other parents in the past, this pilot effort was unique.

Fortunately, feedback on the FIP parent program was very positive. Parents filled out a questionnaire at the last session, "Parents' comments about the FIP Parenting Program." Parents liked the content, the leader, the attendance slips, and the group interaction.

Nearly all parents indicated that there was not enough time to cover things as thoroughly as they would have liked. Some wanted more classes. A few indicated that they would have liked more time for interaction among group members. Some thought the group too large to get as much help with specific problems as they would have liked. Everyone indicated that "knowing that other people have similar problems" was very reassuring.

Leader's Evaluation of the Parent Program

Parents were asked to do homework and hand it in each week. As a group, parents were not particularly conscientious about completing and handing in these assignments despite much reinforcement for doing so in the form of both written comments and class recognition. Nonetheless, the completed assignments indicated clearly that parents were mastering the content. They were asked to indicate when and how they had used the skills taught during the week with their families. They were also requested to indicate whether their application of the skills and principles seemed "helpful, not helpful, or neither." Across the group, responses to this question over the accumulated weekly assignments fell about equally into the three respective categories. Certain individuals tended to report more in the "helpful" category than the others. They had experienced early success with skill application.

No differences were noted in the participation (or parent feedback) from parents who were at risk for abuse and those who were not on most dimensions. The only family who requested follow-up communication skills training were from the at-risk group as a result of emotional abuse. Two high-risk fathers did not participate at any time in the large group interactions and only reluctantly (but good-naturedly) in the small groups where everyone was given an exercise to carry out. Both these men were excessively punitive to their sons but not agency-confirmed abusers. These men were far less educated and had lower level jobs than the other fathers. It is more parsimonious to account for their performance differences on the basis of socioeconomic status, it would seem, than on factors related to risk for maltreatment.

Leaders of both the adults' and children's groups thought that there had been no negative consequences of the heterogeneous grouping arrangement in either the adults' or children's groups. Without comparisons to alternate homogeneous groupings, it is impossible to know whether one strategy is superior. However, it is reassuring to the interventionist to know that no deleterious effects were observed from the use of an unorthodox approach. One might suggest that, in programming for groups that *on average* are not extreme in displaying abusive behaviors, heterogeneous groups would not be inappropriate.

Children's Evaluation. The children's evaluation was not written. In the last class, which nearly everyone attended because the attendance prize was given that night, the two leaders asked the children to use their newly acquired communication skills to express their feelings and ideas about the classes. Since good communication does not include evaluation of persons, per se, but rather focuses on behaviors and other objective phenomena, there was no inherent threat in this exercise. Children indicated that they thought the classes were sometimes too much like school, but they liked everything else about them. Some reported that they disliked having been pressured by parents to attend.

Leaders' Evaluation of the Children's Program

Leaders believed that the children enjoyed the program for the most part, particularly the role-playing and warm-up games. For the more didactic components (none prolonged), leaders really had to try harder to get the youngsters involved. Children were bored and listless if the level of stimulation was not very high. However, the content, per se, was relevant to all the youngsters—even the younger ones. Leaders took great pains to use relevant examples and keep on the children's level.

Leaders believed that the program was rewarding enough to all to justify its employment again. No major areas were considered unsuitable for future use.

A Final Word on the Children's Program

As a result of the FIP case study, no empirical case can be built for the use of a children's program in general or of this specific approach in particular. Nonetheless, what is known about elements for successful interventions would support both the strategy of programming for children as well as their parents and the content and approach of the FIP children's program.

Children at risk (the majority of faithful attenders at the group meetings were in the high-risk category, we later found) need positive adult models such as those provided by the leaders. They need to feel understood and accepted. They also need positive social skills to help them avoid being provocative and to avoid being trapped in the "might makes right" stress-reducing response patterns to which they have been exposed in their families.

Programming for children is both treatment and prevention—the latter in that much of what would be learned in an interpersonal skills-oriented program would be proactive and future-oriented. Finally, there is the potential of greater treatment effects when programming simultaneously for both sets of participants in relationships. This hypothesis would need to be tested experimentally by comparing effects achieved with two already proven programs to those of the children's program alone or the parents' program alone. This author believes that, barring some implementation problems, the effects of the double programming would be clearly superior.

Why not put both youngsters and parents together in a joint program? The agendas for the respective groups are quite different, necessitating different program goals and content. Placing them together for skill and information training, as opposed to family therapy, which would address the specific dynamics of a specific family, would mean compromising on meeting the needs of the respective groups.

Final Comments on the FIP Intervention Program

Without outcome data for the FIP pilot version of the Parenting Skills Program, the following analysis is obviously only conjecture. However, much support for both the strategy (Coufal and Brock, 1979; Guerney and Wolfgang, 1981) and content of the FIP pilot approach exists in the literature (Garbarino, etc.). Garbarino and Vondra (1983a) argue that intrapsychic and social interactional approaches alone are unlikely to lead to permanent change. Garbarino and Vondra state that "the key is nurturance *and* feedback; social resources and social control" and further that "there is a great deal of anecdotal and a systematic empirical evidence to support the contention that families at high-risk for maltreatment can participate in and profit from programs that project social support and control" (1983, p. 3).

The author believes that the FIP pilot parenting skills program contains the necessary elements to provide both. The didactic "skills approach" provides principles and practice that help to establish appropriate expectations and norms for adult behaviors. Feedback on skill mastery is provided by leaders and coparticipants. The empathic stance taken by the leader and soon emulated by the group members in their interactions with each other helps to generate the necessary support. Furthermore, the content per se of the lessons focuses on the affective (nurturant) and control dimensions of relationships stressing the critical importance of balance between them.

Analyses of positive effects of the parenting skills training program (L. Guerney, 1977) have not isolated the contribution of learning empathic responding from the mastery of other skills. The program philosophy is that all of the skills must be learned and each used discriminately and/or in appropriate combinations. Equal attention must be paid to encouraging the group to utilize its full support and feedback powers to stimulate learning and deal with the feelings generated when confronted with challenges to one's typical behaviors. Together, the components of the program (i.e., the focus on feelings of both parents and children, teaching of principles, the practice of constructive behaviors, and the support aspects) make it appropriate to characterize the strategy as Affective, Behavioral, and Cognitive, or, briefly, an A-B-C approach. This approach would represent an integration of "state-of-the-art" elements for changing parental functioning. Care must be exercised in making changes that would reduce any part of the triad.

Until it is empirically established that changes in any or all do not reduce program effectiveness, it would seem important to continue to include all. However, studies of the comparative importance or primacy of individual skills would be of interest. It is hypothesized that empathy would be the most essential content component.

As is always the case, more research is needed to support these conclusions. In the interim, further efforts using similar skills approaches would appear to be conceptually sound and consistent with this experience. Demonstration of lasting change in maladaptive parent attitudes and behaviors, via such programs, would in turn provide support for the concepts from which the skills-oriented interventions were derived.

CONCLUSION: THE PROGNOSIS FOR TROUBLED YOUTH IN TROUBLED FAMILIES

12

JAMES GARBARINO
CYNTHIA J. SCHELLENBACH
JANET M. SEBES

Throughout this book, we have walked a fine line between recognizing the genuine challenges faced by families dealing with adolescence, on the one hand, and buying into the stereotype of adolescence as a time of storm and stress, on the other. In choosing to study a sample of families containing "troubled youth," of course, we ran the risk of implicitly strengthening the storm and stress proposition. Recall that the youth in our sample of families *do* manifest a great deal of such storm and stress. But recall also that their level of difficulty places them at the extreme end of the normal continuum: the average score for our adolescents puts them at about the eighty-fifth percentile on the national norms for the Achenbach Child Behavior Checklist. As we saw in Chapter 1, about one in five adolescents does exhibit a pattern of "tumultuous growth," psychosocial disruption, and maladaptive behavior that befits the storm and stress label. Our concern is with the families in which these troubled youth are embedded, however, for it is this family context that is the key in determining whether high-risk adolescents will make a success of their lives.

Offer (1969) refers to families with adolescents as being in a state of "transitional crisis characterized by confusion." Hill (1980, p. 33) concludes that:

> Studies where family interaction is observed suggest that there may be a period of temporary disequilibrium in early adolescence while the family adjusts to

293

having a "new person" in the household—"new" in stature, "new" in approaching reproductive capability, "new" in cognitive competence—but this disequilibrium in no way approaches the shoot out that many parents are led to expect from media reports. Instead, in most families there appears to be a period of adaptation to the primary changes, a period when both parents and their newly adolescent children work out—often not consciously—what these changes mean for their relationships.

But how does this image of normality and adaptation change if we focus on troubled youth in troubled families? In the chapters that preceded this one, we have explored this issue. We found that the outcome of family dynamics surrounding a troubled youth reflected a complex interaction of personal characteristics and system properties. We found that the attitudes and values of the parents concerning the management of adolescent behavior were significant in establishing the likelihood that parent–adolescent interaction would deteriorate into maltreatment. High-risk attitudes and values are linked to the probable presence of maltreatment: Few families with low-risk values and attitudes become abusive; most families with high-risk values and attitudes do (at least when faced with a high-risk youth).

In comparing high- and low-risk families, we found a general pattern of favoring the low-risk parents and adolescents. High-risk families are characterized as punitive and somewhat less supportive. They are more likely to be "chaotic" and "enmeshed" and thus to be poorly positioned for dealing with high-risk adolescents. They tend to embody more interparental conflict. They are more likely to contain the special challenges of step relationships and, even among a sample of troubled youth, they are faced with very high levels of adolescent problem behavior and a lower level of social competence. All in all, high-risk families are best characterized as social systems with very high demand for adaptive behavior but low social and psychological resources to sustain such desperately needed adaptive behavior.

What are the likely outcomes for troubled youth in troubled families? As we saw in Chapter 3, one is that they will run away from home. Previous research established that conflicted family relationships, indicators of adolescent psychosocial maladjustment, and maltreatment all are linked to running away. How do we see this manifest in our families?

Bear in mind that the average age of our sample of youth was about 13.5 years. This puts most of these adolescents below the typical (modal) age for runaways, which is 16. Thus, it is not surprising that overall, "only" 14% of the youth had run away (as indicated by responses to the Child Behavior Checklist question dealing with running away). Eight of these nine youth were in the 14- to 16-year-old age range.

Eight of the nine known runaways were from high-risk families. This puts the runaway rate at 30% for the high-risk group and only 3% for the low-risk families. What is more, the runaway youth had particularly high overall Child Behavior Checklist scores (34.22 on externalizing problems; 19.00 on social competence; 33.33 on internalizing problems). What is more, four of the nine came from stepfamilies (one was adopted).

Certainly, running away from home is often a symptom of malfunctioning family relationships. The available evidence is clear on this point. Does this mean that we should expect more and more of the youth in the high-risk group to run away from home as they enter the prime years for running away? It certainly would seem so, if we can assume that the high-risk families are uanble to adapt successfully to the challenges of managing a high-risk adolescent. This leads us to consider what we know in general about the outcomes of maltreatment (as a precursor to asking about the prognosis for the troubled youth in the troubled families that we studied).

In a comprehensive review of the consequences of abuse and neglect, Martin (1980) identified three major forms of harm that result: *medical problems* (ranging from nutritional deficiencies to hearing loss to brain damage); *developmental problems* (from mental retardation to language deficiencies to impaired motor skills); *psychological problems* (encompassing the extremes on most dimensions of personality—for example, being either very shy and inhibited *or* very aggressive and provocative—as well as general unhappiness, poor attachment, and inadequate peer relations). Martin sheds some light on the "Dynamics of the Effect of Abusive Environment on Development." He includes the idea that a pattern of transactions develops (cf. Sameroff and Chandler, 1975) in which the damaged child elicits responses that reinforce the damage—for example, brain damage adversely affects personality, a pattern of entrapped parent–child conflict releases a pattern of abuse, mastery languishes, increasingly iatrogenic interventions occur as foster placement occurs then fails. All this is plausible, and the reality of damage appears undeniable. It is the form, severity, prevalence, and duration of harm that remain at issue. It is, therefore, appropriate that we consider a theoretical scheme that may help organize existing knowledge and guide further research and speculation. We find this needed scheme in an ecological perspective.

AN ECOLOGICAL PERSPECTIVE ON THE DEVELOPMENT OF ABUSED AND NEGLECTED CHILDREN

As used here, an ecological perspective on human development focuses on the biological and psychological systems of the individual acting in combination with the social systems of the family, neighborhood, community, and society to generate the ecological niche in which development proceeds (Garbarino and Associates, 1982). It emphasizes a formulation of development that is conveyed in the following statement: "The developmental status of the individual is reflected in the substantive variety and structural complexity of the . . . activities which he initiates and maintains in the absence of instigation or direction by others" (Bronfenbrenner, 1979, p. 55).

The standard aspects of growth and maturation combine with individual differences in constitution and temperament to form the raw materials for child and adolescent development. Even in adulthood, biological timetables play a role (although they are much more variable than in childhood) in shaping the individual's readiness to make use of environmental circumstances. How do we conceptualize these environmental circumstances? We do so through the component parts of an ecological perspective that includes but also extends beyond the individual organism—micro-, meso-, exo-, and macrosystems.

Microsystem

The systems most immediate to the developing individual are microsystems, the actual social–psychological settings in which individuals experience and create day-to-day reality. One of the most important aspects of a microsystem is the existence of relationships that go beyond simple dyads because such $N + 2$ relationships offer the increasing complexity that feeds development. Family, school, and peer group are salient microsystems for most adolescents.

Mesosystem

The interrelations among major settings containing the developing person constitute mesosystems. Mesosystems can exist through links between family and school, peer group and church, and camp and work place, among others. These links include both actual participation and cognitive representations of those settings. Mesosystem is a concept with a large subjective component, and it exists to greater or lessser degrees for different individuals, groups, and cultures. In general, the stronger and more diverse the links between settings, the more powerful the influence of the mesosystem on the individual's development.

Exosystem

Exosystems are settings that have a bearing on the individual's development but in which he or she does not actually play a direct role. They include the major microsystems in which institutional decisions are made (e.g., local government and corporate headquarters) and in which key figures in the individual's life (but not the individual him- or herself) are directly active and which, therefore, indirectly influence the individual (e.g., when the work place influences the worker's behavior at home in the role of parent).

Macrosystem

The meso- and exosystems are set within the broad ideological and institutional patterns of a particular culture or subculture. This is the macrosystem. It is a "blueprint" for the ecology of human development. It reflects a shared assumption of "how things should be done" and of "human nature." It normalizes behavior and provides the foundation for roles and expectations by systematizing cultural axia.

APPLICATION OF AN ECOLOGICAL PERSPECTIVE

This ecological perspective can aid in efforts to generate hypotheses about causation, about unintended consequences, and about alternative avenues for intervening in social and personal problems. This model suggests that contextual factors are particularly influential in cases of individuals at high risk (Willerman et al., 1970). This hypothesis may prove critical in understanding the consequences of maltreatment and the prognosis for troubled youth because it suggests that the impact of socially and economically impoverished environments may be greatest for the victims of such maltreatment (Garbarino and Gilliam, 1980). We can hold it firmly in mind as we proceed to review the consequences of maltreatment in ecological perspective.

Organism

What role do organismic factors play in mediating the consequences of child maltreatment? One influence may lie in affecting the degree of harm. Clearly, some individuals are more vulnerable to harm than others. Garmezy (1977), for example, has argued that "stress-resistant children" (the successor term to "invulnerable children") may overcome the experience of maltreatment, whereas vulnerable children may be developmentally devastated by it. A second organismic difference may be found in effects on the type of harm. Some children are more likely to internalize harm (in the form of somatic complaints, disordered thinking, extreme but unarticulated emotions, etc.), while others externalize it (in the form of aggression, delinquent behavior, and the like). Achenbach and Edelbrock's (1979) research on the two-factor structure of problems assessed via the Child Behavior Checklist documents this differentiation, and we saw some evidence of it in our study.

Finally, evidence derived from observational studies reporting on the role of aversive child behavior in instigating and sustaining patterns of maltreatment implies an active role for the child (Wahler, 1984), perhaps based upon temperamental differences such as those uncovered by Thomas and Chess (1977, 1980). Presumably, this active role pertains to shaping the consequences of maltreatment as well. Biologically based temperamental factors include differences in rhythmicity, basic activity level, and reactivity. Such temperamental variation (on both the child's and adult's part) affects the degree to which family relationships are harmonious and satisfying. Some children are cuddlers; others seem to be stressed by close physical contact. Some parents (and cultures) make greater demands for regular eating and sleeping habits; some children are better able to meet such demands. The match of parental expectations, values, and temperament with the child's temperament—what has been called the "goodness of fit" between child and environment—does much to predict effective socialization (Thomas and Chess, 1977, 1980). It implies that parental ability to flexibly adjust to the individual temperament of the child is important. In cases of extreme asynchrony or incompatibility, temperamental differences may increase markedly the risk for maltreatment and decrease the likelihood of ameliorating it within the family microsystem. This describes what we observe in many high-risk families facing troubled adolescents.

Temperamental differences are part of a more general pattern of interindividual biologic variation with implications for family functioning. The child's capabilities and the demands he or she places on the family derive in part from biology. Biological maturation plays a general role in shaping the sequence and character of shifts in cognitive development, for example. Recent evidence suggests that the shift from more concrete to more abstract forms of reasoning in adolescence places special demands on parents—particularly fathers—to readjust their use of power-assertive techniques in discipline (Garbarino et al., 1984). The onset of puberty may alter the character of family relationships—for example, by reducing the appropriateness and comfortableness of physical intimacy between fathers and daughters.

Microsystem

What role do microsystem factors play in mediating the consequences of child maltreatment? We can break this question into two others. First, what else is going on in the family that may affect the damage done by maltreatment? Second, in what other microsystems does the child participate, and what is going on in those microsystems? As we shall soon see, this second question quickly leads us into a consideration of mesosystem issues.

A study conducted by Hunter and Kilstrom (1979) suggests that the efforts of a nonabusive parent within a family can be very significant in reducing the damage done to the child by an abusive parent. They studied 49 families in which at least one of the parents had been a childhood victim of maltreatment. Those that did not abuse their own (premature) infant within the first year of life ($N = 40$) either were abused by their fathers but not their mothers or were abused by their mothers but were "rescued" by some other adult (a point we will refer to again in discussing mesosystems). In the 9 families that were repeating the pattern of abuse, the mothers had all been abused by their mothers and had not been rescued.

Egeland and Sroufe (1981) reinforce this emphasis on the role of the mother in abuse and its consequences. Their results reveal different consequences of abuse in the first 3 years of life as a function of whether the mother was involved in psychological and/or physical maltreatment. The general finding seems to be that the incidence of psychosocial damage (e.g., as manifest in "insecure attachment") is greatest when the roles of "abuser" and "primary caregiver" are played by the same person, as is usually the case when the mother is abusive. This highlights the importance of assessing the "relationship of the perpetrator to the victim" as a mediating factor in the consequences of maltreatment.

It seems reasonable to expect that different combinations of type and perpetrator of maltreatment will produce different consequences. For example, many students of sexual abuse report that the *reaction* to the abuse by a noninvolved parent (as well as others) is critical in determining the extent of psychological damage that will result (cf. Finkelhor, 1979). Many victims of paternal sexual abuse report that the sense of betrayal they felt when not supported and protected by their mothers was a critical negative influence.

What of nonfamilial microsystems? Little evidence bearing on the role of nonfamilial microsystems in mediating the consequences of maltreatment is available directly. Few intervention programs deal directly with *children* (and fewer still have adequate outcome data), because most interventions concentrate their attention on the task of changing the parents (Martin, 1980). As we saw earlier, many intervention programs do deal with adolescents, but on the basis of their socially incompetent behavior in settings outside the home, rather than as victims of maltreatment.

Mesosystem

What role do mesosystems play in mediating the consequences of maltreatment? Two seem most likely. The first is the degree to which the family microsystem is isolated from other social systems (families, peer groups, religious and civic associations, recreational groups, etc.). The well-documented social isolation and "distancing" of many abusive and neglectful families (Garbarino, 1977; Gaudin and Pollane, 1983; Polansky et al., 1981) highlights this factor. In the absence of such family-other mesosystems, there is less likelihood of compensatory socialization or access to what Emlen (1977) calls "protective behaviors." That these are important is suggested by Hunter and Kilstrom's (1979) study of child maltreatment discussed previously. Among their sample of 49 families in which one or both parents had been abused as a child, the childhood experience of being "rescued" by an adult outside the nuclear family figured prominently in whether or not the parents became perpetrators of maltreatment within a year after the birth of a premature infant. Contemporary presence of adequate social support was also a critical influence— being described as adequate for 73% of the nonrepeaters versus 22% of the repeaters.

A second, related mesosystem influence is the degree to which family-other relationships provide ideological support for maltreatment or provide counter values. We must consider whether or not associations outside the immediate family reinforce abusive or neglectful treatment. Straus et al. (1980) report that where kin are the only or principal association of parents, the result is *more* rather than less physically abusive treatment of the child when the family is subject to significant social and economic stress. This may reflect a process of ideological congruence within kinships groups regarding the treatment of children. Whether such ideological congruence exacerbates or mitigates the *consequences* of such abuse is unknown. It is possible that by "normalizing" it such congruence *reduces* negative developmental consequences. Certainly, the results of anthropological studies (cf. Korbin, 1979) add plausibility to this speculation. However, it may well be that some forms of child treatment such as rejection have a negative influence that is "transcultural" (Rohner, 1975), in which case defining it as normal does not significantly diminish the damage inflicted upon the child. In a society such as our own, it seems reasonable to expect that most adolescents will recognize the discrepancy between societal norms and what they experience at home. In our study, it appears that adolescents are aware of this discrepancy and thus subject to the negative psychological consequences of maltreatment.

Mesosystem factors appear to be important in formal intervention efforts as well. Whether it be residential institutions (Whittaker, 1983), foster care placements (Fanshel and Shinn, 1978), or behavioral modification programs (Wahler, 1984), the power of intervention to produce *lasting* improvement in the lives of children (including maltreated children) appears to depend upon the degree to which a strongly positive home-intervention program mesosystem is established. Where such a mesosystem is lacking, intrafamilial change extinguishes—perhaps most notably among low-income families not having access to sufficient compensatory resources in their social networks (Wahler, 1984).

Exosystem

What role do exosystems play in mediating the consequences of child maltreatment? Put another way, how does institutional policy and practice affect victims of child maltreatment? Efforts to evaluate intervention projects (e.g., Cohn, 1979) suggest that recidivism can be controlled by an intelligently applied mixture of professional expertise and lay helping. Skilled intensive intervention in times of extreme family crisis (such as is provided by the Homebuilders program) can even avert out-of-home placement— even for high-risk families with adolescents (Kinney et al., 1977). The point of all this is to suggest that policy decisions (exosystem effects) can influence all aspects of child maltreatment by shaping the infrastructure, resources, goods, and configuration of human service delivery systems (Whittaker et al., 1983).

Certainly one of the barriers to ameliorating the outcomes of maltreatment is the fact that the motive to rationalize behavior is strong and strongly expressed at all levels of the human ecology. Parents rationalize their abusive and neglectful treatment just as "the general public" favors quick dramatic action that restores a sense of moral legitimacy to community institutions and, indeed, to society as a whole. This may be why foster care is the leading "solution" to child maltreatment in the public mind. "Business as usual" seems to be the message. It implies that progress in dealing with the consequences of maltreatment must come spasmodically, as outbursts of public *need* for moral rationalization are used to achieve concrete institutional change. Interestingly, this same need for cognitive consistency in affected individuals with a strong internal locus of control orientation can produce social leadership, as the affected individual seeks to change society to rationalize their place in it (rather than altering their view of their experience). It also suggests—as many activists have long recognized—that personalizing maltreatment aids in turning the consistency motive toward social change rather than simply internal cognitive reorganization—the easiest solution when personal "investment" is low. Exosystems are crucial, and they are governed by a process of rationalization. We see this particularly in the case of adolescent maltreatment, where the dominant conception is that of the adolescent as perpetrator and the parent as victim.

Masson's (1984) recent critique of Freudian-based psychoanalysis and its handling of sexual abuse illuminates another possible exosystem effect (as well as the power of cognitive dissonance as a factor in clinical and theoretical analysis). By deciding to interpret female reports of sexual abuse as fantasy, the psychoanalytic "community" may well have exacerbated the psychological damage experienced by female victims of sexual abuse. This policy decision and others that punish the victim of sexual abuse (e.g., by removing her rather than the offending father from the home or by forcing her to testify in open court) may contribute significantly to the adverse consequences of abuse. Professional helpers often seem to be operating under the domination of cognitive consonance mechanisms, mechanisms that work to the detriment of adolescents in particular.

On the positive side, policy decisions that lead to improved functioning on the part of abusive parents may well increase the parental ability to rehabilitate the youth through compensatory caregiving. This presumed exosystem affect is the foundation for most parent-treatment programs. It finds support in anecdotal reports from victims and parents alike but has not been subjected to rigorous empirical verification.

Macrosystem

What role do macrosystem factors play in mediating the consequences of child maltreatment? One may speculate that various components of political ideology play a role in macrosystem influences on the consequences of maltreatment. A collectivist, interventionist ideology such as that dominating Chinese institutions may minimize damage by providing for powerful intervention supported across all levels of the human ecology. In contrast, the individualistic, noninterventionist ideology contained in the concept of *family privacy* may maximize damage by permitting the negative patterns begun in the family microsystem to generalize, and even become functionally autonomous. With so little systematic cross-cultural evidence regarding intervention in child maltreatment, it seems impossible as yet to subject these speculations to empirical test. What cross-cultural evidence we do have, however, does seem consistent with the hypothesis that the overall level of support (nurturance *and* feedback) given to parents on an institutionalized basis does translate into differences in the prevalence of maltreatment (Garbarino and Ebata, 1983; Korbin, 1979).

The power of culture to "normalize" experience is enormous. As Korbin's (1979) anthropological review demonstrates, parental behaviors that would be devastatingly abusive or neglectful in one culture seem nearly or actually benign in another. For example, facial scarification that would constitute serious physical abuse in North America or Western Europe is normal and apparently a positive experience in some African tribal cultures. The reverse is true of circumcision. Similar findings exist for homosexual rituals (Kagan, 1984). This leads Korbin to focus on "idiosyncratic" maltreatment—behavior that is outside the realm of acceptable chid treatment in a particular culture. As she correctly acknowledges, however, a totally passive acceptance of a culture's criteria for defining idiosyncratic maltreatment is insufficient. Such extreme cultural relativism completely denies the validity of professional expertise which can act in a dialectical relationship with "community norms" to produce historical improvement in the lives of children and youth (cf. Garbarino and Gilliam, 1980, p. 6). Recent efforts to legitimate adolescents as victims of maltreatment testify to the importance of this process.

Having said all this about the outcomes of maltreatment and the prognosis for high-risk families in general, what can we say about the families in our study? We only have some tentative answers at this point because the bulk of our effort was directed at assessing the families at one point in time. The result is a series of family portraits rather than a set of home movies. When we were conducting our study, funding was unavailable for a full-scale longitudinal study. Nonetheless, we have conducted an informal follow up.

COMPARING HIGH- AND LOW-RISK FAMILIES

We contacted families again at least 2.5 years after the initial interviews and assessments. An investigator, who was unaware of the previous assessments and risk/abuse status of the family, conducted telephone interviews with as many members of as many families as could be contacted. She explored seven topics with them:

1. What would you define as the most important event in your family during the past 2 years?
2. Is the family composition the same as it was 2 years ago?
3. In general, how would you compare family relations now with 2 years ago?
4. Using a scale of -2 (much worse) to $+2$ (much better) how would you compare the adolescent's relationships with other family members now in contrast to 2 years ago?
5. What about problems with school (grades, teachers, etc.), peers, or drugs and alcohol?
6. Did any new problems arise during the past 2 years? If so, what kind and how long did they last?
7. How would you summarize the current situation of the adolescent and his/her transition within the family as a whole?

The responses of family members provide the basis for some interesting hypotheses concerning the prognosis for troubled youth in troubled familes.

The Low-Risk Families: Healthy Adaptation is the Rule

Overall, it appears that the low-risk, nonabusive families have succeeded in overcoming the challenge presented by their high-risk adolescents. They appear to have drawn upon the adaptive resources we documented in our initial assessment to resolve the issues surrounding the adolescent. Over and over again in the interviews, members of low-risk families pointed to improved relations and conveyed a sense of adaptive resolution. These families are finding ways to manage. Some have on-going problems—particularly involving fathers—but they are succeeding.

Some examples illustrate these hypotheses.

> *Family 029:* Although the family is facing a serious medical problem (the mother is undergoing treatment for cancer), relationships within the family have improved. The father rates the adolescent's relationships with other family members as improved (+1 with parents; +1 with siblings) and reports the youth is managing well in school now, despite his learning disabilities. The boy himself says he feels closer to his parents and rates the relationships as much improved (+2). He is not involved in drugs or alcohol and has a positive attitude toward school.

At the time of the initial assessment, when the boy was 14, this youth was rated high on externalizing and internalizing problems by both parents (the mother noted 20 internalizing and 26 externalizing problems; the father reported 10 internalizing and 25 externalizing; the boy reported only 7 internalizing and 2 externalizing).

> *Family 009:* The mother reports that in the past 2 years she finished her course work and now has time "to enjoy the family again." She and the father agree this has had a beneficial effect on the whole family. The parents report that their daughter is getting along better with them (+1), and the girl agrees (+2). All report she is doing well in school, and that family communications seem to be getting better.

At the time of the initial assessment, when she was 11, the mother rated the girl as having 11 internalizing and 11 externalizing problem behaviors, while the father noted 10 internalizing and 19 externalizing. The daughter reported only 2 internalizing and 5 externalizing.

> *Family 025:* The parents report that their daughter's relationship with them is not so good as they were 2 years ago (−1), but she herself says they are much better (+2) due to the fact that she feels she has "better communication" with them. The parents do report that overall family relationships are excellent (+2). The mother thinks the girl is "quieter." Now the daughter is 12.5 and into normal adolescent concerns. Mother and daughter mention a problem the girl had with a teacher last year that caused her a lot of upset. But both report she "learned to cope with it."

At the time of the initial assessment, when the girl was 10, her mother noted 17 internalizing and 10 externalizing problems; the father noted 7 internalizing and 11 externalizing; the girl reported 21 internalizing and 7 externalizing problems.

Family 027: This family is unanimous in identifying the father–daughter relationship as the central issue. The mother and daughter report a strong and improved relationship between them (+2) but cite the father–daughter relationship as problematic (0). The father describes the father–daughter relationship as worse (−1). The mother says her daughter "has done a great deal of maturing and seems to understand her father's trouble with her." The father says he "hates the teenage period because he doesn't communicate with his kids." The mother reports that the daughter is doing well in school and has no problems with drugs or alcohol.

At the time of the initial assessment, when the girl was 14, the father was identified as being rather uninvolved in the family (and overinvolved in his work). This is evident in the fact that the mother and daughter reported the girl had many problems (19 internalizing and 28 externalizing according to the mother; 34 internalizing and 28 externalizing according to the girl). The father was aware of few (3 internalizing; 7 externalizing).

High-Risk Families: Adaptation Means Escaping Conflict

In contrast to the generally positive picture that emerges when we examine the low-risk families after 2.5 years, many of the high-risk families appear to be struggling, often unsuccessfully. We hypothesize that many of these families have been unable to resolve (or even stabilize) the issues they faced when we initially observed them. Many have "resolved" their problems by terminating the troubled relationships—typically by the troubled youth leaving the family. We hypothesize that these outcomes reflect the imbalance of resources and challenges in the family system that we documented at the time of the initial assessments.

Some examples will serve to illustrate these hypotheses.

Family 007: The adolescent quit school when she turned 16 (not long after the initial assessment). She had been running away, and the parents report "they couldn't keep her in school." She then got married, completed a graduate equivalency diploma (GED), went to a trade school (to become a beautician), and had a baby. The parents report that interaction with their daughter is good now: "She seems to be happy and that's all they want." The parents defined the daughter's marriage as the most important family event in the past 2 years. It appears they could not live well together, and the girl's departure has "solved" the family's problem.

At the time of the initial assessment, when the girl was 15, the family was quite troubled. There was a great deal of conflict between the parents (he is her stepfather). All saw the girl as evidencing many problems. The mother reported 12 internalizing and 54 externalizing problems. The stepfather reported 33 internalizing and 46 externalizing. The daughter noted 37 internalizing and 39 externalizing. Her older sister (then 17) had already left home—presumably to "solve" the family problem as her younger sister later did as well.

> *Family 015:* The family presents a mixed picture. The mother has changed her work schedule, and the kids have had contact with their biological father for the first time since they were small children. The adolescent boy is pretty negative about school (and has failed 2 year's worth of English). The mother reports that the meeting with the biological father was very disruptive—precipitating conflict between both the boy and the stepfather and the boy and his sister (because the father favors his son over his daughter). The mother says the stepfather now "feels helpless and can't seem to keep in touch with the kids but keeps on trying hard to keep the family together." The boy rates his relationships within the family as worse (-1) and says he feels confusion now about the stepfather. He states that he "feels pressure for being an adult but yet everyone still treats him as a kid." He "doesn't know how to handle the situation with his real father and his stepfather and wants to know them both but feels torn between the obligations to both, to show emotions when he needs to." But he "can't seem to talk about what he really feels." He also reports that he has experimented with drugs and alcohol but that it is "nothing serious." He feels pressure at home about school and just wants to get out on his own. The stepfather reports that he "resents the natural father for coming into the lives of his kids. . . . It has affected the entire family and the way they get along with one another. There are problems with (the stepson's) interaction with him and his authority."

At the time of the initial assessment, when the boy was 14, the family was having financial troubles. The father is physically handicapped, and there is a suggestion of a parental problem with alcohol. The mother noted 10 internalizing and 38 externalizing problems; the stepfather 18 internalizing and 45 externalizing; the son 68 internalizing and 64 externalizing. The family was described as being highly stressful. During the interview, the mother locked the 15-year-old daughter outside the house so that she would not interrupt.

> *Family 010:* The mother reports that the daughter's running away from home became chronic in the months after the initial assessment. The parents were threatened with court intervention in connection with the girl's truancy, so they approached social services for help. When the agency recommended a juvenile detention facility, the parents refused, and instead found a private group home placement. The day before she was supposed to move in, the girl ran away and ended up in the hospital for a drug overdose. They then arranged for psychiatric help and subsequently discovered that the girl (who is adopted) had been sexually abused by her biological father before she came to live with these (adoptive) parents. She then was placed in a private facility that deals with abused children. She has since graduated from high school and is working and attending school part-time. The parents report that the girl "has never been home since the day she left." She feels she is not ready to come back, and this hurts the parents deeply, but "they understand and hope that some day she will be able to come back home."

At the time of the initial interview, when the girl was 16, the family was struggling with the daughter's problems. They had adopted her when she was 8, and replaced the "chaotic" family she had come from. The parents were noted to be "very religious" (and two observers saw this as the source of the strict, rigid, and punitive child-rearing approach—particularly on the father's part—that they linked to abuse). The father's high AAI score placed the family in the high-risk category. All three family members noted many internalizing and externalizing problems. The mother noted 46 internalizing and 51 externalizing problems; the father 33 internalizing and 46 externalizing; the daughter 34 internalizing and 37 externalizing.

Family 023: The mother reports that the only negative in the family's relationships is the son–stepfather bond (− 1). The son agrees (− 2). The boy is the youngest of seven children, and the only one left at home. The boy says "he knows he is defiant with his mother at times when she gets on his back." He "feels she doesn't trust him," and he "hates the pressure from his mother about furthering his education." He doesn't talk to his parents about matters like drugs or sex—both of which he is experimenting with—because he "feels they wouldn't understand." He feels "the communication is alright as long as they stick to surface items and don't get into anything personal." The stepfather says he still feels a lack of authority with the boy, "but that (the boy) is beginning to respect him more than before." This reduces marital tension. But the stepfather "finds it hard to accept (the boy's) defiance and lack of interest in making his future a good one." He "feels bad he was never able to become real close to (the boy)."

At the time of the initial assessment, when the boy was 15, the relationship between son and stepfather was the major item of concern (in addition to the boy's problem behavior). Both parents had high-risk AAI scores. The mother noted 11 internalizing and 7 externalizing problems; the stepfather 10 internalizing and 17 externalizing; the boy 21 internalizing and 25 externalizing.

CONCLUSION

We believe our review of previous research and the results of our own investigation support our overarching hypothesis that in order to study the dynamics of adolescent maltreatment, we must concern ourselves with the adolescent as an element of a family system. More specifically, we must be attentive to the dynamics surrounding behaviorally problematic youth in families that are themselves at risk due to their high level of stress and low level of adaptive resources. These two factors (adolescent problems and a family's effective capacity) are related yet distinct. On the one hand, we suspect the level of problems exhibited by the adolescent is a function of socialization in the family. On the other, these problems are a challenge to the family. Overall, high-risk families face more seriously troubled youth *and* are less well-equipped to deal with such youth. Low-risk families face less problematic youth and are better able to deal with them. Often it seems the way high-risk families respond is by restructuring the system to exclude the troubled youth, whereas low-risk families adapt by reforming relationships within the system.

In sum, the prognosis for troubled youth in troubled families, like the origins of high risk itself, is a matter of human ecology. Characteristics of the individual organism and the microsystem of the family interact with meso-, exo-, and macrosystems. *Who* an individual adolescent is and *how* that adolescent's family works combine with *what* the school, the peer group, the community, and the culture do to shape the experience of adolescence.

BIBLIOGRAPHY

Abidin, R. *The parent education and intervention handbook.* Springfield, IL: Charles E. Thomas, 1980.

Abidin, R., and Carter, B. In R. Abidin (Ed.), *The parent education and intervention handbook.* Springfield, IL: Charles E. Thomas, 1980.

Abused children more likely to become teenaged criminals. (1983, December). *APA Monitor,* pp. 26–27.

Achenbach, T. M. The classification of children's psychiatric symptoms: A factor-analytic study. *Psychological Monographs,* 1966, *80* (7, Whole No. 615).

Achenbach, T. M. The child behavior profiles: I. Boys aged 6–11. *Journal of Consulting and Clinical Psychology,* 1968, *45,* 478–488.

Achenbach, T. M. The child behavior profiles: I. Boys aged 6–11. *Journal of Consulting and Clinical Psychology,* 1978, *46,* 478–488.

Achenbach, T. M. The Child Behavior Profile: An empirically-based system for assessing children's behavioral problems and competencies. *International Journal of Mental Health,* 1979, *7,* 24–42.

Achenbach, T. M., and Edelbrock, C. S. The classification of child psychopathology: A review and analysis of empirical efforts. *Psychological Bulletin,* 1978, *85,* 1275–1301.

Achenbach, T. M., and Edelbrock, C. J. The child behavior profiles: II. Boys aged 12–16 and girls aged 6–11 and 12–16. *Journal of Consulting and Clinical Psychology,* 1979, *47,* 223–233.

Achenbach, T. M., and Edelbrock, C. Behavioral problems and competencies reported by parents of normal and disturbed children aged 4 through 16. *Monographs of the Society for Research in Child Development,* 1981, *46,* (Serial No. 188).

Achenbach, T. M., and Edelbrock, C. *Manual for the child behavior checklist.* Burlington, VT: University of Vermont Press, 1983.

309

Adelson, J. *Handbook of adolescent psychology.* New York: Wiley-Interscience, 1980.

Adler, I., and Kandel, D. B. A cross-cultural comparison of sociopsychological factors in alcohol use among adolescents in Israel, France and the United States. *Journal of Youth and Adolescence,* 1982, *11*(2), 89–113.

Adult Education Association of the U.S.A. *Training group leaders.* Washington, D.C.: Adult Education Association of America, 1956.

Aldous, J. *Family careers.* New York: Wiley, 1978.

Alexander, J. F. Defensive and supportive communication in normal and deviant families. *Journal of Consulting and Clinical Psychology,* 1973, *40,* 223–231.

Alfaro, J. D. *Report on the relationship between child abuse and neglect and later socially deviant behavior.* Albany, NY: New York State Assembly, 1978.

Alfaro, J. D. Report on the relationship between child abuse and neglect and later socially deviant behavior. In R. J. Hunner and Y. E. Walker (Eds.), *Exploring the relationship between child abuse and delinquency.* Montclair, NJ: Allanheld, Osmun, 1981.

Allen, C., and Straus, M. A. Resources, power, and husband-wife violence. In M. A. Straus and G. T. Hotaling (Eds.), *The social causes of husband-wife violence.* Minneapolis, MN: University of Minnesota Press, 1979.

Altemeier, W. A., Vietze, P. M., Sherrod, K. B., Sandler, H. M., Falsey, S., and O'Connor, S. Prediction of maltreatment during pregnancy. *Journal of the American Academy of Child Psychiatry,* 1979, *18,* 205–218.

Alvy, K. Preventing child abuse. *American Psychologist,* 1975, *30,* 921–928.

Ambrosino, L. *Runaways.* Boston, MA: Beacon Press, 1971.

American Humane Association. *Annual Report of the National Clearinghouse on Child Abuse and Neglect.* Denver, CO: American Humane Association, 1977.

American Humane Association. *Annual Report of the National Study of Child Abuse and Neglect Reporting.* Denver, CO: American Humane Association, 1982.

Anderson, S., and Messick, S. Social competency in young children. *Developmental Psychology,* 1974, *10,* 282–293.

Annual Report on the Runaway Youth Act, 1978.

Austen, Jane (1816–19). *Emma.* London: John Murray, 1816.

Bachman, J. G. *Youth in transition. Vol. 2: The impact of family background and intelligence on tenth-grade boys.* Ann Arbor, MI: University of Michigan Press, 1970.

Bachman, J. G., Johnston, L. D., and O'Malley, P. M. *Monitoring the future: Questionnaire responses from the nation's high school seniors: 1978.* Ann Arbor, MI: Institute for Social Research, 1980.

Bachman, J. G., O'Malley, P. M., and Johnston, L. D. *Youth in transition. Vol. 6: Adolescence to adulthood: Change and stability in the lives of young men.* Ann Arbor, MI: Institute for Social Research, 1978.

Baher, E., Hyman, C., Jones, C., Jones, R., Kerr, A., and Mitchell, R. *At risk: An account of the work of the Battered Child Research Dept., N.S.P.C.C.* London: Routledge and Kegan Paul, 1976.

Balswick, J. O., and Macrides, C. Parental stimulus for adolescent rebellion. *Adolescence,* 1975, *10,* 253–266.

Baltes, P. B. Life-span developmental psychology: Some converging observations on history and theory. In P. B. Baltes and O. G. Brim (Eds.), *Life-span development and behavior* (Vol. II). New York: Academic Press, 1979.

Bandura, A. *Aggressive: A social learning analysis.* Englewood Cliffs, NJ: Prentice Hall, 1973.

Bandura, A. Self-efficacy: Toward a unifying theory of behavioral change. *Psychological Review*, 1977, *84*, 191–215.

Bandura, A., and Walters, R. H. *Adolescent aggression*. New York: Ronald, 1959.

Bandura, A., and Walters, R. H. *Social learning and personality development*. New York: Holt, Rinehart, & Winston, 1963.

Barter, J. O., Swabck, D. O., and Todd, P. Adolescent suicide attempts: A follow-up study of hospitalized patients. *Archives of General Psychiatry*, 1958, *19*, 523–527.

Baumrind, D. Current patterns of parental authority. *Developmental Psychology Monographs*, 1971, *4*, 99–103.

Baumrind, D. Early socialization and adolescent competence. In S. Dragastin and G. H. Elder, Jr. (Eds.), *Adolescence in the life cycle: Psychological change and social content*. New York: Wiley, 1975.

Baumrind, D. A dialectical materialists' perspective on knowing social reality. *New Directions in Child Development*, 1979, *2*, 61–82.

Bavolek, S. J., Kline, D. F., McLaughlin, J. A., and Publicover, P. R. *The development of the adolescent parenting inventory (API): Identification of high risk adolescents prior to parenthood*. Utah State University, Department of Special Education, 1979.

Beck, A. T. *Depression: Causes and treatment*. Philadelphia, PA: University of Pennsylvania Press, 1970.

Beck, A. T. The development of depression: A cognitive model. In R. J. Friedman and M. M. Katz (Eds.), *The psychology of depression*. Washington, D.C.: Winston, 1974.

Bell, R. Q. The effects on the family of a limitation in coping ability of the child: A research approach and finding. *Merrill-Palmer Quarterly*, 1964, *10*, 129–142.

Bell, R. Q., and Harper, L. V. *Child effects on adults*. Hillsdale, NJ: Erlbaum, 1977.

Belsky, J. Three theoretical models of child abuse: A critical review. *International Journal of Child Abuse and Neglect*, 1978, *2*, 37–49.

Belsky, J. Child maltreatment: An ecological integration. *American Psychologist*, 1980, *35*, 320–333.

Belsky, J. The determinants of parenting: A process model. *Child Development*, 1984, *55*, 83–96.

Belsky, J., and Vondra, J. Lessons from child abuse: The determinants of parenting. In D. Cicchetti and V. Carlson (Eds.), *Current research and theoretical advances in child maltreatment*. Cambridge, MA: Cambridge University Press, in press.

Berdie, J., Baizerman, M., and Lourie, I. Violence toward youth: Themes from a workshop. *Children Today*, 1977, *6*, 7–10; 35.

Berdie, J., Berdie, M., Wexler, S., and Fisher, B. *An empirical study of families involved in adolescent maltreatment*. San Francisco, CA: URSA Institute, 1983.

Berger, I., and Schmidt, R. M. Results of child psychiatric and psychological investigations of spontaneous and reactive runaways. *Praxis der Kinderpsychologie Kinderpsychiatrie*, 1958, *7*, 206–210.

Bernard, J. *Remarriage: A study of marriage*. New York: Russell & Russell, 1956.

Bienvenu, M. Measurement of parent–adolescent communication. *Family Coordinator*, 1969, *18*, 117–120.

Bierman, K. L., and Furman, W. The effects of social skills training and peer involvement on the social adjustment of preadolescents. *Child Development*, 1984, *55*, 151–162.

Blechman, E. A., Berberian, R. M., and Thompson, W. D. How well does number of parents explain unique variance in self-reported drug use? *Journal of Consulting and Clinical Psychology*, 1977, 1182–1183.

Blumberg, M. Psychopathology of the abusing parent. *American Journal of Psychotherapy*, 1974, *23*, 21–29.

Boesel, D. *Violent schools—safe schools*. Washington, D.C.: The National Institute of Education, 1978.

Boger, R., Knipers, J., Cunningham, A., and Andrews, M. *Material involvement in day care: A comparison of incentives*. Final grant report to the Office of Child Development, 1974.

Bohannon, P., and Yahraes, H. Stepfathers as parents. in E. Corfman (Ed.), *Families today: A research sampler on families and children*. NIMH Science Monograph. Washington, D.C.: U. S. Government Printing Office, 1979, pp. 347–362.

Bolton, F. G. Personal communication to J. Garbarino, February 1984.

Bolton, F. G., Reich, J. W., and Gutierres, S. E. Delinquency patterns in maltreated children and siblings. *Victimology*, 1977, *2*, 349–357.

Bowerman, C. E., and Irish, D. P. Some relationships of stepchildren to their parents. *Marriage and Family Living*, 1962, *24*, 113–121.

Brayer, H., and Cleary, Z. *Valuing in the family*. San Diego: Pennant Educational Materials, 1974.

Bremner, R. H. *Children and youth in America* (vol. 1). Cambridge, MA: Harvard University Press, 1970.

Brennan, T. Mapping the diversity among runaways: A descriptive multivariate analysis of selected social psychological background conditions. *Journal of Family Issues*, 1980, *1*, *2*, 189–209.

Brennan, T., Huizinga, D., and Elliott, D. S. *The social psychology of runaways*. Lexington, MA: D. C. Heath, 1978.

Bronfenbrenner, U. Socialization and social class through time and space. In E. Maccoby, T. Newcomb, M. E. Hartley (Eds.), *Readings in social psychology*. New York: Holt, Rinehart and Winston, 1968.

Bronfenbrenner, U. *Two worlds of childhood*. New York: Russell Sage Foundation, 1970.

Bronfenbrenner, U. Toward an experimental ecology of human development. *American Psychologist*, 1977, *32*, 513–531.

Bronfenbrenner, U. *The ecology of human development*. Cambridge, MA: Harvard University Press, 1979.

Bronfenbrenner, U., and Crouter, A. C. Work and family through time and space. In C. Hayes and S. Kamerman (Eds.), *Families that work: Children in a changing world*. Washington, D.C.: National Academy of Sciences, 1982.

Brook, J. S., Whiteman, M., Gordon, A. S., and Brook, D. W. Parental determinants of female adolescents' marijuana use. *Developmental Psychology*, 1984, *20*(6), 1032–1043.

Brownstone, J., and Dye, C. *Communication workshops for parents of adolescents*. Champaign, IL: Research Press, 1975.

Bryan, J., and Freed, F. Corporal punishment: Normative data and sociological and psychological correlates in a community college population. *Journal of Youth and Adolescence, 1980, 11*, 77–87.

Bugental, D. B., Caporael, L., and Shennum, W. A., Experimentally produced child uncontrollability: Effects on the potency of adult communication patterns. *Child Development*, 1980, *51*, 520–528.

Buhler, C. Loneliness in maturity. *Journal of Humanistic Psychology*, 1969, *9*, 167–181.

Burchinal, L. G. Characteristics of adolescents from unbroken, broken, and reconstituted families. *Journal of Marriage and the Family*, 1964, *24*, 44–51.

Burgdorff, K. Recognition and reporting of child maltreatment: Findings from the National Incidence Study. Washington, D.C.: National Center on Child Abuse and Neglect, 1980.

Burgess, R. L. *Project interact: A study of patterns of interaction in abusive, neglectful, and control families.* Final report to the National Center on Child Abuse and Neglect, 1978.

Burgess, R. L. Child abuse: A social interactional analysis. In B. B. Lahey and A. E. Kazdin (Eds.), *Advances in clinical child psychology* (vol. 2). New York: Plenum, 1979.

Burgess, R. L. Family violence: Implications from evolutionary biology. In T. Hirschi and M. Gottfredson (Eds.), *Theory and fact in contemporary criminology.* Beverly Hills, CA: Sage, 1980.

Burgess, R. L., Anderson, E. A., Schellenbach, C. J., and Conger, R. D. A social interactional approach to the study of abusive families. In J. P. Vincent (Ed.), *Advances in family intervention, assessment and theory: A research manual* (vol. 2). Greenwich, CT: JAI Press, Inc., 1981.

Burgess, R., and Conger, R. Family interaction in abused, neglectful, and normal families. *Child Development*, 1978, *49*, 1163–1173.

Burgess, R., and Garbarino, J. Doing what comes naturally? An evolutionary perspective on child abuse. In D. Finkelhor, R. Gelles, G. Hataling, and M. Straus (Eds.), *The dark side of families.* Beverly Hills, CA: Sage, 1983.

Burgess, R., and Richardson, R. Coercive interpersonal contingencies as a determinant of child abuse: Implications for treatment and prevention. In R. Dangel and R. Polster (Eds.), *Behavioral parent training: Issues in research and practice.* New York: Guilford Publications, Inc., 1981.

Burke, R. J., and Weir, T. Sex differences in adolescent life stress social support and well-being. *Journal of psychology*, 1978, *98*, 277–288.

Burr, W. R. *Theory construction and the sociology of the family.* New York: Wiley, 1973.

Butler, J. T. Early adolescent alcohol consumption and self-concept, social class and knowledge of alcohol. *Journal of Studies on Alcohol*, 1982, *43*(5).

Bybee, R. Violence toward youth: A new perspective. *Journal of Social Issues*, 1979, *35*, 1–14.

Caldwell, B. M., Heider, J., and Kaplin, B. *The inventory of home stimulation.* Unpublished manuscript, Syracuse University, 1968.

Canter, L. *Assertive discipline for parents.* Santa Monica, CA: Canter & Associates, 1982.

Caplan, G. The family as a support system. In G. Caplan and M. Killilen (Eds.), *Social support and mutual help.* New York: Grune & Stratton, 1976.

Caplan, P. J., Walters, J., White, G., Perry, R., and Bates, R. Toronto multiagency child abuse research project: The abused and the abuser. *Child Abuse and Neglect*, 1984, *8*, 343–351.

Carkhuff, R. *Helping and human relations* (vol. 1). New York: Holt, Rinehart and Winston, 1969.

Carnegie Foundation. *Education of the academically talented.* 1958–1959 Annual Report.

Carr, A. *Final report on analysis of child maltreatment-juvenile misconduct associa-*

tion in eight New York counties. Washington, D.C.: National Center on Child Abuse and Neglect (ERIC Document Reproduction Service No. ED 180 157), 1977.

Carter, H., and Glick, P. C. *Marriage and divorce: A social and economic study.* Cambridge, MA: Harvard University Press, 1976.

Chapman, M. Father absence, stepfathers, and the cognitive performance of college students. *Child Development*, 1977, *48*, 1155–1158.

Cheavens, F. *Leading group discussions.* Austin, TX: The Hogg Foundation for Mental Health, 1958.

Cherlin, A. Remarriage as an incomplete institution, *American Journal of Sociology*, 1978, *84*, 634–650.

Children's Defense Fund. *Children in adult jails.* Washington, D.C.: Washington Research Project, 1976.

Children's Defense Fund. *Children's Defense Fund Reports*, 1981, *3*(9), 6ff.

Chilman, C. Program for disadvantaged parents. Some major trends and related research. In B. Caldwell and H. Riccuitti (Eds.), *Review of Child Development Research.* Chicago: University of Chicago Press, 1973.

Chodorow, N. *The reproduction of mothering.* Berkeley, CA: The University of California Press, 1978.

Cicchetti, D., and Rizley, R. Developmental perspectives on the etiology, intergenerational transmission, and sequelae of child maltreatment. *New Directions for Child Development*, 1981, *44*, 31–52.

Clifford, E. Discipline in the home: A controlled observational study of parental practices. *Journal of Genetic Psychology*, 1959, *95*, 45–82.

Clingempeel, W. G. Quasi-kin relationships and marital quality in stepfather families. *Journal of Personality and Social Psychology*, 1981, *41*, 890–901.

Clingempeel, W. G., Brand, E., and Levoli, R. Stepparent–stepchild relationships in stepmother and stepfather families: A multimethod study. *Family Relations*, 1984, *33*, 465–473.

Coddington, R. D. The significance of life events as etiological factors in the diseases of children. I. *Journal of Psychosomatic Research*, 1972(a), *16*, 1–18.

Coddington, R. D. The significance of life events as etiological factors in the diseases of children. II. *Journal of Psychosomatic Research*, 1972(b), *16*, 205–213.

Cohler, B. J., Weiss, J. L., and Grunebaum, H. U. Child care attitudes and emotional disturbance among mothers of young children. *Genetic Psychology Monographs*, 1970, *82*, 3–47.

Cohn, A. Essential elements of successful child abuse and neglect treatment. *Child Abuse and Neglect*, 1979, *3*, 491–496.

Coleman, J. S., and Associates. *Youth: Transition to adulthood.* Chicago: University of Chicago Press, 1974.

Colletta, N. D. Support systems after divorce: Incidence and impact. *Journal of Marriage and the Family*, 1979, *41*, 837–846.

Colletta, N. D., and Gregg, C. H. Adolescent mothers' vulnerability to stress. *Journal of Nervous and Mental Disease*, 1981, *169*, 50–54.

Collins, J. K., and Harper, J. F. The problem of adolescents in Sydney, Australia. *Journal of Genetic Psychology*, 1979, *125*, 187–194.

Collins, A., and Pancoast, D. *Natural helping networks.* Washington, D.C.: National Association of Social Workers, 1976.

Colvin, B. K., Hicks, M. W., and Greenwood, B. B. *Intrafamilial stress in stepfamilies:*

research findings and theoretical implications. Paper presented at the annual meeting of the National Council on Family Relations, Milwaukee, WI, October 1981.

Cooley, C. H. *Human nature and social order.* New York: Scribners, 1909.

Coopersmith, S. *The antecedents of self-esteem.* San Francisco: Freeman, 1967.

Corbett, J., and Vereb, T. S. Juvenile court statistics, 1974 (Department of Justice Grant Nos. 76-JN-99-0006 and 76-DR-99-0034). Washington, D.C.: National Institute for Juvenile Justice and Delinquency Prevention, 1974.

Corder, B. F., Page, P. V., and Corder, R. F. Parental history, family communication and interaction patterns in adolescent suicide. *Family Therapy,* 1974, *1,* 285–290.

Corder, B. F., Shorr, W., and Corder, R. F. A study of social and psychological characteristics of adolescent suicide attempters in an urban, disadvantaged area. *Adolescence,* 1974, *9,* 1–6.

Coufal, J., and Brock, G. Parent child relationship enhancement: A skills training approach. In N. Stinnet, B. Chesser, and J. DeFrain (Eds.), *Building family strengths: Blueprints for action* (vol. 1). London, NB: University of Nebraska Press, 1979.

Covington, J. Adolescent deviation and age. *Journal of Youth and Adolescence,* 1982, *11*(4), 329–344.

Cowen, E. L., Pederson, A., Babigian, H., Izzo, L. D., and Trost, M. A. Long-term follow-up of early detected vulnerable children. *Journal of Consulting and Clinical Psychology,* 1973, *41,* 438–446.

Craighead, W. E., Smucker, M. R., and Duchnowski, A. *Childhood and adolescent depression and attributional style.* Paper presented at the meeting of the American Psychological Association, Los Angeles, August 1981.

Craighead, W. E., Wilcoxon-Craighead, L., and Meyers, A. W. New directions in behavior modification with children. In M. Hersen, R. M. Eisler, and P. M. Miller (Eds.), *Progress in behavior modification* (vol. 6). New York: Academic Press, 1978.

Crnic, K. A., Greenberg, M. T., Ragozin, A. S., Robinson, N. M., and Basham, R. Effects of stress and social support on mothers and premature and full-term infants. *Child Development,* 1983, *54,* 209–217.

Cronbach, L. J. Coefficient alpha and the internal structure of tests. *Psychometrika,* 1951, *16,* 297–334.

Crouter, A. Paper presented at the Fifth Annual Meeting of the Pennsylvania Council on Family Relations, Lehigh University, Bethlehem, PA, November 1984.

Crowley, M. *Female runaway behavior and its relationship to prostitution.* Unpublished master's thesis, Institute of Contemporary Corrections and the Behavioral Sciences, Sam Houston State University, 1977.

Cutright, P. Income and family events: Marital stability. *Journal of Marriage and Family,* 1971, *33,* 291–306.

Dahlgren, K. G. Attempted suicides—35 years afterwards. *Suicide Life Threat Behavior,* 1977, *7,* 75–79.

Daly, M., and Wilson, M. Child maltreatment from a sociobiological perspective. *New Directions for Child Development,* 1981, (11), 93–112.

Daly, S. J. *Questions teenagers ask.* New York: Dodd, Mead, & Co., 1963.

D'Angelo, R. *Families of sand: A report concerning the flight of adolescents from their families.* Columbus, OH: School of Social Work, Ohio State University, 1974.

DeFrancis, V. *Child abuse—preview of a nationwide survey*. Denver, CO: American Humane Association, 1963.

DeLissovoy, V. Child care by adolescent parents. *Children Today*, 1973, *2*, 22–25.

DeLissovoy, V. Toward the definition of "abuse-provoking child." *Child Abuse and Neglect*, 1979, *3*, 341–350.

DeMan, A. F. Autonomy-control variation in child-rearing and level of alienation in young adults. *Journal of Psychology*, 1982, *112*(1), 71–78.

Demone, H. W., and Wechsler, H. Changing drinking patterns of adolescents since the 1960's. In M. Greenblatt and M. A. Schuckit (Eds.), *Alcoholism problems in women and chidren*. New York: Gruen and Stratton, 1976.

Department of Health, Education and Welfare. Annual Report on the Runaway Youth Act. Washington, D.C.: U.S. Government Printing Office, 1978.

Devereux, E. Neighborhood and community participation. *Journal of Social Issues*, 1960, *16*, 64–84.

Devereux, E. C., Bronfenbrenner, U., and Suci, G. Patterns of parent behavior in the United States and the Federal Republic of Germany: A cross-national comparison. *International Social Science Journal*, 1962, *14*, 488–506.

Devereux, E. C., Bronfenbrenner, U., and Rodgers, R. R. Child-rearing in England and the United States. *Journal of Marriage and the Family*, 1969, *31*, 257–270.

Dinkmeyer, D., and McKay, G. *Systematic training for effective parenting*. Circle Pines, MN: American Guidance Service, Inc., 1976.

Douvan, E., and Adelson, J. *The adolescent experience*. New York: Wiley, 1966.

Dreikers, R., and Soltz, V. *Children: The challenge*. New York: Hawthorn, 1964.

Dreyfus, E. A. *Adolescence: Theory and experience*. Columbus, OH: Charles E. Merrill, 1976.

Duberman, L. *The reconstituted family: A study of remarried couples and their children*. Chicago, IL: Nelson-Hall Publishers, 1975.

Duncan, J. W., and Duncan, G. M. Murder in the family: A study of some homicidal adolescents. *American Journal of Psychiatry*, 1971, *127*, 1498–1502.

Duvall, E. M. *Family development*. Philadelphia, PA: Lippincott, 1971.

Eaton, M. T., D'Amico, L. A., and Phillips, B. M. Problem behaviors in school. *Journal of Educational Psychology*, 1966, *47*, 350–357.

Edelbrock, C. Running away from home: Incidence and correlates among children and youth referred for mental health services. *Journal of Family Issues*, 1980, *1, 2*, 210–228.

Education Development Center. *Exploring childhood*. Cambridge, MA: Education Development Center, 1974.

Edwards, J. N., and Brauburger, M. B. Exchange and parent-youth conflict. *Journal of Marriage and the Family*, 1973, *35*, 101–107.

Egan, K. Stress management and child management with abusive parents. *Journal of Clinical Child Psychology*, 1983, *12*(3), 292–299.

Egeland, B., and Brunquell, D. An at-risk approach to the study of abuse. *Journal of the American Academy of Child Psychiatry*, 1979, pp. 219–235.

Egeland, B., and Sroufe, A. Developmental sequelae of maltreatment in infancy. In R. Rizley and D. Cicchetti (Eds.), *New directions in child development*. San Francisco: Jossey-Bass, 1981.

Elmer, E. *Fragile families, troubled children*. Pittsburgh, PA: University of Pittsburgh Press, 1977.

Eme, R. F. Sex differences in childhood psychopathology: A review. *Psychological Bulletin*, 1979, *86*(3), 574–595.

Emlen, A. *If you care about children, then care about families.* Address to the Tennessee Association for Young Children, Nashville, TN, November 1977.

Empey, L. T., and Erickson, M. L. Hidden delinquency and social status. *Social Forces,* 1966, *44,* 546–554.

Engerman, S. Economic perspectives on the life course. In T. Haveven (Ed.), *Transitions: The family and the life course in historical perspective.* New York: Academic Press, 1978.

Ensminger, M. E., Brown, C., Hendricks, D., Kellam, R., and Sheppard, G. Sex differences in antecedents of substance use among adolescents. *Journal of Social Issues,* 1982, *38*(2), 25–42.

Erickson, M. L., and Empey, L. T. Class position, peers and delinquency. *Sociological and Social Research,* 1965, *49,* 268–282.

Erikson, E. H. The problem of ego identity. *Journal of the American Psychoanalytic Association,* 1956, *4,* 56–121.

Erikson, E. H. *Childhood and society* (2d ed.). New York: Norton, 1963.

Erlanger, H. Social class differences in parents' use of physical punishment. In S. Steinmetz and M. Straus (Eds.), *Violence in the family.* New York: Dodd, Mead and Co., 1974.

Espinoza, R., and Newman, Y. *Stepparenting.* Rockville, MD: U.S. Department of Health, Education and Welfare, DHEW Publications, #48-579, 1979.

Evans, K., Branca, M., and D'Augelli, J. State College, PA: Addiction Prevention Laboratory, 1976.

Fanshel, D., and Shinn, E. *Children in foster care.* New York: Columbia University Press, 1978.

Farber, E., and Joseph, J. The maltreated adolescent: Patterns of physical abuse. *Child Abuse and Neglect,* 1985, *9,* 201–206.

Farber, E. D., and Kinast, C. Violence in families of adolescent runaways. *Child Abuse and Neglect,* 1984, *8,* 295–299.

Farrington, D. P. The family backgrounds of aggressive youths. In L. A. Hersov and M. Berger (Eds.), *Aggression and anti-social behaviour in childhood and adolescence.* Book supplement to *Journal of Child Psychology and Psychiatry* (No. 1). New York: Pergamon Press, 1978.

Fast, I., and Cain, A. C. The stepparent role: Potential for disturbance in family functioning. *American Journal of Orthopsychiatry,* 1966, *36,* 435–491.

Feindler, E., Marriot, S., and Iwata, M. *An anger control training program in junior high delinquents.* Paper presented at the Fourteenth Annual Convention of Association for Advancement of Behavior Therapy, New York, 1980.

Feshbach, N. Learning to care: A positive approach to child training. *Journal of Clinical Child Psychology,* 1983, *12*(3), 266–271.

Finkelhor, D. *Sexually victimized children.* New York: The Free Press, 1979.

Fisher, B., Berdie, J., Cook, J., Radford-Barker, J., and Day, J. *Adolescent abuse and neglect: Intervention strategies and treatment approaches.* San Francisco, CA: Urban and Rural Systems Associates, 1979.

Fisher, B., Weisberg, D. K., and Marotta, T. *Report on adolescent male prostitution* (DHEW contract 105-79-1201). San Francisco, CA: Urban and Rural Systems Associates, 1982.

Fisher, D. D. Managing stress and enriching life. In N. Stinnet, J. DeFrain, K. King, D. Knaub, and G. Rowe (Eds.), *Family strengths* (vol. 3): *Roots of well being.* Lincoln, NB: University of Nebraska Press, 1981.

Flacks, R. *Youth and social change.* Chicago: Markham Publishers, 1971.

Foote, N., and Cottrell, L., Jr. *Identity and interpersonal competence: A new direction in family research.* Chicago: University of Chicago Press, 1955.

Ford, D. H. *The person as an open system.* Unpublished manuscript, Pennsylvania State University, University Park, PA, 1982.

Ford, D. H. *The self-constructing living systems framework.* Unpublished manuscript, Pennsylvania State University, University Park, PA, 1984.

Ford, M. E. Social cognition and social competence in adolescence. *Developmental Psychology,* 1982, *18,* 323–340.

Freedman, D. G. *Human infancy: An evolutionary perspective.* Hillsdale, NJ: Lawrence Erlbaum, 1974.

Freud, A. Adolescence. *Psychoanalytic Study of the Child,* 1958, *13,* 255–278.

Friedenberg, E. Z. *The vanishing adolescent.* Boston: Beacon Press, 1959.

Friedenberg, E. Z. *The dignity of youth and other atavisms.* Boston: Beacon Press, 1965.

Friedman, R., and Ziegler, C. *Therapeutic foster homes.* Unpublished paper, Florida Mental Health Institute, Tampa, FL, 1979.

Friedman, S. B., and Morse, C. W. Child abuse: A five-year follow-up of early case finding in the emergency department. *Pediatrics,* 1974, *54,* 404–410.

Friedrich, W., and Boriskin, J. The role of the child in abuse: A review of the literature. *American Journal of Orthopsychiatry,* 1976, *46,* 580–590.

Gallatin, J. E. *Adolescence and individuality.* New York: Harper & Row, 1975.

Gamble, W., and Garbarino, J. Families and their adolescents. In J. Garbarino and Associates, *Adolescent development: An ecological perspective.* Columbus, OH: Charles E. Merrill, 1985.

Ganong, L. H., and Coleman, M. Stepparent: A pejorative term? *American Psychologist,* 1979, *34,* 118–125.

Ganong, L. H., and Coleman, M. The effects of remarriage on children: A review of the empirical literature. *Family Relations,* 1984, *33,* 389–406.

Garbarino, J. A preliminary study of some ecological correlates of child abuse: The impact of socioeconomic stress on mothers. *Child Development,* 1976, *47,* 178–185.

Garbarino, J. The human ecology of child maltreatment. *Journal of Marriage and the Family,* 1977, *39,* 721–736.

Garbarino, J. *The issue is social welfare: Some thoughts on needs and problems in child protection.* Paper presented to the One hundred-sixth Annual Forum of the National Conference on Social Work, Philadelphia, PA, March 14, 1979.

Garbarino, J. Defining emotional maltreatment: The message is the meaning. *Journal of Psychiatric Treatment and Evaluation,* 1980(a), *2,* 105–110.

Garbarino, J. An ecological approach to child maltreatment. In L. Pelton (Ed.), *The social context of child abuse and neglect.* New York: Human Sciences Press, 1980(b).

Garbarino, J. Meeting the needs of mistreated youths. *Social Work,* 1980(c), *25,* 122–127.

Garbarino, J. Child abuse and juvenile delinquency. In R. H. Hunner and Y. E. Walker (Eds.), *Exploring the relationship between child abuse and delinquency.* Montclair, NJ: Allanheld, Osmun, 1981.

Garbarino, J. Understanding adolescent maltreatment. In C. Trainor (Ed.), *Adolescent abuse.* Beverly Hills, CA: Sage, in press.

Garbarino, J., and Associates. *Children and families in the social environment.* New York: Aldine, 1982.

Garbarino, J., and Crouter, A. Defining the community context for parent–child relations: The correlates of child maltreatment. *Child Development*, 1978, 604–616.

Garbarino, J., and Ebata, A. On the significance of ethnic and cultural differences in child maltreatment. *Journal of Marriage and the Family*, 1983, *45*, 773–783.

Garbarino, J., and Ebata, A. T. Human ecology and competence in adolescence. In J. Garbarino and Associates, *Adolescent development: An ecological perspective*. Columbus, OH: Charles Merrill, 1985.

Garbarino, J., and Gilliam, G. *Understanding abusive families*. Lexington, MA: Lexington Books, 1980.

Garbarino, J., and Jacobson, N. Youth helping youth in cases of maltreatment of adolescents. *Child Welfare*, 1978, *62*(8), 505–510.

Garbarino, J., and Sherman, D. High risk neighborhoods and high risk families: The human ecology of child maltreatment. *Child Development*, 1980, *51*, 188–198.

Garbarino, J., and Vondra, J. *Intervention in child maltreatment*. Paper presented at the Annual Meeting of the American Psychological Association, Anaheim, CA, 1983.

Garbarino, J., and Vondra, J. The psychological maltreatment of children and youth. In M. Brassard, R. Germain and S. Hart (Eds.), *Psychological Maltreatment of Children and Youth*. New York: Pergamon Press, in press.

Garbarino, J., Crouter, A., and Sherman, D. Screening neighborhoods for intervention: A research model for child protective services. *Journal of Social Service Research*, 1978, *1*, 135–145.

Garbarino, J., Sebes, J., and Schellenbach, C. Families at-risk for destructive parent–child relations in adolescence. *Child Development*, 1984, *55*, 174–183.

Garbarino, J., Kelly, A., and Schulenberg, J. Adolescence: An introduction. In J. Garbarino and Associates, *Adolescent development: An ecological perspective*. Columbus, OH: Charles E. Merrill, 1985.

Garmezy, N. Children at risk: The search for the antecedents of schizophrenia. Part 1. Conceptual models and research methods. *Schizophrenia Bulletin*, 1975.

Garmezy, N. Observations on research with children at risk for child and adult psychopathology. In M. F. McMillan and S. Henao (Eds.), *Child psychiatry: Treatment and research*. New York: Brunner-Mazel, 1977.

Garmezy, N. Stress-resistant children: The search for protective factors. In J. Tevenson (Ed.), *Recent research in developmental psychopathology. Journal of Child Psychology and Psychiatry Book Supplement* (no. 4). Oxford: Pergamon Press, 1984.

Garmezy, N., Masten, A., Nordstrom, L., and Ferrarese, M. The nature of competence in normal and deviant children. In M. W. Kent and J. E. Rolf (Eds.), *Primary prevention of psychopathology. Vol. III: Social competence in children*. Hanover, NH: University Press of New England, 1979.

Gassner, S., and Murray, E. Dominance and conflict in the interactions in between normal and neurotic children. *Journal of Abnormal and Social Psychiatry*, 1969, *74*, 33–41.

Gaudin, J., and Pollane, L. Social networks, stress, and child abuse. *Children and Youth Services Review*, 1983, *5*, 91–102.

Gecas, V. The influence of social class on socialization. In W. R. Burr, R. Hill, R. I. Nye, and I. L. Reiss (Eds.), *Contemporary theories about the family* (vol. 1). New York: The Free Press, 1979.

Gelb, L. NIDA: Family skills training. *Alcohol, Drug Abuse, and Mental Health Administration News*, 1984, *10*(3), 8.

Gelles, R. Violence toward children in the U.S. *American Journal of Orthopsychiatry,* 1978, *48*(4), 580–592.

Gersten, J. C., Langner, T. S., Einsenberg, J. G., Simcha, O., and McCarthy, E. D. Stability and change in the types of behavioral disturbances of children and adolescents. *Journal of Clinical Psychology,* 1976, *4*(2), 111–127.

Gil, D. *Violence against children.* Cambridge, MA: Harvard University Press, 1970.

Gil, D. Unraveling child abuse. *American Journal of Orthopsychiatry,* 1975, *45,* 346–356.

Gil, D. The United States versus child abuse. *Journal of Clinical Child Psychology,* 1983, *12*(3), 300–306.

Giles-Sims, J. Expectations, behaviors, and sanctions associated with the stepparent role. *Journal of Family Issues,* 1984, *5,* 115–124.

Giles-Sims, J., and Finkelhor, D. Child abuse in stepfamilies. *Family Relations,* 1984, *33,* 407–413.

Gilligan, C. *In a different voice: Psychological theory and women's development.* Cambridge, MA: Harvard University Press, 1982.

Glaser, K. Masked depression in children and adolescents. *American Journal of Psychotherapy,* 1967, *21,* 565–574.

Glick, P. C. Children of divorced parents in demographic perspective. *Journal of Social Issues,* 1979, *35,* 170–182.

Glick, P. C. Remarriage: Some recent changes and variations. *Journal of Family Issues,* 1980, *1,* 455–478.

Glueck, S., and Glueck, E. *Unraveling juvenile delinquency.* Cambridge, MA: Harvard University Press, 1950.

Glueck, S., and Glueck, E. *Predicting delinquency and crime.* Cambridge, MA: Harvard University Press, 1959.

Glueck, S., and Glueck, E. *Delinquents and nondelinquents in perspective.* Cambridge, MA: Harvard University Press, 1968.

Goertzel, V., and Goertzel, M. *Cradles of balance.* Boston: Little, Brown, & Co., 1972.

Gold, M., and Petronio, R. J. Delinquent behavior in adolescence. In J. Adelson (Ed.), *Handbook of adolescent psychology.* New York: Wiley, 1980.

Gold, M., and Reimer, D. J. Changing patterns of delinquent behavior among Americans 13 through 16 years old: 1967–1972. *Crime and Delinquency Literature,* 1975, *7,* 483–517.

Goldberg, M. Runaway Americans. *Mental Hygiene,* 1972, *56,* 13–21.

Goldberg, S. Social competence in infancy: A model of parent–infant interaction. *Merrill-Palmer Quarterly,* 197, *23,* 163–177.

Goldstein, A. *Structured learning therapy: Toward a psychotherapy for the poor.* New York: Academic Press, 1973.

Goldstein, A., Sprafkin, R., Gershaw, J. N., and Klein, P. *Skillstressing—the adolescent.* Champaign, IL: Research Press, 1980.

Goodman, P. *Growing up absurd.* New York: Vintage, 1956.

Gordon, T. *Parent effectiveness training.* New York: New American Library, 1975.

Gottlieb, B. Preventive intervention involving social networks and social support. In B. Gottlieb (Ed.), *Social networks and social support.* Beverly Hills, CA: Sage Publishers, 1981.

Gould, R. L. *Transformations: Growth and change in adult life.* New York: Simon and Schuster, 1978.

Gove, W. R., and Herb, T. R. Stress and mental illness among the young: A comparison of the sexes. *Social Forces,* 1974, *53,* 256–265.

Gray, C. A study of empathy among abusive parents. Unpublished Ph.D. dissertation, University of Maryland, 1978.

Gray, J. D., Cutler, C. A., Dean, J. G., and Kempe, C. H. Prediction and prevention of child abuse and neglect. *Journal of Social Issues*, 1979, *35*, 127–139.

Green, A. H., Gaines, R. W., and Sandgrund, A. Child abuse: Pathological syndrome of family interaction. *American Journal of Psychiatry*, 1974, *131*, 882–886.

Greenberger, E., and Sorenson, A. B. Toward a concept of psychosocial maturity. *Journal of Youth and Adolescence*, 1979, *3*, 329–358.

Griffin, B. S., and Griffin, C. T. *Juvenile delinquency in perspective*. New York: Harper & Row, 1978.

Grinker, R. R., Sr., Grinker, R. R., Jr., and Timberlake, J. A study of mentally healthy young males (homoclites). *Archives of General Psychiatry*, 1962, *6*, 405–453.

Guerney, B. Filial therapy used as a treatment method for disturbed children. *Evaluation*, 1976, *3*, 34–35.

Guerney, B. *Relationship enhancement: Skill training program for therapy, problem prevention and enrichment*. San Francisco, CA: Jossey-Bass, 1977.

Guerney, B. Marital and family relationship enhancement therapy. In P. Keller and E. Ritt (Eds.), *Innovations in clinical practice: A source book (vol. II)*. Sarasota, FL: Professional Resource Exchange, 1983, pp. 40–53.

Guerney, B., Coufal, J., and Vogel, E. Relationship enhancement vs. a traditional approach to therapeutic, preventive/enrichment parent–adolescent program. *Journal of Consulting and Clinical Psychology*, 1981, *49*, 927–1939.

Guerney, L. A program for training agency personnel as foster parent trainers. *Child Welfare*, 1976, *55*(9), 653–660.

Guerney, L. A description and evaluation of a skills training program for foster parents. *American Journal of Community Psychology*, 1977, *5*(3), 361–371.

Guerney, L. A social skills building approach involving parents and adolescents. Pennsylvania State University, 1979.

Guerney, L. *Parenting: A skills training manual*. State College, PA: Ideals, Inc., 1980.

Guerney, L. Introduction to filial therapy. In P. Keller and L. Ritt (Eds.), *Innovations in clinical practice: A source book, (vol. II)*. Sarasota, FL: Professional Resource Exchange, 1983, 26–39.

Guerney, L., and Moore, L. Phone friend: A prevention-oriented service for latchkey children. *Children Today*, 1983, *12*(4), 5–10.

Guerney, L., and Wolfgang, G. Long-range evolution of effects on foster parents of a foster parent skills training program. *Journal of Clinical Child Psychology*, 1981, *10*(1), 33–37.

Gullotta, T. P. *Runaway: Reality or myth?* Paper presented at the Annual Meeting of the American Association of Psychiatric Services for Children, Washington, DC, November 1977.

Gutierres, S. E., and Reich, J. W. A developmental perspective on runaway behavior: Its relationship to child abuse. *Child Welfare*, 1981, *60*, 89–94.

Haeuser, A. A., Stenlund, J., and Daniel, L. Policy and program implications in the child delinquency correlation. In R. H. Hunner and Y. E. Walker (Eds.), *Exploring the relationship between child abuse and delinquency*. Montclair, NJ: Allanheld, Osmun, 1981.

Haley, J. Family experiments: A new type of experimentation. *Family Process*, 1962, *1*, 265–293.

Haley, J. Towards a theory of pathological systems. In G. Zuk and I. Boszormenyl-Nagy (Eds.), *Family therapy and disturbed families*. New York: Science and Behavior Books, 1967.

Hall, G. S. *Adolescence: Its psychology and its relations to physiology, anthropology, sociology, sex, crime, religion, and education.* New York: Appleton, 1904.

Halperin, S., and Smith, T. Differences in stepchildren's perceptions of their stepfathers and natural fathers: implications for family therapy. *Journal of Divorce*, 1983, *7*, 19–30.

Hamburg, D. A., Coelho, G. V., and Adams, J. E. Coping and adaptation: Steps toward a synthesis of biological and social adaptation. In G. V. Coelho, D. A. Hamburg, and J. E. Adams (Eds.), *Coping and adaptation*. New York: Basic Books, 1974.

Hampton, R. Marital disruption: Some social and economic sequences. In G. J. Duncan and J. N. Morgan (Eds.), *Five thousand American families: Patterns of economic progress* (vol. 3). Ann Arbor, MI: University of Michigan, 1975.

Harris, I. D., and Howard, K. I. Parental criticism and the adolescent experience. *Journal of Youth and Adolescence*, 1984 *13* (2), 113–121.

Harter, S. Effectance motivation reconsidered: Toward a developmental model. *Human Development*, 1978, *21*, 36–64.

Hartup, W. W. Two social worlds: Family relations and peer relations. In M. Rutter (Ed.), *Scientific foundations of developmental psychiatry*. London: Heinemann, 1978.

Hartup, W. W. Peer relations and the growth of social competence. In M. W. Kent and J. E. Rolf (Eds.), *Primary prevention of psychopathology* (vol. 3): *Social competence in children*. Hanover, NH: University Press of New England, 1979.

Haupt, D. N., and Offord, D. R. Runaways from a residential treatment center: A preliminary report. *Journal of Social Therapy*, 1972, *18*(3), 14–21.

Heath, D. *Maturity and competence: A transcultural view*. New York: Gardener, 1977.

Heatherington, E. M., and Martin, B. Family interaction. In H. C. Quay and J. S. Werry (Eds.), *Psychopathological disorders of childhood*. New York: Wiley, 1979.

Helfer, R. E., and Kempe, C. H. *The battered child*. Chicago: University of Chicago Press, 1968.

Helfer, R., and Kempe, C. H. *Child abuse and neglect: The family and the community*. Cambridge, MA: Ballinger, 1976.

Herrenkohl, R. C., and Herrenkohl, E. C. Some antecedents and development consequences of child maltreatment. In R. Rizley and D. Cicchetti (Eds.), *New directions for child development, No. 11: Developmental perspectives on child maltreatment*. San Francisco: Jossey-Bass, 1981.

Hess, R., and Shipman, V. Early experience and the socialization of cognitive modes in children. *Child Development*, 1965, *36*, 869–886.

Hess, R. D., and Torney, J. V. *The development of basic attitudes and values toward government and citizenship during the elementary school years*, Part I. Chicago, University of Chicago Press, 1965.

Hill, J. P. The family. In M. Johnson (Ed.), *Seventy-ninth yearbook of the national society for the study of education*. Chicago: University of Chicago Press, 1980.

Hindelang, M. J., Hirschi, T., and Weis, J. G. Correlates of delinquency: The illusion of discrepancy between self-report and official measures. *American Sociological Review*, 1979, *44*, 955–1014.

Hindelang, M. J., Hirschi, T., and Weis, J. G. *Measuring delinquency*. Beverly Hills, CA: Sage Publications, 1981.

Hinkle, D., Arnold, C., and Crooke, J. Adlerian parent education changes in parents' attitudes and behavior and children's self-esteem. *American Journal of Family Therapy,* 1980.

Hirsch, B. J. Psychological dimensions of social networks: A multimethod analysis. *American Journal of Community Psychology,* 1979, *7,* 263–277.

Hirschi, T. and Hindelang, M. J. Intelligence and delinquency: A revisionist review. *American Sociological Review,* 1977, *42,* 571–587.

Hollingshead, A. W. The Hollingshead Scale. In C. M. Bonjean *et al.* (Eds.), *Sociological measurement: An inventory of indices and scales,* 1967.

Holmes, T., and Rahe, R. The social readjusted rating scale. *Journal of Psychosomatic Research,* 1967, *11,* 212–220.

Homer, L. E. Community-based resource for runaway girls. *Social Casework,* 1973, *54*(8), 473–479.

Hopkins, J. R. *Adolescence: The transitional years.* New York: Academic Press, 1983.

Horan, J., and Williams, J. Longitudinal study of assertion training as a drug abuse prevention strategy. *American Educational Research Journal,* 1982, *19,* 341–351.

Horowitz, B., and Wintermute, W. Use of an emergency fund in protective services casework. *Child Welfare,* 1978, *67*(7), 432–438.

Houghten, T., and Golembiewski, M. *A study of runaway youth and their families.* Washington, D.C.: Youth Alternatives project, 1976.

Hubbell, R. *Foster care and families.* Philadelphia, PA: Temple University Press, 1981.

Hunter, R., and Kilstrom, N. Breaking the cycle in abusive families. *American Journal of Psychiatry,* 1979, *136,* 1320–1322.

Hyman, I., and Wise, J. (Eds.). *Corporal punishment in America: Readings in history, practice, and alternatives.* Philadelphia, PA: Temple University Press, 1979.

Jackson, D. The study of the family. *Family Process,* 1965, *4,* 1–20.

Jacobsen, R. B. An exploration of parental encouragement as an intervening variable in occupational learning of children. *Journal of Marriage and the Family,* 1971, *33,* 174–182.

Jacobson, D. S. Stepfamilies: Myths and realities. *Social Work,* 1979, *24,* 202–207.

Jacobson, N. S. Problem solving and contingency contracting in the treatment of marital discord. *Journal of Consulting and Clinical Psychology,* 1977, *45,* 92–100.

Jenkins, R. L. The varieties of children's behavioral problems and family dynamics. *American Journal of Psychiatry,* 1968, *124,* 1440–1445.

Jenkins, R. L. The runaway reaction. *American Journal of Psychiatry,* 1971, *128*(2), 168–173.

Jenkins, R. L., and Boyer, A. Types of delinquent behavior and background factors. *International Journal of Social Psychiatry,* 1968, *14,* 65–76.

Jessop, D. J. Family relationships as viewed by parents and adolescents: A specification. *Journal of Marriage and the Family,* 1981, *43,* 95–107.

John, R. S., Mednick, S. A., and Schulsinger, F. Teacher reports as a predictor of schizophrenia and borderline schizophrenia: A Bayesian decision analysis. *Journal of Abnormal Psychology,* 1982, *91,* 399–413.

Johnson, B., and Morse, H. A. Injured children and their parents. *Children,* 1968, *15,* 147–152.

Johnson, H. C. Working with stepfamilies: Principles for practice. *Social Work,* 1980, *25,* 304–308.

Johnston, L. D. *Drugs and American youth.* Ann Arbor, MI: Institute for Social Research, 1973.

Justice, B., and Justice, R. *The broken taboo.* New York: Macmillan, 1980.

Kadushin, A., and Martin, J. *Child abuse: An interactional event.* New York: Columbia University Press, 1981.

Kagan, J.R. *The nature of the child.* New York: Basic Books, 1984.

Kalter, N. Children of divorce in an outpatient psychiatric population. *American Journal of Orthopsychiatry,* 1977, *47,* 40–51.

Kandel, D. B., and Faust, R. Sequence and stages in patterns of adolescent drug use. *Archives of General Psychiatry,* 1975, *32,* 923–932.

Kandel, D. B., Lesser, G. S., Roberts, G. C., and Weiss, R. *Adolescents in two societies: Peers, school, and family in the United States and Denmark.* Cambridge, MA: Harvard University, 1968.

Kaplan, S. L., Hong, G. K., and Weinhold, C. Epidemiology of depressive symptomatology in adolescents. *Journal of the American Academy of Child Psychiatry,* 1984, *23,* 91–98.

Kelly, A., and Garbarino, J. Adjustment problems in adolescence. In J. Garbarino and Associates, *Adolescent development: An ecological perspective.* Columbus, OH: Charles E. Merrill, 1985.

Kempe, C. Approaches to preventing child abuse. *American Journal of Diseases of Children,* 1976, *130,* 941–947.

Kempe, R., and Kempe, C. The battered child syndrome. *American Medical Association Journal,* 1962, *181*(1), 17–24.

Kempe, R., and Kempe, C. *Child abuse.* Cambridge, MA: Harvard University Press, 1978.

Kemper, T., and Reichler, M. Fathers' work integration and frequencies of rewards and punishments administered by fathers and mothers to adolescent sons and daughters. *Journal of Genetic Psychology,* 1976, *129,* 207–219.

Kendall, P., and Finch, A. A cognitive behavioral treatment for impulsivity: A group comparison study. *Journal of Consulting and Clinical Psychology,* 1979, *47,* 1020–1029.

Kent, J. A follow-up study of abused children. *Journal of Pediatric Psychology,* 1976, *1,* 25–31.

Kent, J., Weisberg, H., and Marx, T. Understanding the etiology of child abuse: A preliminary etiology of cases. *Children and Youth Services Review,* 1983, *5,* 7–30.

Kephart, W. *The family, society and the individual.* Boston: Houghton Mifflin Co., 1977.

Killilea, M. Mutual help organization: Interpretates in the literature. In G. Caplan and M. Killilea (Eds.), *Support systems and mutual help.* New York: Grune & Stratton, 1976, pp. 37–94.

Kimball, N. H., Stewart, R. B., Conger, R. D., and Burgess, R. L. A comparison of family interaction in single versus two parent abusive, neglectful and normal families. In R. Field, S. Goldberg, D. Stern, and A. Sostek (Eds.), *High risk infants and children: Adult and peer interactions,* pp. 43–59. New York: Academic Press, 1980.

Kimball, P. M. Revitalization of values will help bridge the generation gap. *Phi Delta Kappa Bulletin,* 1970, *36,* 49–52.

Kinney, S., Madson, B., Fleming, T., and Haapala, D. Homebuilders: Keeping families together. *Journal of Consulting and Clinical Psychology,* 1977, *45,* 667–673.

Klagsbrun, F. *Too young to die: Youth and suicide.* New York: Pocket Books, 1981.

Klein, K. M., Plutchik, R., and Conte, H. R. Parental dominance–passivity and behavior problems of children. *Journal of Consulting and Clinical Psychology,* 1973, *40,* 416–419.

Kleinman, J., Rosenberg, E., and Whiteside, M. Common developmental tasks in forming reconstituted families. *Journal of Marital and Family Therapy,* 1979, *5,* 79–86.

Koestler, A. *The ghost in the machine.* New York: Macmillan, 1967.

Kohlberg, L., and Mayer, R. Development as the aim of education. *Harvard Educational Review,* 1972, *42,* 449–496.

Kohlberg, L., LaCrosse, J., and Ricks, D. The predictability of adult mental health from childhood behavior. In B. Wolman (Ed.), *Manual of child psychopathology.* New York: McGraw-Hill, 1972.

Kohn, M. L. *Class and conformity: A study in values* (2d ed.). Chicago: University of Chicago Press, 1977.

Kohn, M. L., and Carroll, E. E. Social class and the allocation of parental responsibilities. *Sociometry,* 1960, *23,* 372–392.

Kohr, R. *Likert attitude scale analysis.* University Park, The Pennsylvania State University Computation Center: June 1974.

Kompara, D. R. Difficulties in the socialization of stepparenting. *Family Relations,* 1980, *29,* 69–73.

Konopka, G. Stresses and strains in adolescents and young adults. In L. A. Bond and J. C. Rosen (Eds.), *Competence and coping during adulthood.* Hanover, NH: University Press of New England, 1980.

Korbin, J. (Ed.). *Child abuse and neglect: Cross-cultural perspectives.* Berkeley, CA: University of California Press, 1979.

Kotelchuck, M. Child abuse and neglect: Prediction and Classification. In R. Starr (Ed.), *Child abuse prediction.* Cambridge, MA: Ballinger, 1982.

Kratcoski, P. C. Child abuse and violence against the family. *Child Welfare,* 1982, *61,* 435–444.

Kratcoski, P. C., and Kratcoski, J. E. Changing patterns in the delinquent activities of boys and girls: A self-reported delinquency analysis. *Adolescence,* 1975, *10,* 83–92.

Kruger, W. *Education for parenthood and school-aged parents.* Washington, D.C.: U.S. Office of Education, 1974.

Kulka, R. A., Kahle, L. R., and Klingel, D. M. Aggression, deviance, and personality adaptation as antecedents and consequences of alienation and involvement in high school. *Journal of Youth and Adolescence,* 1982, *11*(3), 261–279.

Laosa, L. M. Social competence in childhood: Toward a developmental, socioculturally relativistic paradigm. In M. W. Kent and J. E. Rolf (Eds.), *Primary prevention of psychopathology* (vol. 3): *Social competence in children.* Hanover, NH: University Press of New England, 1979.

Larson, L. E. System and subsystem perception of family roles. *Journal of Marriage and the Family,* 1974, *36,* 123–138.

Larson, R., Csikszentmihalyi, M., and Graef, R. Mood variability and the psychosocial adjustment of adolescents. *Journal of Youth and Adolescence,* 1980, *9,* 469–490.

Law Enforcement Assistance Administration. *Sixth annual report of L.E.A.A.* Washington, DC: U.S. Government Printing Office, 1974.

Lederer, W., and Jackson, D. *The mirages of marriage.* New York: Norton, 1968.

Ledingham, J. E., Schwartzman, A. E., and Serbin, L. A. Current adjustment and family functioning of children behaviorally at risk for adult schizophrenia. In A. Doyle, D. Gold, and D. S. Moskowitz (Eds.), *Children in families under stress. New directions for child development* (No. 24). San Francisco: Jossey-Bass, 1984.

Ledingham, J. E., and Schwartzman, A. E. A 3-year follow-up of aggressive and withdrawn behavior in childhood: Preliminary findings. *Journal of Abnormal Child Psychology,* 1984, *12,* 157–168.

Lee, D., Hahlberg, E., and Hassard, H. Effects of assertive training on aggressive behavior of adolescents. *Journal of Counseling Psychology,* 1979, *26,* 459–461.

Lenrow, P., and Burch, R. Mutual aid and professional services: Opposing or complementary? In G. Gottlieb (Ed.), *Social networks and social support.* Beverly Hills, CA: Sage Publications, 1981.

Lerner, R. M. Nature, nurture and dynamic interaction. *Human Development,* 1978, *21,* 1–20.

Lerner, R. M., and Busch-Rossnagel, N. (Eds.). *Individuals as producers of their environment: A life span perspective.* New York: Academic Press, 1981.

Lerner, R. M., Palermo, M., Spiro, A., and Nesselroade, J. R. Assessing the dimensions of temperamental individuality across the life span: The dimensions of temperament survey (DOTS). *Child Development,* 1982, *53,* 149–159.

Lewis, D. Medical histories of aggressive delinquents. Presentation to Conference on Child Abuse and Neglect, April 22, 1985, Albany, NY.

Lewis, D. O., and Shanok, S. S. Medical histories of delinquent and non-delinquent children: An epidemiological study. *American Journal of Psychiatry,* 1977, *134,* 1020–1025.

Lewis, D. O., Shanok, S. S., and Balla, D. A. Perinatal difficulties, head and face trauma, and child abuse in the medical histories of seriously delinquent children. *American Journal of Psychiatry,* 1979(a), *136,* 419–423.

Lewis, D. O., Shanok, S. S., Pincus, J. H., and Glaser, G. H. Violent juvenile delinquents: Psychiatric, neurological, psychological, and abuse factors. *Journal of the American Academy of Child Psychiatry,* 1979(b), *18,* 307–319.

Lewis, J. M., Beavers, W. R., Gossett, J. T., and Phillips, V. A. *No single thread: Psychological health in family systems.* New York: Bruner-Mazel, 1976.

Lewis, M., and Wilson, C. D. Infant development in lower-class American families. *Human Development,* 1972, *15,* 112–127.

Libbey, P., and Bybee, R. The physical abuse of adolescents. *Journal of Social Issues,* 1979, *35*(2), 101–126.

Lieber, L. The self-help approach: Parents anonymous. *Journal of Clinical Child Psychology,* 1983, *12*(3), 288–291.

Liebertoff, K. The runaway child in America. *Journal of Family Issues,* 1980, *1,* 151–164.

Lightcap, J. L., Kurland, J. A., and Burgess, R. L. Child abuse: A test of some predictions from evolutionary theory. *Ethology and Sociobiology,* 1982, *3,* 61–67.

Likert, R. A. Technique for the measurement of attitudes. *Archives of Psychology,* 1932, *140,* 44–53.

Loeber, R. The stability of antisocial and delinquent child behavior: A review. *Child Development,* 1982, *53,* 1421–1446.

Loevinger. *Ego development.* San Francisco: Jossey-Bass, 1976.

Longberg, B., Fischbach, M. and Bickerstaff, M. *Youth helping youth.* Boystown, Nebraska: Boystown Center, 1980.

Lourie, I. The phenomenon of the abused adolescent: A clinical study. *Victimology*, 1977, *2*, 268–276.

Lourie, I. S. Family dynamics and the abuse of adolescents: A case for a developmental phase specific model of child abuse. *Child Abuse and Neglect*, 1979, *3*, 967–974.

Lutz, E. P. Stepfamilies: A descriptive study from the adolescent perspective. *Dissertations Abstracts International*, 1983, *41*(3-A), 992.

Lynch, M. A., and Roberts, J. *Consequences of child abuse*. New York: Academic Press, 1982.

Lystad, M. H. Violence at home: A review of the literature. *American Journal of Orthopsychiatry*, 1975, *45*, 328–345.

McClelland, D. C. Testing for competence rather than for intelligence. *American Psychologist*, 1973, *28*, 1–14.

McCoard, W. D. Ohio project uncovers abuse/runaway links. *Midwest Parent–Child Review*, 1983, pp. 8–9.

McCord, J., McCord, W., and Thurber, E. Some effects of parental absence on male children. *Journal of Abnormal and Social Psychology*, 1962, *64*, 361–369.

McCubbin, H. I., Joy, C. B., Cauble, A. E., Comeau, J. K., Patterson, J. M., and Needle, R. H. Family stress and coping: A decade review. *Journal of Marriage and the Family*, 1980, 855–871.

McCubbin, H., Paterson, E., Bauman, E., and Harris, L. *Adolescent–family inventory of life events and changes (A-FILE)*. St. Paul, MN: Family Social Science, University of Minnesota, 1981.

MacDonald, A. Internal-external locus of control and parental antecedents. *Journal of Consulting and Clinical Psychology*, 1971, *34*, 141–147.

Mace, D., and Mace, V. Enriching marriages: The foundation stone of family strength. In N. Stinnett, B. Chesser, J. DeFrain, and P. Knaub (Eds.), *Family strengths: Positive models for family life*. Lincoln, NB: University of Nebraska Press, 1980.

McIntyre, M. S., Angle, C. R., Wilcoff, R. L., and Schlict, M. L. Recurrent adolescent suicidal behavior. *Pediatrics*, 1977, *60*, 605–608.

Macklin, E. Nontraditional family forms: A decade in review. *Journal of Marriage and the Family*, 1980, *42*, 905–922.

McMorrow, F. *Midolescence: The dangerous years*. New York: Strawberry Hills Publishing Co., 1974.

McMorrow, F. *Midolescence: The dangerous years*. New York: Strawberry Hills Publishing Co., 1977.

Maddox, B. *The half-parent: Living with other people's children*. New York: New American Library, 1975.

Manis, J. Assessing the seriousness of social problems. *Social Problems*, 1974, *22*, 1–15.

Marohn, R. C., Dalle-Molle, D., McCarter, E., and Linn, D. *Juvenile delinquents: Psychodynamic assessment and hospital treatment*. New York: Brunner-Mazel, 1980.

Martin, B. The child and his development. In C. H. Kempe and R. Helfer (Eds.), *Helping the battered child and his family*, Philadelphia, PA: Lippincott, 1972.

Martin, B. Parent–child relations. In F. D. Horowitz (Ed.), *Review of Child Development Research* (vol. 4), pp. 463–540. Chicago: University of Chicago Press, 1975.

Martin, H. The consequences of being abused and neglected: How the child fares. In C. H. Kempe and R. Helfer (Eds.), *The battered child* (3d ed.). Chicago: University of Chicago Press, 1980.

Martin, H. P., and Beezley, P. Behavioral observations of abused children. *Developmental Medicine and Child Neurology*, 1977, *19*, 373–387.

Martin, H. P., Beezley, P., Conway, E. F., and Kempe, C. H. The development of abused children. In I. Schulman (Ed.), *Advances in pediatrics* (vol. 21). Chicago: Year Book Medical, 1974.

Mash, E. J. Families with problem children. In A. Doyle, D. Gold, and D. S. Moskowitz (Eds.), *Children in families under stress*. New Directors for Child Development, No. 24, pp. 65–84. San Francisco: Jossey-Bass, 1984.

Masson, J. *The assault on truth: Freud's suppression of the seduction theory*. New York: Farrar, Straus, and Giroux, 1984.

Masterson, J. F. The psychiatric significance of adolescent turmoil. *American Journal of Psychiatry*, 1968, *124*, 1549–1554.

Masterson, J. R. *Treatment of the borderline adolescent*. New York: Wiley, 1972.

Meichenbaum, D., and Cameron, R. Stress-inoculation training: Toward a general paradigm for training coping skills. In D. Meichenbaum and M. Jaremko (Eds.), *Stress prevention and management*. New York: Plenum Press, 1981.

Messinger, L. Remarriage between divorced people with children from previous marriage: A proposal for preparation for remarriage. *Journal of Marriage and Family Counseling*, 1976, *2*, 193–200.

Meyerding, J. Early sexual experience and prostitution. *American Journal of Psychiatry*, 1977, *134*, 1381–1385.

Mezzich, A. C., and Mezzich, J. E. A data-based typology of depressed adolescents. *Journal of Personality Assessment*, 1979, *43*(3), 238–246.

Miller, J. G. *Living systems*. New York: McGraw-Hill, 1978.

Miller, L. C., Hampe, E., Barrett, C. L., and Noble, H. Children's deviant behavior within the general population. *Journal of Consulting and Clinical Psychology*, 1971, *37*, 16–22.

Mills, D. A model for stepfamily development. *Family Relations*, 1984, *33*, 365–372.

Milman, D. H., and Su, W. H. Patterns of illicit drug and alcohol use among secondary school students. *Behavioral Pediatrics*, 1973, *83*, 314–320.

Minuchin, S., and Fishman, H. *Family therapy techniques*. Cambridge, MA: Harvard University Press, 1981.

Mitchell, R. E., and Trickett, E. J. Task force report: Social networks as mediators of social support. *Community Mental Health Journal*, 1980, *16*, 27–44.

Moen, P., Kain, E. L., and Elder, G. H. *Economic conditions and family life: Contemporary and historical perspectives*. Paper presented for the National Academy of Sciences, Assembly of Behavioral and Social Sciences, Committee of Child Development Research and Public Policy, December 1981.

Mondell, S., and Tyler, F. B. Parental competence and styles of problem-solving/play behavior with children. *Developmental Psychology*, 1981, *17*, 73–78.

Moos, R. H., Moos, B. S., and Kulik, J. A. College-student abstainers, moderate drinkers and heavy drinkers: A comparative analysis. *Journal of Youth and Adolescence*, 1976, *5*, 349–360.

Morgan, R. The battered adolescent: A developmental approach to identification and intervention. *Child Abuse and Neglect*, 1977, *1*, 343–348.

Morse, C. W., Sahler, O. J. Z., and Friedman, S. B. A three-year follow-up study of abused and neglected children. *American Journal of Diseases of Children*, 1970, *120*, 439–446.

Mouzakitis, C. M. An inquiry into the problem of child abuse and juvenile delinquency. In R. J. Hunner and Y. E. Walker (Eds.), *Exploring the relationship between child abuse and delinquency*. Montclair, NJ: Allanheld, Osmun, 1981.

Mouzakitis, Chris. Characteristics of abused adolescents and guidelines for intervention. *Child Welfare*, 1984, 63(2), 149–157.

Myers, J. K., Lindenthal, J. J., and Pepper, M. P. Life events and psychiatric symptomatology. In D. F. Ricks, A. Thomas, and M. Roff (Eds.), *Life history research in psychopathology* (vol. 3). Minneapolis, MN: University of Minnesota Press, 1974.

The National Academy of Sciences. *Towards a national policy for children and families*. Washington, D.C.: Government Printing Office, 1976.

National Center on Child Abuse and Neglect. *Executive Summary: National study of the incidence and severity of child abuse and neglect* (DHHS Publication No. OHDS 81-30329). Washington, D.C.: U.S. Government Printing Office, 1981.

Nelson, M., and Nelson, G. K. Problems of equity in the reconstituted family: A social exchange analysis. *Family Relations*, 1982, *31*, 223–231.

Newberger, E. The helping hand strikes again: Unintended consciousness of child abuse reporting. *Journal of Clinical Child Psychology*, 1983, *12*(3), 307–311.

Newberger, E., and Bourne, R. The medicalization and legalization of child abuse. *American Journal of Orthopsychiatry*, 1978, *48*(4), 593–607.

Newberger, E., Reed, P., Danial, J., Hyde, J., and Kotelchuck, M. Pediatric social illness: Toward an etiologic classification. *Pediatrics*, 1977, *60*, 178–185.

Newson, J., and Newson, E. Cultural aspects of child rearing in the English-speaking world. In M. P. M. Richards (Ed.), *The integration of a child into a social world*. Cambridge, England: Cambridge University Press, 1974.

Nicholsen, M., and Schneider, C. *The family center*. Report to The Department of Health, Education and Welfare, Grant No. 90-C-73, August 1978.

Niemi, R. G. *How family members perceive each other*. New Haven, CT: Yale University Press, 1974.

Noam, G., Hauser, S., Santostefano, S., Garrison, W., Jacobson, A., Powers, S., and Mead, M. Ego development and psychopathology. *Child Development*, 1984, *55*, 184–194.

Novaco, R. The cognitive regulation of anger and stress. In P. Kendall and S. Hollow (Eds.), *Cognitive-behavioral interventions: Theory, research and procedures*. New York: Academic Press, 1979.

Nunnally, J. *Psychometric theory*. New York: McGraw-Hill, 1978.

Nye, F. Child adjustment in broken and unhappy unbroken homes. *Marriage and Family Living*, 1957, *19*, 356–361.

Nye, F. I. *Family relationships and delinquent behavior*. New York: Wiley, 1958.

Nye, F. I., and Edelbrock, C. Introduction: Some social characteristics of runaways. *Journal of Family Issues*, 1980, *1*, 2, 147–150.

O'Dell, Carolyn. Parent education in a community mental health setting. Unpublished Ph.D. dissertation, The Pennsylvania State University, 1973.

Offer, D. *The psychological world of the teenager: A study of normal adolescent boys*. New York: Basic Books, 1969.

Offer, D., and Offer, J. Normal adolescence in perspective. In J. C. Schoolar (Ed.), *Current issues in adolescent psychiatry*. New York: Brunner-Mazel, 1973.

Offer, D., and Offer, J. D. Normal adolescent males: The high school and college years. *Journal of the American College Health Association*, 1974, *22*, 209–215.

Offer, D., and Offer, J. D. *From teenager to young manhood: A psychological study.* New York: Basic Books, 1975.

Offer, D., Ostrow, E., and Howard, K. I., The mental health professional's concept of the normal adolescent. *Archives of General Psychiatry*, 1981, *38*, 149–152.

Ogbu, J. M. Origins of human competence: A cultural-ecological perspective. *Child Development*, 1981, *52*, 413–429.

Oldham, D. G. Adolescent turmoil: A myth revisited. In S. C. Feinstein and P. L. Gioracchini (Eds.), *Adolescent psychiatry* (vol. 6). Chicago: University of Chicago Press, 1978.

Olson, L., and Holmes, W. *Youth at risk: Adolescents and maltreatment.* Boston, MA: Center for Applied Social Research, 1983.

Olson, L., Liebow, E., Mannino, F., and Shore, M. Runaway children twelve years later. *Journal of Family Issues*, 1980, *1*, 165–188.

Olson, D. H., Bell, R., and Portner, J. *FACES: Family Adaptability and Cohesion Evaluation Scales.* St. Paul, MN: Family Social Science, University of Minnesota, 1978.

Olson, D. H., Russell, C. S., and Sprenkle, D. H. Circumplex model of marital and family system II: Empirical studies and clinical intervention. In J. Vincent (Ed.), *Advances in family intervention, assessment, and theory.* Greenwich, CT: JAI Press, 1979(a).

Olson, D. H., Sprenkle, D. H., and Russell, C. S. Circumplex model of marital and family systems: Cohesion and adaptability dimensions, family types, and clinical application. *Family Process*, 1979(b), *18*, 3–29.

O'Malley, J. M. Research perspectives on social competence. *Merrill-Palmer Quarterly*, 1977, *23*, 29–44.

Opinion Research Corporation. *National survey on runaway youth.* Princeton, NJ, 1976.

Orten, J., and Soll, S. Runaway children and their families: A treatment typology. *Journal of Social Issues*, 1980, *1*, 249–261.

Otto, U. Suicidal attempts in childhood and adolescence—today and after 10 years: A follow-up study. In A. Annell (Ed.), *Depressive states in childhood and adolescence.* Stockholm: Almquist & Wisell, 1972, pp. 357–366.

Pagelow, M. D. *Exploring connections between childhood violence and later deviant behavior.* Paper presented at the Annual Meeting of the American Sociological Association, San Francisco, 1982.

Papernow, P. L. The stepfamily cycle: An experiential model of stepfamily development. *Family Relations*, 1984, *33*, 355–363.

Parke, R. Socialization into child abuse: A social interactional perspective. In J. Tapp and F. Levine (Eds.), *Law, justice and the individual in society.* New York: Holt, Rinehart, & Winston, 1977.

Parke, R., and Collmer, C. Child abuse: An interdisciplinary analysis. In M. Hetherington (Ed.), *Review of child development research* (vol. 5). Chicago: University of Chicago Press, 1975.

Pasley, K., and Gecas, V. Stresses and satisfactions of the parental role. *Personnel and Guidance Journal*, 1984, *62*, 400–404.

Patterson, G. R. The aggressive child: Victim and architect of a coercive system. In L. A. Hemerlynck et al. (Eds.), *Behavior modification and families. 1. Theory and research.* New York: Brunner-Mazel, 1976.

Patterson, G. R., Mothers: The unacknowledged victims. *Monographs of the Society for Research in Child Development*, 1980, *45*(5).

Patterson, G. R. Coercive family process. Eugene, OR: Castalia, 1982.

Patterson, G. R., and Reid, J. B. Reciprocity and coercion: Two facets of social systems. In C. Neuringer and J. L. Michael (Eds.), Behavior modification in clinical psychology. New York: Appleton-Century Crofts, 1970.

Patterson, G., Reid, J., Jones, R., and Conger, R. Families with aggressive children: A social learning approach to intervention (vol. 1). Champaign, IL: Research Press, 1975.

Peel, E. A. The nature of adolescent judgment. New York: Wiley-Interscience, 1971.

Pelcovitz, D., Kaplan, S., Samit, C., Krieger, R., and Cornelius, P. Adolescent abuse: Family structure and implications for treatment. Journal of Child Psychiatry, 1984, 23, 85–90.

Perkins, T. F., and Kahan, J. P. An empirical comparison of natural-father and stepfather family systems. Family Process, 1979, 18, 175–183.

Perry, J. B., and Pfuhl, E. H. Adjustment of children in "solo" and "remarriage" homes. Marriage and Family Living, 1963, 25, 221–223.

Perry, M., Wells, E., and Doran, L. Parent characteristics in abusing and non-abusing families. Journal of Clinical Child Psychology, 1983, 12(3), 329–336.

Petersen, A. Personal communication, 1982.

Petersen, A. C., and Taylor, B. C. The biological approach to adolescence: Biological change and psychological adaptation. In J. Adelson (Ed.), Handbook of adolescent psychology, pp. 117–155. New York: Wiley, 1980.

Pfleger, J. The "wicked" stepmother in a child guidance clinic. Smith College Studies in Social Work, 1947, 17.

Phillips, E. L. Human adaptation and its failures. New York: Academic Press, 1968.

Phillips, E. L., Coughlin, D. D., Fixsen, D. L., and Maloney, D. M. Youth care: Programs and progress. Boystown, NB: Father Flanagan's Boys' Home, 1979.

Piaget, J. The origins of intelligence in children (M. Cook, Trans.). New York: International Press, 1952.

Piotrowski, C. S. Work and the family system: A naturalistic study of working class and lower-middle-class families. New York: The Free Press, 1979.

Pleck, J. Changing patterns of work and family roles. Paper presented at the Annual Meeting of the American Psychological Association, 1981.

Polansky, N. A., Chalmers, M. A., Buttenwieser, E., and Williams, D. P. Damaged parents: An anatomy of child neglect. Chicago: The University of Chicago Press, 1981.

Polansky, N., and Gaudin, J. Social distancing of the neglectful family. Social Service Review, 1983, 57, 196–208.

Polansky, N., Hally, C., and Polansky, N. F. Profile of neglect: A survey of the state of knowledge of child neglect. Washington, D.C.: Community Services Administration, Department of Health, Education and Welfare, 1975.

Porteus, M. A. A survey of the problems of normal 15-year-olds. Journal of Adolescence, 1979, 2, 307–323.

Post, S. Adolescent parricide in abusive families. Child Welfare, 1982, 61, 445–455.

Poulin, J. E., Levitt, J. L., Young, T. M., and Pappenfort, D. M. Juveniles in detention centers and jails (GPO Report No. 1980-0-311-379/1413). Washington, D.C.: Office of Juvenile Justice and Delinquency Prevention, 1980.

Radbill, S. A history of child abuse and infanticide. In R. Helfer and C. Kempe (Eds.), The battered child. Chicago: The University of Chicago Press, 1974.

Reid, J. Social interactional patterns in families of abused and non-abused children. In C. Waxler and M. Radke-Yarrow (Eds.), *Social and biological origins of altruism and aggression.* Cambridge: Cambridge University Press, 1984.

Reilly, P. What makes adolescent girls flee from their homes? *Clinical Pediatrics,* 1978, *17,* 996–893.

Reismer, S. A research note on incest. *American Journal of Sociology,* 1940, *45,* 566–575.

Rhoades, P. W., and Parker, S. L. *The connections between youth problems and violence in the home* (DHHS Grant No. 10-4-1-80101). Portland, OR: Oregon Coalition Against Domestic and Sexual Violence, September 1981.

Richardson, R. A., Burgess, J. M., and Burgess, R. L. Family size and age structure and the maltreatment of children: A social interactional analysis. Unpublished manuscript, Pennsylvania State University, 1983.

Richarson, R., and Pfeiffenberger, C. Social support networks for divorced and stepfamilies. In J. Whittaker, J. Garbarino, and Associates (Eds.), *Social support networks.* New York: Aldine, 1983.

Riegel, K. The dialectics of human development. *American Psychologist,* 1976, *31,* 689–699.

Riessman, F. The "helper" therapy principle. *Social Work,* 1965, *10,* 27–32.

Robins, L. *Deviant children grown up: A sociological and psychiatric study of sociopathic personality.* Baltimore: Williams & Wilkins, 1966.

Robins, L. N. Follow-up studies of behavior disorders in children. In H. C. Quay and J. S. Wenny (Eds.), *Psychopathological disorders of childhood.* New York: Wiley, 1972.

Robins, L. N. Follow-up studies. In H. C. Quay and J. S. Werry (Eds.), *Psychopathological disorders of childhood.* New York: Wiley, 1979.

Robinson, E., Ross, A. W., and Eyberg, S. M. *The standardization of the Eyberg Child Behavior Inventory.* Paper presented at the meetings of the American Psychological Association, San Francisco, 1977.

Roff, M. Some life history factors in relation to various types of adult maladjustment. In M. Ross and D. Ricks (Eds.), *Life history research in psychotherapy.* Minneapolis, MN: University of Minnesota Press, 1972.

Roff, M., and Sells, S. B. Juvenile delinquency in relation to peer acceptance–rejection and socioeconomic status. *Psychology in the Schools,* 1968, *5,* 3–18.

Roff, M., Sells, S. B., and Golden, M. M. *Social adjustment and personality development in children.* Minneapolis, MN: University of Minnesota Press, 1972.

Rogers, C. *Client-centered therapy.* Boston, MA: Houghton Mifflin Co., 1951.

Rogers, D. *Adolescents and youth* (4th ed.). Englewood Cliffs, NJ: Prentice-Hall, 1981.

Rohner, R. *They love me, they love me not.* New Haven, CT: HRAF Press, 1975.

Rolf, J. E. Peer status and the directionality of symptomatic behavior: Prime social competence predictors of outcomes for vulnerable children. *American Journal of Orthopsychiatry,* 1976, *46,* 74–88.

Rollins, B. C., and Thomas, D. L. Parental support, power, and control techniques in the socialization of children. In W. R. Burr, R. Hill, F. I. Nye, and I. L. Reiss (Eds.), *Contemporary theories about the family: Research based theories* (vol. 1). New York: The Free Press, 1979.

Rosenberg, M. *Society and the adolescent self-image.* Princeton, NJ: Princeton University Press, 1965.

Rosenberg, M., and Reppuci, N. Abusive mothers: Perception of their own and their children's behavior. *Journal of Consulting and Clinical Psychology*, 1983, *51*(3), 674–682.

Rosenberg, M., Reppuci, N., and Linney, J. *Problems of implementation of parent education for high-risk families.* Paper presented to the American Psychological Association Annual Meeting, New York, September 1979.

Rosenthal, R., and Jacobson, L. *Pygmalian in the classroom: Teacher's expectations and pupil's intellectual development.* New York: Holt, Rinehart, & Winston, 1968.

Ross, A. O. *Psychological disorders of children* (2d ed.). New York: McGraw-Hill, 1980.

Rossi, A. A biosocial perspective on parenting. *Daedelus*, 1977, *106*, 1–31.

Russell, C. S. Circumplex model of marital and family systems III: Empirical evaluation with families. *Family Process*, 1979, *18*, 29–45.

Russell, C. S. A methodological study of family cohesion and adaptability. *Journal of Marriage and Family*, 1980, *6*, 459–470.

Rutter, M., Graham, P., Chadwick, O. F. D., and Yule, W. Adolescent turmoil: Fact or fiction? *Journal of Child Psychology and Psychiatry*, 1976, *17*, 35–56.

Safilios-Rothschild, C. Family sociology or wives' family sociology: A cross-cultural examination of decision-making. *Journal of Marriage and the Family*, 1969, *31*, 290–301.

Salade, J. Report on employee assistance programs written to the Pennsylvania Psychological Association, November 1984.

Sameroff, A. J. Transactional models in early social relations. *Human Development*, 1975, *18*, 65–79.

Sameroff, A. J., and Chandler, M. Reproductive risk and the continuum of caretaking causality. In F. D. Horowitz, M. Heatherington, and S. G. Siget (Eds.), *Review of child development research.* Chicago: University of Chicago Press, 1975.

Sandberg, D. N. *The relationship between child abuse and juvenile delinquency.* Testimony submitted to the Senate Subcommittee on Juvenile Justice, October 19, 1983.

Santrock, J. W. Relation of type and onset of father absence to cognitive development. *Child Development*, 1972, *42*, 455–459.

Sawicki, V., and Brown, R. *Working with troubled children.* New York: Human Sciences Press, 1981.

Schaefer, E. S., Bauman, K. E., Siegel, E., and Hosking, J. O. *Mother–infant interaction: Factor analysis, stability, and demographic and psychological correlates.* Unpublished manuscript, University of North Carolina, 1979.

Scheck, D., et al. Adolescents perceptions of parent–child relations and the development of internal–external control orientation. *Journal of Marriage and the Family*, 1973, *35*, 643–654.

Schellenbach, C. *An evaluation of a preventive parent education program for parents of infants.* Unpublished Master's thesis, Pennsylvania State University, 1979.

Schloesser, P. T. The abused child. *Bulletin of the Menninger Clinic*, 1964, *28*, 260–268.

Schneider, C. J. The Michigan Screening Profile of Parenting. In R. Starr (Ed.), *Child abuse prediction.* Cambridge, MA: Ballinger, 1982.

Schoenfeld, P. Network therapy: Clinical theory and practice with disturbed adolescents. *Psychotherapy*, 1984, *21*(1), 92–100.

Schulenberg, J. E., Crockett, L., Abramowitz, R. A., and Petersen, A. C. *The effects of school transitions on early adolescent functioning.* In preparation.

Schulman, G. L. Myths that intrude on the adaptation of the stepfamily. *Social Casework,* 1972, *53,* 131–139.

Schulman, G. L. Divorce, single/parenthood, and stepfamilies: Structural implications of these transactions. *International Journal of Family Therapy,* 1981, *9,* 87–112.

Schwarz, J. Childhood origins of psychopathology. *American Psychologist,* 1979, *34,* 879–885.

Schwarz, J. D., and Zuroff, D. C. Family structure and depression in female college students: Effects of parental conflict, decision-making power and inconsistency of love. *Journal of Abnormal Psychology,* 1979, *88,* 398–406.

Scientific Analysis Corporation. *The sick, the bad and the free: A review of the runaway literature.* San Francisco: Scientific Analysis Corporation, 1974.

Scientific Analysis Corporation. *Runaways: Illegal aliens in their own land— Implications for service.* Unpublished final report, Scientific Analysis Corporation, San Francisco, 1976.

Sebes, J. M. *Determining risk for abuse in families with adolescents: The development of a criterion measure.* Unpublished Ph.D. dissertation, Pennsylvania State University, 1983.

Sebes, J. M. *Assessing risk for inappropriate parenting during adolescence: The development of a predictor measure.* Unpublished manuscript, 1974.

Seigelman, M. Evolution of Bronfenbrenner's questions concerning parental behavior. *Child Development,* 1965, *36,* 163–174.

Shanok, S. S., and Lewis, D. O. Medical histories of abused delinquents. *Child Psychiatry and Human Development,* 1981, *11,* 222–231.

Shea, M. J. A follow-up study into adulthood of adolescent psychiatric patients in relation to internalizing and externalizing symptoms, MMPI configurations, social competence and life history variables. Unpublished Ph.D. dissertation, University of Minnesota, 1972.

Shellow, R., Schamp, J. R., Liebow, E., and Unger, E. Suburban runaways of the 1960s. *Monographs of the Society for Research in Child Development,* 1967, *32,* 3 (Serial No. 111).

Sheridan, J. *Changing family handbook.* State College, PA: (Available from J. Sheridan, State College School District, State College, PA, 16801.)

Sheridan, J. Structured group counseling and biblio therapy: in-school strategies for preventing problems in children from changing families. Ph.D. dissertation, Pennsylvania State University, 1981.

Siegal, M. Economic deprivation and the quality of parent–child relations. In *Fairness in children.* New York: Academic Press, 1982.

Silbert, M., and Pines, A. *Runaway prostitutes.* Unpublished paper, Delancey Street Foundation, San Francisco, 1981.

Silver, L. B., Dublin, C. C., and Lourie, R. S. Does violence breed violence? Contributions from a study of the child abuse syndrome. *American Journal of Psychiatry,* 1969, *126,* 404–407.

Simpkinson, C., and Redmond, R. *Parents helping parents.* Rockville, MD: Montgomery County Board of Education, 1982.

Smith, C. P., Berkman, D. J., and Fraser, W. M. *A preliminary national assessment of child abuse and neglect and the juvenile justice system: The shadows of distress* (GPO Report No. 1980-311-379:1371). Washington, D.C.: Office of Juvenile Justice and Delinquency Prevention, 1980.

Smith, W. C. *The stepchild.* Chicago, IL: University of Chicago Press, 1953.

Speck, S., and Attneave, L. *Family networks.* New York: Pantheon, 1973.

Spicker, A., and Mouzaketis, C. Alcohol abuse, child abuse and neglect: An inquiry into alcohol abusers' behavior toward children. *The Alcoholism Digest,* 1977, *6,* 1–6.

Starr, R. H. *Child abuse: A controlled study of social, familial, individual and interactional factors.* Grant proposal submitted to National Center on Child Abuse and Neglect, Administration for Children, Youth, and Families, Department of Health, Education and Welfare, 1974.

Starr, R. H. The controlled study of the ecology of child abuse and drug abuse. *Child Abuse and Neglect,* 1978, *2,* 19–28.

Staff, R. H., Jr. A research-based approach to the prediction of child abuse. In R. H. Starr, Jr. (Ed.), *Child abuse predictions: Policy implications.* Cambridge, MA: Ballinger, 1982.

Starr, R. H., Cersnie, S., and Rossi, J. What child abuse researchers don't tell about child abuse research. *Pediatric Psychology,* 1976, *1,* 50–53.

Steele, B. F. Parental abuse of infants and small children. In E. J. Anthony and T. Benedek (Eds.), *Parenthood: Its psychology and psychopathology.* Boston: Little, Brown, 1970.

Steele, B. Child abuse: Its impact on society. *Journal of Indiana State Medical Association,* 1975, *68,* 191–194.

Steele, B. Violence within the family. In R. E. Helfer and C. H. Kempe (Eds.), *Child abuse and neglect: The family and the community.* Cambridge, MA: Ballinger, 1976.

Steinberg, L., and Hill, J. Family interaction patterns during early adolescence. In R. Muuss (Ed.), *Adolescent behavior and society: A book of readings* (3d ed.). New York: Random House, 1980.

Steinmetz, S. and Straus, M. The family as a cradle of violence. *Society,* 1973, *10,* 50–56.

Stinnet, N. In search of strong families. In N. Sinnet, B. Chesser, and J. DeFrain (Eds.), *Building family strengths: Blueprints for action.* Lincoln, NB: University of Nebraska Press, 1979.

Straus, M., Gelles, R., and Steinmetz, S. *Behind closed doors.* New York: Doubleday, 1980.

Strother, J. F. Adolescent stress as it relates to stepfamily living. *Dissertation Abstracts International,* 42(7-A, 3019, 1981.

Stuart, R. *Helping couples change: A social learning approach to marital therapy.* New York: Guilford Press, 1980.

Sugg, M. Review of research related to adolescent maltreatment. Richmond, VA: Region III Child Welfare Training Center, 1981.

Sugg, M. *Services for adolescents and their families.* Richmond, VA: Region III Child Welfare Training Center, 1982.

Sullivan, H. S. *The interpersonal theory of psychiatry.* New York: Norton, 1953.

Sundberg, N. D., Snowden, L. R., and Reynolds, W. M. Toward the assessment of personal competence and incompetence in life situations. *Annual review of psychology,* 1978, *29,* 179–221.

Super, C. M. Behavioral development in infancy. IN R. H. Munroe, R. C. Munroe, and B. B. Whiting (Eds.), *Handbook of cross-cultural human development.* New York: Garland, 1981.

Tanner, J. M. Growing up. *Scientific American,* 1973, *229,* 34–43.

Ten Broeck, E. Group therapy of abusing parents. *Children Today,* 1974, pp. 2–6.

Terr, L. C. A family study of child abuse. *American Journal of Psychiatry*, 1970, *127*, 665–671.

Thomas, A., and Chess, S. *Temperament and development*. New York: Brunner-Mazel, 1977.

Thomas, A., and Chess, S. *The dynamics of psychological development*. New York: Brunner-Mazel, 1980.

Thomas, W. I., and Thomas, D. S. *The child in America*. New York: Alfred A. Knopf, 1928.

Thornburg, H. *Development in adolescence*. Monterey, CA: Brooks/Cole, 1975.

Thorndike, E. L. The newest psychology. *Educational Review*, 1904, *28*, 217–227.

Tolstoy, L. *War and peace*. London: John C. Winston Co., 1949 (orig. 1869).

Trainor, C. *A description of officially reported adolescent maltreatment and its implications for policy and practice*. Denver, CO: American Humane Association, 1984.

Triolo, S. J., McKenry, P. C., Tishler, C. L., and Blyth, D. A. Social and psychological discriminants of adolescent suicide: Age and sex differences. *Journal of Youth and Adolescence*, 1984, *4*(3), 239–251.

Troll, L. Is parent–child conflict what we mean by generation gap? *Family Coordinator*, 1972, *21*(3), 347–349.

Tsunts, M. Dropouts on the run. *Atlas*, 1966.

Turner, R. H. *Family interaction*. New York: Wiley, 1970.

Udry, J. R. Marital instability by race, sex, education and occupation using 1960 census data. *American Journal of Sociology*, 1966, *72*, 203–209.

Ulrey, G. Emotional development of the young handicapped child. *New directions for exceptional children: Socioemotional Development*, 1981, *5*, 33–52.

Uniform Crime Reports for the United States. Federal Bureau of Investigation. Washington, D.C.: U.S. Government Printing Office, 1975.

United States, Congress, Senate, *Runaway youth hearings before the Subcommittee to Investigate Juvenile Delinquency of the Committee on the Judiciary*, 92d Cong., 1st session, 1972, S. 2829, the "Runaway Youth Act."

United States, Department of Health, Education, and Welfare. *Runaway and otherwise homeless youth: Annual report on the runaway youth act (Fiscal Year, 1978)*. Washington: Office of Human Development Services, Administration for Children, Youth, and Families, Youth Development Bureau, DHHS Publication No. (OHDS) 80-32009, 1980.

Urban, H. The concept of development from a system perspective. In P. Baltes (Ed.), *Life-span development and behavior* (vol. 1). New York: Academic Press, 1978.

Van Meter, M. J. S., and Agronow, S. J. The stress of multiple roles: The case for role strain among married college women. *Family Relations*, 1982, *31*, 131–138.

Van Stolk, M. *The battered child in Canada*. Toronto: McClelland and Stewart, Ltd., 1972.

Varcoe, M. A cognitive coping skills program for the training of disruptive adolescents. Unpublished Ph.D. dissertation, Pennsylvania State University, 1983.

Vietze, P. M., O'Connor, S., Hopkins, J. B., Sandler, H. M., and Altemeier, W. A. Prospective study of child maltreatment from a transactional perspective. In R. Starr (Ed.), *Predicting child abuse*. Cambridge, MA: Ballinger, 1982.

Visher, E. B., and Visher, J. S. Common problems of stepparents and their spouses. *American Journal of Orthopsychiatry*, 1978(a), *48*, 252–262.

Visher, E., and Visher, J. Major areas of difficulty for stepparent couples. *International Journal of Family Counseling*, 1978(b), *6*(2).

Visher, E. B., and Visher, J. S. *Stepfamilies: A guide to working with stepparents and stepchildren.* New York: Brunner-Mazel, 1979.

Vital Statistics of The United States, 1976. Vol. II. Mortality (Part 3). Hyattsville, MD: National Center for Health Statistics, 1979.

Wagonseller, B., Burnett, M., Salzberg, B., and Burnett, J. *The art of parenting.* Champaign, IL: Research Press, 1978.

Wahler, R. *Problems of maintaining changes in parenting for "insular" disadvantaged families.* Paper presented at a seminar on Professional and Lay Partnerships in Prevention of Unnecessary Out of Home Care, University of North Carolina, Chapel Hill, NC, March 5, 1984.

Waldo, M., Firestone, L., and Guerney, B. *Wife battery: A theoretical construct of origin, a treatment strategy, and a case report.* Paper presented at the Meeting of the American Personnel and Guidance Association, Washington, D.C., 1983.

Walker, K. N., and Messinger, L. Remarriage after divorce: Dissolution and reconstruction of family boundaries. *Family Process,* 1979, *18,* 185–192.

Wasserman, S. The abused parent of the abused child. *Children,* 1967, *14,* 175–179.

Waters, E., and Sroufe, L. A. Social competence as a developmental construct. *Developmental Review,* 1983, *3,* 79–97.

Watt, N. Patterns of childhood social development in adult schizophrenics. *Archives of General Psychiatry,* 1978, *35,* 160–165.

Weathers, L., and Liberman, R. Contingency contrasting with families of delinquent adolescents. *Behavior Therapy,* 1975, *6,* 566–567.

Webster's New Twentieth Century Dictionary of the English Language, Unabridged (2d ed.). New York: Collins World Press, 1978.

Weinbach, R. W., Adams, D. E., Ishizuka, H. A., and Ishizuka, K. I. Theoretical linkages between child abuse and juvenile delinquency. In R. J. Hunner and Y. E. Walker (Eds.), *Exploring the relationship between child abuse and delinquency.* Montclair, NJ: Allanheld, Osmun, 1981.

Weiner, I. *Psychological disturbance in adolescence.* New York: Wiley, 1970.

Weiner, I. Depression in adolescence. In F. Fisch and S. Draghi (Eds.), *The nature and treatment of depression.* New York: Wiley, 1975.

Weiner, I. Psychopathology in adolescence. In J. Adelson (Ed.), *Handbook of adolescent psychology.* New York: Wiley, 1980.

Weiner, I. *Child and adolescent psychopathology.* New York; Wiley, 1982.

Weinstein, E. A. The development of interpersonal competence. In D. Goslin (Ed.), *Handbook of socialization theory and research.* Chicago: Rand McNally, 1969.

Weiss, R. The contributions of an organization of single parents to the well-being of its members. In G. Caplan and M. Killilen (Eds.), *Support systems and mutual help,* pp. 177–186. New York: Grune and Stratton, 1973.

Welsh, R. S. Severe parental punishment and delinquency: A developmental theory. *Journal of Clinical Child Psychology,* 1976, *5,* 17–21.

Werner, E. E., and Smith, R. S. *Vulnerable but invincible: A longitudinal study of resilient children and youth.* New York: McGraw Hill, 1982.

West, D. J. *Present conduct and future delinquency: First report of the Cambridge Study in Delinquent Development.* New York: International Universities Press, 1969.

West, D. J. *Delinquency, its roots, careers, and prospects.* Cambridge, MA: Harvard University Press, 1982.

West, D. J., and Farrington, D. P. *Who becomes delinquent? Second report of the Cambridge Study in Delinquent Behavior.* London: Heinemann, 1973.

West, D. J., and Farrington, D. P. *The delinquent way of life*. London: Heinemann, 1972.

Westley, W. A., and Elkin, F. The protective environment and adolescent socialization. *Social Forces*, 1956, *35*, 243–249.

Westman, J., Rice, D., and Berman, E. Nursery school behavior and later school adjustment. *American Journal of Orthopsychiatry*, 1967, *37*, 725–731.

White, R. Motivation reconsidered: A concept of competence. *Psychological Review*, 1959, *66*, 297–333.

Whittaker, J. *Caring for troubled children: Residential treatment in a community context*. San Francisco, CA: Jossey-Bass, 1979.

Whittaker, J., Garbarino, J., and Associates. *Social support networks*. New York: Aldine, 1983.

Willerman, L., Broman, S., and Fiedler, M. Infant development, preschool IQ, and social class. *Child Development*, 1970, *41*, 69–77.

Wilson, K. L., Zurcher, L. A., McAdams, D. C., and Curtis, R. L. Stepfather and stepchildren: An exploratory analysis from two national surveys. *Journal of Marriage and the Family*, 1975, *37*, 526–536.

Winn, M. *Children without childhood*. New York: Penguin Books, 1983.

Wolf, L. *A dream of Dracula: In search of the living dead*. Boston: LIttle, Brown, & Co., 1972.

Wolfe, D. Prevention of child abuse through the development of parent/child competencies. In McMahan and R. Peters (Eds.), *Childhood disorders: Behavioral-developmental approaches*. New York: Brunner/Magel, 1984.

Wolk, S., and Brandon, J. Runaway adolescents' perceptions of parents and self. *Adolescence*, 1977, *46*, 185–197.

Wolock, I., and Horowitz, B. Child maltreatment as a social problem: The neglect of neglect. *American Journal of Orthopsychiatry*, 1984, *54*, 530–543.

Wooden, K. *Weeping in the playtime of others*. New York: McGraw-Hill, 1976.

Wordsworth, W. Ode: Intimations of immortality. In M. H. Abrams (Ed.), *The Norton anthology of English literature*. New York: W. W. Norton & Co., 1968.

Yarow, M. R., Scott, P., DeLeew, L., and Henig, C. Childrearing in families of working and nonworking mothers. *Sociometry*, 1962, *25*, 122–140.

York, P., and York, D. *Toughlove: A self-help manual for parents troubled by teenage behavior*. Sellersville, PA: Community Service Foundation, 1981.

York, P., and York, D. *Toughlove for kids*. Sellersville, PA: Community Service Foundation, 1983(a).

York, P., York, D., and Wachtel, T. *Toughlove*. Garden City, NY: Doubleday & Co., 1983(b).

Young, R. L., Godfrey, W., Matthews, B., and Adams, G. R. Runaways: A review of negative consequences. *Family Relations*, 1983, *32*, 275–281.

Youniss, J. *Parents and peers in the social environment: A Sullivan–Piaget perspective*. Chicago: University of Chicago Press, 1980.

Youth Development Bureau. *Runaway youth* (DHEW Publication No. OHDS 78-26054). Washington, D.C.: U.S. Government Printing Office, 1978.

Zigler, E., and Trickett, P. K. IQ, social competence, and evaluation of early childhood intervention programs. *American Psychologist*, 1978, *33*, 789–798.

Zur-Spiro, S., and Longfellow, C. *Support from fathers: Implications for the well-being of mothers and their children*. Paper presented at the Biennial Meeting of the Society for Research in Child Development, Boston, April 1981.

AUTHOR INDEX*

A

Abidin, R., 281, *309*
Abramowitz, R. A., 173, *334*
Achenbach, T. M., 93, 123, 128–130, 138, 140, 143, 145, 159–161, 164, 174, 176, 177, 184, 186, 210, 226, 246, 297, *309*
Adams, J. E., 322
Adelson, J., 9, 15, 94, 151, 178, *310*, *316*
Adler, I., 181, 182, *310*
Agronow, S. J., 202, *336*
Aldous, J., 58, 64, 67, *310*
Alexander, J. F., 189, *310*
Alfaro, J. D., 30–34, 36, *310*
Allen, C., 202, *310*
Altemeier, W. A., 87, *310*, *336*
Alvy, K., 59, *310*
Anderson, E., *313*
Anderson, S., 152, 153, *310*
Andrews, M., *312*

Angle, C. R., *327*
Arnold, C., *322*
Attneave, L., 265, *334*
Austen, J., 16, *310*

B

Babigan, H., 154, *315*
Bachman, J. G., 181–183, *310*
Baher, E., 31, *310*
Baizerman, M., 77, *311*
Balla, D. A., 32, 34, 35, *326*
Balswick, J. O., 11, 14, 16, *310*
Baltes, P. B., *310*
Bandura, A., 11, 35, 229, 268, *310*, *311*
Barrett, C. L., 177, *328*
Barter, J. O., *311*
Basham, R., 199, *315*
Bates, R., 121, *313*
Bauman, E., 91, 124, *327*
Baumrind, D., 14, 16, 57, 67, *311*

*Numbers in italics indicate the page where the complete reference is given.

SUBJECT INDEX

A

AAI. *See* Adolescent Abuse Inventory
Abuse; *see also* Adolescent abuse
  adolescent and spouse, 19
  adolescent compared to child, 22
  adolescent-only pattern, 63
  "at risk" families, studies of, 85–89
  on continuum of maltreatment, 19
  criticisms of research in, 85
  critiques of measurement for, 89–90
  and delinquency, 28
  defined within a system perspective, 58
  differential patterns of, 23
  dynamics of power, 19
  exosystem study of, 85
  gender differences during adolescence, 23
  life-course continuum of maltreatment, 20
  measurement of, 84–85
  microsystem study of, 86
  predictor instruments for, 88, 89, 123–124, 125
  psychological and sexual toward adolescents, 22
  rating scales, 233
  and support resources in community, 85
Abusive families, characteristics of social interaction, 84
Abusive vs. disciplinary incidents, 84
Achenbach Child Behavior Checklist, 123, 129, 138, 140, 143, 145, 159, 210, 226, 248, 293
Adaptiveness, 155
Adaptive parenting, 192
Adolescence
  in context, 3

351

H

High-risk families
  case studies, 137–141
  discrepancies in, 133–136, 148
  escaping conflict, 305–307
  family
    characteristics, 126–133, 147
    composition, 124
  socioeconomic stress in, 150,
    191–230

I

"Idiosyncratic" maltreatment, 302
Interpersonal competence. *See*
  Competence
Intervention
  family/couple approach, 262–264
  group therapy, 265
  individual approach, 258–262
  with parents, 255–265
    problems with, 256
  strategies, professional, 257–265
  stress management, approach,
    260–262
  with youth, 265–266

J

Juvenile delinquency. *See* Delinquency; Delinquents

L

Low-risk families
  discrepancies in, 134
  family
    characteristics, 126–133
    composition, 124
  and healthy adaptation, 303–305

M

Macrosystem, 297, 302–303
Maltreatment. *See* Abuse; Adolescent
Maltreatment psychological conceptualization, 59–60
Mesosystem, 296, 299–300
Microsystem, 296, 298–299
Models, Moen *et al.*
  application of, 201–203
  assessment of, 216–225
  categories of, 208
  empirical operationalizations of,
    204
  evidence for, 199–201
  explanation of, 197
  factors in, 198
  hypotheses, 205
  limitations of, 203–205, 226–227
  understanding and expanding,
    225–226

N

Neglect, 61
Neighborhood parent education,
  276–277
Network therapy, 265

P

Parenting, maladaptive, 193, 195–
  196, 211, 216, 219
Parenting styles, 57
  authoritarian, 18
  and social support in community,
    17
Phenomenological perspective,
  227–230